THE SOCIOLOGY
OF ORGANIZATIONS

McGRAW-HILL SERIES IN SOCIOLOGY
CONSULTING EDITOR
Otto N. Larsen, University of Washington

THE SOCIOLOGY OF ORGANIZATIONS

DEAN J. CHAMPION

Professor of Sociology

University of Tennessee, Knoxville

McGRAW-HILL BOOK COMPANY

New York   St. Louis   San Francisco   Auckland   Düsseldorf   Johannesburg
Kuala Lumpur   London   Mexico   Montreal   New Delhi   Panama
Paris   São Paulo   Singapore   Sydney   Tokyo   Toronto

This book was set in Times Roman by Rocappi, Inc.
The editors were Lyle Linder and Susan Gamer;
the cover was designed by Ronald Bowen;
the production supervisor was Sam Ratkewitch.
R. R. Donnelley & Sons Company was printer and binder.

THE SOCIOLOGY OF ORGANIZATIONS

1 2 3 4 5 6 7 8 9 0 D O D O 7 9 8 7 6 5

Library of Congress Cataloging in Publication Data

Champion, Dean J.
    The sociology of organizations.

    (McGraw-Hill series in sociology)
    Bibliography: p.
    1.   Organization.   2.   Industrial organization—
Case studies.   3.   Industrial management.   I.   Title.
HD31.C454   301.18'32   74-12245
ISBN 0-07-010492-1

Acknowledgments

CHAPTER 1

Richard H. Hall, *Organizations: Structure and Process,* © 1972. Reprinted by permission of Prentice-Hall, Inc., Englewood Cliffs, New Jersey.

Alberta H. Rubenstein and Chadwick J. Haberstroh, *Some Theories of Organization,* Irwin, Homewood, Ill., 1966. By permission of Richard D. Irwin, Inc.

Lawrence K. Frank, "The Interdisciplinary Frontiers in Human Relations Studies," *Journal of Human Relations,* Fall, 1954, pp. 9-23. By permission of *Journal of Human Relations* and publisher, Central State University.

CHAPTER 2

Ralph M. Stogdill, in James D. Thompson and Victor H. Vroom (eds.), *Organizational Design and Research,* table 1, p. 4. Reprinted by permission of the University of Pittsburgh Press. © 1970 by the University of Pittsburgh Press.

George H. Rice, Jr., and Dean W. Bishoprick, *Conceptual Models of Organization,* Appleton-Century-Crofts, New York, 1971. Copyright © 1971 by Meredith Corporation.

Joseph L. Massie, "Management Theory," in James G. March (ed.), *Handbook of Organizations,* Rand McNally, Chicago, Ill., 1965. © 1965 by Rand McNally & Company.

James G. March and Herbert A. Simon, *Organizations,* Wiley, New York, 1958.

Douglas McGregor, *The Human Side of Enterprise,* McGraw-Hill, New York, 1960. By permission of McGraw-Hill Book Company.

Delbert Miller and William Form, *Industrial Sociology,* Harper and Row, New York, 1964.

Alex Carey, "The Hawthorne Studies: A Radical Criticism," *American Sociological Review,* vol. 32, pp. 403-416, 1967.

C. J. Lammers, "Power and Participation in Decision-making in Formal Organizations," *American Journal of Sociology,* vol. 73, pp. 201-216, 1967, illustration on p. 210. By permission of the University of Chicago.

Eugene Litwak, "Models of Bureaucracy Which Permit Conflict," *American Journal of Sociology,* vol. 67, pp. 177-184, 1961. By permission of the University of Chicago.

Alvin W. Gouldner, "Organizational Analysis," in Robert K. Merton et al. (eds.), *Sociology Today,* Basic Books, New York, 1959. By permission of the author and Basic Books, Inc.

Chandler Morse, *The Social Theories of Talcott Parsons,* Prentice Hall, Englewood Cliffs, N.J., 1961. By permission of Max Black.

F. J. Roethlisberger and W. J. Dickson, *Management and the Worker,* Harvard University Press, Cambridge, Mass., 1939. Copyright 1939, 1967 by the President and Fellows of Harvard College.

CHAPTER 3

Herbert A. Simon, D. W. Smithburg, and V. A. Thompson, *Public Administration,* Knopf, New York, 1950.

J. Eugene Haas, Richard Hall, and Norman Johnson, "Toward an Empirically Derived Taxonomy of Organizations," in Raymond V. Bowers (ed.), *Studies on Behavior in Organizations,* The University of Georgia Press, Athens, Ga., 1966. By permission of The University of Georgia Press and the authors.

Norman J. Johnson, "An Empirically Derived Taxonomy Table," cited in Richard H. Hall, *Organizations: Structure and Process,* Prentice Hall, Englewood Cliffs, N.J., 1972, pp. 52-60.

Amitai Etzioni, *A Comparative Analysis of Complex Organizations,* Free Press, New York, 1961, table on p. 12: "A Typology of Compliance Relations." Copyright © The Free Press of Glencoe, Inc., 1961.

Daniel Katz and Robert L. Kahn, *The Social Psychology of Organizations,* Wiley, New York, 1966. This material has been adapted as Table 3-6.

CHAPTER 4

Sanford Labovitz and Robert Hagedorn, *Introduction to Social Research,* McGraw-Hill, New York, 1971. By permission of McGraw-Hill Book Company.

Herbert Spencer, *The Study of Sociology,* 10th ed., Routledge, London, 1882. By permission of Routledge and Kegan Paul, Ltd.

Frederick L. Campbell and Ronal L. Akers, "Organizational Size, Complexity, and the Administrative Component in Occupational Associations," *Sociological Quarterly,* vol. 11, pp. 435-451, 1970. By permission of *Sociological Quarterly* and the authors.

Richard H. Hall, J. Eugene Haas, and Norman J. Johnson, "Organizational Size, Complexity, and Formalization," *American Sociological Review,* vol. 32, pp. 903-912, 1967. By permission of *American Sociological Review* and the authors.

S. N. Eisenstadt, "Bureaucracy, Bureaucratization, and Debureaucratization," *Administrative Science Quarterly,* vol. 4, pp. 302-320, 1959.

Henry Assael, "Constructive Role of Interorganizational Conflict," *Administrative Science Quarterly,* vol. 14, pp. 573-583, 1969.

James Worthy, "Organizational Structure and Employee Morale," *American Sociological Review,* vol. 15, pp. 169-179, 1950.

Thomas A. Mahoney and William Weitzel, "Managerial Models of Organizational Effectiveness," *Administrative Science Quarterly,* vol. 14, pp. 357–365, 1969, table 1, p. 358.
Ronald G. Corwin, "Patterns of Organizational Conflict," *Administrative Science Quarterly,* vol.
14, pp. 507–521, 1969, table 1, p. 514.

CHAPTER 5

Stanley E. Seashore, *Group Cohesiveness in the Industrial Work Group,* Survey Research Center,
Univ. of Michigan, Ann Arbor, Mich., 1954. By permission of the Survey Research Center
and Stanley E. Seashore.
E. A. Fleishman and E. F. Harris, "Patterns of Leadership Related to Employee Grievances
and Turnover," *Personnel Psychology,* vol. 15, pp. 43–56, 1962.
H. Alan Robinson and Ralph Connors, "Job Satisfaction Researches of 1962," *Personnel and
Guidance Journal,* vol. 42, no. 2, pp. 136–142, October 1963. By permission of American
Personnel and Guidance Association.
E. L. Hilgendorf and B. L. Irving, "Job Attitude Research: A New Conceptual and Analytical
Model," *Human Relations,* vol. 22, pp. 415–426, 1969.

CHAPTER 6

Jane Cassels Record in Gideon Sjoberg's book, *Ethics, Politics, and Social Research,* 1967. By
the permission of Schenkman Publishing Company, Inc.

CHAPTER 7

L. David Korb, *Training the Supervisor,* U.S. Civil Service Commission, Program Planning
Division Bureau of Programs and Standards, U.S. Government Printing Office, Washington,
D.C., 1956.
Table 7-2, from "On Organizational Size and Administrative Ratios: A Critical Examination of
General and Specialized Hospitals," by Dean J. Champion and H. M. Betterton, is reprinted
from *Pacific Sociological Review,* vol. 17, no. 1, p. 104, January 1974, by permission of the
publisher, Sage Publications, Inc.
James Worthy, "Organizational Structure and Employee Morale," *American Sociological Re-
view,* vol. 15, pp. 169–179, 1950.
Rocco Carzo, Jr., and John M. Yanouzas, "Effects of Flat and Tall Organization Structure,"
Administrative Science Quarterly, vol. 14, pp. 178–191, 1969; fig. 1, p. 181, and quotation from
pp. 190–191.
Marshall W. Meyer, *Bureaucratic Structure and Authority,* Harper and Row, New York, 1972.
Norman R. F. Maier, *Psychology in Industrial Organizations,* Houghton Mifflin Company, Bos-
ton, Mass., 1973. Reprinted by permission of the publishers.
Cecil A. Gibb, "Leadership," in Gardner Lindzey and E. Aronson (eds.), *The Handbook of
Social Psychology,* vol. IV, 2d ed., Addison-Wesley, Reading, Mass., 1969.

CHAPTER 8

Chester I. Bernard, *The Functions of the Executive,* Harvard University Press, Cambridge,
Mass., 1938.
Philip Selznick, *TVA and the Grass Roots,* University of California Press, 1949. Originally
published by the University of California Press; reprinted by permission of The Regents of
the University of California.
Gresham M. Sykes, *The Society of Captives: A Study of a Maximum Security Prison,* copyright ©
1958 by Princeton University Press, Princeton Paperback, 1971. Reprinted by permission of
Princeton University Press.

CHAPTER 9

J. G. Hunt and J. W. Hill, "The New Look in Motivation Theory for Organizational Research," *Human Organization,* vol. 28, 100-109, 1969.

G. P. Fournet, M. K. Distefano, and M. W. Pryer, "Job Satisfaction: Issues and Problems, *Personnel Psychology,* vol. 19, pp. 165-183, 1966.

Enid Mumford, "Job Satisfaction—A New Approach Derived from an Old Theory," *Sociological Review,* vol. 18, pp. 71-101, 1970. By permission of *Sociological Review* and Enid Mumford.

Ian C. Ross and Alvin Zander, "Need Satisfaction and Employee Turnover," *Personnel Psychology,* vol. 10, pp. 327-328, 1957.

Paul F. Wernimont, "Intrinsic and Extrinsic Factors in Job Satisfaction," *Journal of Applied Psychology,* vol. 50, pp. 41-50, 1966. Copyright 1966 by the American Psychological Association and reproduced by permission.

Donald F. Roy, "Banana Time: Job Satisfaction and Informal Interaction," *Human Organization,* vol. 18, pp. 158-168, 1960. By permission of *Human Organization,* Donald F. Roy, and the Society for Applied Anthropology.

Georges Friedman, *Industrial Society,* The Free Press of Glencoe, Ill., Chicago, 1955. By permission of Macmillan.

William Foote Whyte, *Organizational Behavior: Theory and Application,* Richard D. Irwin, Inc., Homewood, Ill., 1969 ©, pp. 589-590; reprinted with permission.

Harriet Holter, "Attitudes towards Employee Participation in Company Decision-making Processes," *Human Relations,* vol. 18, pp. 297-321, 1965, table on p. 307.

Robert L. Kahn, "Productivity and Satisfaction," *Personnel Psychology,* vol. 13, pp. 275-287, 1960.

CHAPTER 10

George Strauss and Alex Bavelas, "Group Dynamics and Intergroup Relations," in *Money and Motivation* by William F. Whyte. Copyright © 1955 by Harper & Row, Publishers, Inc. By permission of the publisher.

Larry E. Greiner, "Patterns of Organization Change," *Harvard Business Review,* vol. 45, pp. 119-130, 1967; quotation from pp. 124-125, and exhibit 1, p. 126. By permission of the *Harvard Business Review* and Larry E. Greiner.

Garth N. Jones, "Strategies and Tactics of Planned Organizational Change," *Human Organization,* vol. 24, pp. 192-200, 1965.

Warren G. Bennis, "Theory and Method in Applying Behavioral Science to Planned Organizational Change," *Journal of Applied Behavioral Science,* vol. 1, pp. 337-360, 1965. Reproduced by special permission.

D. Katz and R. L. Kahn, *The Social Psychology of Organizations,* Wiley, New York, 1966.

CHAPTER 11

Ida Hoos, *Automation in the Office,* Public Affairs Press, Washington, D.C., 1961.

U.S. Department of Labor, Bureau of Labor Statistics, *Experiences of Workers after Layoff,* Bulletin No. 1408, 1964, p. 18.

U.S. Department of Labor, Bureau of Labor Statistics, *Impact of Office Automation in the Internal Revenue Service,* Bulletin No. 1364, April 1963, p. 2, pp. 20-21, p. 49.

The National Commission on Technology, Automation, and Economic Progress, *Technology and the American Economy,* Report of the National Commission on Technology, Automation, and Economic Progress, vol. 1, February 1966, p. xiv, pp. 109-113.

Contents

Preface

The proliferation of literature on formal organizations in professional journals and trade books over the past fifteen years has imposed upon students the herculean task of sifting and sorting many different approaches, perspectives, typologies, models, variables, and methodological tools. The teacher in the classroom can perform part of the necessary task of integrating existing material into a meaningful whole; but a textbook with essentially the same purpose can complement the teacher's efforts significantly.

Existing texts on formal organizations represent partial attempts to help students understand organizational behavior; they supplement the teacher's orientation. Many texts currently in use reflect positions regarding organizational behavior which are, in a sense, polemical. That is, book A looks at organizations and organizational behavior from perspective A; book B looks at organizations from perspective B; and so on. By implication, the author of book A prefers viewpoint A to viewpoint B. But where does this leave the student? Unless he is exposed to a *variety of perspectives,* the beginning student might cultivate, prematurely, a narrow point of view. One objective of this book, therefore, is to familiarize students with *several* frames of reference, so that they can develop a flexible attitude about what goes on in organizations and why.

I have deliberately designed this book so that students can "see" that the results of organizational research have *not* yielded static and clearly defined conceptual frameworks which explain everything. At present, there is great need for some kind of organization of the accumulated research on organizational behavior. No single approach, model, or typology is completely adequate or accepted by all organizational investigators. Neologisms abound in the field (as in many other related fields of social inquiry), and there is still much to be uncovered and learned about the sociology of organizations.

Many persons are concerned about developing a "theory of organizations," and, in fact, several books have titles which, deceptively, reflect this. In fact, no true organizational theory (in a technical sense) exists today. However, we do have what might be termed "partial theories" regarding specific dimensions of organizational life (e.g., leadership "theory," communications "theory," organizational change "theory"). I believe that it is extremely important to work toward the development of organizational theory, even in the midst of what some people might regard as a conceptual Tower of Babel.

The present fluidity of the field should not necessarily be viewed as detrimental. Rather, we might regard it as amenable to innovative and creative theoretical and substantive contributions. The field is open to inputs of sociologists, psychologists, business administrators, educators, and industrialists. We have not, as yet, established fixed organizational boundaries within which we must operate or carry out our research activities. Prisons, churches, scientific laboratories, linoleum factories, schools, and public utilities are all considered legitimate objects of research. We are not, as yet, shackled to a particular approach or theoretical model as we develop and elaborate explanations for organizational behavior.

This book is *intentionally eclectic,* reflecting the author's view that exposure to a multiplicity of perspectives is both rewarding and challenging. This eclecticism might be called *humanistic;* for I do not believe that organizational behavior can be meaningfully discussed or explained by ignoring one realm (e.g., the psychological individual component) and concentrating exclusively on another (e.g., strictly "organizational" factors—size, complexity, formalization—or strictly social ones—group cohesiveness, interpersonal conflict). My "humanistic" approach considers organizations as affective aggregates of individuals engaged in continuous interaction, as opposed to the rather sterile view of organizations as N members, or N levels of supervision, or N departments.

Basically, three units of analysis are targets of discussion throughout the text: the organizational, the interpersonal (group), and the individual (personality). I believe that the interplay between these units of analysis must be understood before sound theoretical appraisals of organizational behavior can be made. Necessarily, this has resulted in a blending of analytical units in each chapter. The interaction of units of analysis is accounted for by the fact that over the past ten years, I have been exposed to students in a variety of academic disciplines as I have taught the sociology of formal organizations. We cannot ignore the important contribution of the industrial psychologist, nor can we afford to ignore the views of the industrial engineer or the business administrator. All these fields exhibit strengths (as well as weaknesses) which complement one another in the final analysis.

It is my hope that students who read this book will not fervently attach themselves to any single theoretical perspective. My aim is to promote flexibility in viewpoint more than anything else. It is to that end that this book is dedicated.

Dean J. Champion

THE SOCIOLOGY
OF ORGANIZATIONS

Introduction

A PRELIMINARY VIEW

A formal organization is a predetermined arrangement of individuals whose interrelated tasks and specialties enable the total aggregate to achieve goals.[1] It is further characterized by provisions for the replacement of members who resign, transfer, die, or retire; a system of rewards and benefits which accrue to each member in return for his services; a hierarchy of authority which allocates power and delegates duties to be performed by the membership; and a communication system which transmits information and assists in the coordination of the activities of the members.[2]

THE OBJECTIVES OF THIS BOOK

The principal objectives of this book are fourfold:
    To delineate some of the characteristics which most formal organizations share. This will require an examination of several types of organizations,

including banks, insurance companies, public utilities, national associations, hospitals, penal institutions, military units, colleges, department stores, churches, and social service institutions. It is apparent that our investigations will involve virtually *all settings* where the social interactions and procedural arrangements are consistent with the definition of a formal organization stated above.

To highlight statements about the structure and process of organizations which contribute to our explanation for and understanding of the behaviors of these institutions. Formal organizations are dynamic entities, but as Hall (1972b:4) indicates:

> every social phenomenon is static at a particular point in time. The forms taken by each can be compared at this point in time. A static analysis allows some determination of which organizational characteristics are interrelated, and this approach provides indications of why and how organizations reached their present forms. Historical and experimental evidence allows further understanding of the dynamics of organizational development and change. From this analysis of organizations as entities at a point in time, the focus will shift to processes internal and external to organizations that will affect their behavior and that of their members.

To describe some useful methods for the scientific study of organizations, including examinations of some of the more crucial variables used in such analyses. Later in this volume, several key organization phenomena will be presented and described. The decision to include some variables and exclude others in this presentation is based primarily upon the frequency with which these terms are cited in contemporary organizational literature. Several useful research strategies, which may help to facilitate our investigations of organizational structures, will be briefly outlined.

To discuss and describe organizational change in several of its numerous forms. The role of professional organizational agents of change, persons responsible for making recommendations for changing existing organizational arrangements, will be considered. The adaptability of organizations to modifications in technology (the means by which organizations accomplish tasks and perform services) will also be assessed as one facet of organizational change.

In order to bring the interests of students of organizations into greater harmony with the above objectives, real examples from a variety of academic fields (e.g., sociology, psychology, business administration, economics, and anthropology) will be presented. These examples describe organizational behavior from a number of different perspectives.

THE SOCIOLOGY OF FORMAL ORGANIZATIONS

This book examines formal organizations primarily from the *sociological perspective.* Although several different themes currently prevail as *subapproaches* within the field of sociology, it is generally accepted that sociologists focus upon the *structure and functioning of social systems (relatively enduring patterns of association involving several people)* within a variety of organizational contexts. *Social interaction is the principal target of sociological inquiry.* Therefore, the types of social interaction that occur in formal organizations fall under sociological scrutiny. Social scientists frequently ask questions which pertain directly to formal organizational structure, such as: "What kinds of structural patterns are generated from particular kinds of social interaction?" and "How does organizational change modify existing social arrangements?"

In contrast, a psychologist might focus upon the aspirations and attitudes of individuals as personality systems in organizations. He may be led to examine which factors motivate individuals to produce more, which factors contribute to individual adaptability to the job, or what the psychological concomitants of job security, interpersonal relations, and worker anxiety are.

Social interaction in organizations involves individuals with differing personality configurations. Several implications for organizational structure stem, in part, from such factors. Nevertheless, the primary emphasis of this volume is upon *the structure and dynamics of social interaction within formal organizations. Such is the nature and focus of the sociology of formal organizations.*

WHY SHOULD WE STUDY FORMAL ORGANIZATIONS?

An extended treatment of the social dimension of formal organizations should be prefaced by a brief rationale for studying them. Formal organizational researchers reflect a variety of interests in their investigations of organizational phenomena. Some investigators specialize by limiting their analyses to *bureaucratic structures* and the implications of such structures for the organizational membership at various authority levels. Others have as their field of specialization *the study of factors which bring about changes in the sizes and shapes of organizations.* Organizational researchers not only have different interests concerning the topics to be investigated, but frequently they select diverse approaches for assessing specific organizational settings. These differences arise in part because of the variety of reasons which investigators provide for conducting their research.

The list of specialties within the sociology of formal organizations is fairly extensive.[3] Given the rate of increase in the number of subareas grouped under the formal organizational rubric, particularly during the period 1960–1970, it is apparent that no single reason for studying the subject will satisfy all concerned at any given point in time. Therefore, we will identify several popular reasons at the outset which will no doubt encompass most researchers' interests. The short list of motives provided here is designed to be a representative rather than an exhaustive compilation. Some of the more common reasons for studying formal organizations are as follows:

Formal organizations should be studied systematically inasmuch as we are related to them, directly or indirectly, during most of our working lives. Most people either work for, or otherwise belong to, formal organizations of one sort or another. An increased understanding of the structure and functioning of work organizations (or service organizations) would be advantageous to many employees. A knowledge of how a given individual's job fits into the overall organizational work pattern may enable that person to assign greater significance to the work he performs. It is said of Henry Ford that he frequently invited workers from the assembly lines to his office to acquaint them with various aspects of automobile manufacturing. He would show them where their particular job fit into the entire structure of work operations. Supposedly, this manifestation of managerial concern helped the worker to see greater meaning in his job, and he tended to be increasingly satisfied with the importance of his tasks in relation to those performed by others.

Organizational heads and managers can derive certain benefits from organizational research which will enable them to plan more effectively any potential changes of organizational structure. Organizations are dynamic in that they continually change in response to environmental conditions in an effort to achieve organizational objectives more effectively. An understanding of the dynamics of change within organizations can lead to better planning and coordinating, particularly before anticipated disruptive modifications in organizational structure. Dealing more effectively with the potential problems associated with changing organizations can contribute significantly to reducing the dollar costs of change by improving the efficiency of employees' role performance and the nature of interaction between many work roles. By the same token, anticipating potential problems can help to improve manager-employee interactions and lead to a more harmonious work atmosphere as employees are given greater consideration in the crucial planning stages. In the long run, both management and employees realize benefits such as increased productivity and greater employee satisfaction with the conditions under which they perform their work activities.

Apart from the practical concerns of some students of formal organizations, some persons like to investigate the theoretical relationships between various aspects of organizational environments. For some researchers, at least, it is important to study relationships between organizational factors for the sole purpose of knowing about them. In effect, this is the accumulation of organizational knowledge for the sake of knowledge. It is often difficult for the layman looking at any academic area to accept the notion that there are those scientists who concern themselves with "knowing" rather than with becoming involved with the practical and immediately applicable aspects of their inquiry. The *practitioner* most often asks how he can *apply* the knowledge he has obtained. In contrast, the *pure theorist* tends to dissociate himself from such questions.

Many researchers investigating problems of formal organizations (and other topics, for that matter) adopt a balanced position regarding their immediate and apparent research objectives. They ask *both* kinds of questions: (1) "What are the theoretical relationships among the various aspects of organizations?" and (2) "How can this information be of use to others in dealing with their organizational problems?" The balanced position seems to be the most preferred when existing research reports are examined. Nevertheless, it is still the right of the individual researcher to choose his specific motives, however abstract and irrelevant they may appear to others.

Formal organizations can be studied in such a way that the findings derived from one setting can be applied to parallel situations in nonorganizational settings. For instance, community investigators and family sociologists may obtain insights into problems associated with their own subject areas by focusing their attention upon research in formal organizations. Depending upon their level of analysis, the benefits derived from examining related materials from formal organizations may be minimal or substantial. In a later section of this chapter we will examine several levels or units of analysis which attract the attention of researchers, and a comparative view of the relative advantages and limitations of each will be provided.

Explanatory schemes for individual behaviors can be enhanced by a study of the structure and dynamics of formal organizations. The impact of organizational structure on the attitudinal configurations of individuals attracts a great deal of attention from social researchers. Although psychologists and social psychologists are perhaps most concerned about these interactions, it is not unusual to find members of other disciplines (e.g., sociology, economics, and political science) who frequently utilize individual variables in their explanations of organizational phenomena.

Among the questions generated by these researchers might be: "To what extent does personality influence the structure of organizations?" and

"To what degree does the organization elicit changes in personality among the staff who comprise it?" The description of the *organization man* by William H. Whyte, Jr. (1957), is characteristic of a general attempt to attribute personality modification to the organization as a primary agency of socialization.

The list of reasons or motives for studying formal organizations presented above can be extended considerably. The main reason for discussing those listed at this time is to underscore the fact that there are significant substantive and theoretical benefits which are realized by the study of organizations. It is expected that the reader will gradually formulate his own impression of the significance of this topic as various dimensions of the subject are treated in later chapters.

UNITS OF ANALYSIS

Formal organizations may be approached and examined at several different levels. Some researchers prefer the word "unit" to the word "level" in making the following distinction. Three units of analysis which are of significance to us in this book are: (1) the individual, (2) the small, interpersonal work group, and (3) the formal organization.

The Individual Unit of Analysis

When formal organizations are examined with the individual as the unit of analysis, the research is often limited to describing interrelations between psychological factors and work roles. What are the organizational forces which impinge upon the individual and affect his morale, fatigue level, and job satisfaction? What are the major motivational factors which stimulate the individual to perform his work role effectively? Some fairly recent works which emphasize the individual in formal organizations use the terms "organizational psychology" or "business psychology."[4] These publications focus exclusively upon individual motivations in work organizations. Although other units of analysis are covered briefly, the primary emphasis is upon the individual and how he adjusts and adapts to his work environment.

Another major area which has received the continuous attention of social scientists is *personality and the implications of personality for workers' behavior in specific organizational settings.* Agencies that test aptitude and abilities have succeeded in selling organizational managerial personnel on the idea that personality can make the difference between a successful and productive employee and an unsuccessful worker. As a result, prospective employees are carefully scrutinized by company personnel officers and a previously specified core of "ideal" personal job qualities is matched against the applicant's personality profile. There is no doubt that personality characteristics have much to do with human adaptations and adjustments in any organization. The use of personality measures in business and industry for purposes of personnel selection, the analysis of organizational problems, and the analysis of the structure and functioning of work groups is extensive and usually profitable.

The Work Group or Interpersonal Unit of Analysis

Focusing attention on the small group as a special interest includes an examination of some of the following variables: group cohesion, or the extent to which groups on the job band together to promote mutual interests; informal relations in the work group, or the extent to which small work groups in the business-industrial setting are able to complement the formal arrangement of things in the organization; the output or productivity of the work group, or the number of products produced, the amount of paperwork completed (in the case of data processing), or the number of services performed; and the composition of the work group (e.g., age, sex, and educational homogeneity and socioeconomic status (SES) differentials).

The group counterpart of personality for the individual is labeled "syntality" (Cattell, 1951). Syntality is literally the personality of the group. Researchers have noted that work groups manifest characteristics apart from and above and beyond the simple sum of the personal characteristics of the individuals making up the groups. Sayles (1958) has described various kinds of work groups in the industrial setting as being erratic, apathetic, strategic, or conservative, and he has provided detailed characterizations of each type in much the way one would discuss individual attributes (e.g., easily upset, erratic, unpredictable, cohesive, shrewdly calculating, patient, restrained).

It is important to understand that *specific individual characteristics are frequently overshadowed by the group aggregate.* Managers of businesses and supervisors of industrial firms often refer to work groups as "behaving" this way or that, rather than describing the behavior of specific individuals. To a large degree, the group is treated as an independent entity. The *group* thinks. The *group* acts. Sociologists have sometimes expressed this by the term "reification." In subsequent discussion it will be interesting to observe the significance attached to small work groups in business, industrial, educational, and other organizational settings and to investigate the extent to which these collectivities play strategic roles in their respective organizations.

The Formal Organization as a Unit of Analysis

The unit of analysis most relevant to this book is the formal organization. All organizations, regardless of their sizes and shapes, are comprised, in part, of individuals performing roles which are functionally related to other roles. In addition, all organizations have varying numbers and sizes of work groups. Although our discussion of what goes on in a formal organization *could be limited exclusively to describing behaviors of individuals and small groups,* our analysis would be far from adequate if we failed to include some of the general *characteristics of organizations* as a part of our description.

Organizations have unique qualities and characteristics in much the same sense as individuals and work groups possess descriptive attributes. In fact, we will find that formal organizations can be compared according to specific characteristics which are common to all of them. For example, one characteristic which tells us something about an organization is its *size.* We may estimate the size of an organization by enumerating the people on a company payroll, observing the number of teachers receiving salary from a school or school system, counting the number of inmates or guards in a prison, and even identifying the number of beds in a hospital or other type of medical facility. Other organizational characteristics might be *the centralization of authority and decision-making power, the specialization of tasks and the functional complexity of task interrelationships, and the proportionate size of the administrative component.* In subsequent chapters, detailed descriptions and definitions of these variables and some of the others most frequently cited in the professional literature will be presented.[5]

One primary objective of students of organizations is to explain and possibly to predict social phenomena by investigating their relationships with these major organizational properties. Hence, an important task of the formal organizational researcher is to delineate those major characteristics and focus upon (1) their interrelationships with other formal organizational properties and (2) their impact (either directly or indirectly) upon social and individual behaviors.

The units of analysis discussed above are not necessarily mutually exclusive. To a degree, they are complementary. Another aim of this book is to emphasize the formal organizational unit of analysis whenever possible and to describe some selected aspects of interaction between this unit and the others (i.e., the individual and the small group). An attempt will be made to demonstrate the influence of organizational variables on the individual and particularly on the groups of which he is a member. Table 1-1 summarizes the three units of analysis and depicts some of the major differences between them.

THEORY IN THE STUDY OF FORMAL ORGANIZATIONS

Understanding the seemingly complex networks of interrelations among the various dimensions of formal organizations is simplified to a degree by the

Table 1-1 Three Units of Analysis of Formal Organizations and Some Specific Interest Areas as Subcategorizations

Individual	Interpersonal	Large organization
1. Personal motivation	1. Incentives of work groups	1. Organizational commitment
2. Personal productivity	2. Output of work groups	2. Organizational effectiveness
3. Personal goals	3. Goals of work groups	3. Organizational goals
4. Personal adaptability	4. Informal group sanctioning system, flexibility of work groups	4. Organizational adaptability

use of theoretical frameworks or logical explanatory schemes. Such frameworks enable us to structure relationships between things in a consistent and systematic fashion. Therefore, organizational phenomena can be examined within the context of a logical scheme which includes a pattern or map of relationships between organizational events or characteristics. In a general sense, a theory may be defined as *an integrated body of assumptions and propositions which are related in such a way as to explain and predict relations between two or more variables* (adapted from Merton, 1957:96-99). The elements contained in this definition are defined and described as follows:

Assumptions

As used here, "assumptions" are analogous to empirical generalizations or observable regularities in human behavior (Merton, 1957:95-96). Assumptions imply regularly recurring relationships between things. For instance, some assumptions which pertain to organizations might be: (1) a hierarchy of authority relations exists in all formal organizations; (2) a division of labor exists in all formal organizations; and (3) there is a functional interdependence between roles in formal organizations. Such statements generally need little or no confirmation in the real world. They are statements about the observed nature of things which have been confirmed repeatedly so that there is little or no exception to them. We have much confidence in assumptions and take their validity for granted.

In a theory, assumptions provide a foundation for the development of an explanatory framework which will lead to the deduction of more tentative statements which can be tested in actual organizational situations. These statements are labeled *hypotheses. Hypotheses are statements which can be subjected to empirical test in order that the validity of any given theory from which they were deduced can be ascertained.*[6]

Propositions

Propositions have not yet achieved the generality and consistency of assumptions. Yet they provide somewhat tentative reflections of the real world. If we were to place propositions on a continuum together with assumptions, it might look something like the following:

Assumptions   Propositions
Certainty--Uncertainty

In effect, this continuum implies that we can differentiate between assumptions and propositions according to their respective degrees of "certainty" or "uncertainty." Compared with propositions, assumptions have a greater degree of certainty attached to them. However, not all researchers are in agreement as to which statements should be labeled as "assumptions" and which should be labeled as "propositions" at any given point in time.

The theorist constructs a theory of both assumptions and propositions. By carefully integrating empirical generalizations with less certain statements, he is able to advance the theory to a point where phenomena can be explained and understood. The theorist makes his most significant contribution to organizational theory at this juncture by extending his more certain knowledge about things into areas which lack satisfactory explanations or have been studied infrequently. Some examples of propositions might be: *(1) group cohesion varies directly with goal clarity; (2) the frequency of communication varies directly with type of authority;* and *(3) productivity varies directly with type of supervision.* Again, the researcher exercises judgment in determining which statements will be labeled as propositions and which ones will be labeled as assumptions or hypotheses.

In the context of uncertainty versus certainty, hypotheses are closest to the "uncertainty" end of the continuum above. Propositions are possibly former hypotheses which have been supported by empirical test in the real world. Assumptions lie toward the "certainty" end of the continuum, and therefore they often constitute the bases of our social theories. We need building blocks as supports for more tentative statements about things. Our scientific knowledge tends to move gradually toward certainty through continuous reexamination of particular phenomena in real-world social situations.

SOME DIFFICULTIES IN DEFINITIONS

One difficulty in trying to label a statement permanently as a "proposition," an "assumption," or a "hypothesis" is that continuing research in various areas of social phenomena causes such changes that what is a proposition today might well become an assumption tomorrow. New ideas have the effect of altering current definitions of things as well as changing our opinions about them and the strategies we use to investigate them. Of course, the more we learn about a given phenomenon, the better we are able to judge statements related to it as being either propositions or assumptions.

A second difficulty is that different researchers using the same statement or statements in their theoretical formulations may elect to use the statements differently. For example, one researcher may feel that the information currently available about a particular phenomenon is insufficient to warrant a strong assumption about it, whereas another investigator may without question readily include the same statement in his scheme as an assumption. Needless to say, the different uses of identical statements in competing theoretical schemes contribute to various kinds of theoretical and methodological problems for investigators who are concentrating their research efforts on the same dimension of an organizational problem. Such inconsistency promotes conflict, confusion, and disagreement among these researchers.

Although the area of formal organizations currently reflects some degree of consistency concerning *how* organizational phenomena should be defined, there is much disagreement and inconsistency with respect to research findings and their systematic interpretation. It will become increasingly noticeable that the field of formal organizations offers potential investigators an endless reservoir of phenomena to study and explain. Also, it will be seen that a wide variety of approaches (theoretical, methodological or both) to organizational research problems are acceptable within this flexible domain of social activity. Table 1-2 summarizes the basic application of theory to solutions of organizational problems. It should be noted that this diagram is consistent with the conventional approach to general social problem-solving, although it is expected that each researcher will modify and adapt various phases of the process of theory verification to fit his own needs and particular organizational situation.

Briefly reviewing, an organizational event, problem, or phenomenon is observed, and an explanation is developed to account for its occurrence. A theory is developed which links the event to the explanation of it, and testable hypotheses are deduced from the theoretical scheme. The two outcomes of tests of hypotheses are (1) the hypotheses will be supported by what is found, or (2) the hypotheses will be refuted by the empirical evidence. Supporting or refuting hypotheses derived from theory either strengthens or detracts from the predictive and explanatory power of the theoretical scheme. If a theory is supported (i.e., the hypotheses derived from it receive support and are defined as "true"), further study utilizing the same theoreti-

Table 1-2   A Conventional Linkage between Theory and Organizational Problems

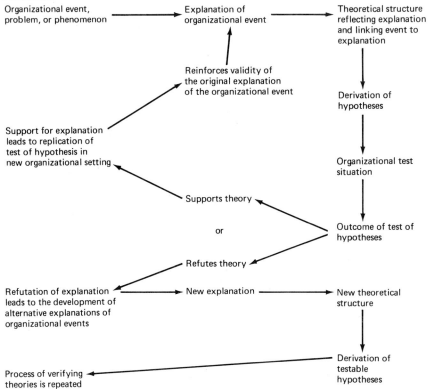

cal scheme is conducted which reinforces the validity of the original explanation. However, if the theory is refuted (i.e., the hypotheses derived from it are refuted and shown to be "false"), either (1) an alternative explanation is provided and subjected to empirical scrutiny, or (2) the explanation is tested again under new organizational circumstances so that it can be shown if it continues to lack predictive power.

The process of verifying a theory is slow and tedious. The truth or falsity of an explanation or theoretical scheme never rests entirely upon the results of a single study. This is why *replication research* (repeating the study under similar conditions in a different social setting) is necessary to increase our confidence in the explanations we provide for various social phenomena. As we discuss various organizational topics in subsequent chapters, inconsistencies will be observed in the findings from several studies investigating the same organizational phenomena. This is to be expected, particularly of research literature in a field which is continually developing new and better measurement procedures and conceptualization mechanisms. Replication research contributes significantly to our understanding of the complexities of social organizational phenomena.

LEVELS OF THEORY

In the same sense that there are levels or units of analysis for investigating organizational activity (i.e., the individual, the interpersonal or small group, and the large formal organization), there are also various levels of theory. In fact, social investigators construct theoretical schemes to fit the particular unit of analysis they choose in viewing organizations. As a result, researchers studying individual motivating factors associated with work behavior or the work-related attitudes of individuals will develop theoretical schemes to account for associations between individual motives and subsequent work actions or between work attitudes and subsequent task behaviors. Researchers who study small groups in formal organizations focus upon the nature of interpersonal relations, and they develop theoretical schemes to account for these associations. Formal organizational researchers develop theories to account for general organizational activity. Their explanatory schemes often include such relationships as organizational size and complexity and the levels of supervision and the functional autonomy of organizational roles in the division of labor. In other words, as the level of analysis moves from the individual, to the work group, to the formal organization, psychological explanations of individual behaviors on the job are replaced by sociological explanations of organizational phenomena.

Some theoretical schemes attempt to integrate all units of analysis with one another. These theoretical formulations are more difficult to construct, but they have the advantage of accounting for a larger share of organizational behavior more adequately than any single unit of inquiry considered separately. As specified previously, the formal organizational unit of analysis will be emphasized throughout this book, but we will certainly not ignore the important contribution of the other units.

SOME DIFFERENCES BETWEEN THEORIES AND MODELS OF ORGANIZATION

A *theory* about an organization is different from a *model* of it. Our conceptions of theories and models of organizations are frequently blurred because the terms are sometimes used synonymously. For example, Litterer (1965:147) begins a discussion of two basic forms of organizational theory by stating that "there are many different theories or models of organizations . . . [and] they tend to fall into two broad generic types." Other researchers add to the confusion of these terms as well. Krupp (1961:54) suggests that "there will be little need to separate a theory from a model. We will normally use these two words interchangeably."

In contrast, Rubenstein and Haberstroh (1966:18) distinguish between theories and models by using the criterion that

> theories are structured such that the conclusions derived from them can be placed into correspondence with (interpreted as) empirical hypotheses and confirmed or refuted by experiments. Models, on the other hand, are systems standing in the place of another, usually more complicated, system or object. Models have structures such that their premises are interpreted, and its conclusions are logical consequences of these. A theory can be refuted by a single contradictory empirical finding; a model is not exposed to refutation, but it is used as long as any benefit can be derived from it. A model can continue to be useful even though it yields many conclusions which are clearly wrong, provided only that it yields *some* conclusions that are correct (i.e., useful). A theory is expected to yield *only* true conclusions.

In this book a sharp distinction is made between so-called "organizational theories" and "organizational models." Consistent with the distinction made by Rubenstein and Haberstroh, a theory, as it has been defined in the preceding discussion, consists of an interrelated set of assumptions and propositions (arranged so that a logical explanatory and predictive scheme is constituted) from which testable hypotheses can be derived. A model, on the other hand, will refer to a set of organizational characteristics which permit portrayal of an organization or organizations from a particular viewpoint or dimension. For example, business and industrial organizations are engaged in continual competition with one another for increased customer patronage and consumption of products. One way of looking at organizations would be in terms of *what the organizations must do in order to remain economically sound*, in other words, competitive with other organizations. We would therefore focus attention on the extent to which departments within each organization examined perform functions which assist overall organizational performance with respect to the improvement of product quality in relation to the product quality of other firms. Some social scientists have termed such a view as the *survival model*, inasmuch as attention is focused upon those things which enable the organization to survive over time in relation to other organizations which compete for similar clientele.

If we agree to view an organization as a predetermined arrangement of individuals whose interrelated tasks and specialties allow the total aggregate to achieve goals, such a definition might be interpreted as reflecting a "goals" model. *The model functions to direct our energies and attention toward certain dimensions of organizations so that our theorizing about them can be enhanced.* In short, *organizational models enable us to grasp different dimensions of organizations which may elicit greater insight into the problems of organizations. Models act as classificatory schemes upon which theories can be constructed.* Therefore, if we choose to perceive an organization from a particular perspective (by application of model X), what can we theorize about interrelationships between various organizational variables?

This discussion is not intended to imply that models and theories are not complementary to one another. The fact is that *theories and models are very much related to one another, but identical in neither form nor function.* Certainly we would not label a frame of reference a "theory." The particular way a person chooses to look at things does not necessarily convey the explanatory scheme involved in linking the explanation of the event to the event itself. The relationship between frames of reference (i.e., ways of looking at or approaches toward problems), models, and theories is illustrated in Table 1-3.

In sum, the field of formal organizations is replete with organizational models which emphasize different dimensions of organizations. By contrast, what little we have which can be labeled as "organizational theory" is considerably less represented in the literature. Organizational theory in the formal sense is conspicuously absent in organizational research today. More often than not, classificatory schemes (models) are regarded as "theories," when, in fact, they do not perform explanatory and predictive functions. *An implicit objective of this book, therefore, will be to assess critically the existing literature and to portray the extent to which organizational theory exists as distinct from organizational models.*

SOME POSITIVE FUNCTIONS OF ORGANIZATIONAL MODELS

Even though organizational models are by their very nature different from theories of organizations, they nevertheless perform several important functions for the organizational researcher. Perhaps the most significant contri-

Table 1-3 The Relationship between Frames of Reference, Models, Theory, and Hypotheses

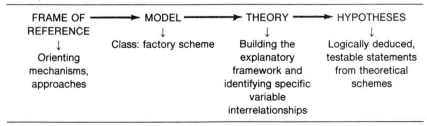

| FRAME OF REFERENCE ↓ Orienting mechanisms, approaches | → MODEL ↓ Class: factory scheme | → THEORY ↓ Building the explanatory framework and identifying specific variable interrelationships | → HYPOTHESES ↓ Logically deduced, testable statements from theoretical schemes |

bution of models is that *they permit the investigator to structure organizational components into patterns which will be useful subsequently in the development of more analytical theoretical schemes.* Each successive model which is developed provides a background for explanatory statements of relationship.

Another function of organizational models is that *they sensitize us to particular aspects of organizations which would go unnoticed were we to apply an alternative model when we view them.* If we consider several competing and alternative models when viewing the same organization, we get different impressions of the organization by viewing it from these different perspectives. This is comparable to examining a topographical map from different positions. What may not be clear according to one view may become clearer when looked at from another angle. *Models, therefore, are the means whereby we structure our thinking about organizations and systematize our investigations of them scientifically.*

There are several drawbacks to models, however. Although each model focuses our attention on specific dimensions of organizations, it is also true that we systematically ignore other dimensions of them. Therefore, an orienting device such as an organizational model may act like blinders on horses: we see certain things quite clearly, but there are other things, equally or more important, which we systematically exclude from our vision and consideration.

There are, then, positive and negative implications for using models. Sometimes a researcher will consider an organizational structure from several different perspectives in order to determine which orientation gives him the best vantage point for assessing problems within the organization. It will be seen in the next chapter that many organizational models exist and that they overlap each other to some degree. The weaknesses inherent in some models may well be offset by the strengths of others. There will always be limitations and strengths accompanying each model selected for organizational analysis.

A NOTE ON THE "STRATEGIES" APPROACH

The general orientation toward the acquisition of organizational knowledge which is followed here derives from the "strategies" approach. This centers upon the development and cultivation of theoretical and methodological skills as strategies designed for organizational problem solving.

The strategies approach is not altogether different from the approaches used to solve problems in relationships between doctor and patient, lawyer and client, and teacher and student. In each of these interactions, the objective is to develop solutions to problems for the purpose of "curing" (doctor-patient), "assisting" (lawyer-client), "improving" (teacher-student), or all three. In each situation there is a *client system* experiencing difficulty: an illness, a lawsuit, or a lack of knowledge. The "helper" or *agent of change* in each case applies skills which are believed to act positively upon the client system. Problem solving is quite difficult at the individual level. Accordingly, at the organizational level, the social scientist is saddled with different kinds of problems, but they are of at least the same seriousness and magnitude as individual ones. Some social scientists contend that organizational problem solving is considerably more complex than individual problem solving. But one thing is clear regardless of the position one takes: solutions to organizational problems are difficult to achieve.

Using a strategies approach in our assessment of organizational problems and identifying interrelations between phenomena will enable us to examine organizations from a variety of perspectives. One objective of this approach will be to develop an impression of the relative strengths and weaknesses of alternative competing schemes as strategies. In order to increase the effectiveness of this book, therefore, it would be helpful for the reader to learn to identify with the role of "helper" as organizational phenomena are examined. In a sense, the reader of this volume becomes a potential "advice giver" or "agent of change" in relation to some client system (i.e., an organization). He acquires a set of useful strategies for the purpose of developing a greater awareness and understanding of the nature and operations of organizations.

At first glance it may seem that a person must memorize several strategies which may function as a "bag of tricks" and can be categorically applied as he moves from one organization to the next in a helping capacity. Although it is useful to have at one's disposal a fund of knowledge about the many facets of organizational activity, the role of the agent of change is far more involved than simply dispensing theoretical cures for organizational problems. The agent of change must not only assess the organization and its dilemmas, but he must also consider seriously his own capabilities and potential contribution toward remedying the existing problem. It is not uncommon for agents of change (professional consultants to business and industry) to find that the information previously acquired in the college classroom is of little or no value in particular organizational situations. In that event, it is necessary for the agent of change to "play it by ear," in a sense. He becomes an artist studying the uniqueness of the client system. Through a close association with the client system he becomes increasingly sensitive to whether the organization (as the client system) has the skills and capabilities to deal successfully with its own problems. His job is to help the client system to determine whether change is necessary at all, and if so, what the direction and nature of change will be as well as its potential theoretical and substantive implications. Accurately forecasting social or organizational change and its results is quite difficult to accomplish, but some appreciation of the potential positive or negative consequences of change should always be provided.

The agent of change most able to benefit client systems usually is the one with (1) the most strategies, (2) the skills to apply the strategies adroitly, and (3) the insight to counsel with the client system concerning the potential implications of organizational change. He must be a good teacher, a good critic, and a good listener. Above all, he must be *flexible in his thinking* and must not allow himself to be drawn toward one solution too quickly and blindly before considering the relative merits of other possible solutions.

To summarize briefly, the strategies approach will be used in the assessment and delineation of organizational phenomena and problems. In several instances to follow in later chapters, problems will be presented and competing solutions will be reviewed and discussed in terms of their weaknesses and strengths.

Some persons contend that books by themselves are poor substitutes for thinking about and dealing successfully with organizational problems. For this reason, in part, numerous sources are cited in the bibliography at the end of this book (indexed according to a variety of topics and variables). These sources will assist the reader in developing greater flexibility in his orientation toward assessments of organizational activity. Logged in many of these references are firsthand experiences and personal accounts of individuals who have studied different kinds of organizations. These accounts should be helpful in expanding the reader's "experience horizon" as well.

THE PLAN OF THIS BOOK

The remainder of this book is designed as follows. Several popular organizational models will be presented and examined. These models provide different ways of conceptualizing organizational activities. It will be shown, for example, that explanations of organizational phenomena vary according to the ways in which organizations are viewed and defined. Using alternative organizational models will draw our attention to different dimensions of organizational structures. One type of model may emphasize the functional interrelatedness of roles in an organizational hierarchy. Another model may emphasize the concerted action of individuals pursuing personal interests as an explanation for more abstract organizational activity. Each model emphasizes one aspect of organizational life, then, and it is not uncommon to find that different organizational models will overlap one another at various points. The reader will find that some models compared with the rest lend themselves more appropriately to certain types of social settings. Learning about some of the more important weaknesses and strengths of each model and becoming familiar with the settings where these models have the greatest explanatory value and application will be two important objectives.

A systematic treatment of selected variables which are cited most frequently in organizational research will follow. Each variable will be categorized according to whether it performs an explanatory function (i.e., does the variable contribute to an explanation of organizational activity and, if so, to what extent and in what ways?) or an indicator function (i.e., is the variable used to determine the impact of other variables?). Each variable will be defined, and several examples will be drawn from the literature to illustrate the usefulness of the variable in organizational research.

Consistent with the strategies approach outlined in the previous section, it is helpful for the researcher to familiarize himself with many organizational variables. The variables which are treated here, therefore, may be regarded as useful strategies in much the same sense as organizational models are viewed as strategies. The variables will also be categorized according to whether they best fit the organizational, interpersonal, or individual units of analysis. The reader will recognize that not all variables are pertinent or useful in explaining all organizational activity under all circumstances. The primary importance of cultivating a familiarity with these variables is to generate flexibility in the analysis of organizational phenomena.

Several research techniques for facilitating investigations of the sociological aspects of organizations will be examined. The administration of questionnaires, interviewing, observation as participants, field research, and case studies will be treated in some detail, with the objective of illustrating the applicability of each technique in the study of organizations. In each case, some of the more important advantages and disadvantages of the technique presented will be discussed. Techniques of collecting research data may be viewed as strategies useful in problem solving as well. It will be shown, for example, that social investigators utilize particular research strategies or procedures for collecting data singly or in combination as a means of demonstrating the validity of the explanations they provide for organizational activity. Again, many of the weaknesses and strengths together with some actual examples of empirical research employing one or more techniques will be presented.

We will also examine the nature of authority systems and patterns of formal organizations. In addition to dealing with the structural aspects of authority hierarchies, we will focus upon the behavior of the leadership under a variety of organizational circumstances. Models of power will be treated together with delineations of some of the major implications of supervisory styles for the behaviors of organizational members.

Communication in formal organizations and its importance for achieving organizational objectives will be treated briefly. The communication functions of formal and informal groupings of persons in organizations will be described and the implications of various types of communication networks will be noted and elaborated. Several organizational factors associated with the satisfaction, motivation, and morale of workers will be considered. Some of the classical literature will be reviewed which describes workers' and employees' behavior in both blue- and white-collar settings. It will be shown, for example, that the nature of interpersonal activities in formal organizations significantly influences organizational development and growth and emerges as a very important dimension which should be considered in virtually every organizational problem.

Finally, we will focus upon the nature of planned and unplanned changes in formal organization. Besides paying attention to the impact of administrative changes in the structure and functioning of organizational activity, the role of agents of change and other external stimuli in relation to organizations as client systems will be discussed. What are the adaptive mechanisms which organizations employ in response to internal and external forces? The general impact of technological change and automation upon organizational structure and the functional interrelationships between organizational members will be described in some detail. Some of the more crucial social effects of automation will be highlighted, and some of the more important implications of displacement of organizational members, possibly resulting from this factor, will be examined.

Following the last chapter of this book, several hypothetical case studies are given which describe some common problems in social interaction in formal organizations. After each case are several questions which require the reader to develop alternative explanations for behaviors which have been described. The questions are designed so that the reader can use organizational models as strategies as well as organizational, interpersonal, and individual variables in developing an explanation for why the problems exist. Since there are no "correct" solutions or analyses of the organizational problems presented in each case, the reader should deal with each by offering several alternative solutions and defend them by citing some of their weaknesses and strengths in application in each instance.

SUMMARY

This chapter has sought to acquaint the beginning student with the broad area of formal organizations and some of the reasons social scientists provide for studying them. Many kinds of organizations are examined by social investigators; and although formal organizations naturally differ from one another, it is the predominant belief of professionals in the field that they share certain common characteristics having to do with patterns of growth, hierarchies of authority, communication networks, and so on.

Organizations can be studied from a great number of perspectives, each giving insights and meaningful explanations which advance our understanding of what is going on in organizations and why. Scientific inquiry is used as the primary investigative medium, and statements about organizations are made in a theoretical context and repeatedly subjected to empirical testing. Theories about various aspects of organizations are developed primarily to explain and predict interrelations between variables at the organizational, interpersonal, and individual level.

A sociological approach to organizations necessarily involves a consideration of how the individual, the group, and the organization as a whole are integrated. How organizations affect groups of employees or volunteers, how groups within organizations affect other groups, and how organizations and groups interact with the individual and other organizations are primary sociological concerns.

There is much to be learned about organizations and their static and dynamic features. The field is currently expanding, flexible, and responsive to new ideas and avenues of scientific inquiry. A *strategies approach* has been suggested to help the reader understand how each topic treated in this text can be of both theoretical and practical value in considering questions about all aspects of organizations.

STUDY QUESTIONS

1 In what respects, if any, do organizational theories differ from organizational models? Explain.
2 What are the three units of analysis to be used in the examination of formal organizations? To what extent are they conceptually different from one another? Can a case be made for integrating them in approaching organizational problems? Explain.
3 Why do researchers study formal organizations? Why is it important to study them? Do you feel that "pure" organizational research is justified? Why or why not?
4 On the basis of your reading, what do you feel are the most important functions of organizational models? Elaborate.
5 Differentiate between an assumption and a proposition. List at least five of each which might be applicable to organizations. (It makes no difference whether you select any particular unit of analysis for the basis of your propositions and assumptions.)
6 Describe briefly the verification process in organizational theory. Why does our knowledge of formal organizations grow so slowly? Explain.
7 Do you feel that inconsistencies in findings in a given field such as formal organizations are necessarily harmful to the development of theories? Why or why not?
8 Differentiate between (and define) an agent of change and a client system. What relationship or relationships exist between them?

9 What complementarity exists between individual personality systems and organizational structure? Give some examples in your response.

NOTES

[1] This definition is a modification of the one provided by Etzioni (1964:3).

[2] A general lack of consensus concerning definitions of social phenomena is characteristic of most emerging social sciences. The social sciences are replete with neologisms, and "outsiders" (i.e., non-social-scientists) have been quick to take issue with and criticize the social researcher for his repeated failure to devise satisfactory definitions for his objects of study which are acceptable to the profession at large. As a result, the social science literature contains a vast array of articles geared to systematize the labels which we apply to social events and individual behaviors. In spite of the state of flux which currently prevails, a significant amount of information has been amassed on the subject of formal organizations. A careful review of research contributions to this important subarea of sociology will reveal that interdisciplinary interests are strong (Rubenstein and Haberstroh, 1966). Contributors to the literature on organizational structure and process represent many fields including sociology, psychology, business administration, social psychology, anthropology, industrial management and engineering, education, political science, and economics. The fact that investigators from different educational fields in the social sciences are involved in the assessment of organizational activity suggests a multiplicity of approaches to a common set of problems. Although there is considerable similarity among these respective investigators concerning the research topics selected, there is also a significant amount of fragmentation associated with the diversity of their contributed information. It is not too difficult to imagine that different approaches to the same problem will eventually lead to competing explanations of them. Seldom are the researcher's efforts directed toward the harmonious arrangement and integration of competing explanatory schemes. More frequently, explanatory frameworks are designed so as to exclude significant amounts of useful information from competing fields. Frank (1954:9–23) has noted the extensive fragmentation of the "helping professions" or social professions in attacking the same problems. He observes that: "surely we must sometimes agree upon an acceptable theory or common assumption about human conduct and how it is produced if our scientific studies are to prosper and our hopes for multidisciplinary studies are to be realized. This does not imply that various disciplines are to give up their chosen fields and problems, but rather, that they construct some acceptable conceptual framework and some shared assumptions which each can use on whatever problems it may study in its field or profession."

Contemporary articles include attempts to clarify and reclarify concepts, lengthy elaborations of new methodologies by which social phenomena can be investigated more thoroughly and scientifically, and revelations of new terms which have greater heuristic value compared with old and obsolete ones. Needless to say, these disagreements and inconsistencies have both beneficial and detrimental implications. On the one hand, a growing field must be flexible enough to welcome and tolerate new ideas and conceptions of things and to permit change in order to improve our knowledge of organizational behavior. Alternatively, the proliferation of paradigms (Merton, 1957:14-16) and the demands for originality in designs and approaches to organizational phenomena retard the accumulation of sorely needed replication research. For it is primarily through the replication of social investigations that we are able to move our present knowledge of things to more advanced and refined levels.

[3] Some of the specialities included in the 1967 *American Sociological Association Directory of Sociologists* include bureaucracy, industrial, occupational, stratification, employee and executive training and development, employee morale and attitudes, job analysis and position classification, labor-management relations, organizational behavior, performance evaluation, criterion development, recruiting, selection, placement, safety research and training, innovation, and invention (pp. ix-x).

[4] Bernard M. Bass, *Organizational Psychology,* Boston, Allyn and Bacon, 1965; Daniel Katz, "The Motivational Basis of Organizational Behavior," *Behavioral Science,* **9**:131-146, 1964; A. P. Quinn and R. L. Kahn, "Organizational Psychology," *Annual Review of Psychology,* **18**:437-466, 1967; E. H. Schein, *Organizational Psychology,* Englewood Cliffs, N.J., Prentice-Hall, 1965; and Arnold S. Tannenbaum, *Social Psychology of the Work Organization,* Belmont, Calif., Wadsworth, 1966.

[5] The problems of measuring organizational characteristics will be discussed in Chapters 3 and 4. For the present, it is sufficient to understand that organizations have measurable characteristics (we may not always agree on how to measure any given phenomenon) and that these characteristics can possibly be used in explaining social phenomena occurring within the organization.

[6] This view of theory is based upon deduction. It is readily acknowledged that inductive models as well may be used for theoretical purposes. The greater simplicity of presenting the deductive model is a primary consideration for its inclusion here.

Chapter 2

Some Organizational Models

INTRODUCTION

An Indian tsar summoned several blind men together and asked them to describe an elephant. Each blind man touched a different part of the elephant (i.e., legs, trunk, tail, head, tusks, and sides), and, as a result, each gave a different account of what an elephant was like to him (Tolstoi, 1928:439-440). In some respects, this story may be adapted to fit organizational researchers who select different approaches for investigating organizational behavior. Depending upon the model chosen for analysis, a different view of organization phenomena will be obtained. A model functions, in part, *to provide the researcher with a way of looking at the organizations he examines.*

Each organizational model stresses a particular dimension or characteristic of organizations. To a degree, models complement one another in that some of them focus upon things which other models tend to ignore. Organizational models are used because of the unique explanatory advantages they give to social investigators as they attempt to account for the observed conditions of organizational structures.

This chapter will examine critically several popular organizational models or classificatory schemes. In each case, the usefulness of the model will be discussed together with its major weaknesses and strengths. It will be seen that most organizational models are subclassifications of or overlap other schemes. One advantage of organizing these models is to permit a more simplified and systematic assessment of their respective contributions for studying particular organizations.

SOME GENERAL LIMITATIONS OF MODELS

Given the rather large number of organizational models currently in existence, the question arises as to which model is the best to use under most organizational conditions. Although this question is easily asked, it is not easily answered. Currently, there are several barriers which prevent unanimity regarding which of several organizational models is most productive and universally applicable. Some of the more significant barriers are identified below.

All organizational models are replete with exceptions. Thus far, organizational models are either too narrow in application (i.e., they fit a limited number of organizations but do not apply to the rest of them) or too broad (i.e., they are so generally descriptive that they are of little value to researchers interested in explaining the differences between two or more organizations which appear on the surface to be identical to one another). Researchers who use "organizational size" as a classification characteristic find that a sufficient number of other organizational properties exist to contaminate relationships between the size factor and other dimensions. For example, two organizations may be of the same size (defined, perhaps, in terms of membership), but the fact that one organization is primarily a voluntary agency and the other is a bureau of highly paid physical scientists makes for marked contrasts between them which are unexplained by size alone.

All models emphasize different dimensions of organizations. Many of these dimensions are equally important. Therefore, the deliberate inclusion of particular characteristics and the systematic exclusion of others renders most, if not all, models inadequate for analyzing organizations.

Many models are derivatives and modifications of others. The terminology used to describe the resulting subclassifications of certain organizational models is inconsistent and confusing. Should a researcher talk about "classical" organizational models, or "machine" models, or "traditional" models when all of these refer to the same thing? Or should the investigator refer to "goals" models, "rational" models, "effectiveness" models, "professional" models, or "human relations" models when discussing "bureaucratic" models? The overlapping of models poses a significant obstacle to researchers who wish to make decisions about which ones should be used for organizational analysis.

Many organizational models are designed for examining static organization arrangements. Given the fact that all organizations are constantly changing, dynamic structures, some models are unrealistic and eventually become inapplicable as organizations change in size, complexity, and function.

All models vary according to the primary unit of analysis selected for investigation. Motivational models, which emphasize personal willingness to become involved in organizational activity and to pursue the organization's goals, focus upon the individual as the unit of analysis. The "human relations" model focuses primarily upon the unit of the work group. The "equilibrium" model selects the entire organization as the basic analytical unit.

Models constructed many years ago continue to generate criticism and dialogue in contemporary social science and organizational literature. More recent schemes are falling under similar scrutiny. The uneven utilization of models in research has no doubt contributed to the extensive investigation of the validity of a few, while other models have not as yet been exposed to specific research applications. Many social scientists legitimately proclaim that, as of now at least, we do not have sufficient information about these models to make competent judgments about their fruitfulness as analytical tools. We are still in the process of inventing new models and conducting ad hoc investigations of these as well as the "old" ones.

Since the development of organizational theory is heavily dependent upon a satisfactory organizational model, the present theoretical void in organizational analysis is not entirely surprising. Given the existing conceptualization and theoretical inadequacies of formal organizational research, an attempt will be made here to place several organizational models in proper analytical perspective in relation to one another. Accompanying each of these models in the following presentation will be brief discussions of their relative usefulness. It has often been said that sociology is an "art." This statement implies that decisions about interrelationships between variables in the social world are not always clear-cut. Rather, the process of determining causal relations between things is complex and tedious, and it frequently demands that the researcher use some degree of imagination in order to locate the best approach for studying the problem as well as the best solution for it. The assessment of various models as strategies for analyzing organizational arrangements is equally arduous. The researcher compares and contrasts, ultimately selecting a model which, to him at least, offers the most strategic explanatory advantage.

ON THE CLASSIFICATION OF ORGANIZATIONAL MODELS

Hall (1972:78) aptly assesses the state of the field regarding models by saying that classificatory schemes are needed in every facet of social life for thought and action. He contends that despite the need for typologies, no adequate scheme for organizations is currently available. One obvious implication of this statement is that we currently have a collection of inadequate models for organizational analysis. In fairness to existing schemes it would be more accurate to say that all schemes exhibit weaknesses as well as strengths, especially in relation to particular organizational research problems. It may be that the development of a universally applicable organizational scheme is currently beyond the reach of organizational theorists, given the shortcomings of our technology and theoretical sophistication. Although organizational theorists attempt to develop all-encompassing models in their endeavors, they are usually among the first to catalog the weaknesses, inconsistencies, and inadequacies of their own schemes. If the word "inadequate" is meant to describe models which are not free from exception in their application, then *all models developed to date are, by definition, inadequate.*[1]

In contrast to the "without exception" criterion used to assess the adequacy of models, each scheme selected for discussion in the present chapter will be assumed to possess weaknesses and strengths complementary to the others. The principle of *relative usefulness* will be applied here. This principle is summarized briefly in a passage from Rubenstein and Haberstroh (1966:18) quoted in the previous chapter: "A model can continue to be useful even though it yields many conclusions which are clearly wrong, provided only that it yields *some* conclusions that are correct (i.e., useful)."

The classification of models is almost as difficult as developing the models themselves. This is particularly true when we consider the pressure upon theorists to make original contributions to their field. In spite of this pressure, there are continuities among various models developed to date. Although some models are distinct from the rest and are not amenable to "grouping," others may be categorized conveniently under several general headings. For instance, all organizations, regardless of their degree of complexity, formality, or size may be viewed as social systems of interaction. One of the basic assumptions of this book, therefore, is that *meaningful explanations of organizational behavior cannot be provided without due consideration to the processes of social interaction within organizations.*

All organizational models reflect particular ways of looking at organizations and the groups within them. Stogdill (1971:4) lists eighteen basic premises and orientations in theories of organization which serve to illustrate the

Table 2-1   Some Basic Premises and Orientations in Theories of Organization

1. Organization as a cultural product
2. Organization as an agent of exchange with its environment
3. Organization as an independent agency
4. Organization as a system of structures and functions
5. Organization as a structure in action over time
6. Organization as a system of dynamic functions
7. Organization as a processing system
8. Organization as an input-output system
9. Organization as a structure of subgroups
10. Subgroups in interaction with the organization
11. Subgroups in interaction with each other
12. Groups as biological-social entities
13. Groups as cultural products
14. Groups as independent entities
15. Groups as interaction systems
16. Groups as interaction-expectation systems
17. Groups as collections of individual members
18. Groups as summations of member characteristics

Source: Stogdill, 1971:4.

differentiation between various organizational schemes. These are shown in Table 2-1. Stogdill notes that the list in Table 2-1 is certainly not exhaustive and is indicative of the current unsatisfactory condition of organizational theory. He suggests, "which concepts and problems are regarded as important in the study of organization are determined in part by the view or combination of views held by the theorist, in part by the philosophical and professional schools to which he subscribes, and in part by the individual conceptualizations he wishes to advance" (pp. 3-4).

Katz and Kahn (1966:18) have suggested that models are either *closed-* or *open-system* schemes. Closed-system models rely almost wholly upon processes within organizations to account for organizational behavior. Open-system models, on the other hand, stress the interrelations of organizations with their environment (i.e., other organizations) and seek explanations of organizational behavior among factors outside of immediate organizational boundaries.

A similar distinction has been made between closed- and open-system analysis. Rice and Bishoprick (1971:164-165) add that:

> The simplest and perhaps the most widely used and most valuable application of the systems concept is that of closed-system analysis. . . . notice that a closed system is a hypothetical construct. Closed systems do not exist in reality. There

Table 2-2   A Reclassification of Stogdill's Organizational Orientations Presented in Table 2-1

Closed-system orientations	Open-system orientations
1. Organization as an independent agency 2. Organization as a system of structures and functions 3. Organization as a structure in action over time 4. Organization as a processing system 5. Organization as a system of dynamic functions 6. Organization as a structure of subgroups	1. Organization as a cultural product 2. Organization as an agent of exchange with its environment 3. Organization as an input-output system

Source: Adapted from Stogdill, 1971:4.

never was, and probably never will be, a completely closed system, because components are always influenced by forces not being considered—that is, by forces outside the system itself. But closed-system analysis as a way of *thinking about* the interaction of components is extremely useful.

If we were to rearrange the orientations toward organizations shown in Table 2-1 and align them under the classifications of closed and open systems, we might generate such a grouping as is shown in Table 2-2.

At least for the present listing of organizational orientations, a simple frequency count of these views under the closed- and open-system classifications offers tentative support for Rice and Bishoprick's contention (1971:164) that closed-system analysis is most widely used in research. Certainly the research advantages of studying an organization without considering external factors as "causes" of organizational behavior contribute strongly to the use of closed-system analysis. Another advantage is the increased simplicity of explanatory schemes of organizational phenomena which do not have to utilize and account for the effects of external factors.[2]

Several popular organizational models have been selected and grouped under the closed- and open-system classification in Table 2-3. It is conceded that several of these models might be grouped under both classifications, given the overlap inherent in them. The grouping in Table 2-3, however, reflects the emphasis of the scheme upon primarily "internal" or upon primarily "external" factors as explanatory tools.

Table 2-3 has been further subdivided into *rational* and *nonrational* systems in the closed-system category. This subdivision evidences the differ-

Table 2-3 A Tentative Classification of Organizational Models within a Systems Context

Organizations as systems		
Closed systems		Open systems
Rational	Nonrational	

1. Machine models
   a. Scientific manage-
      ment
   b. Bureaucracy
2. The goals model
3. The decision model
	1. The human relations
	   model
	2. The professional model
	3. The equilibrium model
		1. The natural-systems
		   model

ent assumptions about organizational participants held by theorists who must contend repeatedly with the potential outcomes of member interaction in organizations. In simplified form, these distinctions are as follows.

The rational assumption is that planned (expected or anticipated) outcomes will follow planned organizational structures and processes. In short, this means that if we arrange the organization according to a set of rules, we can logically expect certain outcomes, such as a smooth-running organization, heightened efficiency, and increased productivity. In contrast, the nonrational assumption is that planned organizational structures and processes sometimes have unplanned consequences or outcomes. For example, Blau (1955) describes an unexpected consequence of the introduction of statistical records to chart the productivity of interviews in a public employment facility. Each interviewer was charged with the responsibility of trying to find jobs for prospective employees and to provide a service to employers as well. The interviewers were divided into two sections, A and B. Members of both sections were assessed in terms of the number of successful job placements over a given time period. The original source is not very clear on this point, but apparently interviewers in section B were *not* evaluated by their supervisor as rigorously as were those in section A in terms of how many job placements they made during a certain period of time; this, combined with the greater job security felt by the members of section B, was the apparent reason that the members of section B were less competitive among themselves than were the members of section A. If any interviewer in section A had a job applicant (job applicants came to all interviewers of both sections according to random assignment) but did not have a suitable job at the moment, it was understood that the interviewer would make known to the other members of his section the availability of the job applicant. The idea of rating the employees according to their individual performance actually backfired in at least one of the sections. Some interviewers would hoard descriptions of jobs or applicants from their fellow interviewers until an appropriate employee-employer match could be found. The result was an overall decline in the effectiveness of the employment agency rather than the anticipated increase in job placements. One of the important reasons given for this decline was that at least one supervisor was using the statistical records as a means of evaluating and promoting the agency personnel under his direct control, thus pitting his subordinates against one another rather than encouraging them to work together as a "team" for the good of the entire agency.

It should be noted that examples of virtually all the models to be discussed in the present section are found in most organizations today independent of their sequential recognition and introduction into the organizational literature. For instance, some firms continue to operate on early-1900 managerial assumptions and models which organizational researchers have repeatedly found in empirical investigations to have deleterious effects on the morale and the levels of work performance of subordinates.

CLOSED-SYSTEM MODELS—THE RATIONAL ASSUMPTION

Machine Models

The forerunner of many organizational schemes today is generally acknowledged as the machine model. Known popularly as the classical or traditional model of organization, the machine model is best portrayed in the work of Fayol (1949), Gilbreth and Gilbreth (1917), Gulick and Urwick (1937), Mooney and Reiley (1939), Taylor (1911), and Weber (1947). Although each of these authors probably regarded his contribution as unique, there are fundamental theoretical principles common to all which dictate that the schemes be combined. For our purposes, the machine model as exemplified by these authors will be treated as a single model category. Some writers feel that it is unfair and misleading to use the terms "traditional" and "classical" to describe certain organizational ideas. One rationale for such a designation is that the models classified as "traditional" are the ones which prevailed in the early development of organizational theory and practice (Carzo and Yanouzas, 1967:24).

Katz and Kahn (1966:71) provide a description of the application of the machine model to organizations: "The organization, though consisting of people, is viewed . . . as a machine, and—[the implication is] . . . that just as we build a mechanical device with given sets of specifications for accomplishing the task, so we construct an organization according to a blueprint to achieve a given purpose." Massie (1965:405) makes explicit some of the more important assumptions of classical theory:

> Efficiency of an undertaking is measured solely in terms of productivity. Efficiency relates to a mechanical process and the economic utilization of resources without consideration of human factors. Human beings can be assumed to act rationally. The important considerations in management are only those which involve individuals and groups of individuals heading logically toward their goals. Members in a cooperative endeavor are unable to work out the relationships of their positions without detailed guidance from their superiors. Unless clear limits to jobs are defined and enforced, members will tend to be confused and to trespass on the domains of others. Human beings prefer the security of a definite task and do not value the freedom of determining their own approaches to problems; they prefer to be directed and will not cooperate unless a pattern is planned formally for them. It is possible to predict and establish clear-cut patterns of future activities and the relationships among activities. The total groups of tasks can be outlined in advance of execution. Management involves primarily the formal and official activities of individuals. The activities of a group should be viewed on an objective and impersonal basis without regard to personal problems and characteristics. Workers are motivated by economic needs, and therefore, incentives should be in terms of monetary systems. People do not like to work, and therefore, close supervision and accountability should be emphasized. Management must lead people fairly and firmly in ways that are not part of their inherent nature. Coordination will not be achieved unless it is planned and directed from above. Authority has its source at the top of a hierarchy and is delegated downward. Simple tasks are easier to master and thus lead toward higher productivity by concentrating on a narrow scope of activity. Managerial functions in varied types of activities, have universal characteristics, and can be performed in a given manner, regardless of the environment and qualities of the personnel involved.

Katz and Kahn (1966:71–72) provide us with a parallel set of concepts which are applicable to machine theory. They include specialization of tasks, standardization of roles, unity of command and centralization of decision making, uniformity of practices, and no duplication function.

The primary objective of machine theory (not unlike several other theories of organization) is to maximize efficiency. Therefore, attention is directed to those aspects of organizations which can be rearranged and structured so as to fulfill this objective. Fayol (1949) believed that certain management principles should be applied, such as a division of work, authority, discipline, unity of command, unity of direction, subordination of individual interest to general interest, remuneration of personnel, centralization, scalar chain (the chain of superiors running from highest to lowest), order, equity, stability of tenure of personnel, initiative, and esprit de corps (Fayol, 1949:20–40). Supposedly one result of the application of these principles is the maximization of efficiency. Two variations of machine theory will be examined here: (1) scientific management and (2) bureaucratic organization.

Scientific Management　Frederick W. Taylor (1911) has exerted perhaps the greatest impact on the entire field of organizational management. Formally acknowledged as the "father of scientific management," Taylor held to ideas similar to those of Fayol, which encompassed many of the characteristics defined by Massie (1965). Basically, Taylor believed that a maximization of efficiency in organizations could be achieved by the segmentation of all tasks involved in production into a series of simple movements and operations. Each worker could be trained to perform a few simple operations, and the combined efforts of all workmen laboring for the common good would maximize efficiency and productivity. Taylor also believed that the average worker is not capable of being self-motivated. He implied that the worker is interested in doing only what is minimally required by management. Therefore, in addition to the redesigning and simplifying of tasks, increased productivity could be achieved by the creation of incentives to work harder during a specified time period. Taylor advocated using a bonus system to reward men who exceeded the minimum of work expected of them. For example, a worker would receive additional compensation for producing ten units of product per day when his normal production expectation is set at only eight units.

Spaulding (1961:189) indicates that "Taylor's most specific contribution was his idea of measuring a suitable day's work, leading as it did to time-and-motion studies and many complex methods of wage payments." In this regard, Taylor suggested that men could be directed, like robots, to perform at command in a predetermined manner. Adhering to a mandatory schedule of rest pauses and work periods, the worker would, at all times during the work day, be at his peak efficiency.

The Bureaucratic Model　Many authors have acknowledged that the writings of Max Weber (1864-1920) have been most influential in the development of modern organizational theory (Merton et al., 1952:17; Etzioni, 1964:50; Mouzelis, 1968:38). Some of Weber's notions (Gerth and Mills, 1946; Weber, 1947) have exerted significant impacts upon general organizational structures and leadership theories. Even workers' orientations toward their jobs have been affected indirectly by the organizational form Weber outlined.[3]

The most popular manifestation of the machine model, the bureaucratic model, prescribes a list of essential components which must be present within organizations in order for maximum efficiency to be obtained. Exploiting the rationality assumption fully, Weber made explicit the following characteristics of an ideally effective organization:[4] (1) impersonal social relations; (2) appointment and promotion on the basis of merit; (3) previously specified authority obligations which inhere in the position, not in the individual functioning in the position; (4) a hierarchy of authority; (5) abstract rules or laws covering task assignments and decisions; and (6) specialization of position.

Weber believed that members of organizations should not relate to one another on a personal basis. His emphasis upon impersonal social relations was a direct assault on the nepotism prevalent in many organizations in his time. Weber assigned much significance to the importance of specific laws which would govern the positions of superiors and decisions made by them. In the general context within which Weber outlined this characteristic, a government should operate according to previously specified laws which would eliminate the possibility of favoring one individual over another in any particular situation. This would reduce substantially, if not entirely eliminate, differential favoritism based on familial connections or personal friendships. Maintaining personal distance between oneself and others meant that less emotion would be involved when it came to enforcing the rules of the organization. The matter of retiring older personnel would be handled more impersonally, and employees could be reprimanded more easily by their supervisors. Guards in prisons must maintain social distance between themselves and the inmates, as an example. Once a guard allows himself to become a "friend" of an inmate or inmates, he supposedly loses a great deal of control over them. Impersonality is conceived to be a strong defense against the potential loss of power should a supervisor consider becoming too friendly with his subordinates.

Again, nepotism becomes the target of Weber's analysis as he specified that employees be selected on the basis of their abilities and promoted according to their performance compared with the performance of others competing for higher positions in the organization. This characteristic eliminates the possibility of hiring the supervisor's son just because he is the supervisor's son. All persons available for particular jobs are thrown into competition for them. The persons rating higher than the rest in terms of their abilities and accomplishments ultimately obtain the positions. This feature ensures that the best-qualified persons will be performing the available jobs.

Each employee should have jurisdiction over his own work activity and be responsible to a supervisor for his role performance. The authority of a position should not change simply because a person is replaced by another upon retirement. The position exists independent of the individual personalities filling that position. For example, there are several expectations of supervisors which do not change as different persons perform the same supervisory job. The person's personal characteristics should have no bearing on how the supervisory job should be performed. A person's authority extends to the boundaries of his present position rather than infringing upon the jobs of others.

Weber also believed strongly that rules of law would enable people to make decisions more objectively rather than allowing their personal judgment to interfere. Also, a system of abstract laws would enable functionaries to succeed one another more easily. This characteristic seems to accompany closely Weber's notion of impersonality. The impersonal implementation of abstract rules or laws in organizational decision making approximates Weber's ideal view of the official behavior of managers.

Each person should develop a high level of competence in a specified task area. By dividing the totality of organizational roles into various basic components, each person would be able to maximize his effectiveness of performance. Each person would exercise absolute control over his job-related activities, but he would be barred from interfering with the ways by which others carry out their role obligations. In essence, Weber endorsed the idea of boundaries within which each official (or worker, employee, etc.) would function. Each would have his own "sphere of competence" and fixed jurisdiction over the aspects of work of his immediate position.

In addition to these organizational requirements, Weber prescribed several ideal characteristics of officials. As Weber saw it, the position of the office holder or official in a "bureaucracy" (the name applied to the organizational form he described) should be consistent with the following: (1) office holding should be viewed as a vocation; (2) the official should enjoy social esteem; (3) the official should be appointed (presumably on merit) rather than elected; (4) the position of the office holder is held for life; (5) a fixed salary and fixed security benefits should accompany the office held; and (6) the official should perceive his occupation as a career.

Weber predicted various outcomes, both organizational and individual, as the result of an organization's conformity to the above requirements. The following listing summarizes many of the "predictable" consequences of his bureaucratic model ideal: (1) The best persons will perform the jobs most closely associated with their personal competence. (2) Each person will have jurisdiction over a designated sphere of work activity, thus eliminating duplication of function. (3) Each person in the organization should logically be more loyal to it as a result of internalizing the "career" orientation noted above. (Considering his job as a career, a person might develop strong vested interests in it; one potential outcome of this might be increased commitment to the organization or greater "loyalty" to it.) (4) Each person will be able to predict what his economic rewards will be from one year to the next. Being able to plan ahead reduces anxiety for many employees. The employee's security within an organization is maximized. The organization continues to protect the employee, even after he retires. (5) Each person will obey the system of abstract rules or laws. Management will be able to anticipate that all persons will conform to stated expectations. (6) Management can expect predictably uniform work of high quality from individuals selected by test and appointed to positions because of their proficiency. (7) The easy replacement of organizational members can be anticipated through selection by test and the system of abstract rules. (8) Finally, as a result of these factors, overall organizational efficiency will be maximized, and the organization will become maximally effective.

Some limitations of the bureaucratic model Inasmuch as the bureaucratic model is perhaps the most advanced and formalized statement of machine theory in application, many of the criticisms which have been leveled against this model specifically may also pertain to machine models in general. The criticisms of bureaucratic theory are extensive. Some of the major criticisms are presented below. In each case, a brief rationale will accompany the criticism cited, and some of the major proponents of the criticism will be included.

People do not behave like parts in a machine. The expectation that individuals will act like automatons in an impersonal organizational environment is quite unrealistic. The cognitive and emotional composition of human beings is such that personal feelings always interfere with the attempt at completely rational behavior. The expected behavior of supervisors in a hierarchy of authority provides an example. According to machine theory in general and the bureaucratic model in particular, supervisory behavior is linked closely with several impersonal rules which govern the definition of the supervisor's role. Supposedly, anyone can carry out the supervisor's role effectively to the extent that the rules governing the role are complied with to the letter. Unfortunately, personality characteristics contaminate the correspondence between what a person should do in that position and what the person actually does.

To illustrate the contrast in supervisory behaviors during and after a changeover in managership of a gypsum company, Gouldner (1954a) provides the following example. Before the introduction of the new manager, Vincent Peele, the company was noted for laxity in rule enforcement. "There were comparatively few rules in the plant, and fewer still that were strictly enforced" (p. 51). After Peele's arrival, the bureaucratic organization of the plant became more pronounced (p. 70), more rules were enforced, and supervisors became much less tolerant of deviation from them. Contrasts given by the workers between Doug (the old manager) and Peele (the new one) cast Doug in the role of treating his subordinates as "one big happy family," being "more intimate with his men," and being "more friendly," while Peele was a "strictly business" type of person (p. 81). No doubt the ability of Peele to maintain impersonal attitudes in the work setting was, in part, a personal contribution to the managerial role, particularly when we contrast his behavior with that of the indulgent Doug.

One implication of this criticism is that we cannot always count on people to do what they are expected to do. This criticism has generated an alternative organizational model to take into account the unpredictability of organizational members. Labeled the "unanticipated consequences" model, it simply emphasizes that we must consider the potential nonrational behavior of individuals in organizations in response to rules designed to elicit predictable task performance (Selznick, 1943).

In most organizations, rules cannot be written to govern every situation (Selznick, 1943). Frequently, events occur which are not clearly within any given department's jurisdictional boundaries. Also, events may emerge that are clearly within a department's jurisdiction, but no clear-cut policy statement may exist to dictate how the situation should be handled. If departments act in response to an event which is not clearly within their domain, they may fall prey to criticisms from higher-ups later for overstepping their authority. As a protective measure against such criticisms, departmental officials often delimit their activities to cover well-defined and predictable events, and they take great pains to avoid any unusual problems which are not clearly within their departmental definition. Almost everyone who has telephoned a large corporation with a specific complaint has encountered the "runaround" from departmental secretaries. In these situations (which are all too common) the customer is transferred by phone from one department to another as each secretary seeks to avoid responsibility for handling the complaint.

Even in the bank setting, where events are supposedly predictable to a high degree, unplanned situations can occur. For example, a bank teller revealed that during her first week on the job, she was approached by an elderly female customer with a $125,000 cashier's check to cash. The customer, appearing somewhat senile, insisted that the teller cash the check. The check itself had been issued years earlier and had been perforated and canceled numerous times by other banks. Hence, it was not a negotiable instrument. Afterward, other bank employees approached the new teller and explained to her that the woman tried to cash the invalid check every day at this and other banks in the immediate area. Apparently, it was common knowledge that the woman was from a nearby rest home and suffered from several psychological disorders. It was also common knowledge that her behavior was tolerated by almost all bank employees who knew of her and that no one had ever had the heart to call the police about the matter. Therefore, a "unique" event for one teller eventually became a predictable one (although the initial encounter generated confusion and was emotionally upsetting for the teller involved).

Conformity to rules and personal expertise can be detrimental as well as beneficial in promoting organizational effectiveness. Merton (1940) suggests that the very skills persons acquire as their specialties in organizations may become barriers to flexibility in handling different, yet related, situations. He uses a term coined by the social theorist Thorstein Veblen, "trained incapacity," to indicate that particularly under conditions of organizational change, "an inadequate flexibility in the application of skills will . . . result in more or less serious maladjustments." In short, the organizational member is unable to adapt to new or changing situations. He is incapable of performing a job different from his own within the organization. Merton contends that

> one adopts measures in keeping with his past training, and under new conditions which are not recognized as significantly different, the very soundness of this training may lead to the adoption of the wrong procedures. Again, in Burke's [1935] almost echolalic phrase, "people may be unfitted by being fit in an unfit fitness"; their training may become an incapacity.

One important implication of this "overconformity" is resistance to change. Since organizations are dynamic and ever-responsive to innovation both internally and externally, bureaucratic rigidity through strict obedience to rules or laws is in direct opposition to organizational progress. The bombing of Pearl Harbor in 1941 provides a glaring example of one of bureaucracy's dysfunctions. As enemy planes strafed military installations, personnel scrambled toward armories where weapons and ammunition were stored. As plane cannons barked overhead and bombs fell everywhere, some armory guards insisted on a formal requisition properly signed according to regulations and following proper channels before weapons would be issued. Needless to say, the bureaucratic rules on this eventful morning were severely violated.

Departmental activities, in time, may be devoted to perpetuating the department rather than benefiting the organization as a whole. In his elaboration of the interests and commitments of groups and individuals in organizations, Selznick (1966) argues that departmental interests may become ends in themselves. In brief summary of portions of his view, each department in an organization has subgoals which contribute to the achievement of overall organizational objectives. At some point in time, however, the subgoals become elaborated and exist as the prime motivators of the behavior of the members. In effect, the department exists to achieve the goals of the department. This condition is not necessarily undesirable unless the effectiveness of goal attainment for the entire organization is affected. When separate departments begin to view their activities apart from the activities of other departments, there is a danger that they will lose sight of the overall goals toward which their separate activities are directed.

Informal groups exist in formal organizations to modify existing impersonal social arrangements. The formal hierarchy of authority and communication channels are often discovered to be in competition with informal social networks of employees who spread information through "grapevines." Informal leaders emerge who do not have the same degree of formal job status as the formal leaders but who nevertheless exert significant influence upon employees' attitudes toward their jobs.

Selznick (1943) notes that every organization creates an informal structure and that the process of modifying organizational goals is effected through such structures. Miller and Form (1964:224-227) discuss some of the characteristics of informal group structure, such as codes of conduct for group members; schemes of ideas, beliefs, and values which underlie and support the codes of conduct; and the informal communication system which is vital to group solidarity and action.

One implication of the presence of informal groups in formal organizations is that rule enforcement is often subject to informal workers' codes and approval. Supervisors frequently find themselves bargaining with subordinates outside of the formal chain of command. The replacement of individuals in various organizational positions is often facilitated or hindered by acceptance or rejection by informal workers' aggregates.

The bureaucratic model of organization, although characterized by high productive efficiency, generates low innovative capacity (Thompson, 1965:1–2). In a competitive economic environment, organizations must manifest some adaptability to change if they are to remain viable. Organizations which are more bureaucratic than others (i.e., those that possess more characteristics of a bureaucracy by comparison) appear to be less responsive to internal or external change. Organizations must change in response to invention and new product markets if they are to compete successfully and survive. Since it has been shown that many bureaucratic departments in organizations are intent on perpetuating the organizational status quo, the bureaucratic model would pose certain structural obstacles which would seriously restrict innovation from taking place.

The bureaucratic model fails to take into account the interrelations between the various subsystems within the organization. Machine theory does not usually deal adequately with the problem of intraorganizational conflict of interests in defining limits of organizational behavior (March and Simon, 1958:33). The interdependency of departments suggests that the exchange of mutually beneficial information or the give-and-take necessary for the satisfactory progression of the organization is not seriously considered as problematic by the bureaucratic model.

The integrity of individuals as autonomous decision makers is completely overlooked by the bureaucratic model. Individuals functioning in various organizational roles have little latitude for varying their behaviors from previously established role definitions. Individual manifestations of innovation for circumventing "red tape" or unnecessary paperwork are often squelched by higher-ups for fear of disrupting the rational order of things. To an extent, the innovation means disorder, a condition which is not compatible with the bureaucratic model.

Selection by test is an inadequate method for replacing organizational members. Gross (1962) describes the wholesale misuses of achievement and interests tests in businesses and industries. Testing is increasingly considered one of the poorer means of selecting employees, inasmuch as almost everyone today has access to mail-order houses which deal in testing literature. For a fee, these mail-order firms will furnish reproductions of the standardized tests (as well as the "correct" answers to them) which are used most frequently in the major employing institutions. The prospective job applicant comes to the organization "primed" to appear as though he might fit the job requirements perfectly. All of this is based, of course, upon the answers he provides to the standardized tests given him by the hiring institution. [The author once applied for a job at five different banks in the greater Los Angeles metropolitan area. Four of the banks used virtually the same aptitude and interests tests in their assessments of job candidates. By the time he got to the fourth bank, he appeared to be a "genius" (owing to the practice he had had on the same tests in the other three banks) and got the best offer there.]

The bureaucratic model is restricted in application to larger organizations. Many formal organizational theorists acknowledge that an increase in the size and complexity of an organization increases the likelihood that a bureaucratic structure will eventually emerge. Bureaucracy connotes the proliferation of departments and a fairly complex division of labor. Smaller organizations (under fifty employees, as an arbitrary figure) are less amenable to analysis by use of the bureaucratic model. They have fewer departments, if any, and role interrelations are simple. Increases in the number of departments and the general complexity of the organization create new kinds of coordination problems. The establishment of an authority hierarchy with an explicit division of labor and chain of command is one solution to the problem of coordination of tasks.

The Goal Model

An alternative organizational scheme functionally similar to the machine model is called the "goal model." The basic elements of the goal model are that (1) the organization exists to achieve stated goals; (2) the organization develops a rational procedure for the achievement of the goals; and (3) the organization is assessed in terms of the effectiveness of goal attainment.

Since all organizations function to achieve goals of one kind or another, it makes sense to focus our attention upon existing organizational goals and the means used to achieve them. The problems of organizations become problems of goal attainment.

The goal model is a deceptively simple strategy for approaching organizational problems. One of the more perplexing questions asked is: "What are the goals of the organization?" The identification of true organizational goals is no easy task. Etzioni (1964:6) defines an organizational goal as "a desired state of affairs which the organization attempts to realize." Thompson (1967:127) suggests that definitions of this genre appear to reify the abstraction "organization" by "asserting that it, the abstraction, has goals or desires." He adds that "there is little to be gained, however, by swinging to the other extreme of insisting that the goals of an organization are somehow the accumulated goals of its individual members" (p. 127). Thompson prefers to view the goals of an organization as the future domain desired by those in the dominant coalition (p. 128). This definition is consistent with that of Vroom (1960c:229), who says that an organizational goal is "a shared goal for the organization on the part of its leaders." Vroom goes on to delineate the difference between organizational goals, the person's own goal for an organization (a region into which that person desires the organization to move), and his perception of the organizational goals (his estimates of the regions into which he thinks the leaders of the organization would like it to move) (p. 229).

Vroom's analysis attacks squarely the ambiguity associated with defining organizational goals and, hence, the ambiguity of the goal model of organizations. Consider the problems encountered by an agent of change entering the client organization. To whom does he turn to determine the organizational goals? If he talks to various supervisors or managers at different levels in the authority hierarchy, he may emerge with several, possibly contradictory, stated organizational objectives. If he reads a published account of organizational goals, he may determine that discrepancies exist between what the organization is supposed to be achieving ideally and what it appears to be achieving in reality. The ideal-real discrepancy poses a significant obstacle to deriving adequate organizational goal definitions.

Several important works exist which bear directly upon the subject of organizational goal definitions (Simon, 1964; Gross, 1969; Thompson and McEwen, 1958; Perrow, 1961a; Wieland, 1969). The consensus seems to be that organizational goals are difficult to define and that the effectiveness of goal attainment is equally difficult to evaluate. A primary implication for the meaningful application of the goal model in organizational analysis is that it is too complex to use on a large scale. The fact that goals may be viewed from multiple positions has led to a proliferation of attempts at classifying goals. For instance, in his study of administrators and faculties of some eighty universities, Gross (1969:286-291) categorized various university goals as output goals, adaptation goals, management goals, motivational goals, and positional goals.

Hage and Aiken (1969:373-374) differentiate between "system goals" and "product-characteristic goals." March and Simon (1958) differentiate organizational goals as "operational" or "non-operational." For that matter, in addition to Vroom's goal distinction noted above, goals may be defined according to the "time dimension" as either "long-range" or "short-range."

Some of the major criticisms of the goal model are summarized below. These center on the usefulness of this model as an analytical tool.

Goals are difficult to define, and therefore the goal model is difficult to apply. It is apparent, in view of the discussion above, that goals of organizations are perceived from several vantage points. Some organizations exist for years without ever realizing several stated goals. Evaluating an organization's effectiveness on the basis of whether or not its stated goals are realized is especially difficult when goal attainment rests on the invention or development of new products or techniques. The Oak Ridge, Tennessee, National Laboratory (a government-sponsored nuclear development facility) as a unit has multiple goals, any one of which may take years to realize. Government scientists and teams of researchers dedicate themselves to the development of new uses of atomic energy and ways of handling nuclear materials. Is it necessarily true that a scientific work team is ineffective if it has worked on the development of a new formula for years without positive results? Are schools necessarily ineffective if they have dropout rates of 50 percent during the first two academic years of student enrollment? Are medical centers specializing in the development of heart-transplant techniques ineffective if a majority of their patients die over a specific time period? No doubt we would concede that the continual improvement of the organization through its members' experiences is evidence of goal attainment, at least indirectly.

In addition, attempts to classify organizational goals have not been very successful from the standpoint of general application to all types of organizations. Replete with exceptions, classificatory schemes for organizational goals have made limited contributions to the development of organizational theory.

The goal model makes the unrealistic assumption of a static organization. All organizations are dynamic entities, ever-changing in size and complexity as well as other dimensions. In addition, the finality of goal attainment is unrealistic. Etzioni (1964:16) argues that most organizations most of the time do not attain their goals in any final sense. The desired state of any organization may be a condition to be maintained daily. The goal, defined as a condition of organizational equilibrium, is a perpetual one. In one sense, goals of this type are reachieved daily or are continually preserved. Existing organizational goals may be supplemented with new ones, modified to fit new markets and service directions, or both. The goal model is not prepared to deal adequately with transformations of organizational goals.

Finally, the goal model tends to stereotype study findings (Etzioni, 1960:257–258). Etzioni (1960) contends that the application of the goal model leads to a comparison between ideal and real organizational goals. This comparison, he believes, is misleading because it almost always implies that the organization investigated is not very effective in goal attainment. As an alternative, he suggests a "systems" model (to be discussed later in this chapter), which deals with the problem more realistically. The question he would raise in this instance is: "How close does the organizational allocation of resources approach an optimum (balanced) distribution?"

The Decision Model

March and Simon (1958:6) describe three assumptions about organizational members which have characterized managerial views throughout various stages during the past hundred years. Organizational members are viewed as (1) passive instruments capable of performing work and accepting directions but not of initiating action or exerting influence in any significant way; (2) sentiment-laden individuals having attitudes, values, and goals who have to be motivated or induced to participate in the system of organizational behavior; and (3) decision makers and problem solvers, with perception and thought processes which are central to the explanation of behavior in organizations. It is likely that manifestations of each of these three views can be found in many organizations today. The third view, identifying an organizational member as a decision maker and a problem solver, is of most interest to us in defining the essential elements of the decision model.

The decision model consists of at least three aspects. Miller and Starr (1967:27) summarize these aspects by stating that "the decision maker wishing to achieve some objective (goal) selects a strategy from those available to him. This strategy, together with the state of nature that exists, and the competitive strategy that occurs, will determine the degree to which his objective is obtained." According to the decision model, organizations are viewed as rational systems consisting of various parts. Each part (such as a department) makes decisions which affect relations with other parts and the organization as a whole. Organizational problems are accounted for, in part, by the quality of decisions pertaining to the utilization of organizational resources and manpower. The decision model has as its guiding theme the rational selection of the best action from several available alternatives with some calculated probability of predictable results. In short, this means to pick the best way of solving the problems with the least amount of financial loss to the organization.

Simon (1957) has provided us with one of the best descriptions of the decision model. He defines organizations as decision-making structures and suggests that the various dimensions of the organization (e.g., hierarchy of authority, division of labor, and specialization of tasks) are designed to enhance the rationality of decision making. Specialization, for example, acts to confine the organizational member within a small sphere of activity. The member is able to have a better grasp of the alternative decisions which he must make in fulfilling his particular decision-making role in the organization. The hierarchy of authority exists, for the most part, to dictate the sphere of activity within which the member will operate.

In some respects, the decision model is not altogether different from the goal model. Both schemes incorporate the notion of achieving goals. An important difference between these schemes, however, is that the decision model emphasizes the *quality of decisions made to achieve goals,* whereas the goal model is concerned about *any* organizational dimension (including the decision-making process implicit in the hierarchy of authority and the division of labor) which is functionally related to goal attainment. Another difference is that the decision model considers as most important the decisions about the means devised for solving problems rather than the actual problem solving (which *is* of primary importance to the goal model).

The decision model, like the goal model, assumes a static organizational arrangement. The decision model neglects to consider external factors (e.g., competition with other organizations and accedence to governmental demands for price controls such as were imposed on a nationwide basis in the early 1970s) as important influences on decisions made by organizational members. The propensity of organizations to change in many crucial dimensions introduces significant factors which influence outcomes and over which members have little or no control.

The decision model assumes access to all possible action strategies. In reality, it is extremely unlikely that decision makers will have a knowledge of all possible solutions to problems. It is also equally unlikely that they will be able to anticipate all possible outcomes of the strategies selected.

Interpersonal processes are not treated adequately in the decision model. Blau and Scott (1962:38) offer the criticism of Simon's (1957) decision model that administration as a decision-making structure deals largely with the effects of the formal blueprint for decision-making behavior and does not include a systematic analysis of those interpersonal processes that are not a part of the formal structure.

All variables typifying the organization (i.e., hierarchy of authority, span of control of supervisors, communication network, etc.) are viewed exclusively in terms of their impact upon rational decision making. No consideration is given in this model to the effect of each of these variables upon the others (Blau and Scott, 1962:38).

Few controls exist to ensure objectivity on the part of the decision maker. The possibility arises for the individual decision maker to make decisions which are beneficial to a particular department but not to the entire organization. The frequency with which individuals act in their own behalf to the detriment of the organization in contrast to the frequency of altruistic, organization-oriented decisions is well-known. Organizational decision making becomes largely an individualized activity in the absence of well-defined guidelines for member behavior.

CLOSED-SYSTEM MODELS—THE NONRATIONAL ASSUMPTION

The Human-Relations Model

Traditional organizational models which focus upon rational factors are criticized, in part, because they assume that human beings will perform tasks without emotion. A logical response to this criticism was the development of the so-called "human-relations school," formally founded during the late 1920s by Elton Mayo. Mayo believed that although organizations exhibit many rational properties, the work attitudes and sentiments of the members must be considered as primary motivating factors affecting variables such as productivity and morale. The "human-relations model," as it was subsequently labeled, reflects the view that man is a collection of sentiments. These sentiments must be considered as strategic in virtually every phase of organizational planning and change.

In order to develop a clearer picture of the relevance of the human-relations model for the period within which it was introduced, it might be helpful to contrast the earlier view of the working man with the emerging conception. McGregor characterizes the earlier view of man in the organization by describing a set of beliefs which he labels "theory X":

> The average human being has an inherent dislike of work and will avoid it if he can. Because of this human characteristic of dislike of work, most people must be coerced, controlled, directed, threatened with punishment to get them to put forth adequate effort toward the achievement of organizational objectives. The average human being prefers to be directed, wishes to avoid responsibility, has relatively little ambition, wants security above all (McGregor, 1960:33-34).

McGregor's "theory Y" depicts an emerging conception of man which fits the human-relations model more closely:

> The expenditure of physical and mental effort in work is as natural as play or rest. External control and the threat of punishment are not the only means for bringing about effort toward organizational objectives. Man will exercise self-direction and self-control in the service of objectives to which he is committed. Commitment to objectives is a function of the rewards associated with their achievement. The average human being learns, under proper conditions, not only to accept but to seek responsibility. The capacity to exercise a relatively high degree of imagination, ingenuity, and creativity in the solutions of organizational problems is widely, not narrowly, distributed in the population. Under the conditions of modern industrial life, the intellectual potentialities of the average human being are only partially utilized [McGregor, 1960:47-48).

The human-relations model examines

> the integration of people into an organization in addition to those factors which motivate them to work together cooperatively and productively. It is action-oriented, relating to people at work in organizations and their economic, psychological, and social satisfactions. It examines variables which contribute toward building a more productive and satisfying worker interrelation (Keith Davis, 1962:18-19).

Much of the scientific evidence compiled by researchers in the early development of this model centered on a series of investigations conducted at the Hawthorne plant of the Western Electric Company near Chicago, Illinois, during the years 1927 to 1932. Some results were published during that period (Pennock, 1930; Putman, 1930), although a more extensive account was released in 1939 by Roethlisberger and Dickson. The "Hawthorne studies" are regarded as classics in the organizational literature. Carey (1967:403) states that "there can be few scientific disciplines or fields of research in which a single set of studies or a single researcher and writer has exercised so great an influence as was exercised for a quarter of a century by Mayo and the Hawthorne studies." The Hawthorne plant was a major assembly point for telephone equipment, including relays and banks of terminals among other things. The studies investigated the impact of the following variables upon employee productivity: rest pauses, new incentive systems, temperature, lighting, length of the workday, humidity, hours of work, pay, and type of social situation. A series of five separate studies constituted much of the material for the later report by Roethlisberger and Dickson (1939). Carey identifies these stages as follows (1967:404):[5]

Stage I: The Relay Assembly Test Room Study. (New incentive system and new supervision.)

Stage II: The Second Relay Assembly Group Study. (New incentive system only.)

Stage III: The Mica-Splitting Test Room Study. (New supervision only.)

Stage IV: The Interviewing Program.

Stage V. The Bank-Wiring Observation Room Study.

Carey observes that Stages I to III contained evidence which presumably led to Mayo's conclusion that social needs and satisfactions are important considerations in explaining employee productivity.

The technical aspects of the Hawthorne studies are well known.[6] Rather than dwell at length on the intricacies of the test conditions, we will focus upon some of the more important findings, which have been of great value in shaping the nature and direction of the human-relations model in modern organizations.

The major outcome was the discovery of the significance of the so-called "Hawthorne effect" (Etzioni, 1964:33). Specifically, increased production appeared to be one result of increased group cohesiveness among workers, significant modifications and improvements in their levels of psychological satisfaction, and "new patterns of social interaction brought about by putting them into the experiment (Relay Assembly Test) room and the special attention involved" (Etzioni, 1964:33). Of course, the increased participation of workers in decisions affecting their work and a greater identification with managerial goals also contributed substantially to their increased productivity, indirectly lending further support to the Hawthorne effect.

The Hawthorne studies have been the target of considerable criticism (Miller and Form, 1964:678–681; Carey, 1967; Landsberger, 1958; Sykes, 1965; and Shepard, 1972). Miller and Form (1964:678) note that "so many critics have appeared and so much has been said about the Hawthorne research that a book on criticisms of the Mayo school was published by Henry A. Landsberger in 1958." Landsberger's (1958) volume is perhaps one of the most objective appraisals of the contribution of the Hawthorne studies to contemporary formal organizations. His review of the criticisms was, for the most part, an attempt to delineate the issues which were the objects of inquiry of Mayo's research.

Carey (1967) offers the most negative appraisal of the Hawthorne studies thus far. He argues that the abundance of methodological and theoretical deficiencies coupled with apparent bias surrounding the inclusion of experimental subjects raises serious questions about the validity of the Hawthorne research. He strongly implies that the vast discrepancy between the evidence and the conclusions of these studies is sufficient to question whether a contribution to organizations has been made at all. Shepard (1971:23–24) has sharply criticized the work of Carey, noting at one point that "if, as Carey argues, the Hawthorne researchers overstated their case, he (Carey) is vulnerable to the same charge."

Miller and Form (1964:678) have summarized some of the basic criticisms of the Hawthorne studies in the following passage:

> The first and most basic criticism takes issue with the group's view of modern society as one in a condition of anomie, i.e., made up of morally confused, isolated individuals surrounded by a society disorganized and full of conflict . . . . as a solution to the problems of modern society the Mayo group is said to propose the reclaiming of individual and society through industrial organizations so managed that there is spontaneous collaboration for a common purpose. Three further criticisms assert that the Mayo group (1) projects an image of the worker which reflects both the acceptance of management's goals and its view of workers, coupled with a willingness to manipulate workers for management's end; (2) fails to pay attention to methods of accommodating industrial conflict such as collective bargaining; (3) fails to take unions into account.

Some basic characteristics of the human-relations model adapted from Keith Davis (1962:14-19) are as follows: (1) *Mutual interest.* This is the assumption of some commonality of interest between employer and employee and among employees. A person's participation is largely voluntary. No two persons will have identical goals, but they can find mutual interest through an organization. In this way people are encouraged to fight the problem at hand instead of each other. (2) *Individual differences.* Each man has unique characteristics, but he is a whole person, rather than a mass of separate traits. He is the unit of feeling, of judgment, of action. He is the one who determines satisfaction and is motivated. The group is secondary. Only a person can take responsibility and make decisions—a group by definition cannot do so. It is powerless until individuals act therein. If, for example, everyone in a group waits for the group to act, there will be no action. A person always has responsibility for action. (3) *Motivation.* Individuals must be encouraged to work together inasmuch as most, if not all, social behaviors are caused by some stimulus or combination of stimuli. Motivation provides a potential cause or initiating factor in this instance. It is the means whereby the manager creates and maintains the desire of his subordinates to achieve the planned goals of the organization. (4) *Human dignity.* Most studies of personal wants show that people want be treated with respect and dignity—to be treated as human beings. The human-relations model accepts human dignity as basic.

From the perspective of the human-relations model, production is the secondary consideration and the individual is the primary one. Organizational structure is designed to accommodate individual attitudes and sentiments. For instance, the nature of supervision over subordinates is "employee-centered" as opposed to "job-centered" (Stogdill and Coons, 1957). The employee-centered supervisor considers the needs of employees and gives them a sense of personal worth (Maier, 1965:130).

Maier (1965:130-131) reports that "another classification of supervisory behavior widely used in research is based on measures of 'initiating structure' and '[showing] consideration.'" Each is treated as a dimension. The dimension of showing consideration reflects the degree to which the leader establishes two-way communication, mutual respect, and a consideration of the feelings of his subordinates. Essentially, it represents a human-relations orientation toward leadership. Initiating structure reflects the extent to which the leader facilitates group interaction toward goal attainment. This involves planning, scheduling, criticizing, initiating ideas, and so on (adapted from Fleishman and Harris, 1962).

The human-relations model maintains some of the rationality associated with the bureaucratic model. Selection by test and a hierarchy of authority are basic components, although the emphasis upon conformity to abstract rules or laws is relaxed considerably. Decisions made by supervisors or managers depend upon personal considerations as well as rationally calculated probable outcomes. Promotions within the organization, for the most part, are dependent upon one's ability to communicate with others effectively. A knowledge of the rules is important, but even more crucial is the "human application of them." Several criticisms of the human-relations model are presented below.

The human-relations model is only selectively applicable. Some organizations simply do not lend themselves to analysis by use of the human-relations model. A military organization, for example, would tend to favor a bureaucratic model in view of the logistical problems of coordinating large numbers of troops. Likewise, prisons are not in the position of being analyzed easily with the human relations model. Social work clinics, on the other hand, would perhaps be more amenable to study by use of this model. Although problems of "human relations" are a part of all organizations, the fact is that better models exist to account for behaviors in a greater portion of organizations.

The human-relations model places too much emphasis upon the importance of social factors. The importance of considering the sentiments of organizational members is self-evident. Certainly the role of the informal group on the job is a significant one. We would be in error, however, if we failed to recognize the significance of attachments which individuals develop to groups or group affiliations external to the immediate organizational setting.

Although the human-relations model emphasizes harmonious superior-subordinate relations and close associations within work groups, we must recognize the importance of conflict as a means of promoting eventual organizational progress. Assuming that one intraorganizational objective is cooperation and harmony among the membership, the human-relations approach seeks to achieve such a state by reducing or eliminating conflicts between work units through mutual understanding and adjustments in personal interactions.

Human relations may bring about a more pleasant social condition within which to work, but this approach does not lessen the tediousness of tasks (Chinoy, 1955).

The human-relations model is functional for those kinds of organizations requiring a high degree of social skills and communicative abilities. Litwak (1961:182) argues that the human relations model is most appropriate for situations in which:

> tasks are relatively not uniform or involve social skills; to illustrate: situations which are not so uniform that government cannot lay down highly specific laws but rather sets up commissions with broad discretionary powers—National Institutes of Mental Health, National Labor Relations Board, etc.; and situations involving the selling of undifferentiated products—large advertising firms.

The Professional Model

One of the primary proponents of the professional model is Litwak (1961). He argues that both the bureaucratic model of Weber and the human-relations model are efficient for dealing with different (but equally important) kinds of organizational phenomena. The bureaucratic model is

> most efficient when the organization deals primarily with uniform events and with occupations stressing traditional areas of knowledge rather than social skills. The human relations model will be most efficient for dealing with events which are not uniform (research, medical treatment, graduate training, designing) and with occupations emphasizing social skills as technical aspects of the job (as that of psychiatric social worker, salesman . . . and politician [p. 177].

Litwak suggests that our contemporary organizations have to deal with both uniform and nonuniform events as a part of their daily activity and that both positions which emphasize traditional knowledge and those which emphasize social skills are needed simultaneously. In an effort to permit two conflicting models of organization to coexist without friction (thereby reflecting greater flexibility in internal functioning and services provided), Litwak identifies four mechanisms of segregation. These are

> (1) *role separation as a mechanism of segregation.* It is necessary to restrict primary group behavior to one set of individuals and formal relations to another.
> (2) *Physical distance as a mechanism of segregation.* Depending upon the phys-

ical facilities of the organization involved, space may not permit great physical distance between departments geared to handle problems differently. However, where possible, physical separation has the advantage of lessening conflict. (3) *Transferral occupations as mechanisms of segregation.* Certain individuals in the organization are charged with the responsibility of bridging interest areas (e.g., the differences between pure scientists' work and the production line) without contaminating either. (4) *Evaluation procedures as mechanisms of segregation.* This means the creation of a position to determine when social relations should shift from one form to another [pp. 182-184].

Table 2-4 illustrates the major differences between Weber's model and the human-relations model. It also shows the additional flexibility achieved by the professional model.

The professional model is suggestive of increased specialization within the organization as a means of obtaining greater flexibility. Expanding the training of organizational members to deal with problematic events more flexibly is professionalizing them. Scott (1966:268-269) characterizes professionals as persons trained in professional schools, possessing complex skills and special knowledge, and equipped with internalized control mechanisms. He contrasts these with bureaucrats who are thought of as relatively special-

Table 2-4 Characteristics of Three Organizational Models

Characteristic	Weber's model	Human-relations model	Professional model
Impersonal relations	Extensive	Minimal	One part extensive; one part minimal
Appointment on merit	Extensive	Extensive	Extensive
A priori specification of job authority	Extensive	Minimal	One part extensive; one part minimal
Hierarchical authority	Extensive	Minimal	One part extensive; one part minimal
Separation of policy and administrative decisions	Extensive	Minimal	One part extensive; one part minimal
General rules to govern relations not specified by above dimensions	Extensive	Minimal	One part extensive; one part minimal
Specialization	Extensive	Minimal	One part extensive; one part minimal

Source: Litwak, 1961:182.

ized in function and as operating in a hierarchical structure under a system of formal rules:

> As members become more professional in their abilities and orientations, organizations run the risk of creating new problems as well as resolving old ones. On the one hand, professionals will be able to operate in organizations more effectively by applying greater expertise with respect to task knowledge and social skills. On the other hand, professionals are increasingly likely to resist or reject various bureaucratic rules, resist or reject bureaucratic standards, resist bureaucratic supervision, and reflect only conditional loyalty to the bureaucracy.

For many organizations the problems of adapting the characteristics of professionals to bureaucratic structure will not emerge because either (1) the organization is able to function adequately without the aid of professionals or (2) mechanisms of separation of function are instituted which will at least minimize the conflict if not entirely eliminate it. Professionals are likely to reject bureaucratic rules because they perceive themselves as capable of establishing a more functional set of behavioral expectations. Their expertise entitles them to operate "professionally," without the "constraining regulations or interference from others" (Scott, 1966:270). They resist standards of bureaucratic organizations because, reflecting a cosmopolitan orientation, they adhere to the standards created by the abstract professional aggregate on a national scale (e.g., the American Medical Association, the American Bar Association, and the American Psychological Association).

Professionals are increasingly discontent with bureaucratic supervision because, in many instances, the supervisors over them are not qualified in their own fields of specialization (Scott, 1966:273; Arensberg and McGregor, 1942; Marcson, 1960). The loyalty of professionals toward their employing organizations cannot be predicted absolutely. Professionals increasingly follow the norms and behavioral expectations of their profession at large (provided that their speciality areas have local, state, or national professional organizations), rather than those of the employing organization.

The Equilibrium Model

Barnard (1938) and Simon (1947) have provided a theory of organizational equilibrium which emphasizes the importance of motivational factors in encouraging member participation. Barnard defines an organization as *a system of consciously coordinated activities or forces of two or more persons.* In essence, the equilibrium model connotes an exchange of rewards (from the organization) for services performed (by organizational members). By motivating members to participate in organizational activities, the organization ensures its "survival" over time. Sometimes, the terms "survival model" and "motivational model" are used to reflect what is essentially contained within the equilibrium model.[7] In support of this view, March and Simon (1958:84) mention that "the Barnard-Simon theory of organizational equilibrium is essentially a theory of *motivation*—a statement of the conditions under which an organization can induce its members to continue their participation, and hence assure organizational *survival.*"

The term "equilibrium" is generally interpreted to mean a state of balance between opposing forces. It carries with it the implicit assumption of the perpetuation of the status quo or little, if any, organizational change. Attention is focused, therefore, on those factors which serve to *maintain the organization in some kind of static state.* Organizational leaders and others may feel that the organization is stable and not in need of undergoing changes of any kind. Each segment of the organization apparently relates to every other segment in a harmonious fashion. Member participation is fairly predictable. Each person does his job, each department performs its designated functions, and things generally run smoothly. The equilibrium model applicable to organizations is very similar to the homeostasis of an organism or a group. As long as each bodily part or group member fulfills its designated tasks, the entire organism or group persists in a kind of constant state. Changes in the stock market, increased competitiveness from other companies, dissatisfaction of the members with the work performed and the remuneration, etc., can act as external and internal factors which could conceivably upset the homeostasis or equilibrium of the organization. Members who quit, die, or retire (or are fired) are replaced by others in order to perpetuate (and maintain) the equilibrium of the organization. Promotions of personnel, transferrals, the phasing out of certain departments, the consolidation of other departments, and changes in the authority pattern and communication network all spell change in the equilibrium of the organization. At least, changes of these sorts can upset the equilibrium of the organization for a short period. But usually the organization fairly rapidly restores the status quo through member replacement, financial rewards, and numerous other adjustments.

The basic assumptions of the equilibrium model of organizations are summarized by Simon, Smithburg, and Thompson (1950:381-382):

An organization is a system of interrelated social behaviors of a number of persons whom we shall call the *participants* in the organization. Each participant and each group of participants receives from the organization inducements in return for which he makes to the organization contributions. Each participant will continue his participation in an organization only so long as the inducements offered him are as great or greater (measured in terms of his values and in terms of the alternatives open to him) than the contributions he is asked to make. The contributions provided by the various groups of participants are the source from which the organization manufactures the inducements offered to participants. Hence, an organization is "solvent"—and will continue in existence—only so long as the contributions are sufficient to provide inducements in large enough measure to draw forth these contributions.

The equilibrium model places significant emphasis upon individual attitudes toward participation in organizational activity. The notion of inducements covers a broad range of motivational factors including psychological rewards as well as financial ones. The survival of an organization, however, is dependent upon many additional factors besides individual incentives. For example, the economic market conditions in any given time period must be considered in an evaluation of the effectiveness of any organization. The factors of size and functional complexity also contribute to organizational equilibrium and to whether or not it survives.

The equilibrium model stresses the interdependence of members and departments in their cooperative effort to perpetuate the organization. The coordination of tasks in the division of labor might very well be handled through skillful planning rather than reliance upon highly motivated participants to carry out cooperative functions. The bureaucratic model plays down the role of motivation in relation to the perpetuation of the organization. A system of abstract rules coupled with unconditional compliance with them defines the basic orientation of members within highly bureaucratized institutions. Bureaucracy achieves stability or equilibrium through norms of compliance, whereas the equilibrium model relies upon personal incentive factors. Neither the bureaucratic nor the equilibrium model is particularly amenable to changes, at least from within the organization. The interdependence of positions allows for the determination of whether or not any particular role is being effectively implemented, however. Within the context of the equilibrium model, conflict may be interpreted as a discrepancy between the values of the individual and the expectations of the organization at large (as represented by management). A summary of some of the more important criticisms of the equilibrium model is provided below.

The emphasis upon motivational factors moves the equilibrium model away from a consideration of organizational factors. Small groups or informal aggregates are not considered as important contributors to organizational stability. Supervisory styles are largely ignored as possible "inducements" to participate. The psychological dimension is present to such a great degree that overtones of Elton Mayo's human-relations school are presumed to underlie the equilibrium model. Barnard was obviously impressed by the emergent humanistic managerial philosophy which highlighted the importance of personal satisfactions in increasing output. His "psychology of participation" has subsequently been elaborated by industrial psychologists, and writers such as French, Israel, and Aos (1960) have incorporated these views into experimental situations in factories and businesses.

The equilibrium model gives insufficient consideration to formal labor agreements. An organization is much more than a collection of cooperating individuals. The superior-subordinate relation rests more upon objective, contractual guidelines and labor laws than upon personal definitions of the value of inducements to participate. Organizational changes are to be expected regularly in a competitive environment. Organizational members are obligated to make adjustments and adaptations to new and improved technologies. Through arbitration between labor and management, agreements are reached concerning wages to be paid and work to be performed. In this sense, whether any given individual perceives the inducements associated with the work performed as adequate or inadequate is quite immaterial. In many organizations today (including all of those with union representation), employee discontentments are taken care of through a simple grievance process.[8] Those grievances which are found to be justified (judged so by one's peers or union stewards) are aired in front of management officials for a decision. Usually, the contracts worked out between management and union include guidelines for deciding the fairness of work expectations and labor output. The organization does not become insolvent because of personal discontent. The availability of labor to replace dissatisfied members is also a factor which must be given careful consideration.

The equilibrium model largely ignores organizational change from within. According to this model, in order for change to occur, organizations must receive some kind of stimulus from their external environment (e.g., a competitive challenge from another organization or the suggestions and recommendations of an agent of change). Mechanisms for promoting change within the organization itself are conspicuously absent. Organizations are dynamic entities, whereas the equilibrium model connotes a static organizational situation. Organizations wish to do much more than simply preserve the status quo, although the maintenance of the formal pattern of interrelations of roles is very important.

OPEN-SYSTEM ORGANIZATIONAL MODELS

The Natural-System Model

The organic analogy has often been applied in an attempt to describe the natural-system model of organizations. In this analogy, organizations are perceived as systems made up of interdependent parts, each part functioning so that the entire system is perpetuated (or survives) over time. The system draws its nourishment or energy from sources in its external environment.

The system has built-in mechanisms for maintaining it and for regulating the relations between its component parts. In the context of the organic analogy, the system develops and grows, becoming increasingly complex. Each of the parts adjusts to the contributions of the other parts so that a type of homeostasis is generated. In some respects, this view is similar to that reflected by the equilibrium model in the previous section. Some of the major contributors to the development of the natural-system model as it applies to formal organizations are Gouldner (1959), Parsons (1956a, b), and Thompson (1967).

The major assumptions of the natural-system model have been extracted from the discussion of Gouldner (1959:405-410) and are outlined below:

> The natural-system model regards the organization as a "natural whole." The component structures of the system are emergent institutions which can be understood only in relation to the diverse needs of the total system. The component parts of an organization are interdependent. The organization becomes an end in itself. The realization of goals of the system as a whole is but one of several important needs to which the organization is oriented. The organization serves to link parts of the system and to provide avenues for controlling and integrating them. Organizational structures are viewed as spontaneously and homeostatically maintained. The equilibrium of the system depends very greatly on the conforming behavior of group members. Changes in organizational patterns are considered the results of cumulative, unplanned, adaptive responses to threats to the equilibrium of the system as a whole. Responses to problems are . . . crescively developed defense mechanisms . . . being importantly shaped by shared values which are deeply internalized in the members.

The natural-system model possesses perhaps the most realistic set of assumptions about formal organizations compared with the other models we have examined. All organizations must, in fact, contend with an external environment replete with other competing organizations. Although the closed-system approach to organizational analysis may offer greater theoretical simplicity (because factors external to organizations do not need to be accounted for in the theoretical scheme), it is far removed from the way things are in the real world of organizational activity.

A major limitation of the natural-system model is its unfortunate association with the organic analogy. Although there are many parallels between a bodily system and an organization, there are also many exceptions, which cause the organic analogy to break down under close scrutiny. An organization does not always "die." Neither does an organization necessarily operate ineffectively on a permanent basis. Many factors external to organizations generate particular conditions which interject new life into them. New managerial philosophies, new product markets, improved technology, organizational growth, improved training methods for supervisors and lower-level personnel, new and changing organizational structures, and an increasingly educated work force differentially contribute to organizational effectiveness and survival.

The natural-system model conceives an organization to be the recipient of various "inputs" from the external environment. A factory system is provided with raw materials from external sources, for example. The organization, in turn, has several "outputs," which are fed back into the external environment. The same factory system converts the raw materials into products, which are marketed to the general public through retail outlets.

The various components of the organization (i.e., the departments) differentially contribute to the perpetuation of the entire structure. Each department is a vital part of the system. If the advertising department does not perform its function well, organizational sales will likely decline and the institution will not prosper. On the other hand, if a company has excellent advertising, the marketing of faulty products manufactured by careless personnel in the production division of the organization will be detrimental to the system as well.

Parsons (1951, 1956a, b) has adopted the natural-system perspective in viewing social organizations in general and formal organizations in particular. Parsons adds to the model by describing four kinds of problems which organizations must resolve in order to survive and progress over time. He states that the "process in any social system is subject to four independent functional imperatives or 'problems' which must be met adequately if equilibrium and/or continuing existence of the system is to be maintained" (p. 16). Morse (1961:113–115) summarizes Parsons's problems in the following passage:

> (1) Goal attainment, or keeping the system moving steadily toward its goals; (2) adaptation, or the process of mobilizing the technical means to achieve goals; (3) integration, or the process of achieving and maintaining appropriate emotional and social relations among those directly cooperating in the goal-attainment process; and (4) latency (pattern maintenance and tension management), or seeing that the cooperating units have the time and the facilities to constitute or recognize the capacities needed by the system.

Various units within the organization function to ensure that each of these problems is resolved on a continuing basis. Some units have planning and coordinating functions, while others have managerial functions. There are also units which oversee the quality control dimension as well as those which make policy decisions.

Using the natural-system model for organizational analysis, a theorist would examine the functional interrelations between departments as well as the relation of the organization as a whole to its external environment.

Another undesirable outcome of the use of the organic analogy applied to organizations is the fallacious assumption that an organization has a "natural history" and follows "natural laws." In reality, organizations usually have units which make rational decisions about the nature and direction of organizational growth. Rather than following a "natural pattern," the destiny of the organization is directed by carefully calculated decisions. Below are some of the more important criticisms which have been raised against the natural-system model.

The natural-system model, while calling attention to the unplanned and spontaneous nature of organizational structures, has the disadvantage of de-emphasizing their rational features (Gouldner, 1959:407). One of Gouldner's appeals to organizational theorists is to harmonize the rational and the natural-system models of organizations because of the complementary contributions each makes to understanding organizational behavior (1959:426). This criticism is consistent with one of the general weaknesses of models cited at the beginning of this chapter. In short, this criticism refers to the fact that when a model focuses upon a specific dimension of organizations, this usually means that other dimensions, possibly equally important from a theoretical standpoint, will not be emphasized by it. Organizations do have many rational aspects which must be considered as important in accounting for organizational behavior. The natural-system model includes events which are not touched upon at all by so-called "rational models" of organization. A most profitable theoretical enterprise would be, in Gouldner's words, "the reconciliation of the rational and natural-system models" (1959:426).

The notions of "natural laws" and "natural development" are somewhat unrealistically applicable to organizations. The obvious influence of intentional and rational actions by members of various departments in organizations has been observed repeatedly in organizational research.

Mechanisms for incorporating planned change into the system are ignored by the natural-system model. There are no provisions for dealing with rational action geared to change the system. The natural-system model views change in the system only as a response to external threats to its survival.

The natural-system model assumes the interdependence of parts in the organization, and therefore it does not examine the variation in degrees of interdependence which likely exist (Gouldner, 1959:419). Gouldner notes that some parts of an organization may be able to survive relatively well without cooperation from other units. He states that "the tendency of the natural-system model . . . is to focus on the system as a whole and to overstate the degree of mutual interdependence and integration among its parts" (p. 420).

SUMMARY

Various organizational models have been presented in order to describe some of the ways researchers view organizations. Each model stresses a different dimension or dimensions of organizations, and in this respect each is competitive with the others. Some of the major advantages and disadvantages of each model have been emphasized.

No single model of organizations is universally accepted. There are obvious overlaps between models, and some models make serious omissions. In this chapter models are examined from the systemic perspective and designated "closed" or "open." Theoretically, the open-system models are more realistic; but the difficulties involved in considering external factors often make it impossible to develop open-system models. Closed-system models are far more popular; in such models, only internal factors need be considered.

Organizational theory depends heavily upon the construction of a satisfactory organizational model. Perhaps the best-known model is the bureaucratic model in its ideal form as elaborated by Max Weber. Certainly it has received the most comment, both pro and con. Weaknesses of Weber's model, apparently inherent, have led to the development of numerous variations. The human-relations model, which emphasizes affective or emotional considerations, has been one of its chief rivals. Litwak's (1961) "professional" model, a blend of bureaucratic (rational) and human-relations characteristics, has been considered by many to possess strengths and overcome the weaknesses of the other two models.

The existence of rational models (including the bureaucratic model) and nonrational models (including the human-relations model) emphasizes the need to take into account both *predictable* and *unpredictable* (anticipated and unanticipated) consequences of organizational activity, even though much of it is planned. We have learned a great deal about human beings and their various groupings in organizations over the years. We have observed managers' concepts of employees change slowly, from robots to sentimental souls to decision makers and problem solvers. And accordingly, we have had to change our organizational models.

Models enable us to develop a perspective potentially useful in our analysis of organizations. We can consider organizational models as sensitizing constructs which focus attention on one set of characteristics or another. Models may be viewed as "strategies" in that they provide us with a way of approaching organizations and making systematic statements about them in the context of certain characteristics or dimensions. Each model, then, constitutes a different strategy.

STUDY QUESTIONS

1 What is an organizational model? What are some functions of organizational models for helping to explain organizational behavior? Explain.

2 Contrast closed- and open-system models in general according to their respective weaknesses and strengths. Which do you prefer and why?

3 The bureaucratic model is usually considered to be an ideal form leading to organizational efficiency. What kinds of factors contribute to organizational inefficiency which are inherent in the bureaucratic model? Elaborate.

4 Do you feel that it is possible to develop an organizational model which will encompass all organizations? Why or why not?

5 Consider the various managerial views of the working man over the last century. How has each view contributed to the type of supervision subordinates receive from higher-ups? Explain.

6 Do members of organizations always want to participate in decision-making processes? Why or why not? Under what conditions would persons tend to avoid having to make decisions affecting their own work or the work of someone else? Explain.

7 Of the models we have examined in this chapter, which one, in your opinion, has the greatest degree of utility for helping to explain organizational behavior? Why?

8 What would be some major drawbacks to applying the professional model of organizations to explaining the behaviors of individuals in the paper-processing department of a mail-order firm? Elaborate. Which model, in your opinion, would be more suitable in this respect? Why?

9 Criticize machine models in general and their lack of predictive value in accounting for organizational behavior. Are organizational models "supposed to" enable us to "predict" behavior or simply lead to a better "understanding" of it? Explain.

10 How does the personality of the individual interfere with the application of most organizational models in research? Elaborate. Is there a complementarity between personality and organizational structure? Why or why not?

NOTES

[1] The quest for developing universally applicable models in other disciplines besides organizational analysis is well documented. Criminologists have sought for years to develop an adequate scheme for classifying criminal behavior. The results have not been altogether dissimilar from those of organizational theorists.

[2] For an extended discussion of the advantages and limitations of applying the open or closed model, see Hall (1972:15-27), Katz and Kahn (1966:14-29), and March and Simon (1958:34-82).

[3] In all likelihood, Weber's writings concerning bureaucracy extended to a broad-scale contrast between a form of government which emerged in the West roughly during the 1700s and that which had preceded it. Therefore, the bureaucratic

nonownership of the means of administration would contrast to the earlier lack of distinction between the king's household and its belongings and any "public" property; similarly, the appointment of public officials such as customs officers or tax collectors on the basis of knowledge or competence and the restriction of their authority to that which was necessary to collect taxes (and no more) would contrast to the nepotistic appointment at an earlier time of "tax farmers," who could commingle "private" and "public" funds, who could collect whatever the traffic would bear, and whose authority was not restricted simply to tax-collecting.

   [4] These characteristics have been modified by Litwak (1961:177–178), and although they do not constitute a perfect replication of Weber's listing, Litwak contends that "they are sufficiently close to do no violence to it." These characteristics of Weber's are identified in Gerth and Mills (1946:196–203).

   [5] " 'Stages I and III constitute a series of partially controlled studies which were initially intended to explore the effects on work behavior of variations in physical conditions of work, especially variations in rest pauses and in hours of work, but also in payment system, temperature, humidity, etc. However, after the studies had been in progress for at least twelve months the investigators came to the entirely unanticipated conclusion that social satisfactions arising out of human association in work were more important determinants of work behavior in general and output in particular than were any of the physical and economic aspects of the work situation to which their attention had originally been limited' [Pennock, 1930:296–313]. This conclusion came as 'the great eclaircissement . . , an illumination quite different from what they had expected from the illumination studies' [Roethlisberger, 1941:15]. It is the central and distinctive finding from which the fame and influence of the Hawthorne studies derive. This 'eclaircissement' about the predominant importance of social satisfactions at work occurred during Stage I of the studies. In consequence, all the later studies are in important ways subordinate to Stage I: 'It was the origin from which all the subsequent phases sprang. It was also their main focal point. It gave to these other phases their significance in relation to the whole enquiry' [Urwick and Brech, 1948:27]. Stages II and III were 'designed to check on' (and were taken to supplement and confirm) the Stage I conclusion that 'the observed production increase was the result of a change in the *social situation* . . . [and] not primarily because of wage incentives, reduced fatigue or similar factors' [Viteles, 1954:185]. Stage IV was an interviewing program undertaken to explore worker attitudes. Stage V was a study of informal group organization in the work situation. The two later studies (IV and V) resulted directly from conclusions based on Stages I–III about the superior influence of social needs. Observations made in both were interpreted in the light of such prior conclusions. Hence it is clear that, as maintained by Urwick, Stage I was the key study, with Stages II and III adding more or less substantial support to it" (Carey, 1967:403–405).

   [6] Stage V, the Bank-Wiring Observation Room Study, was also considered important in view of the attention which it directed toward the sanctioning power of small groups. Below is a summary of the results from the Bank-Wiring Observation Room (Shepard, 1972:325): "(1) Each individual in the group was restricting his output. (2) Restriction of output manifested itself in two ways: (a) The group had a

standard of a day's work which was considerably lower than the 'bogey' and which fixed an upper limit in each person's output. This standard was not imposed upon them, but apparently had been formulated by the workmen themselves. Furthermore, it was in direct opposition to the ideas underlying their system of financial incentive, which countenanced no upper limit to performance other than physical capacity. (b) In each individual case it manifested itself in an output rate which remained fairly constant from week to week. The departmental output curves were devoid of individuality and approximated a horizontal line in shape. (3) The departmental output records were distorted. This was found by comparing the observer's count with the figures compiled by the department during the study period. (4) The inaccuracies in the departmental records were traceable to two factors: (a) differences between actual output and reported output, and (b) differences between standard working time and reported working time. The first factor was assessed by comparing the observer's output count with that reported to the group chief by the wiremen. It was found that no wireman reported exactly what he produced each day; some days he reported more and some less. The second factor was studied by recording and analyzing claims for daywork allowances. It was apparent that most of the wiremen frequently claimed to have been prevented from working by stoppages beyond their control when, in reality, there was little justification for their claims because (i) the stoppage was shorter than claimed, (ii) the stoppage was brought about by the operators themselves, (iii) there was in fact no delay, or (iv) there was a real stoppage but it could have been compensated for by working a little harder or decreasing spare time. (5) Analysis of quality records showed that they reflected not only the quality of the work done by the wiremen and soldermen but also the personal relations between them and the inspector. This was found by separating objectively determined defects from those which were determined by the inspector's personal judgment. Analysis of the former showed that an inspector's rating of a solderman varied with different wiremen, even though the solderman was solely responsible for the defect. It also showed that different inspectors varied widely in their gradings of a specific solderman's work. (6) Differences in weekly average hourly output rates for different wiremen did not reflect differences in capacity to perform. This conclusion was based on the following observations: (a) Most of the wiremen stated definitely that they could easily turn out more work than they did. (b) The observer said that all the men stopped work before quitting time. Frequently, a wireman finished his work quite early and stalled until quitting time. In general, the men who ranked highest in output were the first to be finished. This point was verified by a comparison of individual morning and afternoon output rates, which showed the greatest differences in the cases of the faster wiremen. (c) Tests of dexterity and intelligence showed no relation between capacity to perform and actual performance" (Roethlisberger and Dickson, 1939:445-446).

[7] Barnard (1938) notes that "the initial existence of an organization depends upon a combination of . . . elements appropriate to the external conditions at the moment. Its survival depends upon the maintenance of an equilibrium of the system. This equilibrium is primarily internal, a matter of proportions between the elements, but it is ultimately and basically an equilibrium between the system and the total

situation external to it." The equilibrium model, from Barnard's view, could easily be classified under "open-systems models," although the fact is that internal cooperation factors are most crucial. For this reason, the model has been placed under the "closed-system" designation.

[8] An excellent discussion of the grievance process at work is found in Wolfbein (1970). Wolfbein distinguishes between grievances of workers and industrial conflict, and he outlines the procedures whereby grievance adjustments take place.

Chapter 3

Some Organizational
Typologies

ON THE DEVELOPMENT OF TYPOLOGIES

The problems involved in the development of organizational typologies are similar to those encountered by researchers who attempt to construct models of organizations. In the general case, "a type is a selective, purposive simplification, constructed in terms of certain criteria and constituting a bridge between a theoretical approach on one side and empirical observations on the other" (Caldwell and Black, 1971:66), and "A typology is a collection of types having certain characteristics in common but also sufficiently different to be distinguishable from one another" (Caldwell and Black, 1971:66).[1]

Typologies are ways of describing or labeling differences among organizations. Certain relationships among variables may be true within one type of organization but not necessarily within another. Typologies are useful in that they contribute to explanations of differences between organizations. Although organizational theories are devised and intended to apply to all organizations, the fact that organizations differ in size, shape, complexity, and a host of other factors often means that theoretical statements about them will not be clear-cut. If a theory applies to one organization but not to another, the theorist wants to know why. Is the theory only partially adequate, or is the investigator attempting to apply a theory about "oranges" to "apples"? Classifying organizations according to several key criteria will enable the investigator to unravel some of the complexities surrounding the systematic analysis of these structures.

Unfortunately, organizational theory is not at the level of sophistication necessary to bridge the theoretical gaps between all organizations. Consequently, many theorists have attempted to devise theories which apply to certain *classes* or *types* of organizations (i.e., those which exhibit specific characteristics in common) and not to others. The crucial question raised in the construction of organizational typologies, therefore, is: "Which criteria should be used in such classification schemes?"

Haas, Hall, and Johnson (1966:162-163) provide a partial list of criteria which have been used in the classification of organizations. These are shown in Table 3-1.

A second question which derives from the first above is: "How do we know whether or not we have selected the 'right' criteria for our typology?" Only through systematic research on organizations can this question be answered satisfactorily. Obviously, some typologies will be more "successful" than others, if success is defined according to the usefulness of the particular scheme in predicting differences between organizations. Researchers tend to be quite pragmatic when it comes to developing an allegiance to one typology or another.

In this chapter several typologies of organizations will be examined. The same deficiencies and limitations associated with models also pertain to all typologies constructed to date. No typology is fully comprehensive, and all contain exceptions. *The general usefulness of typologies, however, is that they enable us to sift and sort through the myriad of organizations which exist currently and isolate important similarities between them which have potential theoretical and substantive value.* The decision as to which typologies to include here was based, in part, upon which ones are most frequently cited in the organizational literature. Some typologies were excluded because of an insufficient attachment to the empirical world. Five typologies will be described briefly. These include (1) the Hughes typology (1952), (2) the "tenfold taxonomy" (Haas, Hall, and Johnson, 1966), (3) the "compliance" typology (Etzioni, 1961a), (4) the "prime-beneficiary" typology (Blau and Scott, 1962), and (5) the "genotypical-functions" typology (Katz and Kahn, 1966).

Table 3-1   Some Criteria for the Classification of Organizations*

1. Organizational goals and objectives
2. Major activities of the organization
3. Basic organizational character or orientation
5. Major divisions or departments (horizontal differentiation)
6. Vertical and horizontal complexity (combined index)
7. Geographical dispersion of personnel and facilities
8. Interdependency of departments
9. Concreteness of positional descriptions
10. Committees and boards
11. Organizational control (source of major policy decisions)
12. Centralization of authority
13. Formalization of authority structure
14. Communication structure
15. Dependence on written rules and policies
16. Penalties for rule violation
17. Emphasis on status distinctions
18. Manner in which new members enter the organization
21. Distinctions regarding types of organizational members (nonhierarchical)
22. Number of members, with extent of variation in size of departments
23. Turnover of membership, by level (per year)
24. Planned limit on size
25. Restrictions on membership
26. Dependency on other organizations
27. Other organizations dependent on one studied
28. Competition with other organizations
31. Share of potential customer market
32. Geographic factors as a handicap
33. Primary sources of income
34. Financial condition of the organization
35. Age of organization
36. Shifts in major activities throughout history of the organization
37. Patterns of growth and decline

* Certain items have been omitted because they are, in the opinion of the author, irrelevant.
Source: Haas, Hall, and Johnson, 1966:162–163.

The Hughes Typology

Hughes (1952) identifies five different kinds of organizations which are characteristic of contemporary society. These are *voluntary associations* (e.g., the American Sociological Association, the Lions' Club, and the Catholic church), *military organizations* (e.g., the U.S. Army, military academies, and the National Guard), *philanthropic organizations* (e.g., universities, hospitals, and research institutes), *corporation organizations* (e.g., IBM, General Motors, U.S. Steel, and the Bank of America), and *family business organizations* (e.g., small businesses and the Mafia).

Although Hughes has attempted to differentiate between organizations on the basis of the general *purpose* of each, there are some serious deficiencies inherent in his scheme. First, the scheme is weak because of its inability to differentiate between organizations *within* classes. For example, there are many kinds of voluntary organizations, ranging from the Ku Klux Klan to the ladies' aid society. Needless to say, there are differences between organizations within any given category which have obvious theoretical significance and must be taken into account in any comprehensive analysis of organizations. A second limitation of the scheme is that it is far from being comprehensive. Highly generalized schemes have the disadvantage of failing to make finite distinctions between many types of organizations.

A Tenfold Taxonomy

In a rigorous attempt to classify organizations according to their similarities and differences, Haas, Hall, and Johnson (1966:157-180) developed a taxonomy of ten "prime classes" of organizations. These classes have been listed in Table 3-2.

The primary strengths of their taxonomy are (1) that the taxonomy resulted from an extensive, though not exhaustive, array of organizations and characteristics, (2) that the taxonomy computer program was used to classify the organizations selectively, and (3) that the taxonomy appears to have some degree of analytical and predictive utility.

Hall (1972a:60-61) has noted several weaknesses of the taxonomy, however. Among them he states that:

> (1) the variables selected for inclusion might not have been those that are most crucial for organizations; (2) the data varied in completeness and depth because of the differential knowledge possessed by interviewees of organizations investigated, and (3) the taxonomy covered only 75 organizations and therefore, it did not pertain to *all* types of them.

The Compliance Typology

Etzioni (1961:3-21) has devised a classification scheme for organizations which is based on the nature of the *compliance behavior*. "Compliance," according to Etzioni, "is universal, existing in all social units. It is a major element of the relationship between those who have power and those over whom they exercise it." Accordingly, Etzioni defines "compliance" as "the relation in which an actor behaves in accordance with a directive supported by another actor's power, and to the orientation of the subordinated actor to the power applied" (1961:4).

In all organizations, members are subjected to the orders of members at a higher level in the hierarchy of authority. Higher-level members may exer-

Table 3-2 Haas, Hall, and Johnson's Taxonomy

Organizations	Common characteristics
Class I. Restaurants, governmental regulative agencies, motels, banks, insurance companies, manufacturing plants, parochial school systems, private television stations	Members enter the organization by simple sign-up; members are primary affiliates; no racial restrictions on membership; no physical requirements; geographical factors no bar to organizational success; no shifts in organizational activity over time
Class II. Manufacturing plants, religious service organizations, state schools, public school systems, farmers' federations, post offices, state penal institutions, newspapers, marketing organizations, retail organizations, farm cooperatives, labor union organizations, public utilities, hotels, banks, public transit firms, quarries	Members enter organization by simple sign-up; no religious restrictions on membership; compared to other organizations, the organization faces average geographic situations; no departments engaged in production of goods for internal use
Class III. Delinquent reformatories, state penal institutions	Nonprofit, government organizations; provide a service for nonmembers; strong flexibility and change orientation; no departments engaged in sale of product or service; overall complexity is .020–.029; low concreteness of positional descriptions; written job descriptions at all levels; no intradepartmental committees; three committees in total organization; source of major policy decisions is another organization; authority is not formalized in writing; medium emphasis on status distinctions; some members enter organization voluntarily and others by prescription—i.e., by law; primary members only; some primary members nonvoluntary; upper-level turnover is 0–5%; limit to overall size of organization; limit to size of particular departments; no racial restrictions on membership; no religious restrictions on membership; no physical requirements; no citizenship requirements for membership; being on a blacklist is not a bar to membership; part of a larger organization; no subsidiary organizations; tax supported; geographic factors no bar to organizational success; primary source of income is public tax; compared to other similar organizations, the organization faces average geographic situations; financial condition is satisfactory; one or more shifts in activities in last three years; greater emphasis on some activities previously present

Table 3-2 Continued

Organizations	Common characteristics
Class IV. Municipal airports, educational television stations, governmental regulative agencies	Commonweal organizations; nonprofit, governmental organizations; provide a service to nonmembers; no departments engaged in production of goods for internal use; no departments engaged in production of goods for external use
Class V. Private hospitals, trade associations, private schools, churches, civil rights organizations, private country clubs, universities, trucking firms	Penalties for rule violation not clearly specified; members enter the organization voluntarily; no departments engaged in production of goods for external use; no departments engaged in production of goods for internal use
Class VI. State hospitals, delinquent reformatories	Nonprofit, governmental organizations; strong emphasis on internal efficiency; average emphasis on service to the public; no departments, internal or external; provide a service to nonmembers
Class VII. Private welfare agencies, religious-fraternal organizations	Presence of three goals; nonprofit, nongovernmental; provide service to members primarily; no departments engaged in production of goods for internal use; no departments engaged in sale of product or service
Class VIII. Juvenile detention centers, fund-raising agencies, law-enforcement agencies, city recreation departments, state penal institutions, local religious organizations, private welfare agencies, state church organizations, military supply commands, public school systems, labor union organizations, universities, state psychiatric hospitals	No departments engaged in production for internal use; no departments engaged in production for external use; no departments engaged in sale of product or service
Class IX. State church organizations, county political parties	Two goals; cultural goals; mutual benefit associations; nonprofit, nongovernmental; strong growth orientation; no departments engaged in production for internal use; deepest single division has three levels; penalties for rule violation clearly stipulated
Class X. County medical associations, railroads	Economic goals; provide service to nonmembers; no departments engaged in production for internal use; two departments engaged in internal service or supportive activities; many rules; rules and policies occasionally reviewed

Source: Johnson, 1966: 186–234.

cise authority over subordinates through force or coercion, reward or remuneration, or normative means. By the same token, the recipients of directives, the "lower participants," (generally) vary in the nature of their involvement in the organization according to the nature of the directives focused at them. For instance, it may be that a person will become alienated within the system because he is forced or coerced into complying with directives from above. On the other hand, a person may feel morally obligated to participate and obey the directives from above to the extent that he believes they are normatively based. Finally, a person may calculate the benefits he can obtain by complying with remuneratively based directives. Etzioni has developed a typology of compliance relations that is illustrated in Table 3-3. Types 1, 5, and 9 are designated by him as *congruent,* because, he argues, congruence is more effective, and organizations are social units under external and internal pressure to be effective. Etzioni explains the existence of the incongruent types, in part, as due to external factors which reduce the power of superiors in the organization (e.g., the membership of lower participants in unions) and various value commitments.

These are some examples of incongruent types (e.g., coercive-moral and normative-alienative). A coercive-moral incongruency, for instance, might occur in the armed forces. A person may be drafted into the army, air force, or some other branch, and he therefore feels coerced. However, even though he dislikes doing what his superiors in the situation direct him to do, he does so because of moral considerations (i.e., it is patriotic to do so). A normative-alienative incongruency might occur when a priest or minister in a church organization does what he believes to be normative things (e.g., deliver sermons and counsel persons with marital troubles). Perhaps his position dictates that he remain celibate, and in time, he comes to resent the requirement. Eventually he becomes involved in his work in the church in an alienative fashion, in spite of his belief that it is a normative set of behaviors he has to follow.

Coercive-calculative incongruencies may be observed in the case of an aspiring young executive who feels "coerced" into doing certain things which he believes are below his capabilities and potential. Yet he realizes

Table 3-3 Etzioni's Typology of Compliance Relations

Kinds of power	Kinds of involvement		
	Alienative	Calculative	Moral
Coercive	1	2	3
Remunerative	4	5	6
Normative	7	8	9

Source: Etzioni, 1961:12.

that if he persists in what he is doing, he may eventually get promoted to a position where undesirable work will not be required. As another example, the involvement of graduate students in graduate programs throughout universities may be characterized as a coercive-calculative incongruency. Remunerative-alienative incongruent types may be illustrated by the "soldier of fortune" who, as a mercenary, fights for a country for money, having little or no concern for the ideals and the people of the country itself. A remunerative-moral incongruency might be evidenced by the director of a funeral home who realizes substantial profits in his business but at the same time realizes that his task has moral implications for bereaved families.

Finally, the normative-calculative incongruency is depicted in a professor who believes that it is his task to teach others specialized materials in his subject area. But at the same time it occurs to him that being a professor may mean extensive summer vacations, spring vacations, and Christmas vacations, all of which add up to nearly four months in which little or no academic involvement is expected. The person complies with directives of the higher-ups and does a reasonable teaching job, but at the same time he reaps substantial rewards through more leisure time, more time to write books and obtain royalties, and more time to increase his stature in the profession.

The idea of congruent and incongruent types does not necessarily imply that overlaps cannot exist. It is entirely possible for several types of power to be exerted by the same individual in relation to someone else at the same time. It is also possible for persons to have overlapping types of involvement in the activities they are expected to perform. It is only for illustrative purposes that Etzioni has depicted the types as mutually exclusive. In reality, they are not.

Table 3-4 shows Etzioni's classification of organizations in terms of which compliance types predominate.

Several criticisms have been leveled against Etzioni's scheme. For instance, Perrow (1967) has indicated that schemes which focus upon a single dimension of organizational structure or process neglect other, equally or more important dimensions which should be considered. In the general case, unidimensional schemes tend to be inadequate theoretically and have little explanatory value beyond certain organizational limits. Although multidimensional schemes offer better theoretical promise in this regard, they are more complex to construct. In addition, the question arises as to which variables are more important to include in the typology. On the interpersonal level, however, Etzioni's scheme would appear to have some utility for contributing to an explanation for particular behaviors and attitudes, such as morale, job satisfaction, labor turnover, productivity, and esprit de corps.

Table 3-4   Types of Organizations Corresponding to Particular Compliance Patterns

Organization	Examples
1. Coercive	Concentration camps; prisons; correctional institutions; custodial mental hospitals; prisoner-of-war camps; relocation centers; coercive unions; forced-labor camps
2. Utilitarian	Blue-collar industries and blue-collar divisions in other industries; white-collar industries and white-collar divisions in other industries; business unions; farmers' organizations; peacetime military organizations
3. Normative	Religious organizations; ideological political organizations; general hospitals; colleges and universities; social unions; voluntary associations; schools; therapeutic mental hospitals; professional organizations
4. Dual Structures	
a. Normative-coercive	Combat units
b. Utilitarian-normative	Majority of unions
c. Utilitarian-coercive	Some farms, some early industries, company towns, and ships

Source: Etzioni, 1961:66–67.

It is important to consider that Etzioni probably intended to suggest the compliance factor as one possible comparative base among several equally important alternatives.

The Prime-Beneficiary Typology

Blau and Scott (1962) have created a classification scheme based upon the principle of *who benefits* by the particular organizational activity. Formally designated as the prime-beneficiary typology, this scheme delineates four types of beneficiaries (thus making explicit the identification of four corresponding organizational divisions). The types of organizations and the corresponding prime beneficiaries are shown in Table 3-5.

Blau and Scott are careful to point out that their scheme includes potential inconsistencies and understandable overlaps. It should be emphasized, however, that in organizations which appear to "benefit" *several* interests, the category of persons which is benefited *most* is designated as the prime beneficiary.

Blau and Scott suggest that their classification scheme might be useful for investigating the impact of organizational change on the prime benefi-

Table 3-5 The Prime-Beneficiary Classification Scheme

Type of organization	Prime beneficiary	Examples
1. Mutual-benefit	Members, rank-and file participants	Political parties, labor unions, fraternal associations, clubs, veterans' organizations
2. Business	Owners, managers	Mail-order houses, industrial firms, banks, insurance companies, wholesale and retail stores
3. Service	Clients	Social-work agencies, hospitals, schools, legal aid societies, mental health clinics
4. Commonweal	General public	Internal Revenue Service, military services, police and fire departments, National Guard

Source: Blau and Scott, 1962:42–58.

ciaries. For example, a university (a service-oriented organization) may function for the primary benefit of its students. However, many of the professors may become so wrapped up in the advancement of their own careers that they may fail to provide the necessary services (e.g., counseling and good teaching) to students. The organization slowly drifts from being a service institution to being a business concern of sorts. The growing disenchantment of student groups in such a situation highlights the seriousness of the change in prime beneficiary for organizational growth, development, and change.

The Genotypical-Functions Typology

Katz and Kahn (1966:110-111) argue that "most typologies of organizations tend to oversimplify the complexities of many interacting factors and to propose pure types based upon the presence or absence of a single characteristic." They propose a classification scheme which not only depicts crucial organizational characteristics but also specifies the *degree*, from high to low, to which the characteristic is present.

The major focus of their typology is upon the *genotypical functions* organizations perform. In their words, "genotypic function is the function which an organization performs as a subsystem of the larger society" (p. 147). Table 3-6 lists four different kinds of organizations based upon

Table 3-6   Organizational Types based on Genotypic Function.

Type of organization	Examples
First order	
1. Productive or economic organizations	Manufacturing plants, transportation fa- cilities, communications companies
2. Maintenance organizations	Schools and churches
3. Adaptive organizations	Research laboratories, universities
4. Managerial-political organizations	National, state, and local governmental agencies, labor unions, pressure groups
Second order	
1. Nature of organizational through-put	Distinction between objects and people as the end product of organizational functioning
2. Nature of maintenance processes	Distinction between expressive (intrinsic) rewards and instrumental (extraneous) rewards as ways of attracting and hold- ing members in organizations
3. Nature of bureaucratic structure	Distinction in terms of permeability of or- ganizational boundaries (ease of joining or leaving) and in terms of structural elaboration (degree of role specialization and number of echelons)
4. Type of equilibrium	Distinction between the tendency to a steady state and the tendency toward maximization of organizational return as dominant organizational dynamics

Source: Katz and Kahn, 1966:147–148.

genotypical (first order) factors. Also presented in the table are four second-order factors, which operate in conjunction with the first-order ones.

In contrast to some of the other typologies which have been discussed in this chapter, the genotypical-functions scheme focuses our attention upon the functional interrelations of the organization and the society within which it is found. At the same time, it has the advantage of describing internal organizational characteristics which may be helpful in accounting for inter-organizational differences. The typology is broadly conceived and attempts to cover most types of organizations. However, this merit is also a disadvantage. Schemes which are too general in scope have the unfortunate consequence of not being specific enough for useful predictions of organizational behavior. The typology clearly neglects to cover the nature of functional interrelationships between roles and departments within the organization. It would seem that most attention is devoted to structure, with little emphasis upon the processual aspect of organizational functioning.

A CONCLUDING NOTE

No typology which currently exists is entirely adequate from the standpoint of being universally applicable. All have their respective weaknesses and strengths, and they appear to be differentially appropriate under varied organizational conditions. The existence of numerous schemes is indicative of a continuing interest among organizational theorists to develop analytical tools capable of being applied to all organizations.

Competing for recognition are various ways of looking at and classifying organizations. If we consider each of these schemes as an attempt to develop a set of consistent propositions which will contribute to a general theory of organizations, it is clear that much work remains to be done. The field of formal organizations is "wide open" in this respect.

In the next two chapters we will examine several key variables which may be useful in organizational analysis. These variables may be included within several of the models and typologies of organizations which have been presented in this and the previous chapter. They may function to assist researchers in delineating salient organizational, interpersonal, and individual factors as they impinge upon work environments. Not all variables are equally appropriate for every model or typology described thus far. One challenge confronting the organizational researcher is to identify which variables are most important for explaining social structure and process. Certainly the advancement of organizational theory is contingent, to a great degree, upon whether or not investigators can meet this challenge adequately.

SUMMARY

Organizational typologies are classification schemes by which different kinds of organizations may be grouped according to common characteristics. Typologies and models have proliferated for the same reasons. But typologies differ from models in separating organizations: models, by contrast, can be applied to all organizations across all categories.

The inability to construct useful theoretical statements applicable to all organizations has been a persistent problem in this field. Therefore, typologies have at least one raison d'être—to let researchers make theoretical generalizations about a given class of organizations rather than all organizations. This is tantamount to moving from simple formulations to more complex ones. In effect, we must learn to walk before we can run.

No typology has satisfied the professional demands of all organizational investigators. Hence, several competing typologies currently exist. A few have been described briefly in this chapter. Some typologies, such as those of Blau and Scott and Etzioni, focus upon "who benefits" or on power and compliance; others (e.g., those of Hughes and Hall, Haas, and Johnson) focus on the purposes fulfilled by organizations and the functions they perform. Much work remains to be done in the development of typologies.

Perhaps the primary merit of typologies is that they serve to delimit our theoretical scope and develop singularly useful statements about certain kinds of organizations. Although attempts at constructing typologies have so far been less than perfect, the typologies we have are better than none at all.

STUDY QUESTIONS

1 What is an organizational typology? How does it differ from an organizational model? Explain.
2 Do you feel that typologies of organizations can be developed to apply to all organizations, regardless of size, shape, or complexity? Why or why not? Discuss.
3 List five organizations in the real world (apart from those suggested in the text) which might be likely to fit each of the congruent compliance-involvement types suggested by Etzioni. In each case, write a short paragraph defending your selection.
4 What do you consider to be the major contributions of typologies to social research in formal organizations? Explain.
5 Why are the typologies suggested by Hughes and Parsons restricted in their application to investigations of organizations? What do you consider to be their respective weaknesses and strengths? Elaborate.
6 Try to develop a brief typology of organizations within a given category, such as "manufacturing" or "service." What kinds of difficulties do you encounter as your typology is attempted? Explain briefly.

NOTES

[1] A comprehensive discussion of the problems involved in typology construction in general is found in McKinney (1966).

Organizational Variables

INTRODUCTION

What are the relevant variables in studying organizations and how are they related to cause the phenomena under study? How is one to understand a pattern of variables whose interdependence is highly complex? These are extraordinarily difficult questions to answer. The variables are so numerous and the interrelationships so complex that one must be careful lest he miss the very complexity that is so characteristic of organizations [Argyris, 1960b:6].

The systematic study of formal organizations involves an examination of several key *variables. A variable is any quantity which can assume more than one value.* Some examples of commonly used variables in organizational analysis are span of control, organizational size, degree of job satisfaction, size of the administrative component, and whether the work performed is blue-collar or white-collar. This chapter is designed to familiarize the student of organizations with several important variables characteristic of such structures. Our discussion will include how the variables under consideration can be measured empirically and how they can be used in verifying organizational theories. Several selected variables which are used most often in organizational research will be highlighted. In most instances, we will present some of the ways each has been conceptualized, measured by social scientists, and utilized in actual research projects.

Researchers new to the area of formal organizations are frequently unfamiliar with many of the more critical variables which would be useful in their analyses. Although the treatment of variables in this chapter is by no means comprehensive, we have attempted to identify those factors which are cited most frequently in contemporary organizational literature. This was the sole criterion by which these variables were selected for inclusion.

The variables defined and described in subsequent portions of this section are labeled as "organizational." This label is intended to underscore the fact that each variable is a characteristic of the organization as a unit. Other variables commonly associated with the interpersonal and individual units of analysis will be discussed in the following chapter. The fact that certain variables have been extracted for inclusion in this chapter does not mean that they are not related in some respect to variables characteristic of the small group or the individual. On the contrary, one of the primary assumptions we are making is that there are significant overlaps among the variables of all three units of analysis. Deciding whether to classify a variable as "organizational" rather than "interpersonal" or "individual" is a matter of considering the unit most emphasized by it.

SOME PRELIMINARY GENERAL CLASSIFICATIONS OF VARIABLES

Before the selected organizational variables are presented, it seems appropriate to discuss briefly some important variable functions and characteristics as they pertain to causality. Variables may be classified according to at least the following dimensions: (1) independent-dependent, (2) discrete-continuous, and (3) necessary, sufficient, contributory, and contingent.

The Independent-Dependent Distinction

Variables may be regarded as independent, dependent, or both simultaneously, depending upon how they are used in any organizational investigation. An *independent variable is one which elicits changes in other variables.* For example, if the management of an organization were to change *the type of incentive system* under which the employees are operating, there is a chance that the change will elicit changes in other variables in the work setting. For instance, if changes in productivity rates among employees work groups are observed to occur shortly after the changeover to the new incentive plan, there is a strong likelihood that the incentive plan had something to do with the change in productivity. In fact, the researcher may interpret the change in productivity rates to be causally connected to the change in the incentive system. In this instance, the "type of incentive system" is regarded as an independent variable to the extent that it elicited a change in productivity rates among employees.

A dependent variable is one which receives its value from changes in some other variable (usually an independent one). In the example provided above, the *rate of productivity* among employees might be regarded as a dependent variable inasmuch as it appeared to change in response to a change in the organizational incentive system (the independent variable).

Sometimes, variables function in dual capacities. They may be dependent and independent simultaneously. It could be, for example, that changes in the incentive system of the organization modify the morale of employees. A decrease in morale may be followed by a decrease in the output of work groups. The incentive system acts in this instance as the independent variable in relation to morale. Morale would be considered dependent in relation to the incentive system. But morale could act in an independent capacity in relation to productivity. The productivity of a group would be designated as "dependent" upon the morale of the group (the independent variable in this relation).[1]

The important thing to remember is *that a variable is defined as independent or dependent (or both) according to how it is used in organizational research.* Different researchers working independently but using the same variable X in their analyses of organizations may define variable X differently. One researcher may use variable X as independent, while the other researcher uses it as a dependent one. Obviously, the organizational researcher should clarify the specific function or functions of each variable used in his analysis. He specifies the functions of variables in the theoretical scheme he constructs to account for particular organizational behavior. The rationale for interrelating variables in a particular fashion is developed thoroughly, and subsequently when hypotheses are derived from the theoretical scheme to be tested empirically, there will be little or no question as to which variables are independent or dependent.

The Distinction Between Discrete and Continuous

Another way of looking at variables is in terms of whether they are discrete or continuous. *A discrete variable is one which has a limited number of subclasses. A continuous variable is one which can be infinitely divided.* Variable subclasses are the various divisions of a single variable. For example, *sex* is a discrete variable in the sense that it has only two subclasses: (1) male and (2) female. *The rate of productivity* is continuous in the sense that it may vary infinitely (2.3332615 units of product, 151.7784 units of product, etc.). Attitudes of various kinds (e.g., job satisfaction, aggression, and anxiety) are also regarded as continuous variables in some respects. Variables are designated as either discrete or continuous *depending upon how they are measured by the researcher.* As different organizational variables are presented in subsequent sections, it will be seen that each variable may be measured by alternative means.[2] Whether a variable is discrete or continuous will limit the researcher's choice of statistical tests or techniques (if used in the process of data analysis) and place certain demands or constraints upon him pertaining to the measuring instruments necessary to take the phenomenon into account empirically.

Necessary, Sufficient, Contributory, and Contingent Variables

Our discussion would be incomplete unless we included a description of variable functions in terms of necessary, sufficient, contributory, and contingent conditions. Inasmuch as variables occur in relation to one another in a time sequence (except in the instance of concomitant variation, such as height and weight), it makes sense to view their origination and change from the dimension of *conditions.* We would attempt to answer the general question: "What is the specific impact of a given variable upon another as a result of its presence as a condition?"

"*A necessary condition is one that must occur if the phenomenon of which it is a 'cause' is to occur*" (Selltiz et al., 1959:81). This does not mean, however, that if a given necessary condition is present, a particular phenomenon *will* occur. *Other* necessary conditions may also be required for the occurrence of the phenomenon. *All* necessary conditions must prevail in advance of the occurrence of a given phenomenon.

"*A sufficient condition is one that is always followed by the phenomenon of which it is a 'cause'*" (Selltiz et al., 1959:81). For example, there may be several alternative sufficient conditions which "cause" labor turnover in a factory (e.g., type of supervision, working hours, or physical difficulty of work).

Some variables function in relation to one another as *contributory conditions.* If a particular variable is present in an organization (to a specified degree), it possibly contributes to the occurrence and degree of another variable. A contributory condition does not automatically mean that another variable will be affected to a particular degree. Rather, it implies that the variable will be influenced by the other variable working together with several other contributory factors.

A contingent condition is most readily linked with an "intervening" factor in the presence of a relation between two other variables. We may say that a relation is established between two or more variables, provided that a particular condition (or third factor) exists to a certain degree. In many respects, contingent conditions are closely associated with necessary ones. Although a moderate conceptual distinction exists between the two terms, we will, for purposes of clarifying our present discussion, treat contingent conditions as necessary ones.

It is possible to generate various combinations of variable functions by using these criteria. For instance, a variable may be a necessary (and obviously "contributory") condition, but it may be insufficient to bring about a given phenomenon. Or a variable may be a contributory condition but not necessary for a given phenomenon to occur. Variables can function as sufficient but not as necessary, and so on. The main point of this discussion is simply that *variables can be treated several different ways simultaneously in relation to other variables in the analysis and determination of a causal relation.* The rationale or theory we devise to account for a given phenomenon in the organizational setting provides the necessary structure for delineating the precise nature of the contribution of each variable to the others in formulating testable hypotheses.

Because causal relationships between variables are difficult to establish and verify scientifically, a number of criteria have been devised to assist researchers exploring the nature of potential causal associations. Pertinent here are John Stuart Mill's methods of *agreement, difference,* and *concomitant variation* (Mill, 1930:32-33):

> The so-called *method of agreement* states that if the circumstances leading up to the given event have in all cases had one factor in common, that factor may be the cause sought. This is especially so if it is the only factor in common. . . .
> Another classical method is based on the *method of difference,* which states that, if two sets of circumstances differ in only one factor and the one containing the factor leads to the event and the other does not, this factor can be considered the cause of the event. For example, if batches of rats are fed identical diets under identical conditions except that one batch receives also a certain drug, the fact that the rats in this batch die immediately is evidence supporting the hypothesis that the drug kills rats. But it does not prove it. The result may have been due to chance; perhaps the rats would have died anyway from other causes. The difficulty is connected with the expression 'identical circumstances'; no two circumstances are ever exactly identical; at the very best they must differ either in time or in place and will in fact differ in a practically infinite number of other respects as well. . . . A third principle—*the method of concomitant*

variation—states that if variation of the intensity of a factor results in a parallel variation of the effect, then this factor is the cause. It is seen that this represents a broadened version of the combination of the first two methods. Most of the remarks about them therefore apply to the new principle also.

Additional criteria may be used to establish causality. These are *association, time priority, nonspurious relation,* and *rationale* (Labovitz and Hagedorn, 1971:3-9):

> It is widely accepted that if two or more variables are not associated, one cannot be the cause of the other. . . . an association is a necessary condition for a causal relation. [Also] . . . . to establish cause, the independent causal variable must either occur first or change prior to the dependent variable. . . . A nonspurious relation is an association between two variables which cannot be explained by a third variable. Stated otherwise, if the effects of all relevant variables are eliminated and the relation between the independent and dependent variables is maintained, then the relation is nonspurious. [And finally] . . . the rationale refers to the theory, explanation, or interpretation of a relation stipulating that not only does the independent variable change first, but it also causes changes in the dependent variable. The rationale is the justification for the observed relation, which is often stated in terms of assumptions and hypotheses. . . . A rationale may specify the causal nature of a relation by designating the intervening mechanisms that connect the independent and dependent variables.

These passages underscore the importance of the rationale in establishing causal relations between organizational phenomena. The theory is perhaps the most vital part of the research process, particularly where the objective is to define causal relationships between things as opposed to sheer description.

Establishing a clear-cut causal relation between two or more variables is not as easy as it may appear. The usual assumption (quite erroneous) is that an observed association between variables means that there is also a cause-effect relation between them. Frequently overlooked is the possibility that the observed "apparent" association is no more than a chance occurrence. For example, in a given study of twenty five organizations there might be a high correlation between organizational size and the number of supervisory levels. Does this necessarily mean that for *all* organizations the larger the size of the organization, the greater the number of supervisory levels? One explanation for varying numbers of supervisory levels may be the variety of philosophies of managerial control utilized from one organization to the next. Regardless of the size of the organization in terms of numbers of employees, the number of supervisory levels may actually be dependent upon the particular philosophy of management and the unique arrangement of the hierarchy of operating positions.

Some management philosophies state that a supervisor should have many employees under his direct control, thereby permitting him to channel his energies toward planning and coordinating tasks instead of "riding" one or two employees during the working day. A contrasting view of management behavior may indicate that each supervisor should have fewer than three employees under his jurisdiction. This situation encourages more meticulous attention to the actions of subordinates, and the supervisor can more thoroughly examine the work of his personnel.

Therefore, if we were to compare two companies having identical size (the same numbers of employees) but practicing different managerial methods, we might expect to find fewer supervisory levels in the former (requiring many employees under direct supervisory control) and more supervisory levels in the latter (requiring fewer employees under direct supervisory control). In this situation, there is no direct causal relation between the actual size of the organization and the number of supervisory levels.

We can learn several things from this example. First, an observed association between two variables does not automatically mean that a causal relation exists between them. The apparent relation may be due to a third variable (possibly unknown to the researcher), and the original relationship may "wash out" or disappear if we control for (or hold constant) the effect of the third variable. Relationships between any two variables which are due to a third variable are designated as "spurious." Spuriousness is present in virtually all social research, and therefore the researcher must do everything within his power to rule out the possibility that this factor is significantly influencing any relationships between other variables which he observes in his study. An illustration of the effect of a spurious variable is provided in Table 4-1. In part A of the table it would appear that large organizations have a significantly greater number of levels of supervision compared with smaller organizations. However, when we cast the data into a new form, taking into account the effect of a third variable called "supervisory style," notice that the original relationship between organizational size and supervisory levels disappears. In the latter case, all situations of larger numbers of supervisory levels occur under the close supervision condition, regardless of organizational size, whereas all situations of smaller numbers of supervisory levels occur under the general supervision condition, regardless of organizational size.

One of the guiding principles of this book and of this entire discussion of causality is that the researcher *should exercise conservatism in his analysis of organizational variable interrelations.* Theories exist as tentative explanations of things rather than as definite proofs of them. Replication (or re-

Table 4-1   An Example of a Spurious Relationship between Variables

A. Two-Variable Comparison

Large organization		Small organization	
Many supervisory levels	**Few supervisory levels**	**Many supervisory levels**	**Few supervisory levels**
70	30	30	70

B. Controlling for a "Third Variable"

"Close"				"General"			
Large organization		Small organization		Large organization		Small organization	
Many	**Few**	**Many**	**Few**	**Many**	**Few**	**Many**	**Few**
70	0	30	0	0	30	0	70

Type of supervision (Third variable) — (Subclasses of variables) — Number of supervisory levels

peated) research in a given area is necessary before we can say with a significant amount of assurance that one variable is the cause of another. Tentativeness and conservatism are consistent with the method of science and are particularly crucial in a growing area of knowledge, such as formal organizations, where adequate explanations of phenomena are currently underdeveloped. As one alternative, we might phrase interpretive statements in the following manner: "There appears to be an association between two or more variables"; or "On the basis of our investigations, there is some evidence to support the idea that a relationship exists between the two variables." In short, a correlation between variables in a single study of a single organization or even several organizations does not mean that a causal relations exists between these same variables *for the entire class of organizations of which those studied are only a small part.*

ORGANIZATIONAL VARIABLES—A PRELIMINARY VIEW

All of the variables to be treated in this chapter and the following one may be viewed as strategies to assist the researcher in answering certain questions about organizational behavior. However, not all variables listed below will be equally useful at any given time for explaining the problems of any particular organization. In this sense, the term "organizational problems" refers to any undesirable conditions in organizations as seen by at least some organizational members (e.g., low profits, high turnover, low morale, or interdepartmental hostility). Assessing organizational problems analytically often involves imaginative combinations of several variables. The researcher is not always able to use the same variable combinations for analyzing different organizations, either. In other words, having a knowledge of several possible key variables which would be potentially helpful in explaining organizational behaviors will not necessarily lead the researcher to the solutions he seeks. However, the reservoir of information he mentally compiles will significantly affect his facility for thinking constructively about organizational problems.[3]

In order to encourage practical applications of several of the variables discussed here and in the next chapter, a number of case studies have been included as Appendix I (see pages 281-297).[4] It is particularly important for students of organizational behavior to realize that simply conjecturing about organizational problems is insufficient. In addition, the suggestions geared to correct organizational difficulties should be evaluated in terms of their short- and long-range implications. It is possible, for example, that a suggested change in organizational structure may seemingly remedy an immediate problem, but several new problems may emergy subsequently as indirect results of the change. Herbert Spencer (1882:270-271) offers the following statement, which illustrates by analogy the importance of exploring all possible implications of tampering with organizational structure and process:

> You see that this wrought-iron plate is not quite flat; it sticks up a little here towards the left—"cockles," as we say. How shall we flatten it? Obviously, you reply, by hitting down on the part that is prominent. Well, here is a hammer, and I give the plate a blow as you advise. Harder, you say; Still no effect. Another stroke? Well, there is one, and another, and another. The prominence remains, you see: the evil is as great as ever—greater, indeed. But this is not all. Look at the warp which the plate has got near the opposite edge. Where it was flat before it is now curved. A pretty bungle we have made of it. Instead of curing the original defect, we have produced a second. Had we asked an artisan practiced in "planishing," as it is called, he would have told us that no good was to be done, but only mischief, by hitting down on the projecting part. He would have taught us how to give variously directed and specially adjusted blows with a hammer elsewhere; so attacking the evil not by direct but by indirect actions. The required process is less simple than you thought. Even a sheet of metal is not to be successfully dealt with after those common-sense methods in which you have so much confidence. What then shall we say about a society? "Do you think I am easier to be played on than a pipe?" asks Hamlet. Is humanity more readily straightened than an iron plate?

The classification of variables in organizational research is somewhat complicated because of at least the following factors: (1) Not all organizational researchers agree which variables are organizational and which ones are interpersonal, individual, or both. (2) Several measures of the same variable simultaneously used in different studies compete for professional recognition in the field. (3) There seems to be an excessive number of exceptions to classificatory schemes once they have been constructed and agreed upon, and variables are observed to overlap several units of analysis (i.e., the individual, the interpersonal, and the organizational) which were discussed in the first chapter. (4) Variables take on many different meanings and have any number of different implications depending upon the setting in which the research is conducted (e.g., variable X may not have the same kind of significance for, nor exert the same kind of impact upon, variable Z in a bakery as it does in a bank); therefore the contextual surroundings act as intervening conditions which must be considered when one is interpreting research results. (5) Organizational investigators adopt contrasting and often conflicting philosophies and frames of reference when researching the same organizational problem, inevitably leading to the use of the same variables in different capacities in similar, yet independent, research investigations.

The following grouping of variables represents an attempt at rearranging several key organizational factors into a few generally applicable categories. This grouping should help us to distinguish more meaningfully between them and appreciate their differential contributions to the increasing accumulation of organizational literature. The arrangement also provides us with an estimate of the popularity of certain concepts based upon their frequency of usage in recent books and journals. These variables have been mentioned and cataloged according to their appearance (explicit or implicit) in titles of articles and books in the broad area of formal organizations.[5] Although the variables included here overlap one another to varying degrees, four distinct subdivisions will be used. These are (1) organizational structure, (2) organizational control, (3) organizational behavior, and (4) organizational change.

Organizational Structure

Variables in this category tend to describe the arrangement of formalized positions or departments in an organization. They also describe the amount of differentiation and specialization within it. Three crucial variables pertaining to structure are (1) size, (2) complexity, and (3) formalization.

Size Used primarily as an independent variable, the size of an organization is measured several ways. Most definitions use the number of personnel on the organizational payroll (Hall, Haas, and Johnson, 1967). An alternative definition is *the total number of full-fledged members in the association* (Akers and Campbell, 1970:243). In an independent study of tuberculosis and general medicine and surgery hospitals, Anderson and Warkov

(1961) defined the size of hospital organizations as the "annual average daily patient load." As an alternative, they defined size as "the total hospital labor force."

Since such an extensive array of definitions can be attached to this single variable, it is not surprising that researchers arrive at different conclusions when studying essentially the same topics. The "issue of size has been a compelling one in organizational analysis" (Richard Hall, 1972:109), and one complicating factor is that organizations exist in so many forms. The fluidity of membership, the transiency of employees, seasonal employment fluctuations, and the factor of full- or part-time personnel lend further frustration to researchers intent on conceptualizing this phenomenon.

Complexity or Differentiation Equally nebulous are proposed definitions of organizational complexity. Few attempts have been made to define this variable precisely (Campbell and Akers, 1970:438). Campbell and Akers (1970:438) declare that "complexity is not unidimensional, but can take a number of forms within an organization." They identify two major types of complexity: horizontal and vertical. Horizontal complexity is the "lateral differentiation of functions which in corporate organizations may be duplicated at all levels of authority." Because Campbell and Akers studied occupational associations, it was necessary to modify the term. They note that:

> as applied here . . . it refers to the extent to which there are differentiated activities and divisions at one specific level—the national office of the association. . . . Vertical complexity refers to the extent to which there is differentiated depth or organizational "penetration" below the most inclusive national level . . . . an organization that includes three or four different levels (national, regional, state, and local) is more vertically differentiated [and therefore, more complex] than one which has no additional levels below the national [pp. 438-439].

The example they provide is enlightening:

> The American Medical Association which is a large organization has a great many divisions, committees, and sections at its national headquarters. In addition, it publishes several journels and periodicals. It is, therefore, horizontally complex. It also has state organizations in every state (plus Washington, D.C. and U.S. Territories) and nearly 2,000 local county societies as affiliated subunits below the national level. It is then vertically complex as well. By contrast, the American Chiropractic Association, a small organization, has only a few functional divisions at its national office and publishes only one periodical; it is, therefore, much less horizontally complex. At the same time, there are no regional, state or local groups affiliated as subunits of the ACA (although there

are, of course, state and local associations of chiropractors). Thus, the vertical complexity of the ACA is practically nil—it does not penetrate below the national level [p. 439].

In contrast to these associational distinctions, Anderson and Warkov (1961:582–584) defined complexity in the hospitals which they investigated based upon the number of diseases treated. They concluded that general medicine and surgery hospitals were more complex than tuberculosis hospitals because they treated a greater variety of diseases on a regular basis, including internal diseases and psychiatric illness as well as tuberculosis.

In organizational research, complexity or differentiation is most often treated as an independent variable.

Formalization   For the most part an independent variable in organizational analysis, "formalization" is defined as "how far communications and procedures in an organization are written down and filed" (Hinings et al., 1967:66). In addition, Litterer (1973:331) has defined "formalization" as "a measure of the extent to which rules, procedures, instructions, and communications are written."

One of the most elaborate definitions of "formalization" devised by social scientists is given by Hall, Haas, and Johnson (1967:907):

> (1) Roles: (a) the degree to which the positions in the organization are concretely defined, and (b) the presence or absence of written job descriptions; (2) Authority Relations: (a) the degree to which the authority structure is formalized (clear definition of the hierarchy of authority), and (b) the extent to which the authority structure is formalized in writing; (3) Communications: or (a) the emphasis on written communications, and (b) the degree of emphasis on going through channels in the communication process; (4) Norms and Sanctions: (a) the number of written rules and policies; (b) the degree to which penalties for rule violation are clearly stipulated; and (c) the extent to which penalties for rule violation are codified in writing; and (5) Procedures: (a) the degree of formalization of orientation programs for new members (systematic socialization for all new entrants), and (b) the degree of formalization of in-service training programs for new members (systematic and continuing socialization of new members).

Organizational Control

Associated with the control dimension of an organization are (1) the administrative component, (2) bureaucratization and debureaucratization, (3) centralization and decentralization, and (4) levels of authority (including span of control). These variables are central to the planning and coordinating of tasks within the overall division of labor of an organization. The initiation of directives to subordinate personnel and the formulation and implementation of policy decisions fall within the control realm.

Size of the Administrative Component   The administrative component is that part of an organization charged with coordinating, facilitating, and supporting the activities of the rest of the organizational participants (Campbell and Akers, 1970:437). Campbell and Akers (1970) indicate that the investigation of different types of organizations will necessitate modifying the original definition which they provide. For example:

> In corporate organizations such as industrial firms, the absolute size of the administrative component usually refers to the number of managerial, sales, clerical, and professional-technical employees. In educational institutions these are principals, superintendents, chairmen, deans, presidents, and other officials along with their staffs. The relative size of the administrative component is the ratio of administrative to other employees. We suggest that the appropriate definition of the administrative, or supportive component in voluntary associations (the targets of their investigation) is that which includes all administrative, clerical, technical, professional, and kindred employees of the association. In short, this would include all employees (and equivalent volunteers) to whom associational members usually refer as "staff" [pp. 437-438].

Some researchers use the term "supervisory ratio" to indicate the number of supervisors to the total number of members. Indik (1964b:302), for example, defines supervisors as those individuals whose functional role involves mainly direct interpersonal supervision or key organizational administrative decision-making.[6] This definition excludes those non-rank-and-file personnel higher in the organization who serve mainly clerical functions.

The administrative component is used most in organizational research as a dependent variable. Investigators are often interested in the variation of size in administrative component in response to other organizational variables such as size, complexity, formalization, and goals.

Bureaucratization and Debureaucratization   These terms refer to particular conditions of structure and process generated by a popular organizational form, bureaucracy. In his classic work on the subject, Eisenstadt (1959:312) defines "bureaucratization" as:

> the extension of the bureaucracy's spheres of activities and power either in its own interests or those of some of its elite. It tends toward growing regimentation of different areas of social life and some extent of displacement of its service goals in favor of various power interests and orientations. Examples are

military organizations that tend to impose their rule on civilian life, or political parties that exert pressure on their potential supporters in an effort to monopolize their private and occupational life and make them entirely dependent on the political party.

Blau (1970b:150) notes that "bureaucratization in labor unions refers to the development of centralized control by the leadership, which robs the union rank and file of most of its influence over policies and decisions." Often, and most popularly, "bureaucratization" means increasing specialization, rules and paperwork activities, increased complexity of the division of labor, and an expanding number of departments. In other words, any increased emphasis upon any one or all of these dimensions would be regarded as an increase in bureaucratization. Unfortunately, such a generalized designation for this phenomenon makes it difficult to measure precisely for social research. Not all of the dimensions are linked to the control function. Some characteristics are structural aspects such as departmentalization and specialization of function. Weber (1946:215) has simplified the concept by narrowing what it denotes. He claims that "bureaucratization primarily means discharge of business according to *calculable rules* and without regard for persons."

Bureaucratization is most frequently employed by organizational investigators as an independent variable, although it can be dependent upon the degree of technological change, goals, and labor turnover in any given setting.

"Debureaucratization," the reverse of this process, is defined as: "the subversion of the goals and activities of the bureaucracy in the interests of different groups with which it is in close interaction (clients, patrons, interested parties)" (Eisenstadt, 1959:312).

> In debureaucratization the specific characteristics of the bureaucracy in terms of both its autonomy and its specific rules and goals are minimized, even up to the point where its very functions and activities are taken over by other groups or organizations. Examples of this can be found in cases when some organization (e.g., a parent's association or a religious or political group) attempts to divert the rules and working order of a bureaucratic organization (school, economic agency, etc.) for its own use or according to its own values and goals [Eisenstadt, 1959:312].

Centralization and Decentralization   "Centralization" means the power given to organizational subunits (departments or separate operating units) that could be retained by the central organizational hierarchy at the same level as the subunits to which it is distributed (Richard Hall, 1972:228). A study by Blau (1970b) defined "centralization" similarly. In the same study,

Blau used "decentralization" to mean the delegation of responsibilities from top management (including both the director and his deputy) either to middle managers at the same headquarters or to managers of local offices (p.156).

Centralization and decentralization are used most frequently as independent variables. Although there is little dispute concerning the definition of these terms as they are generally applied to organizations, there is the question as to how much centralization and decentralization should be present in order for the organization to be effective as a competitive economic entity. At present, this question remains unanswered.

Levels of Authority (Including Span of Control)   There is considerable literature on levels of authority and spans of control. The term "levels of authority" refers to the degree of vertical differentiation within an organization. The idea of "levels" connotes layers of different positions, each layer constituting a homogeneous aggregate of employees.

The "span of control" is defined as the number of persons under the direct control of a supervisor or other organizational official.

Although both of these variables are used interchangeably as independent and dependent, most frequently they are manipulated experimentally as independent in relation to such factors as employee's morale and job satisfaction. For example, in a study of the Sears, Roebuck Company, Worthy (1950:178) argued that manipulating the number of supervisory levels in an organization modifies a number of organizational and interpersonal variables, including the span of control. He suggested that:

> in organizations characterized by many levels of supervision and elaborate systems of controls, the individual not only has little opportunity to develop the capacities of self-reliance and initiative but the system frequently weeds out those who do. . . . A number of highly successful organizations have not only paid little heed but have gone directly counter to one of the favorite tenets of modern management theory, to so-called "span of control," which holds that the number of subordinate executives or supervisors reporting to a single individual should be severely limited to enable that individual to exercise the detailed direction and control which is generally considered necessary. On the contrary, these organizations often deliberately give each key executive so many subordinates that it is impossible for him to exercise too close supervision over their activities [p. 178].

Although Worthy's study offers some support for the view that there is a relation between size of span of control and supervisory behavior, the direction of the relationship hypothesized has not been confirmed by subsequent investigations of the same variable interrelations.

Span of control has been the subject of extensive controversy in the literature (House and Miner, 1969:455). Some critics hold that although there may be a limit to the span, it is advantageous to make the spans a great deal wider than any of the numbers usually specified if the work is interrelated. Others believe that the notion of a "small span of control" is mistaken in that it assumes what Likert (1961b) calls the "man-to-man" form of supervision, rather than the man-to-group form (House and Miner, 1969:455).

Fayol (1949:98) was probably one of the first to propose a science of administration, and he stated that whatever his level of authority, one head only should have direct command over a small number of subordinates, less than six normally. Only the superior (foreman or his equivalent) should be in direct command of twenty or thirty men when the work is simple (House and Miner, 1969:452). Currently no conclusive evidence exists for specifying exactly how wide (or narrow) the span of control should be in any organization. Woodward (1965:69-71) implies, however, that the optimum size of the span of control is highly dependent upon the technology of the organization. Her contention is supported by little empirical evidence, though.

Organizational Behavior

The term "organizational behavior" is not meant to personify the organization as an object with emotions and volition; the organization "acts" or "behaves" through the aggregate movements of its living membership. Defining "organizational behavior" is more complicated than simply accumulating the actions of all the individuals in an organization and labeling them as "organizational behavior" (Thompson, 1967:127). Thompson implies that organizational behavior is most frequently equated with the behavior of the power coalition which controls the organization. Expressions about organizational behavior are widespread and are an integral feature of the layman's vocabulary: "General Motors just laid off 3,000 employees." "This organization doesn't pay me enough for my work." "This university is very intolerant of liberal attitudes from faculty members." "That store cheats every customer." From these examples it is quite apparent that organizations are personified extensively, yet we know that the organization, as an abstraction, does not possess these qualities in the same sense as a living person. An organization takes on characteristics and qualities in the same sense that a country develops a "national character" or a "basic personality." Complicating the meaning of "organizational behavior" further is the fact that much organizational research refers to this phenomenon as covering a wide range of attributes.

Three variables which are not directly connected with structure, control, and change in organizations are (1) organizational climate, (2) organizational effectiveness, and (3) organizational goals. These are most often identified as important dimensions of organizational behavior in the collective sense.

Organizational Climate The formalization of the "human-relations school" in the late 1940s contributed significantly to the development of this term. Davis (1962:58) states that:

> climate for an organization is somewhat like personality for a person. The perceptions which people have of that climate produce its image in their minds. Some organizations are bustling and efficient, others are easygoing. Some are quite human, others are hard and cold. They change slowly, being influenced by their leaders and their environment.

This variable is difficult to conceptualize from the standpoint of examining it scientifically with the research tools of the social investigator. Frequently, it is meant to convey the impressions people have of the organizational environment within which they work.[7] It may also be viewed as the degree to which organizational rules are enforced by the administrative component. It may refer to the extent to which persons are treated as "human beings" rather than as "cogs" in a machine (again reflecting the human-relations emphasis).

There are some methodological problems with this term as well. Since climate often is inferred from the subjective impressions workers have of the organizational environment, it is logical to expect that not all individuals will have the same view of that environment. Some will see it as authoritarian, and others will view it as democratic. The location of the defining individual in the organizational hierarchy is an important consideration in understanding the nature of the term. One illustration might be found in an academic department of a large university. Where promotions and salary increases are based, for the most part, on the number of publications a professor has, a highly "productive" professor may see the "publish-or-perish" climate as democratic and rewarding, whereas an unproductive colleague may view the climate as threatening, punitive, and authoritarian (which it is to him).

Organizational climate is used interchangeably as an independent and a dependent variable. It is affected by supervisory practices, group cohesion, variation in managerial philosophies, and personality complementarity. It also effects changes in labor turnover, productivity, job satisfaction, and other related variables.

Organizational Effectiveness Although it would appear that much more has been written about "effectiveness" than about "climate," the concept is equally difficult to define precisely. Often, researchers will use parallel criteria to portray effectiveness. For instance, Etzioni (1959a:43) defines "organizational effectiveness" as "the ability of an organization to achieve its goals." Other researchers include derivatives of this definition in their discussions of organizational "success" or effectiveness (Bass, 1952; Ghorpade, 1970; Price, 1968b).

Ghorpade (1970) suggests that different criteria of organizational effectiveness will be used depending upon the model of organization used by the researcher. As examples he cites the rational and social-systems models, which measure effectiveness in terms of *attainment of goals* and *adaptability,* respectively. The rational model emphasizes the achievement of goals, whereas the social-systems model emphasizes how well the organization can adapt to existing conditions in a competitive environment with other organizations. Bennis (1966a) and Georgopoulos and Tannenbaum (1957) endorse similar distinctions.

Yuchtman and Seashore (1967:891) contend that we are badly in need of an improved conceptual framework for the description and assessment of organizational effectiveness. After contrasting and criticizing several effectiveness models, they define "effectiveness" in terms of its bargaining position, as reflected by the ability of the organization, in either absolute or relative terms, to exploit its environment in the acquisition of scarce and valued resources (p. 898). If we define the objective of an organization as acquiring resources, it would seem that this definition advances us little beyond the "goals" criterion.

One significant attempt to clarify the concept is the work of Mahoney and Weitzel (1969). Their study of eighty-four managers in thirteen companies giving judgments concerning the effectiveness of their subordinate organizational units revealed twenty-four dimensions. Table 4-2 shows these dimensions in detail. These researchers ultimately define "effectiveness" as efficient, productive performance. They indicate that such performance is closely related to, and usually accompanied by, a high degree of utilization of manpower achieved through job assignments which challenge and utilize the skills available, as well as development of manpower resulting from formal training and reliance upon the internal development of manpower resources (p. 360). Reliability and cooperation are singled out by these writers as two important criteria of effectiveness, although they have only an indirect connection with productivity. These criteria cannot be applied consistently to *both* business and research organizations, however. The short-run and long-run nature of goal achievement must be regarded as important here. Many research organizations have goals which are broadly conceived and not achieved in a short period. Managers must have some definition of where they stand in relation to the stated goals of the organization, and often they employ "mid-range" criteria or measures of output in "stages." Some research and development organizations have projects which continue for years with little or no achievement of objectives. Sometimes these projects are terminated before their goals have been attained. One possible explanation is that productivity is a tangible measure of "success" or effectiveness in general business organizations, whereas cooperation and reliability are measures of effectiveness in research organizations, where goals are less tangible and, possibly, take longer to achieve.

Organizational effectiveness is treated most frequently as a dependent variable in organizational research. Effectiveness is seen as dependent upon such things as authority structure, patterns of communication, styles of supervision, employees' morale, and productivity.

Organizational Goals   Gross (1969:277) argues that the central concept in the study of organizations is the organizational goal. He notes that little attention has been given to developing a clear definition of what is meant by the term (p. 278). An "organizational goal" is defined as a state of the organization as a whole toward which the organization is moving, as evidenced by statements persons make (intentions) and activities in which they engage.

One problem of defining organizational goals from this perspective, however, is that persons at different levels of authority and within different departments of an organization see it in the context of their own role definitions. Cartwright and Zander (1960) have highlighted the difference between goals which members may have for an organization and the goals of the organization itself (i.e., on the organizational level of analysis; Wieland, 1969:170). They cite the difficulty in defining the latter conceptualization of goals compared with the former. Although a conceptualization on the organizational level of analysis is preferable on theoretical grounds, the difficulties in formulating such a definition are only now being overcome (Warriner, 1965; Simon, 1964).

The goals of particular departments within an organization may not be recognized by the general public as goals of the organization as a whole. The members of each department have in mind a vague conception of the objectives of the organization for which they work, but all too often they see the overall organizational goals from a biased perspective. The department's existence becomes an end in itself.

The difficulties of defining organizational goals methodologically should not obscure the fact that the term "organizational goals" as used in research most frequently refers to collective ends or objectives of the organization at large. Thompson's (1967) analysis of organizational characteristics suggests that one may define organizational goals by paying attention to the

Table 4-2 Dimensions of Organizational Effectiveness with Standardized Regression Coefficients

Dimension	Model General business	Research and development
Flexibility. Willingly tries out new ideas and suggestions, ready to tackle unusual problems.	.07	−.19
Development. Personnel participate in training and development activities; high level of personnel competence and skill.	.08	.23
Cohesion. Lack of complaints and grievances; conflict among cliques within the organization.	.07	−.00
Democratic supervision. Subordinate participation in work decisions.	.03	.01
Reliability. Meets objectives without necessity of follow-up and checking.	.13	.27
Selectivity. Doesn't accept marginal employees rejected by other organizations.	.02	−.16
Diversity. Wide range of job responsibilities, and personnel abilities within the organization.	−.02	−.03
Delegation. High degree of delegation by supervisors.	.04	−.09
Bargaining. Rarely bargains with other organizations for favors and cooperation.	−.05	.01
Emphasis on results. Results, output, and performance emphasized, not procedures.	.01	.14
Staffing. Personnel flexibility among assignments; development for promotion from within the organization.	.06	.01
Coordination. Coordinates and schedules activities with other organizations, utilizes staff assistance.	−.08	−.08
Decentralization. Work and procedural decisions delegated to lowest levels.	−.01	.19
Understanding. Organization philosophy, policy, directives understood and accepted by all.	−.08	−.04
Conflict. Little conflict with other organization units about authority or failure to meet responsibilities.	−.09	−.01
Personnel planning. Performance not disrupted by personnel absences, turnover, lost time.	−.04	−.06
Supervisory support. Supervisors support their subordinates.	−.12	−.04

Table 4-2 Continued

Dimension	Model General business	Model Research and development
Planning. Operations planned and scheduled to avoid lost time; little time spent on minor crises.	.25	.31
Cooperation. Operations scheduled and coordinated with other organizations; rarely fails to meet responsibilities.	.11	.33
Productivity-support-utilization. Efficient performance; mutual support and respect of supervisors and subordinates; utilization of personnel skills and abilities.	.43	.12
Communication. Free flow of work information and communications within the organization.	−.07	−.27
Turnover. Little turnover from inability to do the job.	.01	.17
Initiation. Initiates improvements in work methods and operations.	.09	.12
Supervisory control. Supervisors in control of progress of work.	.03	.08
Multiple correlation, R.	.76	.79

Source: Mahoney and Weitzel, 1969:358.

definitions provided by the organizational power coalition, a small oligarchy of individuals who establish policy and direct and design the communication networks and the mechanisms of conformity to norms within the organization. Sometimes, organizations publish brochures or other printed matter outlining the major objectives around which most of their internal activities center. Vroom (1960c:229) defines organizational goals similarly. He states that "an organizational goal is a shared goal for the organization on the part of its leaders." "Goal" is used in a Lewinian sense to denote a region of positive valence. Vroom also notes the potential discrepancy between an individual's definition of organizational goals and certain personal goals he might have by virtue of his being a member of a given department: "A person's own goal for an organization is, therefore, a region into which that person desires the organization to move. His perception of the organizational goals, on the other hand, represents his estimates of the regions into which he thinks the leaders of the organization would like it to move" (p. 229). In his study of 1,676 persons employed in two product divisions of an electronics manufacturing organization, Vroom concluded that a person's perception of organizational characteristics is affected by his attitudes and goals in much the same way as is his perception of other persons. An individual tends to attribute his own attitudes, opinions, and goals to persons, groups, and organizations toward which he has a positive attitude and to deny them in persons, groups, and organizations toward which he has a negative attitude (p. 238).

The concept of an organizational goal may be examined more meaningfully and methodologically if we distinguish between system goals and product goals (Perrow, 1967:202). System goals emphasize quantity, substantial profits, and stability, while production goals emphasize growth in size, improved product quality, and innovative research and development (Hage and Aiken, 1969:373).

Organizational goals are treated most frequently as independent variables and as legitimatizations of individual and group activities in organizations. The multidimensional nature of goals (long-range, short-range, individual, interpersonal, organizational, systems, production, etc.) suggests that problems of definition will certainly be encountered; but, in spite of these problems, organizational goals are to be regarded as important factors in the assessment of organizational behavior.

Organizational Change

As organizations grow in size and complexity, new departments are created, membership fluctuates, and technology changes in response to innovation and customer-consumer demand. The variables selected for inclusion in this section are associated with various kinds of organizational change. Frequently, they pertain to various ways of measuring or explaining change. They are (1) labor turnover, (2) organizational conflict, (3) organizational flexibility, (4) organizational growth, (5) administrative succession, and (6) technology (including automation).

Labor Turnover   Turnover, used frequently as a dependent variable, reflects the proportion of persons who leave an organization in the course of a year (Argyle, Gardner, and Cioffi, 1958:31). It is often used to determine the potential impact of such factors as the nature of supervision, employees' morale and satisfaction, or administrative behavior. It can also be used in an independent fashion as a means of accounting for the heterogeneity of workers, as new individuals are introduced into the organizational environment to modify existing formal and informal (interpersonal) interactional arrangements.

Labor turnover is one of the easiest organizational variables to measure. It can be assessed by the records of any given firm. Of course, some distinction may be made between those persons who leave voluntarily and those who are asked to leave (Argyle, Gardner, and Cioffi, 1958:31). In other words, those who are laid off, die, retire, become pregnant, etc., are regarded as a part of the aggregate of *involuntary* labor turnover. Labor turnover in a university might be measured by the ratio of professors who leave of their own accord each year to those who remain. In a hospital, labor turnover might be the number of employees of a nonadministrative capacity who leave voluntarily each year, or during some other time period. The telephone company, for instance, maintains records of operators who leave each month as a means of determining potential seasonal fluctuations in labor turnover among such persons.

Organizational Conflict This term refers to tension within the organizational system. One may observe such tension by paying attention to possible incompatibilities among departments, to incompatibilities among staff members or employees, to complexities of the communication network, and even to the organizational structure itself (Dahrendorf, 1959). The idea of "conflict" has several meanings in the social sciences. In one sense, "conflict" may mean feelings of hostility on the part of one person or group toward another or others. It may also mean emotionally hostile and intentional efforts on the part of one person or group to prevent another person or group from attaining the latter's desires or goals. In the present discussion, "conflict" is used in the former sense and should complement the definition provided by Dahrendorf.

Corwin (1969:507) studied conflict in twenty eight public high schools. He found that size, specialization, hierarchy, complexity, staff additions, and heterogeneity were related to organizational conflict, although these variables were related in different ways depending upon the bureaucratic and professional context and the type of conflict involved. Corwin used "felt tension" and reports of "perceived disagreement," overt disputes, and interpersonal competition as measures of conflict. Warren (1969) used staff disunity and disagreement with administration as measures of conflict.

Organizational conflict (regardless of the source from which it stems) is treated primarily as a dependent variable, although the amount of tension and stress present can influence such factors as effectiveness, clarity of roles, and job satisfaction. It is important to note that there are at least two potential kinds of organizational conflict: (1) intraorganizational and (2) interorganizational. Intraorganizational conflict is conflict of an interpersonal nature or between departments within the system. Interorganizational conflict is conflict between organizations. "Managers and theorists have more frequently been concerned with resolving conflict within the organization rather than conflict between organizations," however (Assael, 1969:573).

In his study of interorganizational conflict between dealer-franchisers for General Motors products, Assael (1969:574–576) identified the following "key issues of concern to dealers" when he conducted interviews with them:

> (1) Factory involvement in retail operations through dealerships owned and financed by manufacturers, (2) too many dealers in a given area, (3) leasing by the manufacturers and direct sales of fleets to large accounts, (4) service and warranty policies, particularly lack of acceptance by manufacturers of dealer warranty claims, (5) cooperative advertising policies, largely managed by the manufacturers, and (6) alleged interference by manufacturer's personnel in dealer store management. Issues which had resulted in conflict in the past, but were not of great concern at the time of the study, included (7) threats of franchise cancellation, (8) manufacturers forcing new cars, (9) pressures to increase investment in the dealership, and (10) pressures to stock manufacturer-owned parts and accessories [pp. 574–576].

Organizational Flexibility The degree to which an organization is adaptable to internal changes (changes in the hierarchy of authority, interpersonal groups, etc.) and external changes (e.g., competition with other organizations, changes in the economic market, marketing innovations) describes the flexibility and accommodation of the organization. Some organizations, particularly those with built-in research and development divisions, have structural means for implementing changes and modifications in organizational structure and process in response to change. Organizations which are deeply entrenched in departmentalization and routine are difficult candidates for change in the absence of such formal mechanisms for change (Denhardt, 1968; LaPorte, 1965).

One of the difficulties in determining the degree of organizational flexibility is in finding how much coordination between units within the organization is required for substantial changes to occur. One way of assessing the flexibility of an organization is to determine the amount of *resistance to change* in the form of intraorganizational conflict. It is entirely possible that a *lack* of *overt* conflict will sometimes accompany a resistance to change, particularly in voluntary organizations lacking effective procedures for working through disagreements. To preserve the semblance of unity, organizational members in such circumstances often avoid dealing with a problem calling for change for fear that unproductive, hostile disagreement will result, leading to no real resolution of the issue. Organizational flexibility may be regarded as an independent variable where it influences the rate of technological change and the implementation of new channels of communication. It may also be used as a dependent variable as the by-product of specific organizational structures, administrative patterns, and supervisory practices.

Organizational Growth Haire (1959) has defined "organizational growth" as the increase of employees over any specified time period. Such a definition is consistent with a biological growth model, that is, the population increase within an organizational context. (Draper and Strother, 1963:194). But the biological model does not seem to be valid for describing or predicting the growth of organizations, nor does it appear to be a source of useful hypotheses for future research (Draper and Strother, 1963:194).

The growth of an organization may also be defined in terms of increases in net assets; the proliferation of departments and job specialties; the increase of contacts with other organizations in symbiotic, exchange relations; and the expansion of new product markets. Usually treated as an independent variable, organizational growth exerts influence upon such factors as organizational complexity, the size of the administrative component, and personal alienation. This variable is, in turn, influenced by the degree of market competition, product innovation, and technological change. In view of the fact that most organizations have the propensity to expand, it is apparent that organizational growth as an explanatory variable is an important consideration in the study of organizational behavior (Barnard, 1938:159).

Administrative Succession This term refers to the degree of turnover among administrative heads in an organization. Carlson (1961:210) indicates that all enduring organizations must cope with succession and that the replacement of an individual in a key office is potentially a significant event in the development of an organization. He emphasizes the fact that administrative succession can be stressful for members and clients in an organization and that, therefore, organizational theory should deal with succession and organizational responses to succession.

Most frequently viewed as an independent variable, succession among administrative personnel is systematically assessed largely in terms of its disruptive effects. Carlson (1961) contends that propositions about succession are seldom developed or tested. His later work (1962) examines administrative succession in school systems, and his studies of school superintendents are generally regarded as significant contributions to the burgeoning field of educational sociology.

Organizational Technology (Including Automation) A small amount of research has been devoted to the effects of technology on organizational structure, interpersonal relations, and individual behavior. In the broadest sense, technology refers to "the mechanisms or processes by which an organization turns out its product or service" (Harvey, 1968:247). The term "technology" may refer to a tool, a machine, or a system of machines and even to ideas or strategies.

Since technology can pertain to so many different things—mechanization, automation, ideas—it is expected that several conceptualization problems will be encountered by social investigators exploring the effects of this variable upon social structure and process. What is the "rate of technological change," for example? Does it refer to the amount of invention or innovation within a given firm? Or does it mean the number of ideas which are implemented in companies each year to improve communication channels? Each of these changes is, by definition, a technological change, although each would make decidedly different impacts.

Little empirical research of a specific nature is available on the social effects of technology. By far the bulk of literature on this subject is speculative. The paucity of information which is available currently suggests that (1) there are significant conceptualization obstacles to overcome (Sultan and Prasow, 1965); (2) there are differential implications of different forms of technology for employees in various fields; (3) there are probable links between technological change and organizational structural change, including modifications in authority hierarchies, spans of control, and job elimination or change, although these links have not been precisely established; and (4) virtually no general theory of technological change exists currently to account for changes occurring within organizations because of the impact of this broadly defined variable.

The methodological problems involved in attempting to measure the amount of technological changes are somewhat difficult, though not impossible, to overcome. In a seemingly simple comparison of two organizations utilizing different production processes, how do we determine which organization is more "automated" than the other? The fact that the distinction between automation and mechanization (the use of machinery of any kind, manually or automatically driven) has not been clearly delineated and is still in dispute raises important questions which impede adequate measurement of technological change.

One attempt to measure "degree of automation" is by Amber and Amber (1962) and is discussed by Hickson et al. (1969), who noted that "as a means of assessing automation of equipment, there was available the classification of automation by Amber and Amber (1962:2) in terms of the degree to which first energy and then information are provided by machines rather than by man. Organizations in the sample were scored on the five ordered categories shown in [Table 4-3.] Unfortunately, the available data were inadequate to do more than represent the automaticity scale by scoring automaticity mode (the level of automaticity of the bulk of the work-flow

Table 4-3   Automaticity Scale

[Scale items]	[Scoring]
Hand tools and manual machines	0
Powered machines and tools	1
Single-cycle automatics and self-feeding machines	2
Automatic: repeats cycle	3
Self-measuring and adjusting: feedback	4

Source: Amber and Amber, 1962: Chart 1-1.

equipment, as estimated by the research team) and the automaticity range (the score of the most automated piece of equipment used, every organization also scoring the lowest possible, zero, by using hand tools)."

The general category of variables amassed under the rubric of "technological change" is theoretically used as independent. Some grandiose theorists speculate about the societal factors which generate the growth and elaboration of technology in its many forms. In this case, technology is treated as a dependent variable. One potentially fruitful attempt to define "technology" is the work of Meissner (1969:13-41), in which a distinction is made between "conversion operations" (p. 16) and "transfer operations" (p. 17) in a production setting. "Degrees" of conversion operations (changing the properties of materials, p. 16) and transfer operations (the movements of materials or equipment, or both, between stations, p. 16) are delineated by Meissner. In spite of his admirable efforts to quantify and categorize such an elusive term, Meissner (p. 19) acknowledges two limitations in the generalized use of his scheme. In the cases he studied (the reported research of others from approximately 1915-1965), the information obtained was insufficient in the number of cases which were available to fill his constructed categories (p. 19).

To recapitulate briefly, this chapter has sought to familiarize students of formal organization with some of the key major organizational variables used in research investigations. The variables presented thus far by no means constitute *all organizational variables which are theoretically useful in organizational analysis.* They do, however, represent some of those most frequently cited in contemporary professional literature on the subject. These are to be viewed as "strategies" or potential explanatory inputs to the development of subsequent theoretical predictive schemes. As was mentioned earlier, Appendix I consists of several "case studies" which are examples of potential organizational behavioral problems. The variables in this chapter and those in the next are presented, in part, to assist students in arriving at possible solutions to the problems dealt with in each case. They are presented in order to help students become more flexible in their thinking about why particular organizational behaviors occur. In the following chapter, variables common to the interpersonal and individual units of analysis will be illustrated. These, too, will contribute to one's flexibility in orientation toward organizational problems, their possible origins, and their possible solutions. We have not, as yet, devised certain rules covering which variables are considered most crucial for this problem or that. The usefulness of any particular variable or combination of variables in an explanation of organizational behavior must be evaluated within the context of the particular set of organizational circumstances under investigation. Later in the book we will examine such specific topic areas as authority structure, communications systems, and organizational change as substantive extensions and elaborations of many of the variables and organizational models treated up to now.

SUMMARY

A serious study of formal organizations should be preceded by discussion, definition, and understanding of general usage of common terminology. Argyris has asked, "What are the relevant variables in studying organizations?" Answers to this question must be provided if a meaningful reading of the literature is to be attempted. Because there is sometimes a tendency to embark on a course of action armed with the necessary tools but not knowing how to apply them, a brief discussion of variables *in general* was given.

In considering the interdependence of variables, we must recognize not only that many different variables exist which may function as explanations or predictors but also that they may be dependent on or independent of one another. Also, we must be aware of the pitfalls accompanying apparent cause-and-effect relations. Spuriousness—the influence of an unknown third variable on two others—must always be anticipated.

Organizational variables were divided into structure, control, behavior, and change. Within each category several commonly used organizational variables were discussed.

One of the most important things to be learned from the overall discussion in this chapter is that organizational terminology is subject to a variety of interpretations and definitions. In short, not everyone defines the same term the same way. By the same token, not everyone uses any of these variables in precisely the same manner from study to study. As a consequence, inconsistencies and even apparent contradictions may be found from study to study, even though the same terms are used. The conceptualization of variables, or the conversion of organizational terminology into a functional numerical language for hypothesis testing, is often characterized by bias and subjectivity. Therefore, we must scrutinize so-called "replication studies" to ascertain whether or not there is consistency in definitions of variables.

A systematic presentation of organizational variables was made so that the reader can utilize these variables in answering questions about various aspects of organizations. In this regard, a variable can be a *strategy* to the extent that it can help explain why things happen in certain ways in organizational contexts. This chapter has dealt exclusively with organizational variables; Chapter 5 will briefly treat interpersonal and individual variables for the same purpose.

In Appendix I several case studies have been provided, with questions following each. There are no "pat" answers to these questions. The reader is encouraged to utilize pertinent variables in this chapter and the next as possible explanations for the existence of a problem or problems. It is hoped that these exercises will encourage a certain amount of flexibility in thinking together with an opportunity to put into practice common organizational, interpersonal, and individual factors as potential "predictor variables."

STUDY QUESTIONS

1 Why is it difficult to develop and find empirical support for causal relations between organizational variables? List some of the factors which must be considered in the establishment of causality relationships, and in each case explain briefly how each functions as an obstacle in this regard.
2 Differentiate between necessary and sufficient conditions. How does each relate to the concept of causality?
3 Differentiate between independent and dependent variables. Can variables be independent and dependent simultaneously? Explain your answer by providing an example.
4 What is a "spurious" relationship between variables? How can social scientists control spuriousness? Explain.
5 Differentiate between organizational control factors and organizational structural factors. To what extent are they complementary to one another? Discuss your answer briefly.
6 In your opinion, which variable discussed in this chapter seems to be most important as a direct explanation of organizational behavior? Why?
7 Define the climate of the class you are attending or have attended in the past. What are some of the problems in conceptualizing climate? Compare your assessment of class climate (if you are a part of a class) with the assessments made by three other students. To what extent are these assessments similar or different? Regardless of the outcome of your comparison, what is your explanation for your findings? Elaborate.

8 On the basis of your reading of this chapter, what appear to be some of the more important problems associated with variable conceptualization applied to organizational analysis?

NOTES

[1] It is quite difficult to isolate the specific impact of a single variable upon any organizational or interpersonal phenomenon. Most of the time, it is more realistic to regard organizational and interpersonal phenomena as products of the "interaction" or "intermixing" of several variables operating in concert with one another. Of course, when the researcher attempts to study the influence of combinations of variables on a single organizational phenomenon, he finds his task a difficult one. Multivariate (or multiple variable) relationships are usually very complex. The researcher frequently has to apply several advanced statistical procedures in his analysis in order to make sense out of any kinds of relationships between the variables he observes. The treatment of multivariate relations between variables will be limited to "two-variable" situations in this book. Not only do the multivariate analytical procedures available currently require more sophisticated and advanced statistical designs beyond the scope of this book, but they also assume greater theoretical sophistication than is necessary as a prerequisite for reading this text. Therefore, our treatment of variables throughout will serve as examples of research strategies and will provide an elementary foundation upon which more complex research designs and theoretical schemes of a multivariate nature can be formulated.

[2] It is likely that the biochemist may define an infinite number of categorizations of "maleness" and "femaleness" by using body chemistry and hormone accumulation as measures of sexuality. Considering sex from this standpoint, we would regard it as continuous rather than discrete.

[3] Those industrial and business consultants who make the most valuable contributions to their clients are usually the ones who have the greatest variety of strategies at their disposal. These "strategies" include not only specific approaches, frames of reference, and theoretical organizational models, but also many organizational variables which lend to their analytical flexibility.

[4] The suggestion is to read each case study carefully, and then answer the questions which follow. There are no "standard" or "pat" answers to the questions raised, although several alternative solutions to the problems portrayed in each case can be generated by the use of some of the variables from this chapter in imaginative combinations. It would also be helpful and instructive to use some of these questions for open class discussion as a means of stimulating flexibility in thinking about organizational problems.

[5] The following areas are represented predominantly through citations of key trade journals and textbooks: sociology, psychology, business management and administration, economics, anthropology, education, and industrial engineering and management.

⁶ Very often, depending upon the size of the organization, the administrative component may be defined as supervisory staff, staff, administration, leaders, coordinators, etc.

⁷ Sometimes, the term "organizational atmosphere" is substituted for "organizational climate" (Pelz and Andrews, 1966), although it appears that both designations apply to essentially the same phenomenon.

Chapter 5

Interpersonal and Individual Variables

INTERPERSONAL VARIABLES

Variables designated as "interpersonal" are characteristics of employees' work groups in organizations. These are not necessarily typical of the organization as a unit. Neither do they describe individual behaviors adequately. Many studies focus upon work groups or cliques of employees in a business setting or industrial organization. The classical "Hawthorne studies" concentrated in part on the cohesiveness of employee aggregates in specific sections of a work plant (Roethlisberger and Dickson, 1939). Among the many questions raised in this research were: "How can the output of work groups be increased?" "How can the morale of specific work groups be modified?" "What is the effect of a particular kind of supervision on turnover or interpersonal conflict in a work group?"

Three interpersonal variables selected for inclusion in this chapter are (1) uniformity or similarity of values, (2) group cohesion, and (3) supervisory methods.

Uniformity or Similarity of Values

This has to do with homogeneity of orientations toward the job. How much homogeneity is there in any group of workers or employees? To what extent are the aspirations of workers similar?

Several examples from business and industrial literature document the influence of this variable upon such factors as employee performance, job satisfaction, and the productivity of work groups. For example, Gouldner (1954a) notes the difference in loyalty orientations among various types of employees of a gypsum mine. The mine workers were distinctly different from the "surface personnel" not only in terms of their life style and residential location but in their orientation toward work and their general belief systems as well.

Employees who perceive that they share certain interests and ambitions with other members of their work group evidently have a more compatible relation with them. Standards of behavior and productivity for work groups as a whole appear to be more readily enforced to the extent that attitudinal uniformity exists. Homans (1950:182) suggests that groups (in general) manifesting similar sentiments toward things will interact more harmoniously and participate in greater numbers of activities. When one generalizes to business or industrial organizations, the same principle should logically be upheld. An important question to raise here is *which attitudes* are most critical for the group members to share. Which values seem to make the most difference in fostering interpersonal cooperation?

Frequently, work groups are composed of members of similar ages, sex, educational level, or socioeconomic backgrounds. These similarities will often generate similar outlooks toward things. Workers who come from the same residential areas and who interact with one another both on and off the job socially as well as formally seem more likely to share similar values. Although it is true that groups may be composed of several individuals with a variety of individual personality characteristics, there is some evidence to indicate that gradual modifications of individual attitudes and behaviors occur toward a "group standard" or "group norm," which typifies none of the individual members' original dispositions about things. In other words, group associations foster characteristics unique to the group as opposed to describing behaviors of any given individual in the group. Therefore, it may be that during the process of interactions of a work group, a heterogeneity of attitudes and orientations observed at the outset may, in time, be replaced by a greater similarity of interests. Formal organizational research conventionally defines attitudinal uniformity as an independent variable.

Group Cohesion

Émile Durkheim (1951) was one of the earlier social scientists to introduce this term to the professional community as an interpersonal factor responsible for increases and decreases (under certain social and psychological conditions) of suicides. Subsequently, many attempts have been made to describe this phenomenon fully.

The term "cohesion" or "cohesiveness" means the tendency of group members to "stick together." It has been variously measured by means of the number of times group members use "we" in referring to their group activities, the number of in-group sociometric choices, and the degree of willingness of group members to leave the group. Some researchers have even defined "cohesion" as the number of times (during a given interval, such as a year) that a work group will process grievances jointly before administrative higher-ups (Sayles, 1958a).

Deutscher and Deutscher (1955:336) have investigated cohesion as it pertains to a group which they studied known as "The Columbia Committee on Racial Equality." Their view of cohesiveness dealt with those factors which held the group together or which kept it from falling apart. They attempted to determine how consensus was achieved by the group on racial matters and policy dilemmas. Some of the conclusions they reached were that small group size, frequent meetings, and clearly defined goals were instrumental in raising group cohesion. Also, a limitation on the number of formal demands made by members of the group on others in the group, altruistically motivated participation in the group, and a feeling that the group was successful in achieving its stated objectives were factors fostering increased amounts of cohesion.

Seashore (1954b:97-102) defines group cohesiveness as "the attraction of members to the group in terms of the strength of forces on the individual member to remain in the group and to resist leaving the group." He investigated the impact of cohesion on other variables (in an independent sense) and also the effects of certain factors upon cohesion (in a dependent capacity). Some of the hypotheses generated were:

1. The degree of cohesiveness with a group determines the power of the group to create forces towards uniformity of behavior among members (group standards). 2. Members of high cohesive groups will exhibit less anxiety than members of low cohesive groups with respect to matters relevant to group activities or the group setting. 3. The degree of cohesiveness developed in a group will be a function of the attractiveness of the members of the group as determined by the prestige of the members. 4. The degree of cohesiveness developed in a group will be a function of opportunities for interaction among members of the group. 5. Group cohesion is positively related to the degree of prestige attributed by

the group members to their own jobs. 6. Group cohesiveness is positively related to opportunity for interaction as measured by (a) size of group, and (b) duration of shared membership on the job [pp. 97-102].

Supervisory Methods

Supervisory style is predominantly an independent variable in formal organizational research. Although it is true that in most organizations supervisors are obligated to follow certain rules and adhere to specific procedures as a part of the superior-subordinate relationship, some latitude generally exists for supervisors to interject personal behaviors into their leadership roles. Supervisory behavior connotes initiating activity for subordinates in the work setting. Leaders must obtain the compliance of so-called "lower-level participants" in the organization. Since several alternative means may be employed to elicit the compliance of subordinates, many researchers have explored the diverse reactions of these individuals to differential supervisory behaviors in a variety of organizational settings (Anderson, 1966; Fleishman, 1953; Lowin et al., 1969; Parker, 1963). The consensus seems to be that differential supervisory behaviors elicit fairly predictable reactions among subordinates. Acting as intervening variables between type of supervisory behavior practiced and reaction of subordinates are such factors as years of education of employees, job seniority, type of job performed, age difference between supervisor and subordinates, and union strength.

One of the most comprehensive discussions of supervisory behavior and its effects upon subordinates is Lucio and McNeil's (1969). Although their emphasis is upon the supervisory behaviors of educators in school systems, much of their information is generalizable to other settings. They define a supervisor (in the school context) as one who holds a supervisory position, who actually makes a difference in the operations of the school by exercising authority or influence, and who spends time on particular organizational functions (p. 45).

The work of Fleishman and Harris (1962) delineates the role of supervisor along a different dimension. They distinguish between supervisors who "show consideration" and those who "initiate structure":

Consideration includes behavior indicating mutual trust, respect, and a certain warmth and rapport between the supervisor and his group. This does not mean that this dimension reflects a superficial "pat-on-the-back," "first-name-calling" kind of human relations behavior. This dimension appears to emphasize a deeper concern for group members' needs and includes such behavior as allowing subordinates more participation in decision making and encouraging more two-way communication. Structure includes behavior in which the supervisor organizes and defines group activities and his relation to the group. Thus, he defines the role he expects each member to assume, assigns tasks, plans ahead, establishes ways of getting things done, and pushes for production. This dimension seems to emphasize overt attempts to achieve organizational goals [pp. 43–44].

This statement implies that a supervisor either initiates structure *or else* shows consideration but not both. This is a misleading implication because structure and consideration are orthogonal dimensions of behavior and a supervisor could be high on both, high on one and low on the other, etc.

Etzioni (1961a:3–21) discusses some of the implications for subordinates resulting from a supervisor's exercise of different kinds of power. He notes that power is the actor's ability to induce or influence another actor to carry out his directives or any other norms he supports. Supervisors may exercise (1) coercive power, where threat of physical sanctions such as pain, frustration, or death are used to obtain compliance; (2) remunerative power, where material rewards are used as incentives to obtain compliance from subordinates; and (3) normative power, where esteem and prestige symbols may be allocated for the benefit of subordinates to enlist their compliance. Following each of these types of power are various kinds of involvement which are predictably expected from subordinates. Subordinates who are coerced into complying with higher-ups may become alienated and reflect a negative orientation or hostile view, while those who comply through remuneration will reflect calculative involvement and the expectation of material gain. Finally, those who comply because of normative power are morally involved and reflect positive orientations of high intensity. Loyal follower and leader, parishioner and priest, political party member and candidate are manifestations of moral involvement in contrast to these other types.

Although supervisory style is not directly organizational in nature (in contrast to such variables as organizational size and complexity), the role of this factor in effecting organizational change is equally important and must be accorded adequate treatment in organizational research.

INDIVIDUAL VARIABLES

Individual variables depict personal perceptions of the work environment and the tasks performed. The employee, worker, or volunteer has numerous attitudes, orientations, and dispositions toward various work roles. It is not uncommon for an employee to define the status of his position in relation to others within the organization. Perhaps the greatest array of variables exists to portray the condition of the organizational member. Three general classifications of individual variables are (1) attitudes of members, (2) job characteristics, and (3) definitions and performance of roles.

Attitudes of Members

The expressed sentiments of employees assume many forms. We will focus upon two work-related attitudes as popular examples.

Levels of Aspiration Maslow (1954) postulated the existence of several needs which are presumably basic to all individuals. These are (1) physiological well-being, (2) security or safety, (3) "belongingness," (4) self-esteem, and (5) self-fulfillment. The idea behind his scheme is that we are motivated to satisfy these needs in our everyday social encounters, and therefore our behavior is in part a manifestation of the attempt to fulfill these needs. There are several interesting interpretations which can be made of Maslow's notions, but of most interest to us in this book is the potential impact of these needs upon individual behavior in organizational settings. Some organizational researchers utilize Maslow's "hierarchy of needs" to account for behavioral variations in work performance. Some workers are highly motivated and produce much. Others are apathetic about their work activity and produce relatively little. Some employees struggle a great deal to advance themselves in their work through promotions. The need for esteem and recognition account in part, for their "achieving" behavior.

W. I. Thomas (1923) presented a scheme of human wishes or desires not altogether different from Maslow's hierarchy of needs. Thomas specified four basic wishes of man: new experience, security, recognition, and response (love). The wish for new experience, for example, may partially account for the frequency with which some persons change jobs or are dissatisfied with their present tasks. The wish for recognition may propel a worker toward his best efforts and output in the work setting, thus enabling him to make a good impression in front of his superiors and to obtain their praise.

Hunt and Hill (1969:107) survey recent research on the relation between performance and motivation. The "Vroom model" (Vroom, 1964) is selected by Hunt and Hill as holding great promise for predicting behavior in organizations. Vroom (1964:6) defines motivation as "a process governing choices, made by persons or lower organisms, among alternative forms of voluntary activity." Briefly, Vroom contends that the *valence* (or strength of an individual's desire for a particular outcome), *instrumentality* (or the extent to which one outcome enables one to achieve a second outcome), and *expectancy* (or the likelihood that a particular effort will lead to a desired outcome) are important motivational factors which account for individual behavior in organizations (e.g., superior performance leads to promotion within the work setting) (Hunt and Hill, 1969:104).

Workers' levels of aspiration are usually treated as independent variables which can be used to account for levels of job satisfaction, productivity, and cooperation and conflict among workers. Using this variable in an independent capacity, for example, Chinoy (1952) discusses the influence of aspirations upon interpersonal relations in the automobile industry.

Job Satisfaction In a detailed analysis of literature dealing with job satisfaction in the early 1960s, Robinson and Connors (1963:136–137) examined the relationships between job satisfaction and the following variables:

> ability, absenteeism, achievement, administration, advancement, aspirations, attitudes, automation, autonomy, colleagues, creativity and opportunity for self-expression, education, efficiency, ego involvement, experience, fatigue, freedom and independence, health, human relations, job enlargement, leadership, life adjustment, longevity, management, marital status, mental health, mobility, motives, occupational level, offspring, opportunity to learn, opportunity to render service, parental influence, peer group, physical hardships of the job, psychological factors, public image, recognition, responsibility, retirement, routine, security, self-esteem, salary, self-realization, sex, size of group, size of plant, skill, social status, students, supervision, tenure, training, turnover, type of work, unemployment, union, variety, work group, work load, and working conditions.

An examination of the findings of the works cited in their bibliography shows that variable relationships with job satisfaction are far from being clear cut. One reason for this is the fact that so many competing definitions and measures of job satisfaction exist.[1] One measure may emphasize a person's satisfaction with the working hours, and another measure will focus upon his satisfaction with work associates. It is advisable to note how each variable is defined whenever interpretations are made of a research report. Often, apparent "inconsistencies" in findings between two studies which investigate the same phenomenon may be attributed to the fact that different measures of the same variables are used.

Job satisfaction is used as a dependent variable to measure the effect of other variables such as the type of supervision or quality of job content. It is also used as an independent variable which affects individual productivity or rates of labor turnover.

One of the continuing issues in organizational research has been the theoretical and substantive value of studies of job satisfaction. Hilgendorf and Irving (1969:415) indicate that early studies of organization, particularly the classic Hawthorne studies, were influential in establishing subsequent research interests and trends toward investigating the impact of job satisfaction on workers' behavior. They add that:

> the state of the organization and the actions which it takes determine job attributes, and that the employee's experience of these attributes determines his

satisfaction or dissatisfaction which in turn affects his behavior. Other factors such as needs, values, and expectations are assumed to affect the various links in the chain . . . the importance of this underlying model is that it has historically provided a rationale for studying job satisfaction with a view to inaugurating industrial change [pp. 415-16].

These authors also note that "the relationship between job satisfaction and overt work behavior remains tenuous, except in the general area of labor turnover and absenteeism."

Early thinking about the importance of job satisfaction to organizational members espoused the philosophy that "a happy employee is a more productive one." Therefore, much attention was devoted to examining this variable under a variety of conditions. For instance, in their study of the job satisfaction of Prudential Insurance Company employees, Morse and Reimer (1956) found that increased involvement in the decision-making process of the organization contributed to greater job satisfaction among employees.

Job Characteristics

Variables which pertain directly to the functional requirements of one's work role include decision-making power, job status, and work routine and monotony.

Decision-Making Power This variable is the amount of freedom an employee has to determine how his job should be performed. Baldridge (1971b:26) defines decision-making as the process by which pressures and power are translated into policy.

Most widely used as an independent variable in organizational research, decision-making power is closely related to the authority structure of formal organizations. In studies of organizations, the question is often asked: "How much decision-making power should employees have?" French, Israel, and Aos (1960), for example, have demonstrated that increased participation in the decision-making process of a Norwegian factory stimulated increased interest in work and induced the workers who participated more to reach production standards more quickly than those who were involved only minimally or not at all.

In a study of motivation and morale in the Prudential Insurance Company, Viteles (1953) found that the productivity of workers increased to the extent that the supervisors were "employee-centered" (i.e., to the extent that supervisors showed the workers consideration and permitted them to be involved extensively in decisions affecting their work) as opposed to "production-centered" (i.e., insistent on meeting production quotas at all costs, regardless of how employees felt about the accelerated pace of work and about job assignments).

Gore and Silander (1959:121) have compiled an extensive bibliography on decision-making research. As a result of their analysis they indicate that nearly five thousand entries in the literature (up to and including 1958) discuss decision making in one sense or another, and they argue that what is needed most is an adequate theory of decision making. They find that the literature on decision making is "uneven and chaotic, and in no respect comprehensive . . . and that many central problems to decision making seldom, if ever, receive adequate attention." Finally, they warn that we must discard old administrative ideologies and embark upon new strategies to deal with the decison-making issue more effectively.

Job Status Several writers have linked job status with such things as job satisfaction, workers' aspirations, and motivation (Duffy, 1960; Edwards, 1969; Lewis and Lopreato, 1963). Within the organization, the status of a job is generally determined by its position in the hierarchy of authority. People tend to evaluate one another in an organization according to the amount of power which they can wield over others.

In some instances, knowledge about work and the interrelations of roles becomes a type of status, particularly in the eyes of novice employees. In bank work, for example, new employees are expected to be thoroughly familiar with numerous forms for completing a variety of transactions. Their first few weeks on the job can be nightmarish, as they run to "older" and more knowledgeable staff members to inquire whether to use Form A-111, CT-103, or R-14 to complete a transaction. Staff members with more seniority frequently take great delight in doling out information to new workers slowly, relishing the opportunity to demonstrate that they know more than someone else.

Of course, job status may be determined by one's occupational title, income, or surroundings at work. Surroundings are particularly important in bank work. The bank officers responsible for making loans and handling real estate matters often sit in areas of greater prestige (e.g., plush offices with carpeted floors and mahogany desks) than operations officers who are of equal rank and income but who are responsible for a different dimension of bank activity (operations officers ordinarily oversee tellers and bookkeepers; they work behind metal desks in areas with linoleum floors).

Job status is heavily dependent upon such things as education and former work experience. Pavalko (1971:132) refers to occupational status as "the education and income associated with an occupation." He differentiates between occupational status and occupational prestige by noting that "prestige refers to the subjective evaluations that people hold of occupations." Since new occupations are being created each year, it makes sense to argue that any present method of ranking occupational status will be out of date almost as soon as it appears in print. There is at least one exception to this statement. If we define job status at a very general level (i.e., professionals, proprietors, managers, clerks amd kindred workers, skilled workers, semi-skilled workers, and unskilled employees), it is possible to classify new jobs in one of these categories as they emerge each year.

Almost exclusively an independent variable in most research, job status influences interpersonal relations, job satisfaction, motivation for achievement, and job security. In turn, it is influenced by such things as income, decision-making power, and position relative to other jobs.

Work Routine and Monotony   In his classic study of the worker performing the repetitive job, Walker (1950) examined problems among workers of the parts manufacturing department of an IBM plant. In brief summary of one aspect of his study, he found that workers preferred job enlargement or a greater variety of things to do in their work as opposed to repetitive work operations.

Friedmann (1955:131–132) states that scholarly attention to the monotony and repetitiveness on the job go back to the days of Adam Smith (1904), who noted that people viewed the task of making "pins" (nails) as a monotonous activity. Assembly-line operations are particularly monotonous. Not only do few opportunities exist for interaction with other workers during assembly-line production, but little intellectual challenge (if any) or job differentiation exists among workmen employed at such tasks (Walker and Guest, 1952).

The amount of routine and repetitiveness involved in any job obviously modifies a worker's satisfaction with it. Too much routine may lead to high labor turnover or low employee morale. Bureaucratic organizations are notorious for creating positions involving repetitive job operations and strict adherence to rules. The routine and monotony associated with any job is defined as an independent variable in many contemporary studies of formal organizations.

Definitions and Performance of Roles

The final set of variables discussed here concerns employees' perceptions of job activity. These variables are productivity, specificity of roles, and conflict among roles.

Productivity   This variable is defined according to the organizational context within which employees are studied. In a factory where workers are paid according to a "piece-rate" system, productivity is measured according to the number of "pieces of product" produced per day. Although pieces of product are easy to count in this instance, it is difficult for anyone to define the meaning of "productivity" for a scientific work team trying to invent a marketable product in a chemical laboratory. The research team may work for years before producing a product which the company officials desire. In some instances, the team may never "produce" this commodity. In this event, the application of effort toward the research objective becomes the measure of group or individual productivity, in spite of the ambiguity surrounding such a measure.

Productivity almost always is used as a dependent variable in relation to such factors as job satisfaction, supervisory style, and technological change. It is determined by the extent to which an organizational member satisfactorily performs his role or fulfills the expectations of higher-ups. Individuals who accomplish much in relation to their role expectations are said to be "high producers." Those who fail to achieve the minimal standards of their role set by administrative definition are viewed as "low producers." This statement simply suggests that productivity is not always a matter of "producing things."

Managers, business leaders, and supervisors are perhaps most interested in workers' productivity, inasmuch as this variable most directly determines the profits and losses of organizations. Much research, therefore, has focused upon the strategies which can increase productivity of workers in a variety of work settings. A plethora of managerial styles, administrative hierarchical models, and fringe-benefit programs for employees have been instituted regularly in businesses and industries in order to influence this variable in an upward direction. The motivational research of the industrial psychologist, for example, is directed toward discovering those factors which cause the worker to produce more.

Role Specificity   "Role specificity" or "role clarity" is defined as the perceived degree of familiarity with the requirements of one's work role in the organization. There is considerable agreement among management writers that clear lines of authority and responsibility are desirable, together with *clear role definitions* (Hickson, 1966:232).

Role specificity is treated predominantly as an independent variable in relation to such factors as workers, commitment to the job, motivation, and anxiety. One argument is that with high role specificity there is a reduction in flexibility and hence much frustration. The more clearly the role is defined, the less deviation is expected as a part of the role performance. Highly bureaucratized organizations are known for imposing numerous rules and regulations as role expectations for their members. An extreme example of high role clarity is the performance expected of assembly-line workers who perform repetitive operations daily. How many different ways can bolts be fastened to the chassis of the automobile?

Sometimes, role specificity is related to certain components of the personality. Some people prefer considerable latitude in their job definitions. Others feel uncomfortable with their work if they do not have a precise knowledge of what their superiors expect of them.

Hickson (1966:237) suggests that organizations may be classified according to the amount of role specificity present within them. And studies of organizational change examine the impact of modifications of jobs, or elimination of jobs, and of reassignments upon role clarity. Specifically, some studies of social organizational consequences of increased automation look at the implications of change for role clarity and other variables related to it, such as labor turnover, absenteeism, and low esprit de corps. In other words, how is role specificity affected, and what are some of the implications of changes in role specificity for other variables in the work setting?

Role Conflict   Completing the discussion of individual variables is role conflict. In a general sense, role conflict may pertain to any number of things. Linton (1936) has defined a "role" as those duties and responsibilities which are a function of a person's status. "Role" conveys the idea of expectations of others in the social relation (Loomis, 1960). Role conflict, then, can occur in several different ways. Dyer (1960) isolates several kinds of role conflicts: (1) Conflict lying in the disparity between the demands of two roles which one person is expected to take. (2) Conflict arising where a person assumes so many roles that he cannot possibly fulfill all the obligations involved. (3) Conflict internal to a given role, (a) where a person accepts a role and finds that he really does not have time to meet its demands but does not know how to get out of them, and (b) where a person accepts a role for which he has time but feels that he has neither the interest nor the ability to carry out its obligations. (4) Conflict arising because of different expectations as to how one's role should be carried out.

Gross et al. (1958) investigated the implications of role conflict for school superintendents and contradictory role expectations that stemmed from their relations with subordinates. Conflict situations pertained to (1) hiring and promoting teachers, (2) the superintendent's allocation of his after-office hours, (3) salary increases for teachers, and (4) the priority the superintendent gives financial or educational needs in preparing the school budget.

Getzels and Guba (1954:166) hypothesize that as role conflict becomes more intensified, persons become increasingly ineffective in role performance. They acknowledge that the intensity of perceived role conflict varies according to certain personal and attitudinal characteristics of the actor, however. Their study of nearly two hundred officer-instructors at the Air Command and Staff School of Air University offered tentative support for the above hypotheses.

Evan's (1965) study of superior-subordinate conflict in two research institutions is indicative of typical role-conflict incidents in formal organizations. Nonsupervisory engineers and scientists, first-level supervisors, and second-level supervisors were questioned about conflicts with their superiors (p. 12). Evan reports that "the incidence of superior-subordinate conflicts is positively associated with organizational position in both laboratories. There is a tendency for technical conflicts to decrease and administrative conflicts to increase with organizational position" (p. 52).

An early study by Wray (1949) implicitly describes the plight of the first-line supervisor or foreman in industry. Wray characterizes the foreman as a "marginal man" between management and the lower-level worker in the organization. Foremen are often regarded by their immediate subordinates as a part of "management," an anonymous body of higher-ups who make up rules and enforce them. Management, on the other hand, considers the foreman as a lower-level participant and treats him not much better than any other worker. Faced with having to implement decisions made by his superiors, the first-line supervisor is indeed a marginal person in industry. As Wray says, "The poor fellow is in the middle, of course, in the sense that a person may be the middle one of three in a bed; he gets it from both sides!" [pp. 300–301).

From a theoretical viewpoint, role conflict is defined as an independent variable in organizational research. Productivity, job satisfaction, role performance, effectiveness of work groups, and interpersonal relations are a few of the many concomitants of role conflict in the workplace.

Throughout the remainder of this book, additional variables will be introduced in conjunction with various topics of specialization. Again, not all variables will be equally useful for any given research project, but a broad grasp of numerous alternatives should enhance the flexibility of any organizational investigator. The variables which we have examined in the present chapter should be particularly useful in contributing to explanations of the personnel problems outlined in the case studies in Appendix I.

SUMMARY

It is difficult to study organizational processes without paying attention to the groups and the individuals making up organizations. In fact, a view of formal organizations which considered only organizational factors would give a relatively sterile product. On the other hand, it would also be sterile to focus only on individual "needs" and characteristics. We must acknowledge that the three units of analysis—the organization, group, and the individual—are blended if we are to comprehend organizational structure and processes.

This chapter has considered interpersonal and individual variables; it would seem, from the frequency with which they are mentioned in the literature, that these variables elicit the greatest response from organizational researchers. Their value, like the value of organizational variables, lies in the fact that they are potential strategies for thinking about and explaining organizational problems and activities.

Inconsistencies in terminology appear in this area, as in the area of organizational variables and for precisely the same reasons. Not everyone sees things (or defines things) the same way. Again, we must be alert to the possibility that inconsistencies in findings might be attributable to variations in definitions for the same terms or variables.

These variables discussed in this chapter, together with those discussed in Chapter 4, can be used strategically in tentatively answering the questions in Appendix I. The student is encouraged to examine the interplay among these variables at all three levels of analysis.

In Chapter 6, strategies for studying organizations, including research designs, methods of collecting data, and potential avenues for initial entry into organizations, will be discussed. Most of these strategies are discussed more completely in social-research texts; Chapter 6, however, has the advantage of applying these strategies in organizational contexts.

STUDY QUESTIONS

1 Differentiate between individual and interpersonal variables. In what ways are such variables complementary to one another? Explain.
2 Which of the individual variables discussed in this chapter do you feel is most difficult to measure empirically? Why?
3 Differentiate between "initiating structure" and "showing consideration" as manifestations of supervisory behavior. Give two examples for each drawn from real or imaginary organizational situations.
4 Under what conditions should employees have considerable decision-making power in the workplace? How much voice should workers have in policy decisions at high administrative levels? Why?
5 How important do you feel "needs" of individuals are in describing job satisfaction? Consider the work of Maslow and Thomas. How would each of these theorists account for organizational ineffectiveness (assuming each uses as major explanatory inputs variables at the individual or interpersonal levels)?
6 Can an organization ever eliminate role conflict in the general sense? Why or why not?
7 Some persons contend that "opposites attract." Explain how "value similarities" can function as mutual interpersonal attractions in view of this contention.

NOTES

¹ For example, see *The Science Research Associates Employee Inventory,* Chicago, Science Research Associates, Inc., 1952; Nancy C. Morse, *Morse Indexes of Employee Satisfaction: Satisfactions in the White Collar Job,* Ann Arbor, Mich.: University of Michigan, Institute for Social Research, 1953; *Guttman Scales of Military Base Morale;* Delbert C. Miller and Nahum Z. Medalia, "Efficiency, Leadership, and Morale in Small Military Organizations," *The Sociological Review,* 3:93–107, 1955; Arthur H. Brayfield and Harold F. Rothe, "An Index of Job Satisfaction," *Journal of Applied Psychology,* 35:307–311, 1951; Robert P. Bullock, *Social Factors Related to Job Satisfaction: A Technique for the Measurement of Job Satisfaction,* Columbus: Ohio State University Bureau of Business Research, 1952; B. J. Speroff, "Job Satisfaction and Interpersonal Desirability Values," *Sociometry,* 18:69–72, 1955; Judson B. Pearson, Gordon H. Barker, and Rodney D. Elliot, "Sales Success and Job Satisfaction," *American Sociological Review,* 22:424–427, 1957. Additional references to job satisfaction under a variety of conditions may be found in Delbert C. Miller, *Handbook of Research Design and Social Measurement,* 2d ed., New York: McKay, 1970; and Charles M. Bonjean, Richard J. Hill, and S. Dale McLemore, *Sociological Measurement: An Inventory of Scales and Indices,* San Francisco: Chandler, 1967.

Chapter 6

Studying Formal Organizations

INTRODUCTION

Studying formal organizations is the primary preoccupation of the organizational researcher, yet comparatively little information currently exists which deals with the problems associated with contacting and entering organizations for the purpose of studying them. Given the many different organizations available for scientific scrutiny, it is all but impossible to prescribe a universally applicable strategy for approaching and studying them. Many organizations openly solicit help from outside researchers, asking them to assist in the resolution of company problems.[1] But probably more often than not, social researchers initiate contact with organizations in one way or another in order to study their characteristics. Some researchers are lucky in the sense that they know a friend of a friend who works for a particular organization and who will do him a favor. Of course, the significance of the "favor" depends upon the friend's authority or position in the organization.

Researchers without inside contacts are less fortunate. Investigators who wish to study hospital organizations, for example, encounter extremely busy administrators who seldom want to interrupt their busy schedules with requests for social scientific examinations of their internal operations. Many organizations are well protected against invasions of social investigators by "main gate" guards or receptionists who request special permits or other appropriate identifying signs for admittance.

Getting into any particular organization for purposes of examining its structural and processual elements is dependent upon a number of factors. Some of the more important of these are outlined and discussed briefly below. The order in which each is presented is not an indication of its priority in relation to the others listed. All the factors below are important and applicable at different times and under appropriate circumstances.

Does the researcher have a sponsoring agency to work through in contacting organizational officials? Studies which are funded and sponsored by such organizations as the Ford Foundation, the National Institutes of Mental Health, the U.S. Office of Education, the Russell Sage Foundation, and the National Opinion Research Center (the University of Chicago) seem more likely to be in the position of obtaining cooperation from target organizations than an unfunded study conducted by an obscure professor at a small college. The prestige of the sponsoring institution obviously lends credence and legitimacy to the study and carries significant weight in eliciting the cooperation of the organization to be studied.

Does the researcher have direct access to organizations through friends or professional associates? Often the influence of friends enables the researcher to enter organizations and obtain the required information. Much depends on the position of the friend in the organization and the influence of the professional associate.

What degree of formal approval is required for the project? Bargaining with hierarchies of authority in bureaucratic organizations is a delicate matter. Often, studies approved at one level in the hierarchy are subject to disapproval or rejection at a higher level. In a proposed study of the social organization of a bank, I was introduced to the bank president through an influential acquaintance. The basic elements of the study were explained to the president in detail; he seemed agreeable and gave me tentative assurance that the study would take place. He said that he would have to "touch base" with the personnel officer "just for the record" before final approval could be given. Two weeks later, the president informed me by letter that he did not feel that the study would be in the best interests of his bank.[2] No other explanation for the refusal was given.

Which type of approach is used by the researcher to contact organizations initially? There are an infinite number of approaches to be taken by investigators for contacting organizations. The researcher's "sales pitch" may emphasize the benefits which may potentially accrue to the organization. Or the investigator may ask the organization to "help" him in an altruistic sense. Students working on doctoral dissertations or master's theses (or other research papers at the undergraduate level) may facilitate the achievement of their research objectives by using this type of appeal.

What is the length and complexity of the proposed study? Does the researcher wish to study staff members on the job over time through nonparticipant observation? Does he plan to interrupt their daily work routine by asking them questions when he chooses and by otherwise interfering with the efficiency of the performance of their work operations? Does the researcher require repeated examination of the organization over time such as is common in before-and-after research designs? Will the employees be subject to social manipulation in some experimental fashion, or will their interpersonal relations with other staff be placed in a state of flux?

To what extent will the research instruments used be viewed as threatening to organizational officials? In a very real sense, tests and measures of individual, interpersonal, and organizational variables are *learning experiences* for employees as respondents. There is some justification for managers of organizations to believe that social scientists will raise questions which their staff members may not have considered relevant before their exposure to the research instruments. Specifically, questions pertaining to job satisfaction, the nature of supervisory practices, and the openness of communication channels might generate enough interest among employees so that they might begin asking the same kinds of questions of their own organizational officials.[3]

Record (1967:38) suggests that

> the unease with which any organization, especially if it operates in sensitive or controversial fields, is likely to view research projects by outsiders is not hard to explain. Findings critical to the organization may cause it to lose face, force, friends, or funds. Critiques by noneducationists of school curricula and teaching methods, for example, particularly after Sputnik, roused public concern and drew a defensive reaction from the education establishment. A private social work agency lost contributions of volunteer services and money to a rival organization in a California community when the rival publicized a few critical comments contained in the report of an academic researcher who had received the cooperation of the first agency making the study.

How much anonymity is guaranteed the participating organization? Many organizations hesitate to become involved in social research because of the possibility that the researcher may reveal their identity and someone may turn an otherwise innocent piece of social research into a bad bit of publicity. In fact, some researchers, by virtue of their university or college affiliation and geographical location, may refer to a local company anonymously, still leaving no question in the minds of readers as to the identity of the company cited. Many investigators provide written guarantees to target organizations that all published accounts of information derived from them will be utilized in an anonymous fashion. References to these organizations will be vague, such as a "small metal-working firm in the Northwest" or "a small liberal arts college in the New England area." Ironically, guarantees of anonymity to the target organization may backfire. It may turn out that the organization *wants to be identified* for publicity reasons or for other motives. Rather than declare a blanket guarantee of anonymity, it would be preferable to offer organizations the option of allowing their identity to be or not to be known.

Details such as the value of the research to the target organization, the amount of time involved on the part of the employees, the nature of the questions to be asked, and the amount of information about the study to be shared with officials of the target organization must not be overlooked.[4] Sometimes, extraneous factors over which the researcher has little or no control may interfere with what otherwise appears to be a cooperative organization. In one situation, I contacted a bank in the Midwest for purposes of conducting a pilot study.[5] Permission for the pilot study was refused outright. Further investigation revealed that the bank had been plagued by embezzlement of funds by one or more employees. The insurance company underwriting the bank insisted that each employee at each hierarchical level submit to a lie detector test. My appeal to conduct a study dealing with employees' attitudes toward their organization came in the aftermath of the humiliating experiences of these employees with the lie detector.

ALTERNATIVE APPROACHES TO THE STUDY OF ORGANIZATIONS

Apart from the direct confrontation of organizational officials for permission to study their organizations, there are other alternatives for acquiring information about organizational behavior. Some social scientists write about organizations of which they are or have been a member (e.g., Carey, 1972; Dalton, 1950, 1955; Roy, 1952, 1954, 1960). As an example, my interest in bank problems was generated chiefly by my former employment in two banking chains during periods of organizational transformation due to the introduction of electronic-data-processing systems. Although this means of acquiring data is a more personal form of participant observation, the acquisition of information should not be the primary reason for occupying an organizational position. Any information which may become useful at some later date (for an article or a dissertation, perhaps) should be viewed as a fringe benefit which is obtained through sheer convenience and being in a right place at a right time.

Another way of obtaining information about an organization is to contact its employees off the job. Although such research practices would appear harmless on the surface, many organizational officials would feel that the researcher is violating their organizational privacy. Some organizations, particularly those affiliated with government at various levels and in different capacities, require oaths from their employees not to divulge any information about their own role or any other information pertaining directly or indirectly to organizational structure and functioning. The matter of ethics involved in such research tactics is currently far from resolved.

ON THE ETHICS OF GRANTING PERMISSION TO STUDY SUBORDINATES

Questions frequently arise concerning the authority of supervisors or managers to permit outsiders (researchers) to study the members of their organization. Some examples might be the following: (1) military officers granting permission to research agencies to study their enlisted personnel; (2) wardens of prisons granting permission to study inmates; (3) superintendents of schools granting permission to study their teachers; (4) teachers granting permission to study their students; and (5) managers of businesses and industries granting permission to researchers to study their employees.[6] The list of instances is endless. The question raised is: "To what extent do superiors (managers, business leaders, etc.) have the right to involve their subordinates in activities which are not directly associated with their assigned tasks?" Although there are no definite answers to this question at present, several implications are apparent.

A predominant concern of many people today is the *invasion of their privacy*. During the 1960s, a significant amount of attention was directed toward the rights of individuals to reveal or not to reveal information about themselves to others. What will the information be used for? How are the respondents to know for sure that any information they provide will be kept confidential and will be used only in impersonal respects? What are the potential psychological and social hazards associated with investigating organizational members? For example, in an attempt to ascertain the nature of the social organization of a work plant, a researcher might ask sociometric questions such as these: "Who do you prefer to associate with most on the job?" "Who do you feel would best represent your interests before higher-ups concerning a company grievance?" "Which employees do you prefer to avoid on the job?" Questions such as "What do you think about the type of supervision you receive from your immediate boss?" or "How do you feel toward employee X?" may seem innocent enough to the researcher during the course of the interview, but the damage to informal group structure in the organization may be irreparable if the researcher inadvertently shares "privileged and confidential" information with others in the work setting. Some employees put the investigator in an awkward position by asking him what other people said about him. One can imagine the tension and conflict of the investigator, particularly when sensitive information about people and situations is requested.

As a safeguard against the misuse of information about human subjects, professional associations such as the American Psychological Association and the American Sociological Association (as well as the U.S. government) are moving gradually toward the formalization of codes of ethics concerning the uses of information obtained. Each year additional protective measures are introduced to prevent respondents from becoming innocent victims of irresponsible researchers who ignore the ethics of their respective fields.

SELECTING THE UNITS OF ANALYSIS

A study of organizational behavior will involve the organization at large, some or all work groups within the organization, the individual or individual motivations pertaining to work behavior, or some combination of these.[7] Decisions about which unit or units of analysis to investigate depend upon the research interests of the investigator. It would probably be safe to state that there are as many research interests as there are researchers.

One way of differentiating between research interests could be in terms of "theoretical" and "applied." Those researchers whose orientation is theoretical are seldom concerned exclusively with the practical problems of real organizations. More often than not, these researchers are content to explore abstract relations between organizational phenomena without engaging in empirical inquiry to support or refute their theoretical statements. Other investigators deal almost exclusively with practical organizational problems. These researchers inquire into how labor turnover can be decreased, how the job satisfaction of employees can be improved, or how productivity levels can be raised. They examine the relative merits of alternative determinants of organizational effectiveness. Frequently, these persons have little interest in generalizing the solutions for one organization to the problems of another.

By far the bulk of organizational researchers (consisting primarily of academicians but including industrial and business consultants as well) lies somewhere in between the extremes of exclusively theoretical or exclusively applied interests. In other words, most researchers are concerned about making *both* theoretical and substantive (applied) contributions to organizational literature. Although any given investigator may study whatever he wishes for whatever reason he chooses, most select a balanced orientation which will ultimately allow their work to have relevance for a broader professional audience.

Investigators may also be differentiated according to the unit of analysis which they prefer to examine. Some like to study small groups, while others prefer to examine large organizations. Still others may be interested in looking at the totality of units of analysis in combination and their interrelation.

Researchers also may be distinguished according to whether they investigate organizations directly or indirectly. Some prefer to acquire information personally from organizations, while others are content to examine data which have been compiled by others for various purposes. Of course, one of the problems associated with using existing information about organizations is that it is often incomplete. It may have been collected for purposes other than those of the present investigator. It is quick to acquire, however, and if the researcher is working within a limited budget or is saddled with time restrictions, he simply may not have the money or time to obtain information from organizations directly. If he elects to study organizations on a firsthand basis, several options are available. Table 6-1 presents several possible organizational research alternatives.

SOME ALTERNATIVE RESEARCH STRATEGIES

A research design is essentially a plan for studying something. Applied to organizations, a research design is a plan to be followed which will enable the investigator to assess various organizational characteristics. It is a blueprint

Table 6-1   Some Possible Research Alternatives for Studying Formal Organizations

1. Studies of a single organization at one point in time (case study).
2. Studies of a single organization at several points in time (before and after).
3. Studies of two or more organizations at one point in time (comparative).
4. Studies of two or more organizations at several points in time (comparative, before and after).
5. Studies of work groups or individuals in a single organization at one point in time.
6. Studies of work groups or individuals in a single organization at several time periods (before and after).
7. Studies of work groups or individuals in two or more organizations at a single point in time (survey).
8. Studies of work groups or individuals in two or more organizations at several points in time (survey, before and after).

which specifies the organization or organizations to be studied. It prescribes the unit or units of analysis, as well as which methods of data collection should be used to acquire information about the organization. Finally, it includes means for analyzing data and interpreting it.

Research designs are primarily exploratory, descriptive, or experimental in orientation (Selltiz et al., 1959:50). Exploratory designs provide information about specific aspects of organizational phenomena about which we have little knowledge. These designs are used when little is known about the organization or the organizations to be studied. A person who studies hospital administration, for example, might find it helpful to become familiar with the hospital's internal social structure, formally and informally, Knowing about the jargon persons use in such settings will enable the investigator to devise a more sophisticated plan of study at a later date. From a very practical standpoint, it is important to know enough about the setting at the outset before one begins an examination of it. The exploratory study, therefore, is meant to increase one's familiarity with the setting or settings to be investigated.

Descriptive designs are oriented toward the assessment and categorization of previously defined organizational characteristics. Such designs are geared to portray various aspects of organizations in detail. For instance, MacDonald and Nichols (1969) described relationships between organizational job activity, the behavior of informal work groups, and power and autonomy of work among employees in seven drawing offices. These descriptions were valuable later, when more analytical research was conducted in similar settings.

Experimental designs test causal hypotheses of relations between variables. They are usually set up so as to control certain environmental conditions so that the researcher can observe the effects of some variable or variables upon "experimental subjects." An example is some research conducted by Day and Hamblin (1964) on the effects of close and punitive supervisory styles on twenty-four groups of students at Washington University (St. Louis). The students were divided into groups of four, and the task consisted of assembling models of molecules using the pegs, springs, and various colored balls often used in chemistry classes. Day and Hamblin simulated general supervisory behaviors by having the supervisor give the *eight* most essential instructions for assembling the molecules to certain groups. Close supervisory behavior involved issuing *forty* instructions to other groups. Also, under the close supervisory conditions, supervisors "hovered" over and watched the groups closely, and they directed many "negative, status-deflating" remarks toward group members as "punitive sanctions." They found that close and punitive supervisory behavior over the workers (in this experimental setting) resulted in the group members' having more aggressive feelings against each other than usual. Another outcome of close supervision was frustration among the workers.

The general nature of experimental studies is the examination of causal relations between variables. Operating in a theoretical framework, the researcher hypothesizes outcomes as results of specific predictor variables. Real organizational settings are testing grounds for relations between such variables as supervision and productivity, group cohesiveness and absenteeism, organizational size and complexity, complexity and formalization, the supervisor's span of control and perceptions of autonomy of the workers under him, and work load and job satisfaction. Typically, few studies are exclusively exploratory, descriptive, or experimental. Most experimental studies, for example, provide elements of exploration and description, although the major emphasis is experimental. But the bulk of organizational research today is chiefly descriptive. There are indications in recent literature of trends toward increased utilization of experimentation in organizational investigations.

Each of the research designs discussed above has its strengths and weaknesses. Exploratory designs are geared to acquaint the researcher with the organizational setting initially and point to specific characteristics of the setting which merit further investigation and description. Descriptive studies provide strong foundations for more elaborate experimental designs to be applied later. Exploration and description, therefore, are essential to our understanding of organizational behavior. Experimental studies enable us to introduce controls into the settings we observe. Observing organizational behaviors under controlled conditions helps us to improve our theoretical understanding of variable interrelations within such structures.

Although many researchers argue that experimental designs are the most relevant for advancing our theories of organizations, these plans are the most difficult to construct and implement. Some people believe that experimental controls are artificially contrived and do not reflect natural organizational behaviors. Currently, this controversy remains unresolved. In the final analysis, each of these designs contributes knowledge about organizations in its own way. It is only through the accumulation of knowledge by diverse means that we will be able to provide answers to the "whys" and the "hows" of organizational structure and process.

SOME COMMON TYPES OF ORGANIZATIONAL STUDIES

Although there are many kinds of studies useful for assessing organizations, only a few appear to be used most frequently. These are *case studies* and *surveys*.

Case Studies

Case studies are intensified examinations of the spatial, processual, and interpersonal characteristics of an organization. Two examples of case studies of organizations will be presented here.

A case study of a Midwestern bank undergoing a changeover to electronic data processing was conducted by Champion and Dager (1967a). The study included (among other things) a description of the bank setting (work layout and spatial arrangement of work roles), a profile of the bank's employees, a portrayal of the hierarchy of authority, a sociometric diagram describing the informal communication network, a detailed examination of job descriptions both before and after the changeover, observations of interworker contact during several workdays, and verbally expressed attitudes of employees toward various aspects of the changeover.

Another case study, by Graves (1970:73), involved a pipeline construction industry. From June 1966 to May 1967, Graves visited construction sites of three companies and their offices in Ohio, Michigan, and Ontario (Canada), where he interviewed workmen and company officials regarding various aspects of their jobs. He spent most of his time with nine workers who seemed to be the most familiar with the different aspects of company operation. His work detailed the problems of forming work crews and finding jobs, and he made extensive use of personal observations of and communications with key workmen in describing certain formal and informal characteristics of the industry.

Case studies usually involve a single organization, although it is not uncommon for researchers to conduct in-depth examinations of several organizations. These types of studies have varying importance for organizational theory. Their significance hinges upon the extent to which the researcher has sought to link them to a general theoretical framework. For example, an investigator may construct a theory of role change consisting of several propositions and assumptions about personal and social characteristics as well as certain task properties. He tests his theory by studying some of the social and personal reactions or organizational members currently experiencing substantial modification in the design and performance of their jobs. The case study suffices as a specific test of the more general theory (e.g., of role change as in the example cited above). The researcher will make certain predictions concerning behaviors manifested by employees and groups after the change. Observing predicted outcomes will lend strength to the researcher's theoretical position and greatly enhances the theoretical relevance of the case study.

On the other hand, if the researcher were to conduct a case study of an organization without linking it to a specific theoretical scheme, the study itself would have little or no theoretical value. It would simply be a description of a single, isolated organization. However, even a study not couched in any specific theoretical scheme can have some practical utility. The findings from it might be suggestive of fruitful strategies which could be applied in a study which is theoretically based. The argument for case studies, therefore, is that *some* information (even though theory is conspicuously absent) is better than *no* information.

A primary strength of case studies is that they offer an in-depth appraisal of organizational behavior. The researcher has the option of considering a wide variety of organizational and interpersonal characteristics in developing his explanation for organizational problems. The major weakness of these studies is that they are most frequently limited to a single organization. It becomes crucial, therefore, to select a *typical organization* for intensive study, particularly if it is the researcher's intention to generalize to the larger class of organizations from which the original one was selected. Unfortunately, the researcher has no way of judging how "typical" his organization happens to be. Again, he is obligated to rely upon his theoretical formulations and to regard the case study as one specific test of the more general organizational theory.

The Field Survey

Surveys of organizations are studies of large numbers of organizations. Officials or administrators are contacted by the researcher and information is acquired (usually by means of questionnaires or interviews) pertaining to certain characteristics of the organizations selected. Several brief examples of surveys of organizations include studies by Marcus (1966), who surveyed 185 unions, the frequency of their conventions, and their respective constitutions; Child (1972), who surveyed 82 British work organizations and obtained from each information describing its formalization, specialization, standardization, centralization, and vertical span, which he contrasted with an earlier survey by Pugh et al. (1968) on a similar topic; and Darkenwald (1971), who surveyed 283 department chairmen at 54 high-, medium-, and low-differentiated institutions in order to assess the relation between the degree of institutional differentiation and conflict between departmental and administrative subsystems in colleges and universities (p. 407).

Surveys may be either limited or extensive, depending upon factors such as the budget of the researcher, his timetable for completing the project, his manpower resources, and his research objectives. Contrasted with the case study, surveys are very superficial in the information they provide about organizational structure and functioning. But the researcher has the advantage of focusing upon specific characteristics of many organizations rather than of just a few of them. While one important consideration in case studies is "typicality," the major consideration of the survey is selecting the most salient variables for examination. For assessing general organizational (as opposed to individual or interpersonal) characteristics, the survey is superior to the case study. Information may be obtained from organizations of various sizes or from the same kinds of organizations. Interorganizational comparisons are easily made, whereas the case study is not designed strictly for comparative purposes. Surveys are more costly in the long run, however. Inasmuch as several organizations must be analyzed, the researcher must allocate his manpower and resources over a broad geographical area (particularly if interviews are used). On the other hand, a case study requires an in-depth examination of a single organization or a unit within an organization. This type of study is more convenient for the researcher in terms of data collection.

Other Types of Studies

Although this chapter is designed to reflect some of the popular methodological tools of the organizational researcher, it is not intended to replace the more detailed discussions found in books about methods of social research. Howver, a superficial exposure to some of the strategies utilized by organizational researchers in their scientific inquiry is helpful in guiding students toward the most appropriate methodological approaches to the problems they are studying. Obviously, it will be necessary for the student to consult more specialized books on specific methodological subjects in order to appreciate the nature and consequences of any given research application. In addition to case studies and surveys, much valuable information about organizations has been "lifted" from the literature by indirect means. Governmental agencies such as the Department of Labor, the Bureau of Labor Statistics, the Department of Health, Education and Welfare, and the National Institutes of Mental Health compile various kinds of information about organizations and their memberships which may be used by researchers. The utilization of such information represents an extremely economical form of data collection. Briefly, two studies will be mentioned here as examples in which sources such as these have been used. Rushing (1969:432) was concerned with the effects of organizational size on surveillance and formal rules (including record keeping to evaluate performance). He obtained information about these factors from population figures for the United States (1960) reported in *Occupation by Industry, The United States Census of Manufacturers and The Statistical Abstracts.* Anderson and Warkov (1961) studied administration in hospitals, paying specific attention to organizational size and functional complexity. They derived their information from monthly reports published by the Central Office of the Veterans Administration. These reports contained figures on the number of hospitals and personnel in various structural categories.

These researchers did not have to encounter organizations directly. Rather, the information in the secondary sources was manipulated or rearranged for their specific purposes and used for testing hypotheses about general organizational and interpersonal variables. The major weakness of such investigations is that the information obtained often does not exactly fit the investigator's theoretical plans. The data compiled may have been selectively obtained for quite different purposes than the researcher's interests.

In order to enhance the validity of their findings, therefore, researchers often resort to using a *combination* of techniques of data collection and study methods and comparing the results obtained by each. This is called "triangulation" and is defined as the simultaneous use of several methods of data collection or tools for examining the same organizational behavior. Naturally, there is more work required of the investigator, but the increased validity of the results is sufficient justification for the additional effort expended. Webb et al. (1966:3) argue that "the most persuasive evidence comes through a triangulation of measurement processes. . . . Once a proposition [about an organization, for example] has been confirmed by two or more independent measurement processes, *the uncertainty of its interpretation is greatly reduced* " (italics added).

A NOTE ON INCONSISTENCIES IN FINDINGS

Few researchers have surveyed literature in preparation for a scientific investigation and found complete accord in the findings of contrasting articles on the same subject. Organizational research as well is replete with inconsistencies in findings. It is almost a convention for investigators to commence their research reports by noting that there are disagreements among investigators concerning relations between particular sets of variables. Inconsistencies and contradictions in research findings occur for many reasons. Some of the more important of these are outlined below.

Different methods of data collection may account for inconsistencies. It is likely that different researchers may arrive at contradictory conclusions regarding the same organization because different methods of data collection are used to obtain the same information.

Different theoretical approaches may lead to contradictory results. Employing different organizational models or typologies may lead independent investigators to different conclusions about the same organizational phenomenon. A "human-relations" perspective versus a "machine" orientation can have interesting implications for the same organizational problems and solutions.

Using different samples (individuals, groups, or organizations) may account for variation in findings. Studies of the same variables under different contextual circumstances (e.g., two studies of job satisfaction and productivity, one in a textile mill and one in an iron works) may yield different results. The variety of differences among employees, including the sex composition of work groups, age similarities, educational background, the length of time on the job, the type of job performed, the levels of authority, and participant functions, used as levels or units of inquiry can all contribute to discrepant results in study findings. Many potentially useful studies have been weakend by a failure to clarify the characteristics of the organization being examined. Yanouzas (1964), for example, collected data on time spent in various activities by foremen in a "job lot plant" and compared them with similar data collected by Walker and Guest (1956) in a study of foremen in an automobile factory. Yanouzas says nothing about the plant he studied except that it was a "job lot" plant. Because we know almost nothing about the technology of this plant, his data are almost meaningless. Faunce (1958) measured some apparent effects of automating machine operations on workers' behavior and interpersonal relationships. But these effects differ in certain respects from effects found by other studies of automation. This may be because the "automation" Faunce studied was itself different in kind or degree; but we can only guess at this, because Faunce says very little about its nature. *This is strong justification for adequate descriptions of organizations as targets of social research.* In other words, even though the exclusive priority of the investigator is examining organizational variables, he should offer an accompanying description of the setting within which he conducts his inquiry.

Different conceptualizations of variables account for differences in findings. As indicated earlier, there are many ways of defining variables in organizational research. Organizational complexity, for instance, could be defined operationally in terms of (1) the number of different functions performed by an organization, (2) the number of interrelations between work roles, (3) the degree of the division of work activity, or (4) the number of supervisory levels.

The validity and reliability of the measures used to describe organizational behavior will affect the outcomes of tests of hypotheses. The validity of a measure lies in the extent to which the instrument measures what it purports to measure. The reliability of a measure is its consistency in revealing the characteristic (of which it is a measure) over time. If our measures of organizational variables (or interpersonal and individual ones) lack these two important properties, the researcher has no way of knowing for sure what he is testing or how to interpret his findings meaningfully.

SOME STRATEGIES FOR DEALING WITH INCONSISTENCIES

Inconsistencies or contradictions in findings can be dealt with in several ways. Some of these follow.

Comparative analyses of similar kinds of organizations may help to reduce contradictions resulting from differences among organizations. The current emphasis on the development of typologies and taxonomies is evidence that researchers recognize that differences among organizations affect the relations of variables. Comparisons of studies within a single industry or business move in the direction of eliminating differences in findings due to situational variations.

Comparing studies utilizing similar measures of organizational, individual, or interpersonal phenomena helps to reduce dissimilarities in the literature relating to common interrelations of variables. Since many definitions of a single variable exist currently, it makes sense to devote considerable attention to those studies which employ the same measures of variables exclusive of the settings investigated. Considering the present state of the field, however, to hope for such comparisons is quite unrealistic.

Improvements in theories and conceptualizations of variables can effectively contribute to increased continuity in independent study results. It goes without saying that as we continue to improve our measures of social and organizational phenomena, our knowledge of organizational behavior will become less diffuse.

Replication studies will serve to enrich our understanding of organizational behavior and lead to the direct accumulation of information which will enable us to retain the most profitable orientations and discard less productive ones. Present demands for originality (particularly in doctoral dissertations and master's theses) function in a positive fashion to broaden our theoretical appreciation of different dimensions of and approaches to organizations. But at the same time, without needed replication research in diverse areas of organizational behavior, it will be a long time before specific statements of general applicability to organizations can be made with a high degree of certainty.

SUMMARY

Chapters 1 to 5 of this text were directed toward presenting a general survey of social theory and its relevance to the advancement of organizational theory, an introduction to variables utilized in the analysis and examination of all sorts of organizations, and a fairly broad coverage of some of the many models and typologies of organizations which presently exist. Little effort was made to specify which models, typologies, and terminologies are "best." Each has strengths and limitations when applied to specific organizational settings. Some professionals endorse one model; others prefer alternatives. Some researchers persistently investigate specific interrelations of variables in a multiplicity of types of organizations. Of course, selecting one scheme over another or one set of terms to study rather than another is evidence of the researcher's interests and biases concerning what is studied, from what perspective, and how. This text is not intended to endorse a specific model or terminology; rather, it is meant to provide the reader with a broad overview of some of the more frequently used existing schemes.

Exposure to some of the key organizational, interpersonal, and individual variables which many persons consider crucial to organizational investigations is only a part of the larger picture. We must also be aware of some of the *means,* or strategies, whereby organizations are examined scientifically. This chapter has focused upon some of the problems of gaining access to organizations, some of the researcher's considerations concerning involvement of employees or volunteers in planned research activity, and some of the ethical questions which must necessarily be raised when human subjects are studied.

Research techniques and procedures which are common to virtually all subareas of sociology and other social sciences have been presented within an organizational context to show more clearly *how* researchers often go about their analyses of organizational settings. The purpose of this chapter has not been to provide in-depth assessments of all potentially applicable research methodologies for studying organizations. There are many specialized texts which provide the specific details of all the research strategies mentioned here. The reader is encouraged to consult such sources in order to become more proficient in selecting and applying the particular research strategies which best suit the organization or organizations to be studied. Some criteria for selecting an appropriate research design or sampling plan have been included as possible guidelines. Finally, this chapter has indicated some of the possible sources of inconsistencies in research findings, including different conceptualizations or definitions of the same variables, variations in organizations sampled, and different approaches to investigating common organizational problems. Some ways of dealing with inconsistencies were discussed briefly.

The remainder of this text treats selected topics which are regarded as some of the more important organizational concerns by many researchers. The intent of each chapter is to convey to the reader an overview of specific dimensions of organizational behavior and some common problems which arise in organizational analyses.

STUDY QUESTIONS

1   What do you consider to be some of the major advantages of case studies over surveys if you wanted to investigate interpersonal interactions on the job? Elaborate.
2   What are some of the problems of entering organizations initially for studying them? How can each problem you list be dealt with most effectively? Discuss.
3   To what extent should a supervisor have the right to allow researchers the opportunity of studying his subordinates? What are some of the ethical considerations which must be made in such situations? Explain.
4   What are some major sources of inconsistencies in organizational research findings? Do inconsistencies in any given topic area within the study of formal organizations necessarily mean the field is "unscientific"? Why or why not? Explain.
5   How can we deal with inconsistencies in findings on organizational behavior? List several examples.
6   In what ways are surveys more economical than case studies for obtaining superficial information about organizational authority hierarchies? How are case studies more economical for investigating internal organizational behaviors? Explain.
7   What is triangulation? Why is it useful in organizational research? Elaborate.
8   What is a research design? What are the three types of research designs which are potentially useful for studying organizations? List some strengths and limitations of each type.
9   What are some major differences between theoretical and applied organizational researchers? What other kinds of distinctions can be made pertaining to researchers' orientations?
10 How can an organizational investigator facilitate access to an organization in order to study it? Explain in some detail the strategy or strategies you list.

NOTES

[1] In late 1971 I was asked to conduct a study of the effectiveness of a large charitable organization in the Southeast. This organization had sixteen affiliate organizations which it subsidized directly through public donations. These affiliate organizations were advised by the central coordinating office to offer me every courtesy by answering any and all questions pertaining to staff expenditures and persons benefited.

[2] In another banking chain in the same area, I approached a branch manager for purposes of studying the single organization under his direct supervision. The branch manager was a personal friend of mine, and permission for the study was granted readily. Two hours later, however, I received a phone call from the manager informing me that unfortunately the study could not take place. The explanation was that the branch manager had had second thoughts, contacted the personnel officer at the main branch, given a vague (and inaccurate) account of what I intended to do,

and been advised not to permit it. I entered a third bank in the same area, and with this additional experience I arranged a meeting with the president, the vice-president, and the personnel officer simultaneously. The proposed study was explained in detail, the advantages to the bank were outlined, and it was pointed out that no costs would be incurred by the participating bank and employees would be allowed to complete their questionnaires in the privacy of their own homes outside of banking hours. Three weeks lapsed, and when I contacted the personnel officer to learn of their decision, he said that the questionnaire I proposed to use would be of no value to the bank and would undoubtedly stir up unnecessary commotion among bank personnel. The next day, I received a call from the bank's vice-president and was informed of the same decision formally, with no reason for the refusal provided. An unusual twist to the otherwise discouraging sequence of events related above happened some weeks later. I was teaching a night class and related the incidents of my encounters with the banks (referring to them anonymously). Two elderly women taking my course approached me afterward and requested a substantial number of the questionnaires which I had prepared previously for the banking personnel. They said that *their bankers* would cooperate and allow these questionnaires to be administered to the employees. I was obviously skeptical about the probability that they would succeed with their bankers, but I gave them the questionnaires. The following week, at the beginning of my night class, they presented me with nearly one hundred completed questionnaires. When I asked them which banks had responded, they named the *same banks which had denied me permission to study them.* Later, I discovered that the women were close acquaintances of the bank officers involved, and passing reference had been made to substantial sums of money which each of the women had deposited in these banks. I have often wondered since then just how much of the bankers' cooperativeness was based on protecting a financial investment by remaining on good terms with the women.

[3] I attempted to study one business organization in 1972 but was refused admission because I was suspected of complicity with an attempt to unionize their employees. In spite of the fact that my university provided adequate authentication of my intentions to the business officials, there was fear on the part of some officers that my information might fall into the "wrong hands." I had to admit, however, that the questions dealing with job satisfaction, pay, supervision, and satisfaction with working hours could theoretically be used in an unscrupulous manner by interested parties.

[4] It is logical to assume that organizational officials will be more amenable to research by outsiders to the extent that the potential information derived may be of value to them. Managers of organizations anticipating significant changes in technology (e.g., automation, new forms of equipment, new methods of organization, new styles of supervision) are anxious to learn about alternative ways of introducing changes more smoothly with a minimum of staff disruption. Attitudinal studies of organizations in such conditions might very well be encouraged. Likewise, projected studies geared to explain such variables as absenteeism, job satisfaction, labor turnover, and productivity may be beneficial to supervisors in a practical sense. There arises a controversy at this point concerning the potential social manipulation of

employees as the direct result of increased knowledge about them gained from organizational research. This is one inevitable consequence of any project in social research. Obviously, this issue cannot be dismissed as insignificant. But there are at least two points of view which appear to offset one another. First, increased information about employees does allow their superiors to manipulate them in ways which will maximize organizational profits ("profits" in the sense intended here would extend to lessened psychological and social stress on employees resulting from organizational changes as well as to financial gains). Second, many forms of manipulation of employees by management (regardless of the ulterior motives involved) make work tasks and general job conditions more pleasant and positive. Increased information about organizational behavior through social research, therefore, is a double-edged sword which is potentially advantageous to both employer and employee.

[5] A pilot study is a preliminary investigation on a small scale designed to determine weak spots in a study design, poorly worded questions, and possible neglected factors for subsequent inclusion. Pilot studies are comparable to experiments with new products before they are marketed. Pilot studies enable the researcher to improve his methods and procedures before his investigation of the target population. Pilot studies are most valuable when they are conducted in settings similar to those to be investigated subsequently. If a bank were to be selected as a study target, then another bank should be used in the pilot study.

[6] Several years ago I discussed a potential study of a business organization with its president. The following morning he called a mandatory meeting of his forty staff members and gave me an opportunity to explain, in layman's terms, the nature and purposes of the study. He ended the meeting by assuring me (in a loud voice and in front of all staff members) that he was *certain everyone would cooperate fully with me.*

[7] Some researchers use the terms "macro" and "micro" to refer, respectively, to situations in which the organization as a unit is investigated or in which the small work group or individual employee is studied. Macroorganizational research might focus on the relation between organizational size and complexity, whereas microorganizational research might be concerned with such factors as group cohesion or individual job satisfaction.

Chapter 7

Patterns of Authority
and Organizational
Structure

INTRODUCTION

All organizations, regardless of their size and shape, have *patterns of authority* which specify functional interrelations between superiors and subordinates. At various authority levels or plateaus in organizations are managers, supervisors, group leaders, work coordinators, bosses, and crew chiefs. Although the list of formal titles by which such persons are designated can be extended indefinitely, at least one common characteristic may apply to all persons performing these roles. This characteristic is *the exercise of power, decision making, or influencing the behaviors of lower-level participants in the organization to varying degrees.*

To put it more simply, there are (1) those who give behavioral commands and (2) those who receive behavioral commands. Persons in positions of exercising control over others may, themselves, be subject to the directives of persons above them in any authority hierarchy. For example, a nurse in a hospital may be able to give commands to nurse's aides, but nurses themselves are subject to directives from nursing supervisors, who are, in turn, subject to orders from physicians, who are, in turn, subject to the orders and decisions of hospital administrators. It should be noted that there is almost always *some* degree of reciprocal initiation from a lower position to a higher one. In any authority relationship, the *direction* of the initiation of order giving is from a higher position to a lower one *more often* than from a lower position to a higher one. Therefore, any organization may be characterized as a sequential pattern of authority relations between individuals at the same or different levels of authority within it.

As has been illustrated in previous chapters, considerable variety exists among organizations with respect to their size, shape, and complexity. On paper, at least, different authority patterns may be observed in organizations which perform essentially the same function (e.g., automobile manufacturing plants, hospitals, legal aid clinics, insurance companies, police departments, National Guard units, and penal institutions). A simplified version of an authority hierarchy in a hypothetical organization is shown in Figure 7-1.

Again, on paper at least, it is apparent that each position in an organization, whatever it may be, is linked with other positions. These "links" have been referred to as *chains of command* and are easily illustrated if we envision the hierarchical relations which exist between various ranks or authority levels in military organizations (e.g., general—colonel—major—captain—lieutenant—private).

The degree to which a formal superior-subordinate arrangement can be maintained in an organization is contingent, to a great extent, upon the

ORGANIZATION A, HIERARCHY OF AUTHORITY

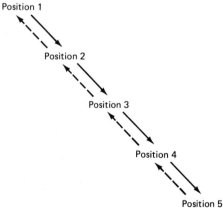

Position 1

Position 2

Position 3

Position 4

Position 5

Figure 7-1 A hypothetical example of a hierarchy of authority in organization A. The arrows indicate the "influence" of a higher position on a lower one. Broken arrows indicate the reciprocity involved in almost all hierarchies of authority.

nature and severity of sanctions (rewards and punishments) which superordinates are capable of imposing. No doubt such variables as organizational size and age make significant contributions to and substantially modify such authority arrangements as well. For instance, a small office of fifteen employees would differ in degree of formality between roles compared with the formality of superior-subordinate relations in an IBM subsidiary organization of five hundred employees. Also, persons who have "grown" with the organization since its inception, regardless of their rank or position at a later point in time, may feel entitled to violate or bend existing rules governing relations between superiors and subordinates by virtue of their imagined or real personal relationship with the company president or some other figure of high authority.

The interests of many organizational researchers regarding authority structures have been twofold: (1) The major focus of attention has been upon the impact of general organizational structure (e.g., authority relations, levels of supervision, communication channels) upon organizational effectiveness, flexibility, adaptability to change and innovation, and climate. (2) A second major interest area has been the analysis of the impact of organizational structure on status relations (e.g., between superiors and subordinates and among individuals at the same authority levels), styles of supervision and leadership styles, the performance and productivity of employees, and job satisfaction, among other variables.[1]

Consistent with these primary points of focus, we will (1) present and review several superior-subordinate schemes both as (a) outcomes of particular organizational structures, and (b) stimuli of particular organizational behaviors (e.g., labor turnover, job satisfaction, esprit de corps or morale, conflict, stress, and employee productivity); and (2) review some of the current literature in an effort to determine several potential implications of authority structures for organizational effectiveness, change, and climate.

Implicit in the discussion of research findings accompanying the topics subsequently addressed is the fact that few, if any, blanket generalizations can be made about authority hierarchies which pertain to all organizations at any point in time. Although formal organizational research has burgeoned considerably, findings—even those pertaining to the same topics or variables—have been uneven and inconsistent, and all too often contradictory. Of course, we may argue that this is to be expected and is typical of a growing field of inquiry and that the differing applications of methodological tools in the analysis of common organizational problems have predictably contributed to these inconsistencies. For the present, we have no general laws of formal organizations which are useful for predicting organizational behavior (to the degree of precision a scientist would deem respectable). And statements which appear to be useful in prediction schemes are severely limited to specific types of organizations. In short, the qualifications which must precede the application of any general statement to organizational behavior at any level of analysis are so numerous that such generalizations are of little real predictive value. This does not mean that we know nothing about organizational behavior or some of the important implications of organizational variables for specific interaction patterns or individual activities or attitudes. On the contrary, a considerable amount of material is available dealing with various facets of the structure of and life within organizations. This chapter surveys some of this material in order to depict the nature of the interplay between various organizational units, particularly with reference to authority relations.

POWER IN ORGANIZATIONS[2]

In the general case "power" may be defined as *a person's ability to influence another person or persons to carry out orders* (Parsons, 1951:121). Many organizational variables (including individual and interpersonal ones) are linked to varying degrees with the nature of the power hierarchy in organizations. Organizational effectiveness is frequently attributed, in part, to the nature of power relations between various positions within organizations. Likewise, labor turnover, job satisfaction, productivity, group morale, and organizational change are believed to be influenced significantly by the organizational power dimension.

Power is most visible in the behavior of supervisory and managerial personnel in any organization. Supervision over the work of others is a manifestation of a power relation. Managerial control over the production divisions of a company or a dean's position relative to the various departments of a university are indicative of power relations as well.

The exercise of power by an individual in an organization is affected by several important factors. Organizational structure may impose constraints upon persons who exert power over subordinates. Rigidly defined behavioral prescriptions for deans of colleges and universities, for example, obligate them to adhere to a high degree to the policies and practices of these institutions. The number of persons over which one exercises power (i.e., the span of control, whether it be wide or narrow) induces persons in positions of power to modify their mode of supervisory behavior accordingly. Logically, we would be led to assume that a person who has fifty subordinates under his direct supervision cannot behave toward each of them in the same manner as a person who has two subordinates under his immediate control. As the number of persons one supervises increases, the time he can devote to directing or criticizing the actions of any specific employee decreases.

Another factor which influences the kind of power of persons in organizations is personality configuration. In his classic study of workers in a gypsum mine, Gouldner (1954a) has illustrated one potential impact upon the miners of a change in plant managership. The change in managership provided an interesting contrast between the former manager (who, in the judgment of the workers, was quite permissive regarding violations of various rules) and the new manager (a person who "went by the rules" and was regarded by the men as considerably more strict). One supervisor directly under the new manager's control reflected the general sentiments of the workers by saying, "Vincent is a stickler for running the plant according to the main office. Vincent says that if that's the way they want it, that's the way they get it" (Gouldner, 1954:78).

A study of an office of a coast-to-coast insurance company involving different kinds of supervisory behaviors in various divisions lends support to the argument that the personality characteristics of a supervisor deserve important consideration (Mullen, 1966b). Mullen notes that:

> these investigations have led to the confirmation of initial perceptions, namely, (1) that the leadership modes in the three divisions [studied] did vary significantly because of the differences in personalities, attitudes, value systems, and methods of articulation and demonstration of the three leaders, and (2) that people who knew the three division managers described these differences in a way which was essentially consistent with the terms used to describe them through[out] this study (P. 111).

In addition, he provides evidence to show that the organization itself (as indicated at the beginning of this discussion), whatever the personality characteristics of the managers, "forced managers to conform to certain standards of comportment or suffer the consequences" (p. 128).

Up to now we have examined power from the standpoint of factors which affect and modify it. Indeed, supervisory or managerial behavior is influenced by many things. By the same token, *there is a reciprocal relation between that which is affected and that which affects.* For example, organizational structure, the number of subordinates, and personality differentially contribute to the nature of power exercised by a supervisor or manager. At the same time, the supervisory or managerial behavior elicited by these factors affects several crucial organizational variables, including structure, goal attainment, effectiveness, and change. Before we explore further the interaction between authority, power, and organizational structure, let us first examine several popular schemes of classification which differentiate among the various kinds of power potentially employed by managerial or supervisory personnel at virtually any level within the organizational hierarchy.

SOME POWER CLASSIFICATION SCHEMES

Three power schemes will be discussed in this section. In large part their selection for inclusion is based upon (1) their relevance to the origin and development of authority patterns in organizations, (2) their usefulness and explanatory utility relating to organizational behavior, and (3) their frequency of citation in contemporary organizational literature. We will examine sequentially the work of Weber (1947), French and Raven (1959), and Etzioni (1961a).

Max Weber's Legitimate Authority Types

Although there are much earlier discussions of authority in organizations and society,[3] a fairly formalized treatment of the topic is found in the work of Weber (1947). (The work cited here is a reprinting of Weber's papers on the subject of authority written during the early 1900s.) He defined three types of what he termed "legitimate authority" found throughout all social aggregates. These authority types have more or less set the pace for later social scientific classificatory schemes. Essentially, Weber argued that the legitimatization of authority has three roots: (1) charismatic, (2) traditional, and (3) legal-rational.

Charismatic Authority This type of authority is evident in the relation of a leader to the followers where the leader possesses and exhibits considerable attraction. Charisma, or the "gift of grace" or the "divine gift" has been attributed to such persons as Alexander the Great, Napoleon, and Adolf Hitler. Their commands to subordinates were typically obeyed without question. Followers would conform to a degree paralleling religious zeal or sacred devotion. The inability of social scientists to measure this property, charisma, as a valid indicator of an authority pattern has relegated this type to an obscure position as an explanatory and predictive factor in superior-subordinate relations in contemporary organizations.

Traditional Authority This type is evident in kinship systems in which the rules of descent are patrilineal or in which the rights of the father at the time of his death pass on to the oldest male child. Kingdoms are usually structured around traditional authority, and power over others is passed on to the next person of royalty in line. Persons living within such social systems support this authority pattern primarily out of custom or "tradition." Some organizations, particularly small ones, manifest characteristics of traditional authority in the same sense. It is expected that the president's (or owner's) son will assume his father's duties whenever the father is unable to discharge them, usually through death, disablement, or retirement.

Legal-Rational Authority This type is best illustrated by reference to our discussion of bureaucratic organizations in an earlier chapter. The authority of superiors in such organizations is legitimized by systems of abstract rules and norms. Rights are bestowed upon persons within an authority hierarchy by persons at a higher level and by rules which govern the particular position or role. Governments are run by persons elected or appointed, and the positions they hold entitle them to exericse authority over their subordinates.

Militaristic organizations operate on similar grounds. A major has legal authority over a captain, a captain has legal authority over a lieutenant, and so on. In school systems, superintendents possess authority over their assistants, over principals, and over teachers in the classroom. They usually have the power to relocate staff where needed to meet shortages and crises in particular parts of the city. Often they have the authority to hire and fire and to promote or decline to promote their subordinates to higher positions. Law enforcement agencies such as police departments and sheriff's offices operate on the principle of legal-rational authority as well. There are jurisdictional boundaries to which each department's authority extends. A department head in a university has the authority to determine teaching loads and committee assignments for professors. For example, depending upon the strength and influence of the American Association of University Professors in any particular academic setting, there are variable limits within which deans and department heads can exercise authority over their subordinates with little or no resistance.

Certainly, the legal-rational form of authority defined by Weber is characteristic of most large-scale organizations in contemporary society. Almost every large business or industrial firm, service institution, or philanthropic organization possesses the legal-rational authority pattern defined above. Most of these organizations are rationally conceived, have a hierarchial authority arrangement or chain of command, and have explicit (sometimes implicit) rules and norms which govern all roles and interrole relations.

French and Raven's Bases of Social Power

French and Raven (1959) have isolated five kinds of power which are present under certain interpersonal conditions. They adapt their power scheme to fit the perspective of the subordinate toward some superior in an authority relation. The scheme is presented independent of any specific kind of organization, although it will be apparent that there are several logical connections between the different kinds of power defined and various organizational types. Also, although the power types presented below are arranged so as to appear independent of one another for purposes of conceptual distinction, it should be recognized that persons in authority positions possess the potential for applying several types of power simultaneously in relation to subordinates. Therefore, the distinctions made do not necessarily rule out the combination of power types in hierarchical relations.

Reward Power   According to French and Raven, persons in authority over others are in positions to reward them. Such rewards may include promotions, verbal praise for work well done, more released time for leisure activities off the job without a pay cut, special favors such as relaxing certain rules in the work setting, giving subordinates easy jobs to perform, and salary increases. Depending upon the kind of organization we are discussing, rewards may come in many forms. If we were examining the reward power of guards in prisons, we might define rewards as overlooking violations such as smoking against rules and providing candy, cigarettes, liquor, and other things to prisoners. In university settings the reward power of department heads in relation to staff members may be in the form of improvement in salary, rank, teaching loads, and office space. Reward power is based upon the ability of superiors in the superior-subordinate relation to administer positive valences and to remove or decrease negative valences (French and Raven, 1959).

Coercive Power   The ability to administer negative valences or remove or decrease positive valences is defined as the coercive power of the superior (French and Raven, 1959). Teachers in the classroom often use coercive power to get students to comply with their demands and expectations. The threat of giving low grades or dispensing failing marks for not complying with what teachers want is a form of coercive power. In the military, the raw recruit is subject to considerable harassment from noncommissioned officers in "boot camp" or during the initial training and orientation period.

Supervisors and managers in companies can conviently "overlook" an employee for promotion or transfer to a better-paying job if he does not dress or behave in a manner which is consistent with the company image. In periods of low employment, when jobs are scarce, rumors circulate about mistreatment of employees by supervisory personnel. The rationale is that the subordinate "puts up with" verbal (and sometimes physical) abuse because of the difficulty in trying to get another job elsewhere.

Of course, in prisons punishments are explicit for particular violations of rules. Visitation privileges may be withdrawn for a prolonged period, or the prisoner may be assigned difficult and unpleasant tasks (e.g., cleaning lavatories and handling garbage). The military institution, not altogether dissimilar from the prison, possesses similar means of punishment for those who fail to obey the rules. Brigs, stockades, and other forms of "lockups" are held over the heads of all recruits as a form of coercion or threat. And the military has many unpleasant jobs to assign stubborn subordinates as well. One of the most severe forms of punishment in the military, apart from being placed in a military prison for disorderly conduct for a specified period, is the "dishonorable discharge." Such a discharge will follow the individual for the rest of his life, exerting a profound impact upon his chances for employment and his potential for promotion.

Volunteer workers in hospitals—"candystripers" or "pink ladies"—are sometimes verbally assailed by physicians, nurses, or other hospital personnel as though they were on the hospital payroll and were obligated to accept such humiliations and insults. As was stated earlier, coercion comes in many forms.

Expert Power   Expert power is contingent upon the amount of knowledge or expertise a superior has (or is believed to have by subordinates). Obviously, if Albert Einstein, the great physicist, were alive today and working with a team of other physicists, his statements about things relative to his field would be regarded as very important by his colleagues. It has often been said that "knowledge is power." There is a great deal of support for this statement in the organizational literature. Airplane pilots must master numerous instruments and controls in order to fly their aircraft safely. Orders from a pilot to a copilot or other subordinate during times of crisis (or at any other time during a given flight, for that matter) would likely be obeyed without question. Expert power is operating in this instance. The expertise of the pilot is sufficient to bestow upon him much confidence from his subordinates. A physician giving orders to a nurse during brain surgery would likewise be obeyed because of the physician's expertise and previous training. A foreman in a factory who has worked up to his present position "the hard way" usually has earned the respect of subordinates and is admired for what he knows about his work and the facility with which he performs it. When he gives orders to his subordinates, they seldom hesitate to fulfill his demands. Again, expert power is evidenced.

Referent Power   This type of power is based upon the degree of friendship felt by the subordinate toward the superior. In short, the subordinate says implicitly, "I will do what you tell me to do because of my friendship with you." Switchboard operators for telephone companies often swap shifts with one another out of friendship in order to keep a date on a particular evening. A supervisor over one shop in an industrial firm may come to the aid of another supervisor in a different shop because of friendship. Although it is difficult to imagine that friendship can be the primary source of power in superior-subordinate relations, such situations occur occasionally, particularly when the subordinate is not directly under the control of the supervisor giving commands in the setting.

Legitimate Power This power type is based on the belief of the subordinate that his superior has the right to give orders to him. Again, we can turn to the military organization for an example. It is an integral feature of the chain of command (i.e., the hierarchy of authority) in any military establishment that higher-ranking officers have the right to give commands to any lower-ranking officer. There are exceptions, such as when a lower-ranking officer is given temporary authority by someone who outranks the higher-ranking officer present in the situation. Parents ("superiors") supposedly have a legitimate power relation with their children ("subordinates"). By law or legal decree, a child must obey his parents until the age of majority. A policeman's command to a crowd to disperse is considered the policeman's right and obligation, and such an act is a form of legitimate power (even though some members of the crowd may feel that such an act is coercive, harassing, or in some other way illegitimate behavior). The President of the United States has certain rights and privileges and so do congressional members, Cabinet officials, and other political functionaries.

Etzioni's Compliance-Involvement Scheme

In Chapter 3 Etzioni's compliance typology was described as one way of looking at organizational behavior, particularly in relation to organizational compliance structures and lower-level participant involvement. To review briefly, Etzioni (1961a) identified three forms of power found in organizations: (1) coercive, (2) remunerative, and (3) normative. These closely resemble three of the power types identified by French and Raven in the discussion above: coercive power, reward power, and legitimate power, respectively. In addition to differentiating among these three power types, Etzioni postulated that subordinates (as recipients of certain kinds of managerial orders) would become involved in their work activity consistent with the type of power exercised over them. He suggested that the following power-involvement associations would be congruent with types of power he distinguished: (1) coercive-alienative, (2) remunerative-calculative, and (3) normative-moral.

    In his discussion of power-involvement congruencies, he used as an example for (1) the inmate of a prison who becomes highly alienated from the coercive prison organization. Examples for congruent type (2) might be a salesman who works harder to make more money and to be promoted more quickly than other salesmen in the organization (reflecting a calculative type of involvement in response to potentially greater remuneration) and a drill-press operator who is paid on a piece-rate system (i.e., payment according to the number of units of product produced per day rather than a fixed monthly or weekly salary) and works faster to increase his earnings. And finally, congruent type (3) is illustrated by the political party member who has a high degree of commitment to the party and therefore feels that it is his moral obligation to donate his money and time for the ultimate benefit of the party. Table 7-1, which juxtaposes the three schemes of Weber, French and Raven, and Etzioni, shows some interesting parallels between them.

Summarizing briefly, *all organizations have hierarchies of authority which involve interactions between subordinates and superiors. The nature and type of interaction between each level of the hierarchy may be prescribed in detail by predetermined organizational rules (e.g., a highly bureaucratized setting).* To some extent, however, the type of hierarchical arrangement between any pair of levels in the organization may be modified by the personality systems of the respective role occupants, the number of subordinates under any single individual's direct control, interpersonal friendships, built-in control devices such as closed-circuit television sets which scan entire departments or divisions of an organization and are monitored by rule-conscious managerial personnel, and the flexibility of the organization itself (measured by the nature of the functional and spatial arrangements of positions relative to one another).

What has been presented above is designed to illustrate that managerial personnel in organizations are capable of wielding different kinds of authority and power (subject to certain kinds of organizational constraints, e.g., rules and norms). Theoretically, at least, persons react differently according

Table 7-1 A Comparison of the Power Schemes of Weber, French and Raven, and Etzioni*

Types of power or authority		
Weber (1947, translated version)	**French and Raven** (1959)	**Etzioni** (1961a)
Charismatic ←——————→ Referent		
Traditional ←——————→ Legitimate ←——————→ Normative		
Legal-Rational ←——————→ Expert		
	Reward ←——————→ Remunerative	
	Coercive ←——————→ Coercive	

* The arrows in the table merely reflect similarities among the three schemes. They are not intended to portray the *influence* of one scheme on another. The emergence of three separate, yet similar, power schemes lends credence to the previously postulated continuity of authority structures in organizations. Certainly such similarities among these classifications mutually validate one another in a sense.

to the various kinds of power exerted over them. If we accept the assumption that an organization is vitally interested in achieving its goals, remaining competitive, and being effective, then we must also view the nature of authority of managerial personnel as a prime contributor to the success of achieving these organizational aims. The organization, in Weber's view, is successful, in part, to the extent that persons within the organization are capable of performing, and in fact do perform, their functions successfully. The concerted action of participants at all levels within the organization, provided each person functions optimally in the position he holds, will by implication enable the organization to achieve its goals (i.e., be effective and competitive in relation to organizations of the same type).

Digressing momentarily, what we are talking about is *human motivational factors in organizations.* What kinds of inputs will motivate the individual to maximize the performance of his personal role? The reasoning is as follows. If a particular kind of power is exercised over subordinates, predictable behavior on the part of employees or workers, commensurate with the power exercised, will emerge. Etzioni's compliance-involvement scheme discussed above is an excellent example of such thinking. Predictable—or, in Etzioni's own words, "congruent"—behaviors will follow as a result of the application of a particular kind of power to obtain the compliance of subordinates. However, Etzioni is careful to point out that "incongruent" relations between power and involvement may be observed as well and that these interfere with the congruent schematic representation of things in organizations.

The relation between power exerted and the type of involvement of subordinates (e.g., the degree and nature of motivation, productivity, and morale) is not a simple one. It cannot be viewed in a vacuum, immune from the other external factors impinging upon it and modifying it. Power is important, to be sure, but we must grasp and understand the organizational structure within which power is exercised in order fully to appreciate its significance for enhancing (or perhaps being detrimental to) organizational effectiveness.

SOME SELECTED FACTORS WHICH INFLUENCE
SUPERIOR-SUBORDINATE RELATIONS

To a great degree organizational structure determines the nature of power exercised by managers and supervisors over subordinates. Organizational structure may be "seen" on paper as a work-flow chart or a pattern of authority relations between all positions. Relationships between all persons in the organization may be clearly defined by explicit rules and norms. In addition to the detailed role definitions provided by an organization, other factors contribute to and affect authority relations between superior and subordinate. These are organizational size, complexity, the number of levels of supervision, the span of control, and technology.[4]

Organizational size is likely to affect the nature of superior-subordinate relations to the extent that greater formality between positions is found in larger organizations compared with smaller ones.[5] Logically, organizations with more members require greater coordination, although it is not difficult to see how easily such a statement is contradicted by organizations in which many individuals perform the same function (e.g., assembly-line work) and are within the full view of a single supervisor. For example, an entire floor of accountants working at desks in neat rows can be scrutinized by a supervisor fairly easily, and little or no coordination is required among the individual accountants on that particular floor.

In order to make our statement of relation between size and the nature of power relations more plausible, we need to introduce the variable of complexity. "Complexity" may be defined as the number of different functions an organization performs, regardless of its size (number of members). Suppose that we have a relatively large organization and furthermore that it is considerably complex (compared with other organizations of a similar type). Greater complexity within an organization does require greater coordination between operational units or divisions, and it is very likely that supervisor-subordinate and even supervisor-supervisor interactions will be affected accordingly. One implication of such an arrangement is possible increased formality and adherence to rules on the part of all the individuals involved.

The size and complexity of an organization can have important implications for the supervisory component as well. For example, in a study of fifty hospitals (general medicine and surgery hospitals compared with tuberculosis hospitals),[6] Champion and Betterton (1974) found that (1) proportionately smaller administrative or supervisory components are found in larger hospital settings (where size was determined by the average daily patient load); (2) tuberculosis hospitals, controlling for hospital size, had significantly smaller administrative components throughout all size categories used in the research (i.e., under 100, 100-200, 200-300, and 300-400) compared with general medicine and surgery hospitals; and finally, (3) hospitals reflecting greater complexity (the number of different functions performed by the hospitals) had proportionately larger administrative components. Table 7-2 shows all hospitals (general medicine and surgery and tuberculosis) compared according to complexity and relative size of the administrative component. Clearly, a positive relation exists between these two variables. Although this study did not examine the nature of superior-subordinate relations existing in the hospitals of different sizes and with different

Table 7-2   All Hospitals (General Medicine and Surgery and Tuberculosis) Ranked According to Complexity (the Number of Different Services Performed) and Accompanying Administrative Component-to-Organizational Membership Ratios (A/P Ratios = Administration/Total Personnel)

Complexity	Sample size	Average A/P ratios
14 (High complexity)	12	.18
13	9	.12
13	10	.11
12	6	.08
10	3	.06
10	2	.05
8	2	.04
7	3	.03
4	3	.03
	Total N = 50	

Gamma = +1.00 between complexity and average A/P ratios.
Source: Champion and Betterton, 1974:104.

administrative components, one may speculate that the presence of a proportionately larger administrative component would place subordinates in more frequent contact with greater numbers of supervisory personnel. However, in this study there is no empirical evidence to support such a statement with any acceptable degree of validity.

In a similar study by Anderson and Warkov (1961) mentioned in Chapter 4, the proportionate size of the administrative component was examined in relation to organizational size and complexity. They studied forty-nine Veterans Administration hospitals of varying sizes and degrees of complexity. Although their findings were inconclusive, they did offer tentative support for the hypothesis that organizational size and the relative size of the administrative component are negatively associated. Of greater importance is the fact that their study offered tentative support for the notion that complexity, in comparison with organizational size, was the more important of the two variables in determining the proportionate size of the administrative component. Their thinking modifies to some extent the earlier views of traditional sociological theorists such as Durkheim (1933) and Weber (1947), who argued that organizational size and complexity are positively related. Spencer (1898) and Simmel (1903) supported this thinking as well by claiming that an increase in an organization's size necessitates more complex forms of communication, hence, greater "complexity." Anderson and Warkov countered rather convincingly with the argument that the complexity of any organization (hospitals, in their case) would depend to a greater extent upon the number of different services provided rather than upon the actual number of people in the organization. Again, the extent to which different degrees of organizational complexity affect superior-subordinate relationships was not explored. But more elaborate communication arrangements between departments or groups performing essentially different functions would seem to increase the number of supervisor-subordinate and supervisor-supervisor contacts.

The organizational structural variable, the number of supervisory levels, has been examined extensively in the literature (Carzo, 1963; Carzo and Yanouzas, 1969; Worthy, 1950). Two studies are exemplary here. Worthy (1950) investigated approximately 100,000 employees over a twelve-year period in several hundred Sears and Roebuck company units. Among other variables, he studied the number of supervisory levels and the supervisors' span of control. He notes that

> a number of highly successful organizations have not only paid little heed but have gone directly counter to one of the favorite tenets of modern management theory, the so-called "span of control," which holds that the number of subordinate executives or supervisors reporting to a single individual should be severely limited to enable that individual to exercise the detailed direction and control which is generally considered necessary. On the contrary, these organizations often deliberately give each key executive so many subordinates that it is impossible for him to exercise too close supervision over their activities. In this type of organization structure, the individual executive is thrown largely on his own to sink or swim on the basis of his own ability and capacity. He cannot rely to a more limited extent on those above him, and these superiors, by the same token, cannot too severely restrict, through detailed supervision and control, their subordinates' growth and development [p. 178].

He adds that such a system "contributes strongly to morale because employees work in an atmosphere of relative freedom from oppressive supervision and have a sense of individual importance and personal responsibility which other types of arrangements often deny them" (p. 178). His study tentatively supports the notion that a flat organizational structure (with fewer supervisory levels and wider spans of control) is more beneficial to employees in terms of morale, self-sufficiency, and satisfaction than a tall organizational structure (with many supervisory levels and comparatively narrower spans of control).

There is much disagreement, however, concerning the relation between flat and tall organizational structures and organizational effectiveness and goal attainment. In one of the more convincing scientific tests of this relationship, Carzo and Yanouzas (1969) examined the performance of several simulated organizations in the laboratory setting. To test their hypotheses about tall and flat organizational structures, they selected subjects "randomly from the male, junior and senior class enrollments of the College of Business Administration at The Pennsylvania State University. The flat and tall structures were assigned to the groups on a random basis. Four different groups of 15 subjects were selected, with two groups performing under each structure" (p. 185). Table 7-3 illustrates the flat and tall structures created by these researchers.

The fifteen positions within each structure were assigned according to the individual student's grade-point average, meaning that the student with the highest grade-point average in any group became president, the student with the next highest grade-point average became vice-president, and so on.

**Table 7-3   Carzo and Yanouzas's Organization Chart:
(a) Tall Organization; (b) Flat Organization**

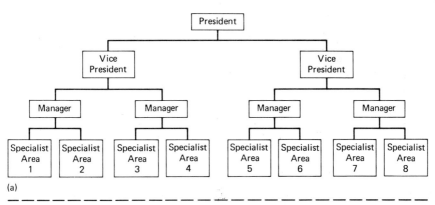

(a)

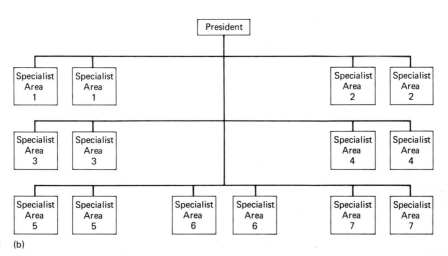

(b)

The groups were tested on three successive evenings, having to make twenty decisions during each evening, the same problems being assigned all groups. The authors focused upon organizational structure in relation to its effect on performance as well as organizational experience over the three successive trials.

Carzo and Yanouzas's (1969) summarization of findings revealed the following:

> The flat organization structure had two levels, with 14 subordinates reporting directly to the president. The tall structure had four levels, with each supervisor limited to two subordinates. Each position had an assigned task which required decisions on a market-order problem. The president was responsible for making an over-all decision for the organization, which he made after receiving recommendations from subordinates on the amounts to order. His main task was to reconcile differences among recommended orders, a capacity restriction, and his own estimates of optimum order quantities. Group performance was measured on three variables: time taken to complete decisions, profits, and rate of return on sales revenue. On all three performance variables, groups under each structure showed patterns of improvement as they gained experience with the task. . . . the pattern of improvement was not significantly different for the two structures; the patterns for decision time appeared to follow a function similar to learning curves found in industrial settings. For each structure, patterns for profits and rate of return on sales revenue was erratic on the first 20 decisions, and transient (that is, steadily improving on the stable pattern) on the third twenty decisions. Structure had no significant effect on decision time. This result was attributed to counteracting forces in the flat structure and to the elimination of some of the barriers to communication in the tall structure. Structure did not have a significant effect on performance as measured by profits and rate of return on sales revenue. Groups under the tall structure showed significantly better performance than groups under the flat structure. This result was explained by the fact that the tall structure, with a greater number of levels, allowed group members to evaluate decisions more frequently, and that the narrow span of supervision provided for a more orderly decision process (pp. 190-191).

A recent study by Meyer (1972a) has focused upon coordination and control factors in 254 governmental agencies and deals directly with the problems of authority structure, supervisory practices, and organizational effectiveness. Specifically, Meyer studied 254 finance departments in all states and in the larger cities and counties of the United States, with the information being obtained by means of a questionnaire sent to department heads and personnel officers.

According to Meyer, "the attempt [was] to study the internal dynamics of bureaucratic structures: How do changes in certain attributes of organizations have implications for other attributes, particularly the distinction of authority and discretion within an organization?" (p. 9). He goes on to say that "the relationship of organizational structure to rationality and authority practices in organizations will be the central focus of this study. We hypothesize that formal organizational structure *does* influence whether or not decisions are made, who makes them, and how more or less predictable behavior is elicited from members" (p. 11).

Meyer tested the following hypotheses:

1   Large organizations have more intermediate levels of hierarchy than small ones.

2   Spans of control are quite narrow at intermediate levels.

3   Yet, intermediate supervisors spend considerably more time supervising than first-line supervisors.

4   Vertical differentiation, the proliferation of supervisory levels in an organization, is associated with decentralization of authority to make decisions.

5   Horizontal differentiation, the proliferation of subunits, is associated with centralization of decision-making authority.

6   Vertical differentiation is associated with formal rules and with rules that partly determine decisions in advance.

General support for the above hypotheses was found in Meyer's research, although he argues that:

> relationships among variables describing organizations are rarely simple. If there is a general pattern, it is that variations in organizational structure have mulitple and inconsistent effects. The direct effect of increased size is to promote economies of supervision, but the indirect effect is to decrease such economies because of added intermediate supervisory levels. Vertical differentiation leads simultaneously to decentralization and rules that largely determine decisions in advance; horizontal differentiation has the opposite effects (p. 104).

Meyer's research also provides tentative support for the findings of Carzo and Yanouzas (1969) pertaining to flat versus tall organizational structures and organizational effectiveness.

In addition to the above variables which affect authority relations, we must consider the significant impact of change in organizational technology, or the ways of getting things done (whether they be material devices for reducing physical labor in the work setting or simply ideas about rearranging and processing things). Although Chapter 11 examines the interaction of various forms of technology and organizational behavior in great detail, we will briefly remark about the specific impact of technology on authority relations between supervisor and subordinate. Organizations are dynamic entities. They are often improving the quality of the product, service, or whatever commodity they deal with. These changes may be defined as changes in technology. For instance, a firm which decides to install an electronic-data-processing system to handle customer accounts (e.g., a bank or an insurance company) must make changes (to one degree or another) in the spatial and processual relationships of personnel (implying a rearrangement of the authority hierarchy, the reallocation of work assignments, and redefinitions of the sanctioning mechanisms).

A Midwestern banking chain became "automated" in the early 1960s with the installation of an electronic-data-processing system. The initial result was that the system subsumed many previously separate tasks under one electronic function. Several supervisory personnel experienced a dramatic decrease in status after the new equipment had been installed. Not only were there new operations and information to master and acquire, but new employees fresh from automation training schools were brought in to work with the updated equipment (consistent with their previous educational experience). Some supervisors became supervisors in name only because their subordinates knew more about the job than they did (Champion and Dager, 1967c). One can imagine how threatening it is to be placed in a supervisory position over people who are considerably more informed about performing complex job operations.

Changes in technology not only affect power linkages between supervisors and subordinates, but they often affect the spatial rearrangements of personnel. Decision making usually becomes more centralized as the use of electronic-data-processing equipment makes more information available to fewer and fewer people in the higher echelons of the organization. This centralization tends to minimize the effectiveness and the decision-making power of middle-level supervisory personnel, not only in terms of organizational function but in the eyes of subordinates as well.

Looking at the authority patterns of supervisors and subordinates as relationships modified and impinged upon by a variety of organizational, interpersonal, and individual factors, we might develop for illustrative purposes the diagram shown in Figure 7-2.

At this stage of accumulated knowledge on authority relations in organizations, we are unable to specify with reasonable precision the relative contribution of each of these variables. The growing amount of literature on the topic of "supervision" is staggering (see the Bibliographical Index in Appendix II). Depending upon the specific field involved, patterns of authority in any organization may be viewed as the result of whatever theoretical notions are popular at any given point in time. Researchers in the field of business management see organizations from one perspective, while indus-

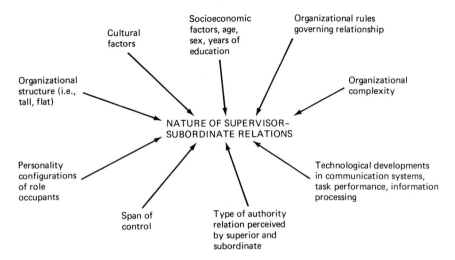

Cultural factors

Socioeconomic factors, age, sex, years of education

Organizational rules governing relationship

Organizational structure (i.e., tall, flat)

Organizational complexity

NATURE OF SUPERVISOR-SUBORDINATE RELATIONS

Personality configurations of role occupants

Technological developments in communication systems, task performance, information processing

Span of control

Type of authority relation perceived by superior and subordinate

Figure 7-2 Some of the more important factors affecting the nature of relationships of authority in an organization.

trial psychologists see them from another. Likewise, sociologists have their own particular orientations toward organizations and their structural and processual properties. And it has been amply illustrated in this chapter that analyses of authority patterns within organizations made by persons within the same field need not coincide exactly. Indeed, there are numerous contingencies which appear to affect the nature and type of authority exhibited by any organization.

MODES OF LEADERSHIP BEHAVIOR IN ORGANIZATIONS

An organization's effectiveness, climate, and ability to attain goals are influenced by many things. In the preceding section, various schemes of authority were presented to describe the interaction between organizational structure and manifestations of power of one type or another. Closely related to power characteristics of supervisors and managers is *leadership behavior*.[7]

Leadership in organizations has received considerable attention from theorists and practitioners (e.g., agents of change, consultants, organizational researchers, and analysts).[8] Most of the empirical studies of this phenomenon have focused upon the impact of various kinds of leadership behavior on motivation, morale, and the performance of individuals or work groups. Of course, the findings vary according to the setting within which the research is conducted (e.g., business as opposed to industrial) and the socioeconomic, personal, and interpersonal attributes of the study targets (e.g., the job status of the persons being led, their education and age, their sex, their cohesiveness as a group, their personality traits, and so forth). In this section we will examine some of the literature on leadership as it defines leadership as a vital component of organizational structures. Some of the more popular competitive notions about leadership behavior will be presented.[9,10] Each notion of leadership is usually projected into a cause-effect relation such as the following:

Leadership behavior X elicits social climate X

Then,

Social climate X elicits group behavior X

with accompanying rationales in varying detail. The notions to be discussed are (1) the leader as a great man (with inborn traits); (2) the leader in a particular situation; (3) leadership behavior which can be learned; (4) styles of leadership; and (5) multiple leaders who fulfill several organizational functions.

The Notion of the "Great Man"

Persons endorsing the "great man" notion of leadership believe that to become a leader a person must possess the genetic qualities of leadership, whatever they are. Lippitt (1955) calls such a view the "trait approach" to leadership behavior. Leaders possess certain traits, and one either has leadership traits or does not have them. It is assumed that such characteristics cannot be acquired through learning or specialized training. Although this view is currently regarded as archaic by the social science professions, one does hear on occasion that someone is a "born leader." From the standpoint of genetics there is little, if any, evidence to support the idea that leadership qualities are inherent in a person at birth and are destined to emerge at a later date, presumably in adulthood. Incidentally, this view parallels closely the idea of "charisma" discussed earlier in Weber's forms of legitimate rule.

The Leader in a Particular Situation

A more plausible explanation of leadership behavior places emphasis upon the situation a person is in. Under certain conditions, persons who lack the so-called "inborn" qualities of leadership have risen to take command of situations when others (supposedly in possession of such qualities) have failed to do so. Panel members of a jury have been influenced significantly by the logic and cool thinking of persons who, under other circumstances, would be regarded as having little or no influence upon anyone. Senior board members of large corporations have been swayed in the direction of opinions expressed by junior board members who happen to have the skills and useful ideas which help to minimize or eliminate the problems at hand. Under other conditions, such junior board members would be thought of by almost everyone else as having little or nothing significant to contribute.

In business, industrial, or voluntary organizations, leadership is usually defined by rules and norms. Superior (leadership) positions are defined and interrelations among roles are made explicit by some preestablished pattern. Hence, the situational notion of leadership behavior is not conveniently applicable to such circumstances. It is interesting to note, however, that organizational structure and hierarchies of authority provide avenues for persons to expose their faults and limitations, especially through promotion. Peter and Hull (1969) have popularized the "Peter Principle," which notes facetiously (although the principle does appear to be remarkably plausible) that "in a hierarchy, every employee tends to rise to his level of incompetence" (p. 172). Their argument is based on the fact that individuals in organizations are promoted to higher positions because of their acceptable performance in lower positions. With higher positions, however, come additional responsibilities and duties. Newly promoted individuals may not be capable of (or may dislike) performing their new tasks. The result, according to Peter and Hull, is poor performance. In turn, the poor performance of individual members adversely affects the overall effectiveness of the organization and its ability to attain goals.

Contrasting the "great man" notion with the "situational approach" briefly, it seems that there are two distinct issues at odds with one another. The first issue is whether certain traits or abilities are inborn or are learned. The second issue is whether a given trait or ability (regardless of its source) almost automatically guarantees leadership regardless of the situation or whether, instead, those traits or abilities or behaviors that are associated with leadership depend on the situation, so that an ability that may result in a person's being chosen or legitimated as a leader in one certain situation may *not* have the same result in a different situation.

Leadership Behavior Which Can Be Learned

The existence of an ability to internalize various behaviors, to function effectively socially, and to learn different methods of guiding and directing the actions of others has considerable validity, particularly when contrasted with the first two leadership notions discussed above. Many works have appeared bearing such titles as "How to Be an Effective Leader" or "The Key to Successful Leadership." They may be in the form of training manuals which specify those characteristics necessary for good leadership (e.g., a good leader must be a good listener, a good follower, a good director, patient, thoughtful, and considerate of the feelings of subordinates). A typical example of this sort of thing is a manual entitled *Training the Supervisor: A Guide on How to Set Up and Conduct a Supervisory Training Program*, put out by the U.S. Civil Service Commission (Washington, D.C., 1956). This short monograph contains a checklist questionnaire which has been used in supervisory training (and leadership training as well); it is shown in Table 7-4.

Miller (1970:302–314) discusses several instruments for measuring leadership in connection with business and industrial firms. Two of the more outstanding measures of leadership behavior presented are (1) Ralph M. Stogdill and C. L. Shartle, *Methods in the Study of Administrative Leadership*, Columbus: Ohio State University Bureau of Business Research, 1955; and (2) Edwin A. Fleishman, *A Manual for Administering the Leadership Opinion Questionnaire*, Chicago: Science Research Associates, 1960. Fleishman's questionnaire, for example, measures two leadership behaviors: (1) "initiating structure" and (2) "showing consideration." Structure "reflects the extent to which an individual is likely to define and structure his own role and those of his subordinates toward goal attainment. A high score on this dimension characterizes individuals who play a more active role in directing group activities through planning, communicating information, scheduling [and] trying out new ideas" (Miller, 1970:304). Consideration "reflects the extent to which an individual is likely to have job relationships characterized by mutual trust, respect for subordinates' ideas, and consideration of their feelings. A high score is indicative of a climate of good rapport and two-way communication. A low score indicates the superior is likely to be more impersonal in his relations with group members" (Miller, 1970:304). "Showing consideration" on the part of the supervisor should extend, in actual practice, to soliciting subordinates' ideas and then attempting to obtain rewards and benefits for them.

Other researchers place emphasis upon the amount of "influence" supervisors must have with higher-ups as a means of distinguishing between effective and ineffective leaders (Pelz, 1952). Still others associate group performance with various leadership behaviors (Patchen, 1962).

Maier (1973), endorsing the learning orientation to leadership, lists nine basic leadership skills particularly suitable for group-discussion situations. These are: (1) the ability to state a problem in such a way that the group does not become defensive but instead approaches the issue in a constructive way; (2) the ability to supply essential facts and to clarify the area of freedom without suggesting a solution; (3) the ability to draw persons out so that all members will participate; (4) the ability to wait out pauses; (5) the ability to restate accurately the ideas and feelings expressed and in a more abbreviated, more pointed, and more clear form than when initially expressed by a member; (6) the ability to ask questions that stimulate problem-

Table 7-4 A Sample Questionnaire to Train Supervisors as Leaders

Directions: Read over this list carefully and then circle the "Yes," "?" (question mark, for "Uncertain"), or "No," according to your own needs for improvement on your own job. Mark all statements. Mark the ones "Yes" that are most vital to you.

Example: How to get out more work   [Yes]   ?   No

I need a better knowledge of and ability to apply the following items:

1. How to train people quickly and easily	Yes	?	No
2. How to be a "good boss"	Yes	?	No
3. How to plan	Yes	?	No
4. How to organize	Yes	?	No
5. How to interpret and apply company policies	Yes	?	No
6. How to get out more work	Yes	?	No
7. How to discipline workers	Yes	?	No
8. How to correct workers	Yes	?	No
9. How to improve the job methods	Yes	?	No
10. How to keep up to date on methods	Yes	?	No
11. How to learn a new job	Yes	?	No
12. How to improvise equipment for a new job	Yes	?	No
13. How to break down a job into elements	Yes	?	No
14. How to work out new ideas	Yes	?	No
15. How to develop my own manual skills	Yes	?	No
16. How to keep machines in working condition	Yes	?	No
17. How to keep things in order	Yes	?	No
18. How to evaluate and rate employees	Yes	?	No
19. How to reduce waste (time, ideas, material)	Yes	?	No
20. How to improve my performance	Yes	?	No
21. How to improve the morale of my department	Yes	?	No
22. How to sell ideas to a superior	Yes	?	No
23. How to manage the boss	Yes	?	No
24. How to delegate responsibility	Yes	?	No
25. How to delegate authority	Yes	?	No
26. How to get people to work together	Yes	?	No
27. How to be diplomatic	Yes	?	No
28. How to improve my written and oral expression	Yes	?	No
29. How to recognize details that count	Yes	?	No
30. How to read blueprints and drawings	Yes	?	No
31. How to read charts and tables	Yes	?	No
32. How to improve my reading ability	Yes	?	No
33. How to judge the importance of instructions	Yes	?	No
34. How to recognize causes of fatigue	Yes	?	No
35. How to improve my memory	Yes	?	No
36. How to reduce disagreeable factors on jobs	Yes	?	No
37. How to sell safety to my workers	Yes	?	No
38. How to work more comfortably	Yes	?	No
39. How to avoid tensions	Yes	?	No

Source: U.S. Civil Service Commission, *Training the Supervisor,* Washington, D.C.: U.S. Government Printing Office (Sept. 1956), p. 27.

solving behavior; (7) the ability to summarize as the need arises; (8) the need for practicing the skills; and (9) the ability to deal with deadlock (pp. 141-142). Maier notes that these skills "seem to be essential," although we would contend that persons possessing all of them would be extremely rare. Ideally, such skills would be quite functional for the successful accomplishment of group tasks, particularly if all of them were found in one person.

There is little doubt that programs for developing leadership have been successful in enabling leaders to internalize certain skills and cultivate a better understanding of people. It should be apparent from a cursory examination of organizational literature that the quality of leadership at various levels in hierarchies of authority has played a major role in the effectiveness of organizations. The potential to acquire leadership skills through learning must certainly be counted as a major input affecting organizational behavior.

Multiple Leadership to Fulfill Several Organizational Functions

Perhaps the most realistic view of leadership in organizations is considering various group needs and relying upon *several persons* to fulfill leadership roles specifically designed to meet each need rather than depending upon a single person to perform such an overwhelming diversification of tasks. Lippitt (1955) suggests that leadership in any social aggregate is chiefly the responsibility of the group. His notion reflects the concept of "division of labor," where some persons are responsible for certain tasks while others see to different tasks. The major point of the idea of multiple leadership is that *no single person performs or assumes all leadership functions.* In fraternities at colleges and universities, for example, the president usually is task-oriented, while simultaneously, another person in the group is informally responsible for managing the social rapport among the membership. He may tell jokes, or he may be the "group clown," but he does hold a position of leadership in an important area which differs markedly from the role of the president (who may perceive his own role as organizing, coordinating, and delegating).

Newcomb, Turner, and Converse (1965:474) support the idea that groups do not necessarily have to have a single leader. Particularly with reference to small, task-oriented groups, they note that

> during the course of one or more group sessions the role of principal facilitator shifts back and forth between two or more persons. It is often impossible, even with respect to one particular kind of contribution, to assert that any single person is *the* special facilitator. Such considerations suggest that it may be more harmful than helpful to think of leadership as necessarily concentrated in a single person.

Watson (1966:177) discusses *distributed leadership* in much the same sense as Newcomb, Turner, and Converse (1965). He points out that different persons in a group may have a special facility for calling the group to order, others may be able to quell a troublesome situation, others may be highly respected because of their judgment and character, and still others may be respected because of their expertise and because they have more facts to contribute than any other member.

LEADERSHIP IN RETROSPECT: AN ORGANIZATIONAL VIEW

The literature on leadership has been somewhat inconclusive with respect to attempts to establish continuities in distinguishing "leadership traits." However, it does have several merits with regard to organizational applications. Gibb (1969:210-215) has provided us with an insightful approach to examining leadership behavior, particularly leadership behavior in organizations. He makes the following distinctions among several definitions of "leadership" and "leader":

    1 The leader as an individual in a given office (very likely the most appropriate definition for our interests and purposes)
    2 The leader as a focus for the behavior of group members
    3 A definition of the leader in terms of sociometric choice (or a function of preference relations among members)
    4 The leader as one who exercises influence over others
    5 Leadership as headship (as in a university setting) where the organization confers such recognition upon the person rather than the group itself (again, such a view in this context is of interest to us in our consideration of leadership in schools as formal organizations)
    6 The leader defined in terms of influence upon syntality (or group personality, performance, and behavior)
    7 The leader as one who engages in leadership behavior, which places the person in the position of being able to "initiate structure" (Hemphill, 1956)
    8 Focused versus distributed leadership.

Gibb (1969:215) summarizes his sentiments regarding each of these views by noting the major advantages of number 8 above. He states that

> leadership is probably best conceived as a group quality, as a set of functions which must be carried out by the group. This concept of "distributed leadership" [see Watson, 1966:177, discussed above] is an important one. If there are leadership functions which must be performed in any group, and if these functions may be "focused" or "distributed," then leaders will be identifiable both in

terms of the frequency and in terms of the multiplicity or pattern of functions performed. Such a precursory conception appears to accord well with the needs of contemporary research in this area. Heads may be distinguished from leaders in terms of the functions they usually or frequently assume. Similarly, differentiation between all types of influential persons may be possible in terms of the pattern of functional roles characteristic of each.

Students of organization cannot omit for consideration the conceptions of authority and leadership as important components contributory to schemes of the prediction and explanation of organizational behavior. Weber placed considerable emphasis on the fact that organizational effectiveness is highly dependent upon the expertise, initiative, loyalty, and quality of the organization's membership, including persons in various leadership roles in the hierarchy of authority. Those persons who are in positions of control over organizational resources and who are responsible for the guidance of their respective institutions toward improvement must be scrutinized as carefully as (if not more carefully than!) the structure within which they operate and the complexities and processual arrangements of their functional interrelations.

Organizational constraints (rules, norms) act to define and delimit the extent and nature of the powers of functionaries in leadership roles. Such constraints (role definitions) may, in fact, establish the "climate" of the situation, thus setting the stage for functional or dysfunctional behavior on the part of subordinates.[11]

SUMMARY

In this chapter we have examined power relationships which exist between superiors and subordinates in organizations as they are embodied within hierarchies of authority. Assuming that subordinates in all organizations accept the rules and provisions of their structures (an "ideal" seldom found in any organization where employees are expected to be perfect conformists), this acceptance places them in a power relation with those above and below them in the chain of command or formal organizational hierarchy of authority. Authority encompasses one's rights (and duties) to direct others to perform specified tasks. In this sense, authority and power are closely aligned. Power is usually regarded as the ability to obtain compliance from others.

Supervisors in organizations are obviously an important part of the hierarchy of authority. Each supervisor has a certain amount of authority (and power) over others (subordinates). By the same token, there are those who exert authority (and power) over supervisors in the overall chain of command. Traditional organizational definitions of supervision contain authority and power, either implicitly or explicitly. A supervisor is in a position of authority and is capable of exercising power over persons designated as his subordinates.

Weber's forms of legitimate rule (e.g., charismatic authority, traditional authority, and legal-rational authority), French's and Raven's types of power (reward, coercive, expert, etc.), and Etzioni's compliance-involvement scheme were presented to describe various dimensions of authority and patterns of authority. *Forms of authority through legitimation, types of authority through the differential use of power, and implications of types of authority for subordinates (the compliance-involvement scheme)* are essential to meaningful interpretations of superior-subordinate relationships.

Various organizational, interpersonal, and individual variables were examined, and their importance to the superior-subordinate relation was assessed. Organizational size, complexity, and technology, as well as characteristics of informal groups and individuals were viewed as direct and indirect determinants of the configuration of patterns of authority in organizations.

Finally, leadership and some of its more important dimensions were assessed in relation to response by subordinates. Whether or not supervisors admit it, they are leaders in a certain sense. They "lead" subordinates by guiding their behaviors toward fairly explicit objectives and expectations. Varying patterns of leadership is tantamount to altering supervisory styles. Fairly successful attempts have been made to ascertain subordinates' reactions to changes in leadership or behavior of supervisors.

STUDY QUESTIONS

1 Discuss the difference between authority and power. Is a person who is assigned "authority" in an organization always in a true position of power in relation to subordinates? Why or why not?

2 What is meant by "distributed leadership?" Is this concept a more fruitful way of looking at leadership contrasted with the notion of "styles of leadership"? Why or why not? Discuss.

3 Identify the five basic power forms suggested by French and Raven. How would each type of power elicit different reactions from the objects of power (i.e., subordinates in relation to superiors)? Explain.

4 How is authority related to organizational structure? Why is authority necessary to all organizations?

5 Do all organizations have the same pattern of authority? Why or why not? Give some examples from your own experience of organizations with different kinds of hierarchies of authority. How does each type of hierarchy of authority affect organizational members?

6 Weber discussed three types of legitimate rule as authority forms. Define each and discuss their respective weaknesses and strengths for formal organizational analysis.

7 Discuss the significance of Etzioni's power-compliance typology. What are "congruent types"? What does he mean by "incongruent types"? Do you think Etzioni intended his congruent types to be reflective of real situations, or would he allow for possible overlapping incongruencies? Explain.

8 What do you consider to be the relation of organizational size to the nature of supervisory behavior? Elaborate.

9 Give an example of a "flat" organizational structure as well as a "tall" one. How would flat versus tall organizational structures affect such factors as group morale and job satisfaction?

10 Define leadership. Which approach to leadership do you feel is most valid for organizational behavioral analyses? Explain.

NOTES

[1] There are many books on supervisory behavior within organizations at present. Among some of the better sources showing the relation between organizational structure and authority patterns are Applewhite (1965), R. V. Bowers (1966). Lucio and McNeil (1969), and Zald (1969a).

[2] The terms "authority" and "power" are used interchangeably throughout this chapter and discussions in other portions of the text. Both terms refer to similar phenomena, although some organizational researchers may prefer to make conceptual distinctions between them.

[3] For example, Plato's *Republic* (circa 369 B.C.) is an example of an early discussion of hierarchies of authority applied to social structures at the societal level.

[4] It is apparent that several variables have been excluded from this list which might be regarded by researchers as equally or more important. The personality of the functionary, the content of the job, and the degree of professionalism associated with the tasks are linked, to one degree or another, with organizational effectiveness.

[5] At present, there is no agreement as to what constitutes a "large" or a "small" organization. Therefore, we must confine ourselves to comparisons between organizations (usually, though not always, the same kind) with different memberships (e.g., 50, 100, 200, 500, and 1,000).

[6] General medicine and surgery hospitals are, by definition, more complex than tuberculosis hospitals because they perform a substantially greater number of functions.

[7] Although some social scientists would equate leadership behavior with the exercise of authority in the capacity of a superior, the phenomenon of leadership seems to be more a function of individual attributes as opposed to behaviors induced by organizational constraints (e.g., rules, norms, interpersonal role sets, and expectations).

[8] Among the various authors who have investigated this phenomenon are Bass (1960), Bennis (1969b), Day and Hamblin (1964), Fiedler (1967), Hollander (1971), Rossel (1970), Sales (1966), and Wager (1965).

[9] The word "notion" is preferred to "theory" inasmuch as little, if any, true leadership "theory" exists in the formal sense. Most leadership notions are limited to specific situations and cover isolated individual behaviors as opposed to being generally applicable and universally upheld.

[10] These leadership notions have been based primarily upon an article by Lippitt (1955).

[11] The differential climates stemming from certain kinds of leadership behavior have been demonstrated time and time again to be important inputs as modifiers of organizational behaviors such as productivity, group morale, and, as a consequence, organizational effectiveness and goal attainment.

Communication In Formal Organizations

INTRODUCTION

Closely paralleling the authority hierarchies of organizations are *communications systems*. *"Communications systems" are defined as networks which are designed to transmit information to and from all positions within an organization.* In short, communication networks are official defined patterns defining what persons, or persons in what positions, are supposed to send and receive what kinds of information or messages from what other persons. During the past twenty years, increasing importance has been attached to communication networks by business administrators, industrial consultants, and, of course, organizational researchers. In fact, there was a time when the word "communication" was regarded as the answer to most problems occurring within organizations (in some cases it still is). The proliferation of research on organizational communication networks in the professional literature is evidence of the emphasis placed upon this dimension of organizational process. The following is a typical statement underscoring the theoretical central-ity of this phenomenon: "Without communication, there can be no organization and, hence, no group productivity because communication is the only process by which people are tied together in a work group. If there is no communication, there can be no group. Communication is the bridge over which all technical knowledge and human relationships must travel" [Davis and Scott, 1969:255].

The formal communication network of any organization is inherent in the chain of command or authority hierarchy, including the horizontal as well as the vertical functional relations between departments in the overall division of labor. The communication pattern formally outlined is usually directly related to the work-flow sequence. This sequence defines the channels through which information and materials must pass in order for the organization to fulfill its overall production objectives. Such objectives can be exclusively material (e.g., assembly of automobiles, manufacture of furniture, assembly of toys, production of typewriters), but need not be: an organization may have less tangible goals (such as performing services for clients—(hospitals, psychiatric clinics, schools, legal firms, banks, detective agencies, and so on). Communication enables organizations to accomplish their objectives whatever they may be.

Although formal communication networks are found in every organization, vital information may be disseminated by other means. Grapevines or informal channels of communication usually exist as a normal part of any organizational environment.[1] It is highly unlikely that employees will restrict communications with one another exclusively to job-related matters at all times during the performance of their tasks or at lunch or coffee breaks. It is also naïve to believe that communication initiated at any level of authority will follow a perfect downward path commensurate with the organizational chart or the hierarchy of authority. Interdepartmental communications may occur among supervisors with common statuses or among lower-level personnel from one department or division to another. It is virtually impossible to restrict information transmission to formal communication channels. Rumors can spread throughout an organization by word of mouth on the basis of something overheard or seen by any individual. There may be no immediately apparent pattern to such information distributions on an informal basis.

Apart from informal and formal communication networks which function to disseminate information to various positions within the organization, other forms of information "processing" are frequently used, sometimes simultaneously with these. An organization may publish a periodic newsletter announcing recent organizational developments, promotions among staff members, departmental reorganizations, and anticipated technological changes. Of course, organizations which are housed under a single roof (as opposed to organizations with numerous divisions spatially separated from one another or located in different geographical regions) may convey information to members by assembling them together in a large conference room. The president, the administrative officer, or some other high-level functionary may address the entire group directly. Usually, conferences such as these involve the organization at large and do not pertain to a specific unit or department apart from the others. A hospital administrator may notify all hospital personnel of plans for new hospital additions or the anticipated implementation of new procedural rules for the admission and care of patients. A warden of a penitentiary may inform all guards in a general conference about new policies relating to the processing and handling of inmates or to correctional reforms to be instituted. Of course, interoffice memos, letters, telephone calls within and between organizations, and so on, are alternative means of transmitting information from one point to another.

Besides reviewing some of the salient literature currently available which describes communication within organizations, this chapter seeks to (1) delineate the functions and dysfunctions of both formal and informal communication networks within organizations; (2) compare and contrast formal and informal communication networks and their complementarity and conflict; (3) examine the impact of various factors upon different kinds of communication networks in organizations and how such factors modify their nature; and (4) determine some of the more important implications of different communication forms and processes for an organization's effectiveness and ability to attain its goals.

FORMAL COMMUNICATION NETWORKS

Max Weber originally outlined a plan for maximizing organizational effectiveness and efficiency. His bureaucratic model of organizations (see Chapter 2) made elaborate provisions for the ordering of social relations necessary for the most rapid and perfect means of goal attainment. An apparently crucial component of the "ideal" bureaucratic organization was impersonal, impartial, and strict obedience to a system of abstract rules by individuals at each level in the hierarchy of authority. Communication between departments within an organization was to be exclusively task-related and was essential as a part of the processes leading to success and progress.

But as our discussion of some of the primary weaknesses of the bureaucratic model revealed earlier, seldom, if ever, do organizations succeed fully in fostering completely impersonal relations among members in any division or department or at any level of authority. The inevitability of interpersonal associations unrelated to work and simple verbal exchanges between persons on the job concerning matters or incidents completely unrelated to any of their work tasks is well documented. Barnard (1938:121-122), for example, was one of the first to acknowledge this fact in the social scientific literature. He states that

> informal organizations as associated with formal organization, though often understood intuitively by managers, politicians, and other organization authorities, have only been definitely studied, so far as I know, at the production level of organizations. In fact, informal organization is so much a part of our matter-of-course intimate experience of everyday association, either in connection with formal organizations or not, that we are unaware of it, seeing only a part of the specific interactions involved. Yet it is evident that association of persons in connection with a formal or specific activity inevitably involves interactions that are incidental to it.

Selznick (1966:251) also makes explicit the emergence of social aggregates apart from the formal organizational arrangement of things. He specifies that "an informal structure within the organization . . . will reflect the spontaneous efforts of individuals and subgroups to control the conditions of their existence." He argues that persons will resist being treated as cogs in the organizational machinery and will manifest their uniqueness as individuals as opposed to behaving in the "expected" fashion as automatons. In a later section of this chapter we will examine closely informal organizational interactions and their relative importance for ongoing formal activities.

Bearing in mind the simultaneous existence of informal communication networks in organizations, we first turn our attention toward the formalized aspects of the communication process. At the outset we should recognize that because there are many kinds of organizations, it is unlikely that a particular communication network common to one type of organization (e.g., a social welfare agency) will necessarily be applicable to all other types (e.g., prisons, petroleum refineries, fire departments, or schools). We may tentatively conclude that formalized communication networks are essential and important to the perpetuation of all organizations, regardless of their types or sizes. Therefore, it seems proper to focus upon some of the functional concomitants of such networks as they relate to intraorganizational activities.

SOME FUNCTIONS OF FORMAL COMMUNICATION NETWORKS

It seems that the necessity for a formalized communication network increases as the organizational membership increases (i.e., as organizational size increases). Some earlier sociological thought on this subject tends to be supportive of this statement. For example, Spencer (1898) and Simmel (1903) both argued that an increase in an organization's size requires more complex and hence more formalized communication patterns. What functions, then, do such formalized communication networks serve? There are several answers to this question. Some of the more important functions of formal communications systems are listed below.

Formal communication networks facilitate the coordination of work activity which constitutes the division of labor within an organization. As the organizational membership grows and the tasks performed become increasingly diversified and specialized, communication is necessary to coordinate these various tasks with one another. Consider the potential chaos which would result if formalized communication networks did not exist within a large automobile assembly plant. Departments A, B, C, D, . . . N manufacture different automobile components A', B', C', D', . . . N'. How is department A supposed to know how many A's should be produced to accompany the number of items produced by departments B and C? Different departments responsible for ordering bolts and nuts of specific sizes and in sufficient quantities for divisions where such items are used in each phase of automobile assembly would be in a quandary if any of the bolts and nuts ordered were of the wrong size. In fact, the entire organization could be brought to an absolute standstill if a particular bolt's diameter was off by as little as 1/64 inch. Interdepartmental coordination is especially important as precision demands (e.g., in manufacturing organizations) are increased to higher levels. Formal communication channels convey information from one level of authority to another and from one department to another. Each department is presented with a picture of what other departments are doing in relation to it. Accordingly, departmental planning and action are improved considerably.

Directly related to the first function described above, formal communication networks provide the feedback necessary to stabilize task performance. Feedback is the assessment by certain departments of the quality and quantity of work performed by other departments. Such assessments are necessary to give each department (as well as each member within it) impressions and evaluations of output. If feedback from one department to another indicates that something is amiss, mechanisms can be brought into play to identify existing problems and develop solutions for them. Bringing to the attention of department A that item A' is 1/64 inch too small will enable that department to make the necessary mechanical adjustments to manufacture an item A' which is compatible with the items produced by other departments. Imagine some problems a restaurant would encounter if whoever ordered the food were to order 50 pints of some staple (e.g., sour cream) instead of 50 quarts.

Of course, feedback becomes increasingly important to the extent that departments are interdependent. This means, in essence, that in order for department B to perform its functions satisfactorily, it must wait for the work or information to be passed on from department A. If department A has not done a good job with the "product in process," potential frictions will ensue between the two departments. This friction results because department B must either correct the deficiencies of department A (thus slowing down department B's efficiency and possibly getting a low effectiveness rating for it from higher-ups) or send the product in process back to department A to do over (which results in lost time and drops in efficiency ratings for *both* departments).

Stemming in part from the first two functions listed above, formal communication networks enable an organization to decrease waste or spoilage of product, eliminate unnecessary work operations (duplication of function), and improve its overall efficiency and effectiveness. By now it should be clear that perhaps the most important function performed by an effective, formalized communication network is general improvement in organizational effectiveness. And since organizational effectiveness is closely associated with goal attainment, formal communication networks presumably facilitate the achievement of organizational goals. Through feedback and smooth interdepartmental coordination, the primary activities of an organization are completed with little or no difficulty (particularly of an interpersonal nature).

Finally, formal communication networks reinforce or lend strong support to the existing organizational structure and hierarchy of power. The transmission of information to all points in an organization is generally characterized as vertical and downward. The typical pattern is for persons in superior positions to dispense information to subordinate personnel, usually under their direct control in the hierarchy of power. In many respects, knowledge is an important medium of power. Members of organizations who possess information about planned changes or decisions about reorganization by higher-ups pertaining to personnel promotions or transfers or to specialized task requirements are in strategic positions to utilize the information in a manipulative fashion. Deference is afforded to persons with superior knowledge (or simply more knowledge) by other persons who are less aware of the internal affairs of the organization. We have already alluded to the existence of employees' grapevines, or informal communication networks which ignore existing formal means of communication for spreading information. Because of such grapevines, it is quite possible for a person with a low formal job status to possess superior knowledge. Of course, this particular situation would yield the person involved high returns in terms of *informal* status. Although the informal employee's communication network is present in most organizations, formal channels of communication still help to solidify a member's formal status in the hierarchy of authority.

SOME DYSFUNCTIONS OF FORMAL COMMUNICATION NETWORKS

Although formal communication networks appear to be a vital component of organizations because they provide invaluable assistance in the coordination of work activity, convey important information to all sectors of the organization, and enhance smooth relations between departments, there are some inherent limitations and problems associated with such networks. Since the structures of formal communication networks "on paper" so often parallel the formal authority structures of the organizations within which they are found, it is at times questionable which structure (i.e., communication or authority) should be "blamed" for particular intraorganizational problems. At any rate, some of the more important dysfunctions of formal communication networks are outlined below.

Formal communication networks are sometimes criticized for disseminating important information too slowly. Military personnel are quite familiar with the delays encountered in the formalized communication network in bringing to their attention matters such as authorizations for "early outs" (sometimes a branch of the service will allow enlisted men to shorten the length of their enlistment by as much as six months in order for them to enroll at a university or college by a certain date), transfer to other duties or bases (fields, sites, posts), or promotions. The speed with which information is transmitted becomes crucial to the extent that the information is significant in affecting the roles of various subordinates or total departments.

The speed of the flow of information through formal communication channels can become a critical factor. A hospital situation is a good case in point. In order for a nurse to give a patient a particular kind of injection (possibly requested by the patient or determined to be necessary by the nurse or attendant), permission must be obtained from the physician assigned to the patient. Frequently, prolonged delays are encountered while various personnel attempt to locate the physician in question. It is possible that during such periods of delay, the patient may die or develop a more serious condition.

Formal communication networks are traditionally conceived as channeling information vertically and downward. This statement follows Weber's bureaucratic organizational model, which has been popularized in the literature and which specifies the rationality of superior to subordinate communication flow. However, in instances where subordinates are in positions of expertise in relation to their superiors, formal communication networks are, at times, dysfunctional. Blau (1968) takes the position that experts as subordinates are in more strategic positions to know what is going on with respect to their own work than their immediate superiors. Scientific research might be an example of a situation in which communication flow would be more meaningful if it were to emanate from the lower positions (in this case, "expert positions") upward toward higher-level supervisors. Blau (1968:458–459) notes the importance of such upward flow of communication from experts "not alone because experts tend to be more alienated by one-sided directives but because they make greater contributions through feedback than persons with poorer qualifications." No doubt the nature of the information being communicated would be an important consideration here. If it is assumed that information generated from upper echelons to lower ones is work-related and affects the quality or quantity of the final product, the dysfunctional implications of downward communication flows are quite understandable. However, if the information generated is of an innocuous nature with respect to the outcome of the product, this would not be a meaningful criticism. Brewer (1971:483) has investigated the nature of communication flow and superior-subordinate expertise. He concludes that "the need for upward communication appears to be high only when there is high differentiation of superior and subordinate roles which removes the superior from first-hand contact with operating problems and from close contact with his subordinates."

Formal communication networks are inherently strained. Interdepartmental contacts are inevitable in organizations if effectiveness is to be achieved and maintained. Although feedback from one department to another or from one echelon to another often lessens the potential for friction and strain, a certain amount of intraorganizational strain is consistently observed in most, if not all, organizations (possibly a result of interactions between departments as well). Georgopoulos and Tannenbaum (1957:535–540) have defined intraorganizational strain as "the incidence of tension or conflict existing between organizational subgroups." In their study of an industrial service specializing in the delivery of retail merchandise, they found that intraorganizational strain was an important factor in the effectiveness of the organization. They defined effectiveness of organization as the "extent to which an organization, as a social system, fulfills its objectives without incapitating its means and resources and without placing undue strain upon its members."

As one important criterion of organizational effectiveness, intraorganizational strain is contingent, in part, upon the nature of the formal communication network. Stymne (1968) has investigated the relation between interdepartmental communication and intraorganizational strain in the home office of a large chemical firm in the United States. Preceding a discussion of the study results, Stymne notes that "the description of a social structure can generally be said to include an account of the constituent units and of the relations between them. In describing the structure of formal organizations, the flows of information or material can represent the relations between the roles" (p. 82). He states, "The communication system is of decisive importance to the functioning of an organization as a goal-oriented system. Traditionally it has also held a position of prime importance in the relevant fields of research. The communication network can . . . be seen as a number of interdependent organizational units" (p. 85). In particular, Stymne focuses upon the coordination of decision making and resource allocation as major communication functions. Intraorganizational strain "consists of tension and mutual stress between different units in the same organization" (p. 86).

The primary argument is that the importance of each unit of an organization is different from that of the other units. One implication of the evident inequality of, and necessity for, intradepartmental contact is, according to Stymne, that "differences in influence between units of equal formal importance will generate strain in communications" (p. 88) and that "strain will arise in the communications between two units if one of them has to control the other without the control being properly legitimized" (p.89). The findings seem to support these arguments, although not strongly. In conclusion, Stymne makes an interesting remark about the "inevitability of strain" within organizations: "A certain minimum level of intraorganizational strain is probably to be found in all organizations. Moreover, too little strain is likely to have a negative effect on the functioning of the organization" (p. 96).

Within the framework of the traditional orientation toward organizational structure (usually depicted by Weber's bureaucratic model), formal communication networks are necessary for several reasons. Attainment of goals, interdepartmental coordination of work activities, and a general reinforcement of the formal authority arrangement are several "positive" outcomes of the formalized flow of information through specific communication "terminals." The ultimate objective and the underlying theme of this entire discussion seems to focus on organizational effectiveness. Ideally, adhering to the formal communication network prescribed by organizational leaders will have predictably favorable consequences for effectiveness. However, as we have seen above, there are conditions accompanying formal communication networks which make it somewhat difficult always to achieve the desired degree of organizational effectiveness. Some of the dysfunctional concomitants of formal communication networks are the slowness of information dissemination, the lack of important feedback, especially in the case of experts placed in low-level hierarchical positions (e.g., researchers in a government laboratory or a comparable institution), and of course, the so-called "inevitable" intraorganizational and interdepartmental strains. One of the natural strategies characteristic of organizational members, which serves to overcome formal communication dissatisfactions and problems, is the informal communication network.

ON INFORMAL COMMUNICATION PATTERNS: THEIR ORIGIN, FUNCTIONS, AND DYSFUNCTIONS

Organizational researchers will probably acknowledge that one of the most important and irritating intervening variables affecting their investigations of relations between organizational phenomena is the presence of an informal group structure distinct from the one which is formally defined. We have already alluded to informal work aggregates in organizations and to some of the behaviors exhibited by them which place administrators in positions of consternation and conflict. That informal groups exist and exert important influence over the affairs of the organization at large is not in question. We may concern ourselves with how they come into being and, more importantly, with why they appear to persist in virtually every type of organization irrespective of size and shape or degree of formality. These are, correspondingly, questions of (1) origin and (2) function. Both questions have been given considerable attention in the professional literature during the past forty years.[2] Of course, in this particular section we are concerned about informal groups insofar as they relate to or interact with formal communication networks and the outcomes and implications of such interactions. But a brief discussion of the origin of informal groups will be useful regarding their subsequent communicative behaviors in formal organizational settings.

The Nature of the Origin of Informal Communication Networks in Organizations

Delbecq (1968) has provided us with a provocative essay on the evolution of informal organization in formal settings. He suggests that:

> attractions and repulsions occur among individual members of an organization, often under conditions of short-lived acquaintanceship. Moreover, individual sociometrically isolated choice patterns are shown in a number of studies to persist over time, and even to become more apparent. Therefore, we can talk of the configuration of such choice patterns as an element of informal group structure, and of such group structures as part of the informal-organization overlay which permeates formal organizational decision-making [pp. 17–18].

Delbecq isolates the following factors, which he notes are apparently salient in the evolution of informal groups on the job: (1) proximity, (2) similarities or attractiveness in terms of work activities, interest or values shared, complementary personality profiles, and individual social characteristics (social class, status, rank, etc.) (pp. 17-18).

Considering these factors operating simultaneously within the formal organizational environment, Delbecq is saying, in essence, that persons who work closely with one another (i.e., in proximity) and perform similar tasks will likely share certain interests or values. To the extent that the persons involved develop a liking for one another and that social class or one's formal position in relation to another is not an overt factor in the social relation, informal collectivities will arise and persist.

Homans (1950) has developed a model of group behavior and interaction which appears to coincide with the prominent factors cited by Delbecq. Homan's model (applied to formal and informal intraorganizational activity) contains three basic terms which are of importance to us. These are (1) interactions, (2) activities, and (3) sentiments. Although Homans developed more thoroughly the interrelationships among these factors in an elaborate theoretical scheme, a perhaps oversimplified version of their relations and application to the origin of informal groups may be stated as follows: Persons who interact frequently with one another are more likely to develop similar interests and sentiments compared with those who interact less frequently. Persons who perform similar or identical activities are likewise disposed to develop similar outlooks toward things. The reciprocal impact of one factor upon each of the others functions to reinforce the social bond which emerges and persists.

Informal groups do not necessarily have to perform the same activities on the job, nor do they have to be of the same socioeconomic level in terms of their occupational affiliations. But the similarities of tasks performed and the frequency of interaction of these individuals on the job daily enhances the solidarity of their informal social bond rather than detracting from it.

Selznick (1966:251-253) is particularly helpful in elaborating the formation and persistence of informal groups in formal organizations. In an attempt to portray the most salient dimensions which should be considered in the development of a formal theory of organizations, Selznick identifies some preliminary and fundamental elements:

1. All formal organizations are molded by forces tangential to their rationally ordered structures and stated goals. Every formal organization—trade union, political party, army, corporation, etc.—attempts to mobilize human and technical resources as means for the achievement of its ends. However, the individuals within the system tend to resist being treated as means. They interact as wholes, bringing to bear their own special problems and purposes; moreover, the organization is imbedded in an institutional matrix and is therefore subject

to pressures upon it from its environment, to which some general adjustment must be made. As a result, the organization may be significantly viewed as an adaptive social structure, facing problems which arise simply because it exists as an organization in an institutional environment, independently of the special (economic, military, political) goals which called it into being. 2. It follows that there will develop an informal structure within the organization which will reflect the spontaneous efforts of individuals and subgroups to control the conditions of their existence. There will also develop informal lines of communication and control to and from other organizations within the environment. It is to these informal relations and structures that the attention of the sociologist will be primarily directed. He will look upon the formal structure, e.g., the official chain of command, as the special environment within and in relation to which the informal structure is built. He will search out the evolution of formal relations out of the informal ones. 3. The informal structure will be at once indispensable to and consequential for the formal system of delegation and control itself. Wherever command over the responses of individuals is desired, some approach in terms of the spontaneous organization of loyalty and interest will be necessary. In practice this means that the informal structure will be useful to the leadership and effective as a means of communication and persuasion. At the same time, it can be anticipated that some price will be paid in the shape of a distribution of power or adjustment of policy. 4. Adaptive social structures are to be analyzed in structural-functional terms. This means that contemporary and variable behavior is related to a presumptively stable system of needs and mechanisms. Every such structure has a set of basic needs and develops systematic means of self-defense. Observable organizational behavior is deemed explained within this frame of reference when it may be interpreted (and the interpretation confirmed) as a response to specific needs. Where significant, the adaptation is dynamic in the sense that the utilization of self-defensive mechanisms results in structural transformations of the organization itself. The needs in question are organizational, not individual, and include: the security of the organization as a whole in relation to social forces in its environment; the stability of the lines of authority and communication; the stability of informal relations within the organization; the continuity of policy and of the sources of its determination; a homogeneity of outlook with respect to the meaning and role of the organization. 5. Analysis is directed to the internal relevance of organizational behavior. The execution of policy is viewed in terms of its effect upon the organization itself and its relations with others. This will tend to make the analysis inadequate as a report of program achievement, since that will be deemphasized in the interests of the purely organizational consequences of choice among alternatives in discretionary action. 6. Attention being focused on the structural conditions which influence behavior, we are directed to emphasize constraints, the limitation of alternatives imposed by the system upon its participants. This will tend to give pessimistic overtones to the analysis, since such factors as good will and intelligence will be deemphasized. 7. As a consequence of the central status of constraint, tensions and dilemmas will be highlighted. Perhaps the most general source of tension and paradox in this context may be expressed as the recalcitrance of the tools of action. Social action is always mediated by human structures, which generate new centers of need and power and interpose themselves between the actor and his goal. Commitments to others are indispensable in action: at the same time, the process of commitment results in tensions which have always to be overcome.

For our purposes it is crucial to recognize the importance Selznick attaches to the informal group structure as a system of delegation and control through communication and persuasion. This is apart from (but perhaps natural to and complementary to) channels of formal authority and communication. Informal groupings of employees, then, are common to most, if not all, formal organizations. We are sensitive to the fact that informal groups in any work context perform innumerable functions (as well as dysfunctions) which influence the formal organizational arrangement of things as well as the sentiments and behaviors of members of such informal aggregates. We will now direct our attention toward the communication dimension of intra-organizational behavior and its interaction with informal employees' collectivities.

Some Important Functions of Informal Groups for Communication Networks

The interactions of employees on the job are, for the most part, related to their work tasks. In many organizations employees are formally reprimanded for exchanging comments with one another about matters unrelated to the job, although under certain conditions (e.g., in large offices) it is difficult for supervisors to distinguish between contacts which are "official" and those which are "unofficial." But regardless of the rigidity of supervisory control over verbal interactions, it is usually the case that employees (or volunteers) are able to get by with so-called "informal interactions" (i.e., communication unrelated to the job). Such informal interactions may occur at coffee breaks or lunch periods or during actual work activities. At these times information is exchanged concerning a variety of topics.

In a study of the introduction of electronic data processing (EDP) in a bank, Champion (1966a) found that the informal groups existing in the departments to be affected were helpful in certain ways, especially in relation to employees' anxieties concerning what to expect with the new EDP system. An obvious discrepancy existed between what the supervisor (in charge of implementing the changeover) believed she had told employees about what to expect and what the employees said they had been told. For instance, at the outset, the operations officer (the supervisor in charge of the installation) conferred with other bank officials and helped to determine what kind of processing system to introduce as a means of increasing banking efficiency as well as improving and expanding the flexibility of customer services. The lower-level bank members, including the women in this study (consisting of thirty-one female operations staff members), first became aware of a possible future change through informal channels of communication. The changeover to EDP was later announced officially to the entire staff, and a tentative date was set for the new installation.

This announcement generated a series of questions, mostly pertaining to which jobs the machines would eventually replace or modify and whether the staff would be reduced. As a part of the orientation phase of the changeover, the operations officer assured each employee in an official meeting that no one would lose her job. In addition to the official announcement and reassurances of continuing employment after the installation of EDP, the officers of the bank provided films at subsequent staff meetings which showed similar installations in operation in New York and other large cities. In spite of the information provided by the bank officers, there were mixed reactions among the staff to the changeover. One bookkeeper said, "I was concerned with what my job was going to be. I think everybody was." When asked if the computer system would replace many people at the bank, another bookkeeper replied, "They said it wouldn't. They [the bank officers] said they wouldn't let anybody go, or fire anybody or anything like that. But at first I thought . . . I didn't know where they were going to put all of those people [remaining after the changeover]." Another bookkeeper expressed a contrasting reaction: "No, I'm not worried about it [the changeover]. They told us that they would not fire anyone, and keep everybody here . . . unless the person just wants to quit."

The operations officer insisted that she had fully informed all personnel about what to expect with respect to the changeover. She believed the films and discussions to be adequate psychological preparations. During and shortly after the changeover, several staff members (responding to personal interviews by this researcher) made comments which indicated that they were not adequately informed as to what was going on. One bookkeeper said, "Everybody hates it [the EDP system] with a passion. I imagine when it starts running smoothly, they will like it, though." Another added, "Well, some call it a big mess. But really, sometimes it's pretty difficult. The changeover brought about problems. . . . On statements day we had to stay here until 1:00 in the morning. We had to balance four books to one total. That took quite a while." A supervisor who overheard other staff members conversing about the change commented, "They [the other staff members] think it is stupid. They don't think it is going to do what it is supposed to do. They have yet to see the day when it'll replace us. There are a lot of remarks being made."

Several employees continued to remark on the fact that they were not being kept informed. A bookkeeper said, "We don't know from one minute to the next what is going on. . . . We may know five minutes before our job will probably be changed. That's another thing I hate about it. They should tell us what we are going to do . . . prepare us; like I never knew that I was going to get this other girl's assignments." The operator of a proof machine stated, "It frightens me when you are asked to do a new job all of a sudden. I wanted to stay in my old department." And one of the supervisors commented, when asked how well she was kept informed as to the way the EDP system would change her own job, "To answer that honestly might mean my job. Because they don't tell us things. Really, they don't. We should be shown. . . . We have never been shown really the different steps [in performing certain tasks related to the EDP system]. And of course they may think that we see right there in the department, but we don't have time to watch it."[3]

The amount of information each employee received appeared to be one of the most significant factors affecting her reaction to change. The information which related directly to their jobs was used in determining each employee's degree of role clarity (i.e., how much each person knows about her own job expectations). There is evidence from this study to support the notion that the informal group was instrumental in providing an information medium whereby anxieties and tensions were lessened, at least for some of the employees who were part of it.

It should not be inferred from this discussion that the mere existence and provision of information will allay fears and anxieties of employees in organizations where changes are anticipated or implemented. Information is similar to a double-edged sword: it cuts both ways. Distorted or incorrect information disseminated extensively throughout the organization by the grapevine may have many deleterious effects upon staff members. Ultimately it depends upon the accuracy of the information transmitted and the extent to which the information is "threatening" to staff members (i.e., the extent to which it means changes in their jobs with which they cannot cope, adjustments in hours of work which will impose hardships, or even loss of their jobs).

In the operations division (the target of change), sociometric charts revealed the existence of several informal groups apart from the formal organizational arrangement.[4] In subsequent interviews with employees, it became apparent to the researcher that although there were, indeed, several informal aggregates among the thirty-one employees, only one was singled out as being extremely cohesive. This so-called "cohesive" group (and several members of the operations division both inside and outside of this group referred to it as "cohesive" in interviews) consisted of eight proof-machine

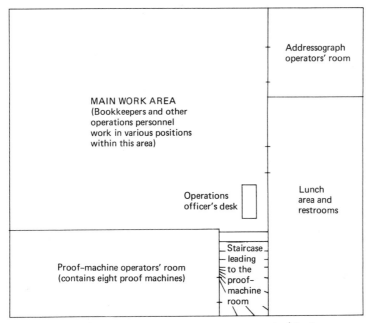

Figure 8-1 A diagram of the operations division showing the locations of various staff positions.

operators. These operators were spatially segregated from the main work area of the operations division. Figure 8-1 shows the general work arrangement before the changeover.

Under these conditions, the sharing of information about changes in jobs and other matters was an integral feature of their association with one another (again, supported by personal interviews), while other employees did not enjoy the advantages of an efficient grapevine system to the same degree.

In order to determine some of the implications of membership in the clique, or informal group, of proof-machine operators, several variables were selected which figured prominently in the changeover to the new EDP system. These factors were (1) role clarity, (2) level of information, and (3) anxiety. Table 8-1 compares the mean scores for each of these three factors for the cohesive group (eight proof-machine operators) and the rest of the staff involved in the change. Measures for each of the three variables were taken for all employees in the operations division both before and after the changeover to EDP. In each instance, the larger the score, the greater the presence of the particular variable. (For example, an information score of 9.57 compared with an information score of 9.00 would mean that, on the average, the employees with the mean score of 9.57 had greater information

Table 8-1   A Comparison of Role Clarity, Information, and Anxiety Scores (Averages) for Cohesive Group Members and Other Staff Before and After a Change-over to Electronic Data Processing

Cohesive group				Main staff		
Before change	N = 8	After change	Variable	Before change	N = 23	After change
$\bar{X}$		$\bar{X}$		$\bar{X}$		$\bar{X}$
40.00		36.43	Role clarity	34.50		33.93
9.14		9.57	Information	9.73		9.00
19.14		16.42	Anxiety	17.22		17.60

Source: Dean J. Champion, "Role Change in a Bank: Some Consequences of Automation," unpublished doctoral dissertation, Lafayette, Ind., Purdue University, 1965.

or at least *perceived* that they had greater information than those with an average score of 9.00.)

Briefly summarizing the information presented in Table 8-1, the changeover caused a general decrease in role clarity for both groups, although the cohesive group was significantly higher in both time periods. The level of information from one time period to the next (before and after the changeover) increased for the cohesive group but decreased substantially for the other staff members. As to the anxiety variable, although the cohesive group appeared to have higher anxiety than the main body of staff members before the change (possibly because of the potential disruption of their strong bond), anxiety decreased significantly for the cohesive group after the changeover. Anxiety scores for the remaining staff members increased from one time period to the next, however. In fact, after the changeover, the cohesive group members had, on the average, lower anxiety scores compared with rest of the staff. These findings lead us to at least one tentative conclusion about the function of informal (and cohesive) groups, at least in this particular instance. *Informal groups provide a channel of communication apart from formal structure which supplies employees with information concerning changes in jobs and other important matters affecting them.* In the study reported above, it was clear that the informal group was instrumental in providing its members with information about their jobs and future changes which lessened their anxieties. They shared more information compared with other staff members and they exhibited higher role clarity. These conditions are directly attributable to the communication function which the group served.

Informal groups also provide more rapid means of disseminating information compared with "official channels" of formal organization. The fact that the staff members at lower levels knew about the proposed changeover to the new EDP system before the official announcement by bank officials gives us some idea as to the rapidity with which information (and rumor) spreads. Roethlisberger (1941) has emphasized the importance of informal social communication systems in making the difference between successful or unsuccessful programs of job change initiated by administrators and passed on to lower-level personnel by formal means. He argues that if management fails to understand its entire social structure (including the informal complement), then it does itself and the organization a disservice regarding its overall effectiveness.

A sentiment consistent with Roethlisberger's, but dating from some years before his work, is that of Barnard (1938). In his classic work, *The Functions of the Executive,* Barnard has written about the indispensability of informal groups in organizations with respect to performing a communication function. He maintains that informal groups are not only necessary in this respect but that they function to promote group cohesiveness and preserve the integrity of the individual. In an increasingly bureaucratized organizational environment, it is not difficult to see the utility and logic of Barnard's statements.

The informal group is more flexible than the formal organization as a communication medium. If formal communication networks are blocked for one reason or another (if one person at a higher level fails to pass on information to a subordinate because of forgetfulness or intentional withholding of it), the informal grapevine will usually become aware of the information some other way.

The transmission of information through informal channels of communication may be of benefit to organizational members on many occasions, but sometimes the network of informal interaction functions to their detriment. According to Sykes (1958:87), "the flow of information in any social group is always imperfect, if we define perfect communication as the transmission of all information to all group members with equal speed and without error."

Some Dysfunctions of Informal Communication Networks

Apart from the fact that the informal group "competes" with the formal communication network for the transmission of information and, possibly, for power, it is inevitable that at some point in time, a breakdown in communication or some distortion in the transmission of information will occur.

Informal communication networks are dysfunctional to the extent that distorted or wrong information is disseminated to group members. Whenever rumors circulate from one person to another, there is evidence to indicate that, because each person interprets the message differently, a transformation of information (rumor) will occur. By the time the original information reaches its intended audience through the informal grapevine, there are strong possibilities that such information has undergone some distortion depending upon the nature of the information flow (Roger Brown, 1965:756–759; Newcomb, Turner, and Converse, 1965:73).[5] Caplow (1964:252–253) also calls our attention to the potential distortion of information in organizational communication networks, whether they be formal or informal. He says, "All organizational networks have mechanical defects so that messages go astray, lag excessively, are misunderstood or distorted without any intention. In the admirable jargon of cybernetics, any message includes a component of noise."

Distorted rumors transmitted by informal grapevines to organizational members can lead to all kinds of serious outcomes. Misunderstandings between superiors and subordinates (latent or expressed) can foster apathy among employees and deliberate slowdowns or absenteeism. To the extent that distortions of information are perceived as bringing about changes in one's job, employee fears and anxieties are aroused, and the workers lose trust in those over them. Another concomitant of distortion of information may be resistance to change or new programs introduced by higher-ups.[6] Although subsequent formal channels of communication may provide the members of the organization with accurate information, sufficient damage may already have been inflicted upon organizational effectiveness.

An alternative communication network in relation to the formal communication network can be a deterrent to effective norm enforcement and supervisory authority. The informal communication network may be viewed as a parallel set of power relations, where knowledge of organizational events is a tool of manipulation over others. Formally authorized or legitimized officials are placed in awkward and humiliating positions when they discover that information about organizational affairs, particularly knowledge common only to their levels of authority and supposedly confined within their office boundaries, has become available to lower-level participants or subordinate personnel without their awareness. Under such circumstances it is likely that supervisors and other functionaries feel that their authority has been undermined, and the importance of their official position in the eyes of their subordinates wanes substantially.

A NOTE ON THE COMPLEMENTARITY OF FORMAL AND INFORMAL COMMUNICATION NETWORKS

A generally accepted phenomenon is that formal organizations are always accompanied by informal groupings of employees or members. We have seen in the previous discussions that both formal and informal organizational structures tend to generate parallel communication networks, authority patterns, and, perhaps, reward systems. Problems are encountered when information is transmitted too slowly through official formal channels or when the information disseminated by either the formal or informal communication network becomes distorted as it is passed on from person to person, from position to position, and from level to level.

Communication is vital to the organization. A sound communication system may help significantly to promote organizational effectiveness, whereas a communication network with several defects and limitations will tend to deter the organization from achieving its goals satisfactorily. For many years, managers of large firms and business administrators have analyzed the problems of communication in organization from diverse points of view. For example the presence and significance of informal groups in organizations must be considered as equally important with the formal arrangement of the hierarchy of authority and the communication network. The inevitability that both kinds of "organization" will exist under one roof simultaneously makes it mandatory that we take into account the theoretical and substantive complementarity of these structures in our organizational research. Figure 8-2 illustrates the interplay between formal and informal communication networks as well as showing other salient factors which act conjointly upon the formalized flow of information.

The variables shown in Figure 8-2 are certainly not exhaustive when we consider all potential factors which could exert an effect upon the formal communication network. Formal organizational structures are dynamic entities, as are their dimensions and attributes. As one significant attribute, the communication network of an organization is impermanent and transitory. It is a malleable dimension responsive to changes in many organizational variables. We must consider the nature and effectiveness of it within the context of change. Organizational effectiveness, evaluated according to the type of organization under investigation, is most often a major dependent variable in relation to the communication network and its nature.

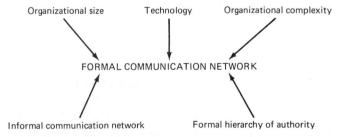

Figure 8-2 The impact of several important variables and conditions on the formal communications network of an organization.

Whyte (1969:70-72) has cautioned that research on formal and informal organizations may impose misleading dichotomous distinctions upon us. He states that "in fact, it may be a characteristic of the most effective superior-subordinate relationships that formal and informal elements are inextricably mixed." In essence, Whyte suggests that in order to understand organizational behavior more fully, we should pay attention to the discrepancy between what the management of an organization says should be going on according to written rules or stated ones and what the employees or organizational members are actually doing. He adds that "any attempt to divide all of behavior into formal and informal categories is bound to lead to confusion."

A study of the intraorganizational behavior of newsmen in a large newspaper office seems to be supportive of Whyte's statements. Breed (1955) investigated so-called "formal" and "informal" behaviors of staff members, including reporters, rewrite men, copyreaders, and others. In the course of his study, he discovered that almost all newspapers have policies which are set by executives but seldom overtly conveyed to the staffers. The observance of company policy by any staffer is based upon the "socialization" he receives from his peers. In addition, there are informal "wrist slaps" or reprimands from superiors whenever a staffer does something he isn't supposed to do (e.g., writing a story which assigns fault for some community problem to a particular city official who happens to be a friend of the newspaper publisher or editor). The newspaper office setting is unique because few overt norms are present. Rules are, for the most part, implicit, and sanctions are doled out in very unobtrusive ways (e.g., editors can ignore stories or assign "safe" staffers to cover a sensitive event of a political or social nature). Breed states that "fear of sanctions" rather than their invocation is the primary reason for conformity to the norms of the newspaper organization. This is, indeed, a clear case of an inextricable blend of formal and informal intraorganizational activity.

In his study of the inmates' culture in a maximum-security prison, Sykes (1958) has also illustrated the apparent inseparability of formal and informal communication networks and conformity to norms. He says, "It is the structure of social relationships formed by imprisoned criminals which concerns us; an inmate may enter these relationships in a variety of capacities for varying periods of time, but it is the structure itself which lays the main claim on our attention." (p. 106). He describes a prison system wherein formal codes of conduct are prescribed. But he carefully notes that without inmate cooperation (i.e., informal sub rosa exchanges of favors, goods, and services between guard and guarded), it would be all but impossible to maintain stability within the prison system. The communication system within informal inmate culture is a highly efficient vehicle for transmitting information about a variety of things. Necessarily, guards grudgingly participate and collaborate with prisoners so that the prison will retain a high degree of equilibrium. Sykes adds that

> the greater the extent of "cohesive responses"—the greater the degree to which the society of captives moves in the direction of inmate solidarity—the greater is the likelihood that the pains of imprisonment will be rendered less severe for the inmate population as a whole . . . [and] . . . inmate solidarity, in the form of "sharing" or a reciprocity of gifts and favors, attacks one of the most potent sources of aggression among prisoners, the drive for material betterment by means of force or fraud [p. 107].

Sykes describes in amazing detail the nature of the complementarity between formal and informal prison culture within the broader context of organizational change. The following is an exemplary statement to that effect:

> The balance struck between the theoretical extremes of perfect solidarity and a war of all against all is, then, of vital significance—not only to the prison officials but to the inmates as well. This balance point, however, is not fixed. Rather, it represents a compromise of a host of competing forces which change through time and thus the structure of social relationships formed by imprisoned criminals is in a constant state of flux. These shifts in the balance point between cohesion and alienation among inmates are in turn part of a larger series of changes embracing the prison as a whole. In short, the social system of the New Jersey State Prison, like every social system, is marked by social change and it is only by examining the nature of this change that we can come to a full understanding of the society of captives [p. 108].

SUMMARY

Communication networks are necessary for the survival of any organization, regardless of its degree of formalization. In many respects, the configuration of communication networks is as varied from one organization to another as is the configuration of hierarchies of authority. Davis and Scott (1969:255) have underscored the significance of communication networks by noting that without them there can be no organization.

This chapter has described certain functions and dysfunctions of two major communication networks—formal and informal. Formal communication networks are usually closely aligned with hierarchies of authority, and often such networks can be portrayed graphically on paper by lines connecting various roles and departments. Simultaneously, informal networks of communication exist. Such networks appear to emerge spontaneously, but a close inspection might reveal more integration and systematization than is apparent at first glance. Selznick (1966) has emphasized the inevitability of informal communication networks in organizations. He has also called our attention to some of the potential modifications informal groups in general (and their communication channels in particular) can engender within formal communication networks and overall organizational structure.

Formal communication networks or channels contribute to greater coordination between tasks and departmental functions, to greater feedback between departments and up and down the hierarchy of authority, to improved performance and better organizational effectiveness, and to a perpetuation and solidification of existing organizational structure. Such networks, however, have been criticized for disseminating information to departments too slowly. This criticism has no doubt provided support or a raison d'être for informal communication networks, whose members take great pride in passing on information from higher echelons with greater dispatch. A counterargument has been that informal communication channels are inadequate for accurate distribution of information, and too much distortion of fact occurs in the process of passing on information from one department to another.

Regardless of whether informal and formal communication networks are compatible or incompatible, the fact that both networks exist is unquestioned. We must learn to appreciate the functions (and dysfunctions) of both networks if we are to more fully comprehend what is going on in an organization and why. We cannot afford to simply ignore informal communication networks and hope that they will go away. We must acknowledge their presence and come to grips with the subtle complementarities existing between formal and informal communication networks in organizations.

STUDY QUESTIONS

1   Discuss briefly the complementarity between informal and formal communication systems. How do informal networks interfere with or enhance formal communication networks? Explain.
2   Why is communication important in formal organizations? What are some ways in which information is disseminated to lower-level participants in organizations? Evaluate briefly the potential effectiveness of each.
3   What are some primary functions of formal communication networks? What are some dysfunctions of them? Elaborate.
4   How would you account for the emergence of informal groups in formal organizations? How would you go about evaluating the importance of specific informal groups in relation to decisions you make as a formal organizational authority?
5   Briefly discuss the relation among the interactions, activities, and sentiments of group members and how such factors perpetuate informal aggregates of employees.

6   How can informal communication networks make the difference between successful and unsuccessful programs of job change initiated by administrators and passed on to lower-level personnel? Explain.

7   Briefly assess the potential contributions of experimental studies of communication patterns and decision-making behavior in small groups.

NOTES

[1] For instance, Blau and Schoenherr (1971:5) state that "not everything that goes on in formal organizations follows an explicit design. . . . Within formal organizations informal organizations arise, because the daily social interaction and activities in the various work groups give rise to regularities of their own and thus manifest an implicit social structure."

[2] The classic Hawthorne studies, reported on in Chapter 2 and elaborated by Roethlisberger and Dickson (1939), provide early documentation of the existence of informal work groups. Taking these studies (conducted between 1927 and 1931) as our starting point, we can see a proliferation of material related to informal groups and their functions and dysfunctions emerging in the organizational literature in later years.

[3] It should be noted that what may have been mistaken for a deliberate withholding of knowledge from staff members by the bank officers and the operations officer herself was their own lack of knowledge of what was going on and what changes and innovations would take place. Consequently, many of the decisions and actions of some of the officers were perceived by lower-level personnel as unusual or erratic behavior.

[4] "Sociometry" is a term developed formally by J. L. Moreno (1934). It is designed to reveal information about the interaction of group members (Selltiz et al., 1959:268-269). Questions such as "Whom do you associate with most frequently on the job?" and "Whom do you invite to your home for a social evening among your colleagues or job associates?" are sociometric and are supposed to reflect informal patterns of communication and interaction in the organization in contrast to the formalized arrangement of things.

[5] Some additional sources to consult on the transmission and distortion of rumors are Back, K., et al., "The Methodology of Studying Rumor Transmission," *Human Relations,* **3**:307-312, 1950; Davis, K. (1953); and Knapp, R.H., "A Psychology of Rumor," *Public Opinion Quarterly,* **8**:22-37, 1944.

[6] Resistance to planned organizational change will be discussed in detail in Chapters 10 and 11.

Chapter 9

Motivation, Satisfaction, and Morale of Employees

INTRODUCTION

Organizational effectiveness is, to some degree, dependent upon the work orientations of members and on their successful performance of tasks— whether they be hourly, salaried, or voluntary personnel. The nature and complexity of the hierarchy of authority and the complementarity between formal and informal communication networks are primary considerations as well. Throughout this volume we have continually emphasized the interdependency between so-called "organizational," "interpersonal," and "individual" variables as well as the specific importance of each as a unit of intraorganizational analysis.

Consistent with the above view, this chapter explores the importance of the motivations, job satisfactions, and morale of employees as each supposedly functions in relation to overall organizational effectiveness. Our major focus of attention will be upon some of the more crucial factors which exist in organizations to elicit predictable changes in these variables. Of necessity, we will include in our scope of inquiry the individual organizational member and the attitudes he possesses which influence his work orientations and performance. It is difficult, if not impossible, to gain adequate knowledge of intraorganizational activity without giving some consideration to the psychological attributes and attitudinal perceptions of organizational members. This does not mean that sociological factors in organizations will be ignored. Rather, our intention is to investigate the interplay of sociological and psychological variables insofar as they conjointly contribute to the effectiveness of organizations. The principal objectives of this chapter are (1) to examine some of the salient literature on motivation, job satisfaction, and morale in a variety of organizations and (2) to delineate and discuss some of the more important interrelations between particular organizational, interpersonal, and individual variables and their conjoint action upon personal satisfactions with tasks performed, motivation toward work, and group morale.

ON THE LOGIC OF CONSIDERING PERSONAL
MOTIVATIONS IN ORGANIZATIONAL RESEARCH

An important variable was introduced in an earlier chapter: organizational effectiveness. Although there are certain problems of conceptualization associated with this variable, organizational effectiveness (the degree to which an organization achieves its goals and adapts to its external environment successfully) is the overwhelmingly predominant preoccupation of organizational leaders. The bulk of existing literature pertaining to organizational behavior is directly or indirectly stimulated, in large part, by a generalized concern for organizational effectiveness and its diverse concomitants. Some persons believe that virtually all literature about organizational behavior is designed to provide management with new and more effective means of manipulating the lower-level membership for some kind of personal gain. Although it is true that various benefits accrue to management as the result of much organizational research, it must also be acknowledged that commensurate benefits are obtained by the lower-level membership as well. Strong arguments may be formulated for each view, but it is not our intention to discuss the "goodness" or "badness" of organizational research and its implications in terms of values, for the deliberate manipulation of organizational behavior. Rather, our attention will be directed toward delineating the presence or absence of conditions (i.e., organizational, interpersonal, or individual) which correlate highly with the motivations and satisfactions of employees.

Drawing upon the work of Mahoney and Weitzel (1969), we find that a considerable number of factors associated with organizational effectiveness are identified as individual attitudes and orientations toward the work performed and strong attachments to small work groups. Table 9-1 shows a common approach to organizational effectiveness based upon personal and interpersonal considerations. It is not difficult to follow the logic underlying the relationships portrayed in Table 9-1. The individual is considered by this logic to be the central figure in all functional organizational operations. If certain key factors are introduced, eliminated, or altered in the life space of the individual (i.e., the person's external environment), then it is argued that changes in the individual's psychological disposition will occur. The resulting dispositions will lead to noticeable increases or decreases in individual effectiveness in the performance of tasks. Improvements in the performance of most, if not all, individuals in an organization will generally improve overall organizational effectiveness. Therefore, we find ourselves turning to a fundamental question pertaining to intraorganizational behavior: "What motivates a person to perform tasks with maximum effectiveness?" Almost all organizational research can be seen as providing potential partial answers to this question.

Max Weber's conception (Gerth and Mills, 1946) of an "ideal type" of bureaucratic organization incorporated elements similar to those which will be discussed here. In addition to prescribing the duties and responsibilities of functionaries in a formal hierarchy of authority relations with abstract rules, Weber outlined certain "dispositions" which functionaries should have toward the tasks they perform (e.g., they should view their work as a career or a predominant life activity and manifest strong loyalties toward their employing organization). In Weber's view, the end result of such disposi-

Table 9-1   The Individual and Organizational Effectiveness

Environmental factors as behavioral inputs (e.g., nature and type of supervision, closeness of person to work group, job content, hours of work, perceived and real prestige or rank associated with tasks performed, etc.)

↓

N individual dispositions*

↓

Alterations in N individual dispositions

↓

Task effectiveness improvements

↓

Organizational effectiveness increases

* "N Individual" dispositions refers to a multiplicity of personality or attitudinal attributes which are directed toward what one does within the definition of the work role in an organization. No single attribute or characteristic of individual sentiment or orientation is believed to be a direct causal factor in relation to task effectiveness. Rather, many of these sentiments operating conjointly make up a profile of an individual disposed to improve quality or quantity of performance or both.

tions would be the maximization of organizational effectiveness and efficiency (supposedly achieved by the hiring of "loyal" personnel who are "expert" in specialized spheres of competence and are highly committed to the goals of the organization). As will be seen shortly, this view has some merit and deserves consideration, but it is regarded by many researchers to be an oversimplification of the relation between employee sentiment and overall organizational effectiveness. It seems more productive to regard individual motivations and satisfactions as contributing to rather than determining the effectiveness of organizations. To what extent such factors function to promote greater effectiveness is consistent with one of our chapter objectives.

JOB SATISFACTION AND MOTIVATION OF EMPLOYEES

What is the relation between job satisfaction and motivation to produce in organizations? This question is inevitably asked because there is the prevailing belief that a satisfied employee is a more productive one. Thus far, the evidence supporting this belief is inconclusive, inconsistent, and often contradictory. The formalized search for variables leading to increased job satisfaction (i.e., contentment of employees with a variety of work dimensions) and, presumably, greater productivity is generally acknowledged to have commenced with the Hawthorne studies.[1] It will be recalled that these studies focused upon the manipulation of environmental factors, such as the frequency and length of rest pauses (and the like), insofar as they were observed to be associated with improvements in the performance of tasks by industrial workers in a division of the Western Electric Company (Roethlisberger and Dickson, 1939). One of the more important implications of these studies was that satisfactions were more a function of humane treatment by supervisors and the cohesive relations among workers rather than a function of any specific financial rewards or physical conditions (e.g., rest pauses or temperatures of workrooms). Although numerous statements have been made for and against these studies, the fact remains that the findings (regardless of the degree of their validity) prompted a proliferation of investigations of similar relations among variables in a variety of work settings (Hilgendorf and Irving, 1969:415).

In a way, it is discouraging to report that the accumulation of information on workers' satisfaction with various job dimensions and motivation to produce during the most recent thirty-year period has been descriptive and speculative at best. This unfortunately is true in spite of the fact that much of the research has been largely experimental. Some examples from relatively recent literature should serve to indicate where we stand at present. In a promising article entitled "The New Look in Motivation Theory for Organizational Research," Hunt and Hill (1960) discuss the relative merits of the following motivational schemes: (1) Maslow (1954) sees motivation as a function of the degree to which an organization can meet certain needs which he has postulated to exist in a hierarchy (needs of physiology, safety, belonging, esteem, and self-fulfillment). (2) Herzberg et al. (1959) and Herzberg (1966) advance a dual-factor theory of motivation of workers, a theory which specifies that different factors account for satisfactions ("motivator" factors such as characteristics of job content) as opposed to those factors which stimulate dissatisfactions (e.g., "preventative" factors, including environmental conditions, company policy and administration, status, technical supervision, and interpersonal relations with superiors, subordinates, and peers). (3) Vroom (1964:6) defines motivation as a "process governing choices, made by persons or lower organisms, among alternative forms of voluntary activity" and sees satisfaction with work in terms of the relationship between expectations and outcomes. Hunt and Hill note that, according to Vroom,

> "instead of assuming that satisfaction of a specific need is likely to influence organizational objectives in a certain way, we can find out how important to the employees are the various second-level outcomes (worker goals), the instrumentality of various first-level outcomes (organizational objectives) for their attainment, and the expectancies that are held with respect to the employees' ability to influence the first-level outcomes" [pp. 101—105].

These researchers evidently endorse Vroom's theory of motivation, inasmuch as they present and elaborate on four studies[2] which utilize this model. Their conclusion is of particular interest to us as a reflection of how much more we need to know compared with what is known at present:

> Taken together, the four studies discussed in the previous section [in their article] seem to show that Vroom's model holds great promise for predicting behavior in organizations. There still remain some unanswered questions. We do not know all of the goals that have positive valence in a work situation. We do not know how much of a difference in force is necessary before one kind of outcome is chosen over another. Nor do we know what combination of measures yields the best prediction in a given situation. The answers to these and other questions await further research. . . . More work must be done before we can make any statements concerning the overall validity of Vroom's model. But the rigor of his formulation, the relative ease of making the concepts operational, and the model's emphasis on individual differences show considerable promise. We are also encouraged by the results of relatively sophisticated studies testing the theory. We believe it is time for those interested in organizational behavior to take a more thorough scientific look at this very complex subject of industrial motivation, and Vroom's model seems a big step in that direction [pp. 107-108].

In an article designed to review and assess the literature pertaining to the issues and problems of job satisfaction, Fournet, Distefano, and Pryer

(1966) have surveyed sixty articles and books on the subject. Initially, they noted the difficulty of trying to compare studies of job satisfaction because of the diversity of methodological approaches used and the variations in definitions of key concepts (p. 166). Throughout their work they identify several factors associated with job satisfaction (as identified by different researchers), such as individual differences, age, education and intelligence, sex, occupational level, characteristics of the job, organization and management, immediate supervision, social environment, communication, security, monotony, and pay. As potential consequences of job satisfaction, they cite performance, absenteeism, and turnover as major dependent variables. Again, as with Hunt and Hill (1969) above, their summary is of significance here:

> This article has attempted to survey the literature on job satisfaction published since the review by Brayfield and Crockett (1955). In doing this, a number of salient features were discussed which have substantial influence on the understanding of this important area of worker behavior. The literature on job satisfaction has been developed by use of various experimental methods, each having some effect on the findings. Characteristics of both the individual and the job appear to be related to job satisfaction, but they are intercorrelated to such an extent that it is extremely difficult to isolate them for scientific investigation; in fact, to attempt this isolation may mean the loss of the interaction effect among variables. Similarly, it is difficult at the present time to understand how these factors are related to such behavior as performance, absenteeism, and turnover. Because of this complexity, theoretical attempts to describe job satisfaction have many shortcomings. Many of the formulations which now appear contradictory may eventually be found to be complementary. In spite of the apparent confusion and complexity in job satisfaction as an area of study, there is a large amount of literature emerging which should help to clarify the issues [p. 180].

For further emphasis, a third summarization of findings and general recommendations has been extracted from the work of Mumford (1970). This investigator has proposed that a more appropriate way of defining job satisfaction is "in terms of the degree of 'fit' between organizational demands and individual needs, and that the employee's satisfaction with his job and the employer's satisfaction with work performance will only be high when this fit is a good one" (p. 72). Figure 9-1 shows Mumford's view of various factors as they affect satisfaction. Mumford argues that the approach suggested by Figure 9-1 possesses certain favorable attributes. For instance:

> If employee need dispositions are obtained by means of regular attitude surveys, it becomes possible to check the fit between need dispositions and role

expectations—and thus the level of job satisfaction—and to identify areas where the fit is not good. The next step is to refine this approach in such a way that it can be readily used in firms which are interested in monitoring job satisfaction in staff groups. This will require devising a much broader type of job analysis than is commonly used; one which extends into the environment of the firm and identifies the pressures exerted on role expectations by the product market. It also requires the development of simple survey techniques to ascertain need dispositions, together with tools for monitoring changes in the labour market which are likely to affect need dispositions [p. 99].

The three articles surveyed above should not necessarily be taken as the "final word" on the relation between job satisfaction, motivation, and productivity (performance). Obviously, there are findings from other studies which have not been considered here. We seem to be fairly certain that job satisfaction exerts an impact on motivation, but we are quite uncertain as to how. We are also somewhat confident that a highly motivated worker is

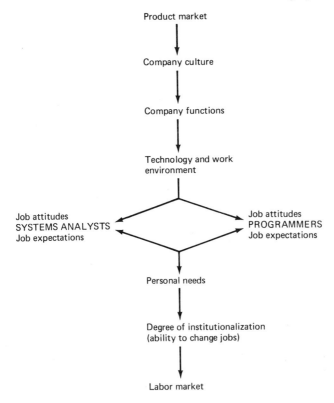

Figure 9-1 Factors influencing job satisfaction. (Mumford, 1970:71-101, especially p. 74.)

likely to be more productive than one who is less motivated. Therefore, within the context of an acknowledged degree of uncertainty surrounding the relationship between satisfaction and motivation, we will proceed to examine what, in our judgement, appear to be some of the more crucial factors associated with these variables.

A REVIEW OF RESEARCH ON JOB SATISFACTION IN ORGANIZATIONS

A common and generally applicable definition of job satisfaction is provided by Vroom (1964:99): "Job satisfaction is the positive orientation of an individual towards the work role which he is presently occupying—which can be restated as an individual liking more aspects of the work than he dislikes."[3] Some of the more fruitful factors affecting job satisfaction which are a part of intraorganizational behavior and which have been investigated as independent variables in relation to this term are (1) style of supervision or leadership, (2) the intrinsic interest of the job, the amount of challenge or change, (3) the cohesiveness or cohesion of work groups (possibly interpersonal conflict or harmony), (4) work load and pressure, (5) the prestige or status of the job in relation to other jobs (possibly involving perceived opportunities for advancement or enlargement of the job, (6) the type of reward structure associated with the work (e.g., payment—hourly, daily, weekly, monthly, or yearly—and voluntary tasks, such as social services in various types of clinics and hospitals or other organizations where volunteers are accepted and incorporated into the membership), and (7) participation in decision making.

Style of Supervision or Leadership

In Chapter 7 various styles of leadership and supervision were presented and inferences were made about the impact of such styles upon the behavior of employees and work groups. Research on job satisfaction has devoted a great deal of attention to delineating particular styles of leadership or supervisory behaviors which function to alter one's attitude toward the task performed. There is some evidence to indicate that job satisfaction is affected by certain styles of leadership in predictable ways. An early study which explored this relation directly was by Worthy (1950). He was primarily concerned with the impact of organizational structure on employees' morale. This study focused upon the Sears, Roebuck Company as the research target. Essentially, Worthy found that "tall" structures (those with many supervisory levels and narrow spans of control) were less conducive to job satisfaction than so-called "flat" structures (those with few supervisory levels and wide spans of control). The argument was that supervisors with narrow spans of control supervised their subordinates closely, whereas in "flat" structures, supervisors were forced to spend their time coordinating work activity rather than concentrating their attention on the performance of any given employee. The general implication of Worthy's research appeared to be that the more persons supervised, the more general the supervision, and the more the employees working under these conditions liked their jobs.

Following this rationale, other studies lend support to the contention that styles of leadership or supervision which allow subordinates a high degree of freedom of movement or autonomy will engender greater job satisfaction among those subordinates.

Consistent with the above findings, Zander (1961) found that supervisors who exhibit interest in their subordinates and support them in the tasks which they perform are significantly more likely to stimulate increased job satisfaction among lower-level personnel. However, other researchers such as Fournet, Distefano, and Pryer (1966:172) caution that simply being employee-centered and showing consideration or permissiveness will not automatically lead to increased job satisfaction among employees. Pelz (1952) examined superior-subordinate relations in the Detroit Edison Company and found that a critical factor in determining whether or not an employee would be favorably responsive to a supervisor's consideration toward him was the amount of influence the supervisor had "up the line" with his own superiors. Supervisors who had much influence up the line and who were also permissive toward their subordinates elicited higher job satisfaction from them, while those supervisors with little or no influence up the line generated job dissatisfaction among their subordinates, even though these supervisors sided with them or "went to bat" for them.

Certainly, factors in addition to supervisory behavior must be considered as possible intervening variables affecting the results of these investigations. For example, blanket generalizations cannot be made about which style of leadership is universally applicable. There are obvious variations in the socioeconomic status of subordinates, age, educational achievement, seniority in the organization, and many other factors which are likely to interact with the styles of leadership exhibited at a given time and place. Although the statement may appear trite, there does appear to be considerable consensus among researchers that humanistic, permissive leadership is a fruitful means of managing subordinates. At least, few researchers fail to condone permissive leadership practices in relation to the satisfaction and productivity of workers.

The Challenge and Intrinsic Interest of the Tasks Performed

Job satisfaction is frequently viewed from the position that jobs which offer challenge (as opposed to more simplistic tasks) and contain intrinsically satisfying characteristics are inherently rewarding to the employee.[4] For example, Faunce (1958b) found this to be a strong corollary of employees' perceptions of their work experiences in nonautomated automobile engine plants compared with subsequent experiences in automated ones. He noted that workers with more education found automated tasks less satisfying than workers with less education. One implication is that the more education a person has, the more challenging he expects a job to be in order for it to be satisfying and rewarding. Faunce also reported that many workers felt alienated by newly automated jobs. He observed that workers made comments such as the following: "[I don't like] the lack of feeling responsible for your work. The feeling that you're turning out more work but knowing it's not yours really and not as good as you could make it if you had control of the machine like before" (p. 72). "It's a completely different feel of work. On my old job, I controlled the machine. On my present job, the machine controls me" (p. 72).

A more explicit statement about the intrinsic factors which elicit satisfaction has been made by Myers (1964). In his study of the job satisfactions and motivations of employees in Texas Instruments Incorporated, Myers identifies "a challenging job [as one] which allows a feeling of achievement, responsibility, growth, advancement, enjoyment of work itself, and earned recognition" as a constellation of attributes which serve to increase these variables significantly (p. 73). He found that "dissatisfiers" in organizations were conditions external to the job being performed, such as seniority rights, fringe benefits, and coffee breaks. Endorsing Myer's position regarding factors in job satisfaction, Herzberg (1968:62) emphasizes "job enrichment," which may lead to increased satisfaction with tasks and can be obtained if employees exhibiting certain abilities and skills are matched with challenging jobs "commensurate with" such skills (p. 62). Herzberg offers a somewhat harsh, yet practical, solution to the problem of motivating personnel to perform more effectively. He says that "the argument for job enrichment can be summed up quite simply: If you have someone on a job, use him. If you can't use him on the job, get rid of him, either via automation or by selecting someone with lesser ability. If you can't use him and you can't get rid of him, you will have a motivation problem" (p. 62).

Some of the early research on the influence of responsibility and challenge upon satisfaction reveals findings essentially consistent with contemporary investigations. For example, Walker (1950) studied drill-press operators in the parts-manufacturing department of an IBM plant. The job involved extremely boring and repetitive activities for the workers. From 1940 to 1950, various changes took place in the plant which upgraded the jobs by raising the level of skill required and instituting more complex operations. The end result of the change was "job enlargement." Walker reported that job enlargement was accompanied by a substantial rise in efficiency and job satisfaction. More interest, variety, and responsibility were perceived by workers to be integral aspects of their changed jobs.

By now it should be fairly clear that much of the research we have discussed is, in a sense, "need-related" and potentially associated with the work of Maslow, who emphasized the importance of recognition, esteem and self-actualization as motivating factors for behavior. If his need scheme is applied to the work setting, there is much evidence to support its validity. Several examples are provided here which are couched in the context of Maslow's scheme. Carey (1972) studied Catholic priests in an effort to determine some of the reasons for variations in satisfaction among them. He found strong support for the idea that priests who felt that their positions allowed them greater opportunity for self-expression were significantly more satisfied with their work than those who did not (p. 190). Satisfaction of needs and a "feeling of doing work that is important" are two important factors in increased job satisfaction identified by Ross and Zander (1957). Their research on 2,680 skilled female workers in forty eight sections of a "large company" revealed that during a four-month period, there were 169 resignations. Those who resigned were interviewed and completed questionnaires, and their responses were compared with those of the continuing workers (1957:329-330). Table 9-2 shows the results of the comparison. From an examination of this table it is seen that those who quit, compared with those who remained, (1) perceived lower degrees of recognition, (2) were more dissatisfied with recognition, (3) were more dissatisfied with their personal achievements, (4) perceived considerably less autonomy, and (5) were significantly more dissatisfied with their autonomy.

Table 9-2 Differences in Satisfactions between Resigned Workers and Matched Continuing Workers

Measurement	Mean difference* between resigned workers and matched continuing workers	P
Strength of need for recognition	.08	ns
Degree of recognition received	− .56	.0025
Dissatisfaction with recognition	.64	.0025
Strength of need for achievement	.15	ns
Degree of achievement received	− .08	ns
Dissatisfaction with achievement	.23	.05
Strength of need for autonomy	.09	ns
Degree of autonomy received	− .44	.025
Dissatisfaction with autonomy	.53	.025

* The negative difference (−) means that the scores of the resigned workers were lower.
Source: Ross and Zander (1957:335).

Finally, some investigators have examined positive and negative motivations among scientists and engineers in a large military research and development laboratory (Friedlander and Walton, 1964). Interviewing eighty-two workers, these researchers asked, among other things, "What would you say are the most important factors that are operating to keep you here with this organization?" (p. 199). They discovered that "among the prime satisfiers that serve to attract the scientist toward his organization are his interest in his work and his technical freedom" (p. 206).

On the other hand, there are those who say that we should not place too much stress on job enlargement and challenge as means of stimulating increases in satisfaction. Hulin and Blood (1968) seem to feel that the case for job enlargement has been "drastically overstated and overgeneralized" (p. 50). These investigators highlight the important, but seldom considered, dimension of workers' backgrounds as mitigating factors in the relationship between job enlargement and job satisfaction. Homans (1961: 271) tends to support this argument by noting that two workers performing identical functions in the same organization and receiving equal pay may not assess their job in the same way or to the same degree. The explanation provided is that the men have different work values which suggests that cultural backgrounds and individual aspirations have a latent effect.

Throughout this discussion we have mentioned at various points such things as "positive" and "negative" motivators which function to elicit satisfaction or, as the case may be, dissatisfaction. Positive motivators have often been linked with factors intrinsic to the job itself, while negative motivators (i.e., those factors which theoretically cause dissatisfaction with work) are extrinsic in nature. Wernimont (1966) has listed the following factors as intrinsic: (1) recognition, (2) achievement, (3) the work itself, (4) advancement, and (5) responsibility. The factors considered as extrinsic by him are: (1) salary, (2) company policies, (3) the technical competence of the respondent's supervisor, (4) interpersonal relations, and (5) working conditions. The thrust of the argument developed by Wernimont is that two entirely different sets of factors account for job satisfaction and dissatisfaction. His summary statement is relevant in this regard and demonstrates the argument explicitly:

In summary, satisfaction with the job can be due to high levels of satisfaction with intrinsic factors, and dissatisfaction can be due to low levels of satisfaction with intrinsic factors. Extrinsic factors cause both satisfaction and dissatisfaction less readily than do the intrinsic factors, but individuals are more likely to say they have bad or dissatisfied feelings about these extrinsic factors. Measures of satisfaction with salary and working conditions may show these two factors to be dissatisfiers, as Herzberg, et al. (1959) claim, but for very different reasons than those invoked in their interpretations. Two different sets of expectations were seen to be major determinants of how job-attitude factors affect overall job satisfaction [p. 50].

Other researchers have reached the conclusion that job satisfaction is a multifaceted variable, dependent upon many things above and beyond the intrinsic factors associated with the content of the job (Palola and Larson, 1965). The work of Friedlander and Walton cited above concluded that "satisfaction and dissatisfaction are, for the most part, unrelated and non-complementary functions, rather than related poles of a single bipolar continuum" (p. 207). This means, in essence, that the presence of a particular factor may not necessarily increase satisfaction, but its absence may be conducive to a general decrease in satisfaction, possibly leading to dissatisfaction. We must be constantly aware that there is not necessarily a one-to-one relation between variations (increases and decreases) of particular variables and changes in satisfaction. The dual approach is evidently the most fruitful one at present.

Cohesion of Work Groups

The argument relating cohesion to job satisfaction is as follows. An employee who has harmonious relations with his work group and is integrated into it will, by definition, be a happier employee than one who is not solidly integrated into a work group. This argument has some merit. Certainly a factor contributing to whether or not a person will like or will not like his job is the nature of the relationship he achieves with his co-workers. Few people will argue that having to work around persons one dislikes will promote greater job satisfaction.

An investigation of the practices in production planning in two similar Indian textile mills has revealed that the managerial techniques within the mills differed markedly from one another (Chowdhry and Pal, 1957). Findings dealing with workers' satisfaction and the stability of membership in work groups were that as the stability of the groups increased, so did satisfaction within the groups. A general positive relation between the cohesiveness of work groups and job satisfaction has also been reported by Viteles (1953).

Several investigators endorse the notion that cohesiveness or identification with a work group is a positive factor in increased satisfaction with the general work environment (Trumbo, 1961; Zaleznik et al., 1958). For example, Trumbo's research on changes involving automation in an office with 46 supervisory and 232 nonsupervisory workers revealed that attitudes toward change were found to be associated with membership in work groups

(p. 344). In fact, members of cohesive groups were more resistant to the changes to automation than other employees. Trumbo interpreted this as "giving support to the view that less favorable attitudes toward change may indicate that change poses a threat to the satisfaction of social needs through informal social structure" (p. 344). Consistent with these findings is the work of Faunce et al. (1962). They, too, were concerned with the adaptation of employees to office automation. One particularly relevant observation was that "it appeared that where change in the job implied change in the work group, those who attached higher value to social satisfactions in work had less favorable attitudes toward change" (p. 66).

A more colorful portrayal of the importance of group cohesion for satisfaction at work is provided by Roy (1970). In the incident to be described, it is evident that the first-line supervisory personnel were accomplices in the deviations by groups from work norms. It may be that in some small way, the supervisors themselves derived satisfaction from an otherwise boring sequence of activities. Roy recounts the following:

> I recall a factory job in my early work experience in which the massive boredom of performing simple repetitive operations as a member of a cooky machine crew was alleviated by the lewd antics of a moronic operative whose job it was to feed our trays of stamped-out cooky dough into the revolving shelves of a large oven. This mentally but not sexually deficient fellow would rescue the rest of us from our pit of painful boredom at intervals by flashing an erection and whirling back and forth with it, to and from the oven, quite gracefully in fact, and by responding to the cheers, laughter, and obscene suggestions of his workmates by imbecilic grinning. Lest it be wondered how such highjinks escaped the watchful eye of management, I report that our first-line supervisor, a man of misanthropic stare, ready profanity, and all 'round disheartening personality, was an occasional witness, but his watching involved no move toward restoration of cooky-baking decorum. Perhaps observing the phallic drolleries made his own problems more bearable; he would appear in the background for an appreciative moment, a smile breaking out beneath glowering brows, like an indulgent gorilla watching its offspring at play [pp. 2-3].

Roy (1960) has also focused upon the importance of informal interactions and group cohesiveness in job satisfaction among a small work group of factory operatives. The operatives were obligated to perform repetitive and simple job operations over a six-day week, with extra-long days (p. 158). He referred to the most critical problem faced by these operatives as the "beast of monotony." He suggests that "revelation of how the group utilized its resources to combat that 'beast' should merit the attention of those who are seeking a solution to the practical problem of job satisfaction, or employee morale. It should also provide insights for those who are trying to

penetrate the mysteries of the small group" (p. 158). He reported that considerable horseplay and informal group antics appeared to be necessary to
relieve the men of the monotony of their tasks. They developed various
diversions such as "banana time" (each day one employee would pilfer a
banana from the lunchbox of a co-worker, shout "banana time!" and devour
the banana before his co-worker could retrieve it). There were other "times"
such as peach time, fish time, Coke time, and lunchtime (p. 162). All of these
times tended to relieve monotony for the work group, and most, if not all,
members went along with the horseplay (even to the point of engaging in
make-believe "fights" or "intentions" to fight, as at "banana time").

Tentatively, we may say that attachments to work groups are generally
important to members of organizations. Of course, some individuals prefer
to work by themselves and to have nothing to do with other people, but such
"isolates" are probably more the exception than the rule. Group cohesion
serves many functions, among which is increasing the satisfactions of the
members of such groups. We must remember, however, that the interactions
of informal groups and the satisfactions derived from them constitute only a
single dimension of intraorganizational behavior. We must not be too quick
to conclude that a happy employee in a cohesive work group will necessarily
be a high producer. In some instances, highly cohesive groups can effectively
operate to "restrict" the production of members, thus making a dysfunctional contribution to the organization. The attraction of the group for the
individual is like a double-edged sword: it is a source of satisfaction on the
one hand, but it can also operate to restrict output.

Work Load and Pressure

In many respects work load and pressure are associated with the amount of
challenge or intrinsic interest associated with various tasks. We have already
discussed job enlargement and challenge and their relation to job satisfaction. "Work load" and "pressure" refer to the amount of work assigned and
the existence of "deadlines" or schedules to which one must adhere. Job
enlargement differs in that it pertains to a greater diversification of work
assignments or variety in routine. The challenge of the job pits the skills and
talents of the worker against the requirements of the work itself.

As a part of a report of employees' reaction to EDP in a bank, Champion and Dager (1967c) noted that during the course of the study, questionnaires, observation of the work setting, and tape-recorded interviews with
employees at various stages of the transition to the new accounting method
revealed inconsistent statements by employees. In the questionnaires, for
example, employees responded that they felt there was greater work load
and pressure after the changeover to EDP than before. In the same question-

naires, a follow-up probe revealed that they were generally dissatisfied with such increases in the work load and the new deadlines. In contrast, personal interviews with these same employees exposed feelings which ran counter to the questionnaires. Most employees told the interviewer that less work load was associated with their new tasks than their old ones. The new deadlines associated with the computer system were simply "givens" and therefore tolerated. Needless to say, the deadlines created anxiety for many staff members. Formerly, they could determine their own pace fairly easily. This condition was not a concomitant of the new system. One of the most interesting things was the fact that on paper, at least, each employee felt obligated to complain about more work, even though interviews revealed that most persons performed less work in the aftermath of change. It may be considered a traditional feature of employees' behavior to complain about "too much work" and the like. But beneath this artificial role expectation was the fact that most employees orally related to the interviewer (through in-depth probes) that they really preferred more work over less. Their almost unanimous explanation for this phenomenon was that when they were kept busy with more work, it seemed to them that the day went by more quickly. In reality, the majority of tasks in this bank setting were repetitive and more boring than before the changeover. Having a greater work load would seem to make time pass more quickly for these banking personnel, thus alleviating much of the monotony associated with the new tasks.

Friedmann (1955) has reported research on the influence of monotonous and constrained work on personality structure. He distinguishes three types:

> First, those whose entire personality has to be interested in their work and who need to become absorbed by it. When their thought and attention are not thus absorbed by their work they feel a growing discomfort which they call "tedium" or some similar term. Second, for others, in monotonous work distraction may serve as a diversion. But they cannot coordinate the psychological series of ideas and images thus aroused with the physical series of movements demanded by their monotonous work; the two series are reciprocally inhibitive. In short, they are incapable of automatic action. Third, others can completely automatize their processes of work. The mind, wholly independent, may wander at will without the performance of physical movements being any less certain. It is for this type of mind that monotonous work is least pleasant [p. 139].

Currently, we are not in a position to specify the precise amount of work a person should be assigned as his optimum work load. Neither are we able to determine precisely the influence of deadlines on specific personalities. It is plausible that different people work differently under various work loads and deadlines. This relation has not, as yet, been sufficiently explored for a more definitive statement to be made on the subject. We know that deadlines create anxiety and that they can lead (in some instances) to dissatisfaction with the job. On the other hand, more and more organizational members today are becoming accustomed to working with deadlines and variations in work loads as technological change in various forms takes over their work settings. It is likely that in time, employees will come to define these conditions as essential and tolerable. Through interaction in informal groups and the other variables we have mentioned above, there may be some offsetting intervening variables which will become primary considerations in an assessment of the importance of the amount of work load and pressure employees are assigned.

Job Prestige and Status

It seems logical that persons occupying positions with high prestige and status should be more satisfied with their work than those individuals who perform more menial and demeaning tasks. However, it may also be argued that persons occupying positions with higher prestige may have greater pressures upon them to perform their jobs well. Early social thought records the recommendations of Niccolò Machiavelli (1469-1527) in a treatise entitled *The Prince.* Machiavelli wrote about the ways in which men can control other men. One of these ways was to dole out "titles" unaccompanied by power. People given such titles would think they held high-status positions, and this would, in turn, elicit their cooperation. Dispensing titles freely was one means of manipulating subordinates in one's kingdom. Applied to present-day organizational situations, this tactic has enjoyed some success. Managers of corporations and other high-level executives give people new titles (without commensurate raises in pay) and find that this is often sufficient to keep them happy with their work. In some industries and businesses, this practice is called "horizontal promotion," implying no promotion at all. But as long as the person *believes* that he has been promoted, almost everyone appears to be happy in the long run. The findings of some social research on this subject will be helpful to review here.

Two interesting examples of the same strategy being employed but yielding inconsistent results are discussed by Whyte (1969:589-590):

> Can symbols be used to elevate the status of jobs? . . . A restaurant owner was having trouble with high turnover and inefficiency on his dishwasher jobs. He recognized three interrelated status problems: (1) the title of the position suggested a very lowly valued position; (2) the wages he paid were at the bottom of his scale and around the bottom paid for unskilled labor in his area; and (3) the work of handling dirty dishes was universally looked down upon. To meet these problems, the owner took three interrelated actions: (1) he changed the job title

to dish machine operator, (2) he gave the position a substantial increase in hourly pay; and (3) he installed a large and complex dishwashing machine for the dish machine operators to operate. The owner reported that after these actions the dishwashing department no longer presented special problems of turnover, absenteeism, and low efficiency.

Another owner of a large restaurant thought he was applying exactly the same strategy, but to his surprise it did not seem to work. He already had modern dish machines. He called in the men of that department to tell them that their job classification had been changed from "dishwasher" to "dish machine operator" and that furthermore they were getting a substantial pay increase. For the first few days, he reported that the men seemed pleased, and the owner thought he was beginning to see the improvements in morale and efficiency that he had counted on, but the improvement was short-lived. The men were soon performing in the old and unsatisfactory pattern. Puzzled, the owner called one of the men aside and asked what he and his fellows were unhappy about. Taking his pay envelope out of his pocket, the worker showed it to the owner. On the envelope were typed these words: "Juan Romero, dishwasher." The owner had informed the payroll clerk about the pay increase for these men, but he had neglected to inform him of the change in title!

In a study of 545 manual workers in automobile and metal fabrication, Form and Geschwender (1962) found support for the notion that job satisfaction varies directly with occupational level. They remark that "workers with ten years or more of tenure are significantly more satisfied than those with less tenure, workers earning $2.00 and over an hour are significantly more satisfied than those earning less, and those in higher occupational prestige categories (sales, clerical, skilled and foremen) are significantly more satisfied than those in lower prestige categories (semiskilled and unskilled)" (p. 235).

Bonjean and Grimes (1970) have alluded to a similar finding in their investigation of the relation between bureaucracy and alienation. Alienation as a "negative motivator" was found to exist to a lesser degree among managerial personnel than among lower-level personnel, although the differences were slight. These researchers offer one possible explanation for this difference by stating that "managers and businessmen may have better developed means of coping with bureaucratization than hourly paid workers. Their higher education, social status, and income may provide them with a better rationale and more opportunities to experience feelings of integration both on and off the job" (p. 371).

Rather than consider each of these studies reported above to be indicative of a direct association between prestige and satisfaction, we must recognize the existence of other factors which we have mentioned as variables. For instance, job content, work load, and pressure play important roles in determining job satisfaction in many instances. Examples can always be cited of individuals who have qualifications for high-prestige jobs but prefer lower-level jobs because of their intrinsic interest. Some people shy away from high-prestige positions because of a fear of the responsibility accompanying them. In the military, a person may turn down a chance for a promotion in order to avoid additional duties and superfluous activities. A promotion might also mean a psychological as well as rank separation from one's peer group where satisfactions are paramount. And there are instances of individuals with master's degrees and Ph.D.s who accept jobs which carry no educational prerequisites and are lower in social status than positions for which these persons are obviously qualified. A teacher may turn down a deanship of a college because of a dislike for administrative chores and a preference for teaching. The matter of job prestige and satisfaction is not at all clear-cut.

Type of Reward Structure

In much of the early work on motivation and the satisfaction of organizational members, there are continual references to the potential importance of monetary rewards as influences upon these variables. The argument is that the more a person is paid, the more satisfied he will be with the job he performs and the harder he will work in performing his tasks. The ultimate result, according to this argument, is increased productivity among organizational members. Maier (1965: 443-444) writes, for example, that "money, in itself, has no incentive value. Since our economic structure has made it a medium of exchange, however, it can be used to obtain the real incentives. Money is sought after in our society because of what it represents." Maier goes on to say that money reflects the satisfaction of various kinds of worker needs. If monetary rewards are seen within a need framework, it becomes easy to understand the underpinnings of the "money leads to job satisfaction" argument. Organizational researchers see the importance of monetary rewards in a different light, however.

In virtually all organizations in which volunteers are not an integral feature of intraorganizational structure, there are several kinds of payment systems in operation. A person may be paid by the hour, the week, the month, or the year. An employee may be paid according to the number of units of product he produces (such a method of payment is called the "piece-rate system"). Persons who perform teaching functions in elementary, secondary, college, and university settings are frequently paid on a nine- or ten-month basis (inasmuch as their teaching activities are primarily restricted to the period between September and May). Salesmen for organizations may be paid strictly on the basis of commission (a percentage of the amount of the product sold) or a combination of salary and commission (i.e., if a person sells more than a certain predetermined quota, he earns a commission on the excess in addition to the regular salary rate). Given the diversification of payment systems in existence, it is not surprising to see the emergence of invidious distinctions between each method of payment. For instance, a person working "by the hour" may not have as much "prestige" compared with another person (possibly performing an identical task and making an equivalent amount of money) who is paid on a monthly or yearly basis.

Before considering some of the implications of varying payment methods for satisfaction, we should be aware of the following facts. Money is essential for the survival of most people (with the exception of farmers, who may "live off the land" rather than depend upon wages of any kind). Money constitutes a means to multiple ends (e.g., new houses, cars, clothes, scarce or exotic foods, or swimming pools). Money is an intermediate reward for work or services performed. In turn, it can be exchanged for other things which people want. As it is a variable common to all organizations of the type we are discussing, we must inevitably raise certain questions about money as a potentially significant input into satisfaction. Is there a relation between money and job satisfaction? If so, what is the nature of the relation? Is there a relation between the method of payment and job satisfaction? If so, what is the nature of this relation?

There are those who argue that little or no relation exists between money and job satisfaction. Wernimont (1966:49) reasons that persons bring to their jobs particular expectations pertaining to salary requirements. The employee-employer relation is a bargaining one. Once an agreement is reached, the employee performs his functions, receives the sum agreed upon from the organization, and feels "satisfied" to the extent that the organization has lived up to its part of the "bargain." Future salary increments may be viewed by the employee as "expected" or "deserved," and under such circumstances, it is unlikely that the employee's level of satisfaction will rise significantly, if at all. On the other hand, if a person assumes additional duties and responsibilities with little or no increase in financial rewards, a strong possibility exists that he may become dissatisfied with that particular arrangement.

In a study cited earlier, Form and Geschwender (1962:235) provide some support for a positive relation between wages and satisfaction. Their investigation of the levels of satisfaction of 545 manual workers in Lansing, Michigan revealed higher job satisfaction among those workers earning $2.00 or more per hour compared with those earning less than $2.00 per hour. Viteles (1953) has provided very tentative evidence to arrive at a similar conclusion.

However, Fournet, Distefano, and Pryer (1966:174) have concluded that too much attention has been assigned to pay. They cite the work of Herzberg et al. (1957) and Troxell (1954) to illustrate that pay as a significant factor affecting the satisfactions of employees does not have the importance or the priority which managers generally assume. They feel that the primary difficulty in demonstrating the relation of pay to satisfaction is "that it is confounded with other factors, such as age, occupational level, and education" (p. 174).

It is perhaps better to look at the various methods of payment in evaluating the importance of pay in relation to satisfaction. A postal carrier, for example, may derive much satisfaction from his job. He receives a fixed monthly salary for his labors. His productivity is determined in terms of the territory he covers, including the number of pieces of mail delivered and the number of persons along his route (Harper and Emmert, 1963:224). If he delivers his mail fast, and if this information becomes known to his supervisor, his territory may be increased, with his basic salary remaining at a constant level. He derives his satisfaction, in part, by "beating the system." He does so by finishing his deliveries early in the day away from the direct observation of his superiors. This gives him increased leisure time to do whatever he wishes (Harper and Emmert, 1963:224-225).

Probably the most visible example of the influence of method of pay upon satisfaction is the piece-rate system commonly used in factory settings. Workers are encouraged to work harder to produce more in order to earn more. They are given "quotas," and any excess units of product above their quotas will result in bonuses or additional pay. Although the piece rate method of payment is primarily a device to increase one's incentive to work, theoretically it does have some merit for increasing a worker's satisfaction. In reality, however, the piece-rate system generally fails to achieve the desired expectations of management. Roy (1952, 1954, and 1960) has vividly depicted the impact of informal group norms upon individual members operating under a piece-rate method of payment. Workers who overproduce or exceed their quotas are punished in some way by the other employees. These persons who exceed their quotas are often called "rate busters" because they "bust" the assigned quotas. Informal group norms operate to "restrict output" because of a generalized fear among the workmen that management will reset quotas if the men produce too much. An engineer may come into the workroom, paint the machine a different color, change a knob or two, and pretend to tamper with the insides of the mechanism. When the engineer leaves, the machine has been "improved" so that the worker can produce at a higher level. New quotas are assigned the individuals who exceeded their production level as well as all other workers performing the same task. Naturally there is just cause (from the standpoint of the informal work groups) to impose rate restrictions in order that subsequent resetting of rates will not occur. The incentive in the form of a bonus fails to attract group members any longer, and such unscrupulous managerial behavior receives its just rewards.

In summary, then, methods of payment appear to be only moderately influential in relation to job satisfaction. The operation of informal work-group norms is sufficient to act against the potential satisfactions derived from exceeding quotas under a piece-rate system. Job expectations, including commensurate salary requirements, make it difficult to determine the precise impact upon the level of satisfaction. Receiving remuneration below one's expectations is more likely to produce dissatisfaction than receiving payments above the quality of one's work is to produce satisfaction. In other words, pay is more likely to be associated with negative motivators than with positive motivators.

Participation in Decision Making

Probably no other variable has received so much attention as a prerequisite and determinant of job satisfaction as participation. The concept of "psychology of participation" is that the more a person participates in a decision, the more likely he is to stick with it and to enjoy his work. A more recent phrase which expresses this notion is "participative management."

Perhaps the formalized origin of employees' participation in decision-making and other work-related matters was the Hawthorne studies, conducted at a plant of the Western Electric Company during the late 1920s and early 1930s. Elton Mayo and Roethlisberger and Dickson gave the principle of participation considerable importance in their later writings, which have been examined in earlier chapters of this volume. Subsequent research on the relation between participation in decision making and job satisfaction has, for the most part, revealed a positive association.[5] We will now examine briefly some of the more current investigations which deal directly with correlations between these two phenomena.

Holter (1965) offers impressive evidence to support the relationship between participation and job satisfaction. Although her study was conducted in Oslo, Norway, we may consider her findings as supplementary to American research carried out under similar work conditions. She obtained her data from employees of industrial firms, insurance companies, and factories by administering a questionnaire. The resultant sample consisted of 591 blue-collar[6] and 397 white-collar employees in insurance companies and 64 white-collar employees in industry. All of the employees involved were non-supervisory personnel (p. 300).

In response to the question, "Do you feel that the employees in general participate sufficiently in decisions that concern the management of the establishment as a whole?" the majority of employees in all three categories (i.e., blue-collar, white-collar-insurance, and white-collar-industrial) said, "No." A follow-up question was, "Do you feel that you personally participate sufficiently in decisions made at your place of work, or do you wish to participate more in them?" Again, an overwhelming majority across all categories reported that either (1) they would like to participate more in decisions that directly concern their own work and working conditions, or (2) they would like to participate more in decisions that concern the management of the whole enterprise. The most crucial question related to participation in decision making and job satisfaction is best depicted by the results shown in Table 9-3. Approximately 39 per cent of the blue-collar employees and 37 per cent of the white-collar employees reported that joint decision making would increase their job satisfaction (p. 307). Almost all of the remaining respondents revealed that it would be "just" and that it would lead to greater efficiency. In her summary, Holter concludes that "the idea of joint decision-making—or more democratic processes of decision-making in industry—has fairly wide support among non-supervisory employees" (p. 318).[7]

In a study by Carey (1972) of priests in Chicago that was cited earlier, it was found that priests were more satisfied with their tasks to the extent that they were allowed a greater degree of self-expression and influence with respect to decisions affecting them (e.g., choice of location, perceived degree to which opinions could be expressed which conflicted with church beliefs and practices). As a major change to improve the satisfaction of priests (and thereby reduce "labor turnover" among them), Carey recommends that "a

Table 9-3   Reasons Given for Desiring More Joint Decision Making

Question: There may be various reasons for feeling that the employees should participate more in decision-making concerning the whole establishment; nevertheless, we ask you to indicate below the reason which you find most important in this connection.

Most important reason for more joint decision-making:	Respondents desiring more joint decision-making, %	
	Blue-collar	White-collar
It would increase *satisfaction* among employees.	39	37
It would be more *just*.	29	22
It would lead to greater *efficiency* in the work.	27	39
No reply, etc.	5	3
Total % =	100	101
Total N =	463	236

Source: Holter (1965:307).

continuing effort be made to promote opportunities for priests to use the skills and abilities they have, or think they have. The creation of a personnel board in Chicago has without doubt done much to have priests appointed in parishes or positions where they have shown a desire to serve. This is a big improvement over former years when a priest had no voice in the time or place of his transfer from one assignment to another" (p. 195).

There has been some research which has led to different conclusions about the relation between job satisfaction and participation. Pugh (1966: 241-242) suggests that a "growing body of data . . . indicates that satisfaction and productivity are not necessarily complementary." He also mildly implies that the same is true of participation in decision making.

A seldom considered, but nevertheless important, factor has been brought to our attention in the work of Hulin and Blood (1968). Given the many individual differences which exist among the personnel of any organization, it is likely that greater participation in decision making and job satisfaction may, in fact, be inversely related for some. They make explicit the fact that "at the very least, we should allow the possibility that some workers prefer the safety of not being required to make decisions" (p. 42). They also cite the work of Vroom (1960), who "has demonstrated that not all workers are satisfied when they are allowed to take part in the decision-making process about their jobs, and there are significant individual differences . . . between workers who respond positively to the opportunity to make decisions and those who do not. While not exactly to the point, these data at least indicate that some workers prefer routine, repetition, and specified work methods to change, variety and decision making" (p. 42).

Given the significant amount of evidence above, it is clear that the relationships between participation and job satisfaction are dependent upon a number of factors at the social and psychological levels. We know that most of the organizations with which we are familiar follow a bureaucratic format not only in structure but in intraorganization relationships (i.e., impersonality, selection by test, specialization of task performance, rigid adherence to a body of abstract rules, etc.). Hierarchies of authority exist which are based on the fallacious assumption that persons at higher levels in the hierarchy are more educated or more knowledgeable than members at the lower levels. On the surface, at least, it would appear that increased involvement in decision making at all levels is in direct contradiction to bureaucracy. In most respects, this is true. Hicks (1972), for example, reminds us of research organizations or universities in which the subordinates in the situation are at least as educated and informed as the superiors in such institutions (pp. 488-489). Hicks among others is quick to recognize that there have been numerous changes in the profile of professionals and nonprofessionals in organizations during the past forty years. He refers to the so-called

"knowledge explosion" as one such change which reflects the fact that workers at all organizational levels today are much more educated and informed
than their predecessors of yesteryear (p. 488). He refers to Warren Bennis's
suggestions for drastic alterations in the administrative philosophies still
practiced. Bennis (1966a) has suggested that we must change many of our
outmoded ideas about the relationship of the organization to the individual.
Some of the more important developments he recommends are (1) a new
concept of man based on an increased knowledge of his complex and shifting needs; (2) a new concept of power based on collaboration and reason;
and (3) a new concept of organizational values based on humanistic-demo-
cratic ideals to replace the depersonalized mechanistic value system of bureaucracy (p. 55).

The notions of "needs" and "need fulfillment" have been introduced at
various points and juxtaposed with particular organizational forms, supervisory styles, job content and challenge, and participation in decision making.
No doubt the needs of the individual employee are integral factors which are
responsive to various kinds of intraorganizational conditions and interpersonal relations. The "ability" of an organization to satisfy employees' needs
is likely to exert a direct impact upon levels of satisfaction. The list of
variables which has been explored above in relation to job satisfaction is
certainly not exhaustive. Realizing that there are many additional inputs
into employees' satisfactions in the organization, we have selected what are
believed to be some of the more salient variables.

We might also conclude that job satisfaction is a direct contributor to
the morale of aggregates of employees. Morale is not so much an individual
variable as an interpersonal one. It generally refers to a property of groups
wherein the members share common values, interests, goals, and—especially—a feeling of "weness." The impact of group morale upon productivity is
similar to that of job satisfaction, although it has been shown by Roy (1960)
and others that the morale of a group can work to the detriment of the
organization by enforcing "restriction of output."

When it comes to discussing the relations among satisfaction, morale,
and productivity, there is much pessimism throughout the literature. Bennis
(1966a) says it clearly when he writes that "the fact of the matter is that we
are not at all clear today about the relationship of morale to productivity,
nor, indeed, are we sure that there is any interdependence between them;
Likert and his associates have found organizations with all the logical possibilities—high morale with low productivity, low productivity with low
morale, etc." (pp.69-70). In an essay on the same topic, Kahn (1960) has
concluded that if there is a relationship between job satisfaction, morale,

and productivity, it has not, as yet, been delineated and demonstrated empirically. He states that:

> with regard to the hypothesized relationship between productivity and satisfaction, an all-out effort was made in the tractor company study [cited earlier in this chapter]. Four identifiable factors resulted from this analysis and were labeled: Intrinsic job satisfaction, satisfaction with the company, satisfaction with supervision, and satisfaction with rewards and mobility opportunities. None of these factors was significantly related to the actual productivity of employees in the tractor factories. For purposes of our present discussion, the completion of the study in the tractor company represents the end of a cycle. We decided that the evidence from these three studies was sufficiently powerful so that we should abandon, in our future research, the use of satisfaction or morale indexes as variables intervening between supervisory and organizational characteristics on the one hand, and productivity on othe other. This, perhaps, is the major conclusion so far as the topic of this paper is concerned [pp. 286—287].

It seems appropriate to conclude the chapter on this note. Next, we will direct our attention to organizational change. Chapters 10 and 11 are arranged so as to describe planned change in organizations and various implications of change for intraorganizational behavior and to describe some of the specific impacts of technological change (particularly in the form of automation) upon organizational structure and process and on interpersonal and personal behavior.

SUMMARY

This chapter has explored some of the interrelations between job satisfaction and motivation and productivity of employees. Needless to say, attempts to establish causal relations between such variables and to link them with organizational effectiveness are hampered by imprecise and inconsistent applications of terminology, by spuriousness, and by the contamination of interrelations of variables from different organizational settings. What, if anything, can be stated about the nature of the relation between job satisfaction, motivation, morale, productivity, and organizational effectiveness?

First, there is some agreement that factors which contribute to satisfaction and high motivation to produce are not necessarily the same factors which generate dissatisfactions and low motivation. The importance of a dual approach to the study of satisfaction and motivations has been stressed particularly by researchers such as Vroom and Herzberg. A happy employee is not necessarily a more productive one; but an unhappy employee may not have as much enthusiasm to perform the job well as an employee who is more content.

Whether an employee is unhappy or happy with his work is related, directly or indirectly, to such matters as the type of supervision received, the interest and challenge of the work, perceptions of the worth or importance of the work compared with that of others, relationships with associates, the amount of responsibility and decision-making power accompanying the job, and the pay. The last factor—pay—has typically been considered a poor predictor of motivation, although many employees would probably complain if they didn't feel they were rewarded enough. Intrinsically rewarding characteristics of the job have tended to play a more crucial role in this regard. If the person likes what he is doing (and possibly feels that it is important in relation to other jobs), he is likely to be *more* motivated to produce than someone who dislikes his work (and its lack of challenge and interest).

Perhaps the most important thing which can be learned from this chapter is that numerous social and psychological (as well as organizational) factors are responsible in varying degrees for the behavior of employees both as individuals and as groups. Present and past efforts to delineate conditions which generate greater motivation and satisfaction among employees (or volunteers in voluntary organizations) have made us increasingly aware that we still have much to learn about virtually every organizational, interpersonal, and individual dimension. But we have moved a considerable distance from the former "carrot-and-stick" philosophy which was so dominant in organizational writing at the turn of the century. Furthermore, we have generally discarded single-factor explanations of events occurring within organizations and have moved toward the development and refinement of multiple-factor predictive schemes as a means of cultivating a better understanding of the sociology of organizations.

STUDY QUESTIONS

1 Evaluate the importance of job satisfaction as it relates to increasing the productivity of workers or employees.
2 To what extent does participation in decision making by lower-level organizational members increase their satisfactions? What are some factors which affect the relation between participation in decision making and job satisfaction? Discuss the impact of each factor you list.
3 Does the fact that an employee is satisfied with his work mean that he will automatically work harder for the organization? Why or why not? Explain.
4 How important is personality in determining individual job satisfactions? Discuss briefly.

5 What is Herzberg's "dual-factor" theory of motivation? Compare this notion with that of Vroom. Which do you feel has the greater predictive utility for use in the organization? Why?

6 Cite some examples of "horizontal promotion" either from your own experience or from the experiences of others known to you. How successful do you feel "titles" are in improving one's job satisfaction and motivation to work? Explain.

7 The informal group often sets norms apart from those imposed by the formal arrangement of things in an organization. What kinds of factors would tend to mitigate the influence of informal groups upon individual group members in relation to their performance? How?

8 How important is money as a "positive job motivator"? Discuss.

9 Why has so much attention been paid to the job satisfaction of employees? Do you believe management is justified in manipulating the environment of workers in order to raise their job satisfaction or contentment with tasks? Why or why not? Discuss.

10 Some people view motivations to work as "need-fulfilling" behavior. How do they arrive at such a view? In your own words, explain the process of "need fulfillment" in the workplace.

NOTES

[1] One of the earliest studies of this type was reported by S. B. Mathewson, *Restriction of Output among Unorganized Workers*, New York, Viking, 1931. Later, following the account of Roethlisberger and Dickson (1939), Morris S. Viteles published an extensive description of industrial workers and their work attitudes in his book *Motivation and Morale in Industry* New York, Norton, 1953.

[2] These studies were, respectively, V. H. Vroom, "Organizational Choice: A Study of Pre- and Postdecision Processes," *Organizational Behavior and Human Performance,* **1**: 212-225, 1966; J. W. Hill, "An Application of Decision Theory to Complex Industrial Behavior," unpublished dissertation, Wayne State University, Detroit, Michigan, 1965; J. Galbraith and L. L. Cummings, "An Empirical Investigation of the Motivational Determinants of Task Performance: Interactive Effects between Instrumentality—Valence and Motivation—Ability," *Organizational Behavior and Human Performance,* **2**:237-257, 1967; and E. E. Lawler and L. W. Porter, "Antecedent Attitudes of Effective Managerial Performance," *Organizational Behavior and Human Performance,* **2**:122-142, 1967.

[3] Mumford (1970:71) uses this definition as a part of a general review on the topic.

[4] Blauner (1964) has investigated the Marxian notion that alienation of labor leads to estrangement of laborers in a factory system, which, in turn, leads to dissatisfaction. It is his contention, however, that on the basis of present research, most people tend to like the jobs they perform.

[5] Among those endorsing the positive relation between participation in decision making and job satisfaction are French, Israel, and Aas (1960), Leavitt (1951), McGregor (1960), Morse and Reimer (1956), and Viteles (1953).

[6] These individuals were made up of factory workers in various firms.

[7] French et al. (1966) conducted a study of participation in a company which had an effective appraisal system. The experimental design which they used allowed them to control the level of participation of 92 volunteers out of a total of 122 managers (p. 5). In general, it was found that the high-participation subjects in comparison with the low-participation subjects expressed more favorable attitudes toward their company's appraisal system.

Chapter 10

Planned Change in Organizations

INTRODUCTION

In this chapter and Chapter 11, we will examine various aspects of organizational change. Organizations are dynamic entities constantly in states of flux, responding to different kinds of internal and external stimuli in many forms. From one point of view, organizations are seen as paralleling organisms, which tend to change over time through the process of evolution. So-called "natural" processes within organizations account for evolutionary changes such as those accompanying managerial succession, labor turnover, and continual redefinitions of overall organizational goals in response to external market demands. Another view of organizational change, contrasting sharply with the evolutionary view, is that of planned change, or purposeful decisions by professionals in collaboration with organizational power coalitions to effect improvements in organizational systems through the skillful application of scientific knowledge (Lippitt, Watson, and Westley, 1958:3-19).[1]

The major objectives of this chapter are: (1) to highlight the importance of studying planned organizational change by focusing upon some of the more significant implications of planning as opposed to change as the result of spontaneity or evolutionary process; (2) to describe the nature of planned change in organizations; (3) to examine some of the more popular strategies for implementing organizational change and their potential implications for improving organizational effectiveness; and (4) to describe the interrelatedness of organizations with the broader environment of organizational units and the effects of this environment upon internal organizational change.

SOME PRELIMINARY CONCERNS AND DEFINITIONS

The traditional literature dealing with planned change in organizations has successfully developed several general objectives and orientations as well as some key terminology.[2]

Before launching into a discussion of these aims and this terminology, we should indicate that planned change is not restricted entirely to organizations. According to Lippitt, Watson, and Westley (1958), planned change may apply to individuals, small groups, and communities as well as formal organizations. The psychiatrist is seen as a primary factor in change in individuals. Training-groups or T-group coordinators are perceived as facilitating the solution of problems in small groups.[3] Community planners, social work agencies, and public health institutions offer different kinds of aids and services to community leaders (e.g., mayors, city councils, metropolitan planning commissions, and city service directors) in the solution of problems associated with urban and suburban life.

In each of the instances cited above, a target (individual, small group, or community) exists as a major focus of interest for various kinds of planners of change. Such a target is commonly referred to as a "client system." "Client systems" are defined as entities in need of some kind of "help" or treatment (Lippitt, Watson, and Westley, 1958:12). Persons or groups of persons providing professional assistance to client systems are designated as "agents of change" (p. 10). Agents of change may or may not be a part of the client system (in the cases of small groups, formal organizations, and communities). Usually, they are persons external to the client systems they assist.[4]

In addition to client systems and agents of change, there are an infinite number of objectives (changes) as "target goals." These are commonly defined as specific states or conditions which client systems, with the help of agents of change, want to achieve. In the case of the person who is mentally ill, other persons may define that person as in need of help and seek the assistance of an agent of change (usually a physician, a psychiatrist, or a psychiatric social worker). It is certainly not unusual for client systems to be unaware of the need for change. By the same token, we must recognize that sometimes client systems will seek assistance for solutions to "imagined problems," and the agents will determine that their relation to such client systems is unnecessary and possibly harmful (under certain conditions). Most agents are the first to recognize whether or not they are needed by a client system and, if so, what their limitations are in relation to the problems for which assistance is sought. Obviously, the particular skills and insights of prospective agents are quite important with reference to specific problems of client systems to be investigated.

So far we have identified "client systems," "agents of change," and "target goals" or "objectives" as traditional terms employed in discussions of planned change in the literature. Also, we have mentioned the possibility that client systems may sometimes "feel" that change is necessary for their improvement and that assistance from external sources (i.e., agents of change or, in some cases, internal sources from within small groups, organizations, or communities) is required in order for their problems to be ameliorated. Agents of change called upon for assistance may or may not feel that changes will lead to improvements in the existing condition of the client system. In fact, it may be the professional judgment of an agent that change of any kind within a given client system would have only detrimental results.

In a classic study by Bavelas and Strauss (1955),[5] problems alleviated in one part of a company gave rise to new and more severe problems in other departments. Their study concerns the Hovey and Beard Company, which manufactured different kinds of toy products (e.g., wooden animals and pull toys) (p. 90). According to these authors, "one part of the manufacturing process involved spraying paint on the partially assembled toys and hanging them on moving hooks which carried them through a drying oven. This operation, staffed entirely by girls, was plagued by absenteeism, turnover, and low morale" (p. 90). The story continues:

> Shortly before the troubles began, the painting operation had been reengineered so that the eight girls who did the painting sat in a line by an endless chain of hooks. These hooks were in continuous motion, past the line of girls and into a long horizontal oven. Each girl sat at her own painting booth so designed as to carry away fumes and to backstop excess paint. The girl would take a toy from the tray beside her, position it in a jig inside the painting cubicle, spray on the color according to the pattern, then release the toy and hang it on the hook passing by. The rate at which the hooks moved had been calculated by the engineers so that each girl, when fully trained, would be able to hang a painted toy on each hook before it passed beyond her reach [pp. 90-91].

Bavelas functioned as the consultant in this case and worked closely with the foreman who supervised the women's operations.

As the result of several meetings with the women to discuss problems associated with their low morale and high turnover, a series of changes were introduced, including the installation of ventilation fans and a speed-control device so that that the women could have complete control of the speed at which hooks passed them. Since the women were being paid on a group-bonus plan (meaning that each time their group exceeded the expected group-production rate predetermined by engineers and management, they received additional earnings as a bonus), complete control of their own production quotas apparently stimulated them to work even harder than before. Morale improved, and so did their individual earnings (inasmuch as the bonus plan was in effect). Compared with other personnel in the company doing similar tasks, these women were receiving substantially higher remuneration for their efforts. The friction resulting from the jealousy of other workers and the foremen and engineers of the other departments made it necessary for the plant superintendent to reinstate the original job specifications for the women. This meant that "the hooks moved again at their constant, time-studied designated speed" (p. 94).

Bavelas and Strauss note that "production dropped again, and within a month all but two of the eight girls had quit. The foreman himself stayed on for several months, but, feeling aggrieved, then left for another job" (p. 94).

An important moral implication of the study by Bavelas and Strauss is that agents of change should do as much as possible to project the potential, far-reaching effects of any changes considered for an organization as a client system. Reemphasizing a portion of a quotation by Spencer (1882) presented earlier in this volume, one does not necessarily remove "cockles" in wrought-iron plates by striking down directly upon them with a hammer, inasmuch as other defects in the plate may occur as a result. Such defects may be more serious that the original one. Strategic planning is a necessary requirement for ensuring success for agents of change as they seek to provide assistance and alternative remedies for the many problems of client systems.

A BRIEF NOTE ON THE NECESSITY OF PLANNED
CHANGE IN ORGANIZATIONS

Because of the high degree of interrelatedness of departments and functional roles within organizations, changes occurring in one area of organizational behavior or in a particular departmental unit will have varying implications for other organizational sectors. Only extremely naïve agents of change will consider even minute modifications in work roles in one organizational department inconsequential insofar as other departments and other work roles are concerned. Changes of any kind relating to the hierarchy of authority, individual work roles, rearrangements of the formal communication network, interrelations of functional roles, new work assignments or new jobs created as a result of technology, pay differentials, working hours, fringe benefits, managerial succession, promotions, and the like—are conspicuous to most, if not all, organizational members. Eventually, even the most innocuous of changes will be brought to the attention of all persons in the organization, probably through the informal communication network or grapevine.

The planning of organizational change must be assessed not only in terms of short-range implications but also in terms of long-range ones. It seems to be the case in numerous instances of organizational change that the lower-level participants collectively view change as a serious threat to the status quo (which it is) and to their jobs (which it might be). Personal anxieties and apprehensions are to be expected in the face of planned change. Potential obstacles which could interfere with changes or prevent them from taking place must be anticipated. Strategies must be devised which take into account many factors, including those which we have mentioned above. Sound planning is necessary, therefore, in order for an organization to minimize the conflicts which may occur.

Utilizing our skills in human relations and understanding employees' needs for predictability in their lives and for reassurances concerning their future roles in the organization are insufficient means of dealing with organizational change adequately. Often, we must turn to a professional agent of change to provide us with additional ideas and expertise in an effort to implement change smoothly and effectively. A primary organizational objective resulting from planned change is improved effectiveness not only in operations and production but in the human sector as well. Below are summarized some of the more important contributions agents of change can make toward organizational effectiveness in all senses of the term:

1   Through close contact or collaboration with the organization, they are frequently able to help in determining the nature and extent of any apparent problems. At the same time, they may be able to call to the attention of the soliciting organization previously unrecognized areas of difficulty which merit substantial consideration.

2   Again, within the framework of a collaborative relation, they may be able to enable the organization to utilize existing resources and skills (e.g., certain personnel with relevant educational background or training in an important area of organizational behavior) to resolve present problems. Certain forms of psychiatric therapy force the individual with problems to deal with them himself rather than receive external inputs (e.g., shock therapy and drugs) as "cures." Usually, one of the first things an agent of change

does is attempt to determine whether or not his direct involvement and the imposition of strategies are necessary. Does the organization exhibit the potential for dealing with the problems confronting it? Is the collaborative relation between the agent and the organization primarily one of helping the system to recognize its strengths and how to use them effectively in the process of eliminating problems?

3 Obviously, the professional abilities of agents of change may be of significant value in sensitizing organizational leaders to anticipated resistance to change from the lower-level membership (and even from middle-level managerial personnel). These abilities may include workable strategies whereby resistance to change may be overcome. Through the teaching and learning process, certain organizational members can be made aware of ways by which the successful implementation of change may be maximized.

4 Perhaps one of the most important functions of agents of change (assuming that change is determined to be necessary) is to help the organizational leaders anticipate the potential long-range consequences of immediate changes, regardless of their apparent short-term value.

Of course, all these contributions are contingent on whether or not the organization (1) has resolvable problems, (2) wants them resolved, and (3) wants the agent, possibly an outsider, to assist in achieving the desired state of affairs. Since there are many persons who act as agents of change, and since there are so many strategies to apply to a limitless number of organizational problems, there is seldom, if ever, an easy solution or blanket strategy which functions as an organizational panacea.

THE EMERGENCE OF A PATTERN OF "SUCCESSFUL" PLANNED CHANGE

To what extent do patterns exist relative to planned change in organizations? If there are identifiable patterns associated with planned change, do these patterns have significant implications for the "success" or "failure" of the client organization in adopting the changes, whatever they may be? In an effort to answer these and other questions, Greiner (1967) has conducted a survey of studies of planned change in organizations. Essentially, he observed eighteen empirical investigations in which changes of one type or another were planned or implemented. On the basis of the conclusions reached by the individual researchers in each case, Greiner was able to delineate a potential "success" pattern (which was defined according to the long-lasting nature of the change involved). The primary characteristics of "successful" attempts at change were:

1. The organization, and especially top management, is under considerable external and internal pressure for improvement long before an explicit organiza-

tional change is contemplated. Performance and/or morale are low. Top management seems to be groping for a solution to its problems. 2. A new man, known for his ability to introduce improvements, enters the organization, either as the official head of the organization, or as a consultant who deals directly with the head of the organization. 3. An initial act of the new man is to encourage a reexamination of past practices and current problems within the organization. 4. The head of the organization and his immediate subordinates assume a direct and highly involved role in conducting this reexamination. 5. The new man, with top management support, engages several levels of the organization in collaborative, fact-finding, problem-solving discussions to identify and diagnose current organizational problems. 6. The new man provides others with new ideas and methods for developing solutions to problems, again, at many levels of the organization. 7. The solutions and decisions are developed, tested, and found creditable for solving problems on a small scale before an attempt is made to widen the scope of change to larger problems and the entire organization. 8. The change effort spreads with each success experience, and as management grows, it is gradually absorbed permanently into the organization's way of life [pp. 124–125].

Notice that the "new man" described by Greiner might probably be designated as the "agent of change." In collaboration with members of high-level management in the organization, the agent provides information, elicits suggestions and information from all managerial levels, and conducts discussions with several levels of organizational members. Several alternative solutions to problems are generated through these discussion sessions and tested on a small scale. Reinforcement of the solutions (through "successful experiences" by organizational members) results in the change's being introduced on a much larger scale and ultimately being accepted and internalized by all members of the organization.

Greiner makes explicit the notion that a redistribution of power is essential in successful change experiences (pp. 125–126). He projects a continuum of power distribution such as is shown in Figure 10-1. Although no such continuum was actually constructed by Greiner, his discussion of the hypothetical continuum parallels that shown in Figure 10-1. At one end of the continuum is unilateral authority. Greiner (1967:120) explains such authority as traditional, hierarchical authority, where action is initiated by top-level managers and passed to the lower echelons in the organization by (1) decree (one-way orders to change), (2) replacement (replacing old personnel with new personnel in strategic positions), and (3) structure (redesigning the shape of the organization to accommodate the change). Such techniques were labeled as "unsuccessful" in implementing changes by authors of studies about them (pp. 120–121).

According to Greiner, the most successful changes occurred through the "sharing of power." Sharing of power was achieved through (1) group

Figure 10-1 Greiner's hypothetical power-distribution continuum. (Greiner, 1967:119-130; this figure was adapted from the general discussion.)

decision making and (2) group problem solving (p. 121). In the "moderately successful" changes, authority was delegated completely to the lower-level participants. Greiner noted that delegated authority occurred through either (1) case discussion (in which a group leader or teacher helped members arrive at a decision to accept change without imposing his will on the group) or (2) T-group sessions (which were supposedly designed to lead group members toward self-analysis, insight, and behavioral change) (pp. 121-122).

Greiner's study led to the identification of six phases of the "successful" process of change. These are summarized briefly in Figure 10-2.

Jones (1965) has attempted to accomplish a task similar to that of Greiner. He suggests that:

> The whole concept of planned organizational change rests upon the premise that some person, group or organizational unit (agent of change or social engineer) may work consciously, deliberately, and collaboratively, toward attaining goals of change which have been planned in advance. The purpose is improved performance and operation of organizational systems (client systems) through the application of appropriate knowledge and social technology. The concept is designed to lead to a program of action and study, and not to provide a specious description of accomplishment. Involved, among other considerations, are mutual goal-setting by one or both parties in the change process, some type of power relationships, and rational planning and action. The final objective sought is that a new situation of social equilibrium will be reached for the proper functioning of the client system (i.e., a condition where all of the significant elements in the social system are in support of each other). In such a state, the individual member of the system is able to find psychological security because of the absence and/or reconciliation of conflicting values, beliefs, and attitudes. In sum, all of the major elements of the social system are in a state of adjustment, both from the place of the individual's position and from that of the organization. Built into the changed state, if it did not exist previously, is a tendency toward movement (change), development, and growth [p. 193].

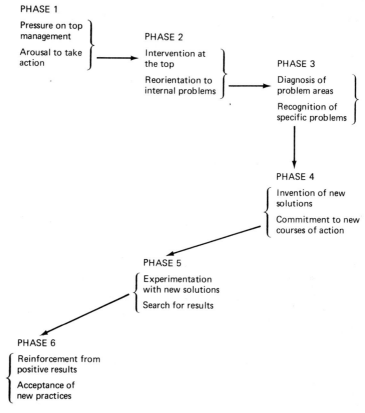

Figure 10-2 Greiner's dynamics of successful organization change. (Greiner, 1967:126.)

In the set of processes involved in change identified by Jones, he identifies "six major elements: (1) agent of change, (2) client system, (3) goals, (4) strategies and tactics, (5) structuring of change, and (6) evaluation. Each of these elements are major topics by themselves, although each in some way or another is inextricably tied to the others in some whole" (p. 193).

For additional emphasis, a third set of elements will be presented here which reflects the views of one of the most active contributors to the subject of planned change. Bennis (1965:358-359) perceives that social scientists are taking an increasingly important role in relation to organizations undertaking programs of change. He acknowledges that the topic of "acceptance of change in organizations" has been researched extensively and that we have acquired much information pertaining to it. He believes that "adoption requires that the type of change should be of proven quality, easily demonstrable in its effects, and with information easily available. Its cost and accessibility to control by the client system as well as its value accord have to be carefully considered" (pp. 357–358).

He presents a lucid argument setting forth "acceptance" conditions in organizations:

> 1. The client system should have as much understanding of the change and its consequences, as much influence in developing and controlling the fate of the change, and as much trust in the initiator of the change as is possible. 2. The change effort should be perceived as being as self-motivated and voluntary as possible. This can be effected through the legitimization and reinforcement of the change by the top management group and by the significant reference groups adjacent to the client system. It is also made possible by providing the utmost in true volition. 3. The change program must include emotional and value as well as cognitive (informational) elements for successful implementation. It is doubtful that relying solely on rational persuasion (expert power) is sufficient. Most organizations possess the knowledge to cure their ills; the rub is utilization. 4. The change agent can be crucial in reducing the resistance to change. As long as the change agent acts congruently with the principles of the program and as long as the client has a chance to test competence and motives (his own and the change agent's), the agent should be able to provide the psychological support so necessary during the risky phases of change. As I have stressed again and again, the quality of the client-agent relationship is pivotal to the success of the change program [pp. 358–359].

It is apparent that successful programs of change utilize members of the organization to a high degree. Such a statement seems tantamount to the doctrine of "participative management" espoused in business administration circles. Stated in simple terms, the theme which runs throughout all of the above programs of change is that meaningful participation by employees in changes which are designed to affect them will yield greater cooperation, higher morale, and a change of considerably longer duration than programs dictated to organizational members by writ from figures of authority.

Another thread common to each of these schemes is the role of the agent of change and his ability to work closely with the organization in a meaningful collaboration. The agent is not someone who enters an organization, renders a rapid diagnosis, dispenses a prescription for the malady, and then leaves. Rather, especially if he comes from outside the client system (organization), he must work at all levels in the hierarchy of authority and with all organizational members to develop rapport and trust. The importance of incorporating a humanistic philosophy into the role of an agent of change cannot be neglected or overemphasized. This does not mean that the agent should seek to abandon the organizational view. Organizational variables are very much a part of his orientation toward problems within organizations. But it is through individuals as participants in decision-making situations that changes in organizational variables are effected.

Bennis (1965:347) gives us his impression of an effective agent of change. A good agent of change is professional and undoubtedly possesses a doctorate in one of the behavioral sciences. Bennis assumes that the agent is interested in the improvement and development of the effectiveness of organizations. By the same token, he is preoccupied with people and the importance of social interaction as it relates to the structure and functioning of organizations. And he recognizes his limitations and possible strengths, ever aware of the needs of the client system and intervening where he feels a significant contribution toward improvement can be made.

SOME FUNCTIONAL APPROACHES TO PLANNED CHANGE

In the preceding section there was much significance attached to the involvement of organizational members in planning changes affecting them. There does appear to be a considerable amount of consensus regarding the participation of employees or workers in decisions which pertain to their patterns of work and social interaction. Students of planned change have formulated many schemes for how change in organizations can best be achieved, minimizing both the costs to the organization and the emotional and social costs to its members. In a study of some of the major theoretical and methodological problems in the investigation of planned organizational change, Clark and Ford (1970:30-31) have represented as two main types of approach the following: (1) the individual-interpersonal approach, in which an attempt is made to change the organization by changing individuals' attitudes; and (2) the systemic approach, which recognizes the existence of structured relations in groups and in organizations and seeks to bring about change by both diagnosing the structural aspects and using structural means to achieve change.

The Individual-Interpersonal Approach

The very thought of working with each and every employee in an organization on an individual basis in order to hasten the planned change (whatever it may be) is indicative of the utilization of the humanistic philosophy to the greatest degree. Such an approach to change emphasizes the personal and emotional concerns of organizational leaders for the subordinates. The approach is "employee-centered" as opposed to "production-centered," or so it would appear. However, some persons may react to the individual-interpersonal approach toward planned change as another in a lengthy list of acts perpetrated upon employees to obtain more from them (e.g., job satisfaction, esprit de corps, lower labor turnover, greater productivity, and increased loyalty to the organization). Regardless of the motives of administrators of change, we are obliged to consider the recurring observation that, generally, employees who are consulted and who become actively involved in planning operations affecting their own jobs seem to feel better about subsequent changes than those who are simply forced to accept change or leave.

A typical study of planned change in a nonunionized industrial organization by Morse and Reimer (1956) illustrates some of the positive implications of the involvement of employees in decisions affecting them. The change was defined as experimental and involved changes in the jobs of "rank-and-file" employees assigned to clerical work. One program, defined as the "autonomy program," increased each person's role and significance in the anticipated changes. The other program, designated as the "hierarchically controlled program," was set up to decrease each person's influence (i.e., high-level managers made decisions for the lower-level personnel). They found that in general individual satisfactions increased substantially in the autonomous program and decreased substantially in the hierarchically-controlled program.

In an earlier study, Coch and French (1948) investigated the impact of the increased involvement of employees in a change in operations in a garment factory. They matched four groups, three experimental and one control, according to several production and interpersonal characteristics. Two of the experimental groups were allowed to participate totally in the decisions affecting their work. The other experimental group was allowed to participate in the change through a representative. Implicit in Coch and French's findings was the fact that those individuals most directly involved in the decision-making process achieved the anticipated production levels associated with the new work faster than those members who were less involved at the outset. In addition, there was markedly less resistance to change among those who fully participated in the planning of change than among those only represented by one of their members. One interpretation of these findings is that those who fully participated became more content and satisfied with the subsequent change, although this is highly speculative.

A later study by French, Israel, and Aas (1960) lends support to the findings of Coch and French. Although their study was conducted within a Norwegian factory manufacturing footwear, French et al. came to similar conclusions regarding increased participation in decision making affecting job changes. Apparently, greater individual participation engendered less resistance to the change.

The individual approach to planned change obviously is designed to maximize one's perceived importance in the organizational decision-making hierarchy. However, it seems that such an approach is relatively restricted to smaller organizations or to independent departments within large organizations. At the same time, we must take into account the nature and magnitude of proposed changes. General organizational overhauls may require the involvement of extremely knowledgeable persons at high administrative levels. In these instances, attempts to involve lower-level organizational members meaningfully may be quite irrational and impractical. Large-scale organizational changes may have little or no meaning for many lower-level personnel. And if we view individuals in various departments as specialists in their tasks, an orientation paralleling Max Weber's bureaucratic model, we might find that employees have minimal interest in affairs which extend beyond their immediate sphere of competence.

The individual approach to change has greater application on a smaller scale. As we have seen from some of the studies discussed above, the increased involvement of employees appears to effect positive orientations toward subsequent changes. It should be noted, however, that these studies focused upon the involvement of employees in decisions which directly affected their work routine. If impending changes pertain to a reorganization of hierarchies of authority, the implementation of new technologies (e.g., automation in various forms or substantial improvements in the mechanization of heavy or routine labor), or important modifications in the work-flow sequence and in functional processual relationships, it is most unlikely to expect the average lower-level employee to possess the knowledge and skills to be of significant value in decision making related to such changes. Although suggestion boxes may be placed in conspicuous positions throughout the organization and employees may be urged to submit their ideas about how large-scale changes should be made, a typical reaction is apathy.

We must closely examine administrative motives for wanting to bring about attitudinal changes among employees. After all, if the power coalition of an organization decides that any particular change is necessary in order to survive in an increasingly competitive economic environment, such changes are made and transmitted throughout the entire organization via formal channels of authority. Individual organizational members may like or dislike the changes in their work routine which result from those decisions, but in conditions of crisis, interorganizational competition as a priority may subordinate concerns for the satisfactions and comforts of lower-level members. However, inasmuch as most large organizations are made up of several parts (i.e., departments) and rely heavily upon the successful performance and functioning of each part in order to maintain or increase overall organizational effectiveness, it is clear that the individual approach to planned change has some utility. Absenteeism, labor turnover, job dissatisfaction, poor work performance, and low productivity may be attributed, in part, to negative attitudes by employees toward planned change. Strategies for implementing changes which help to overcome resistance in a positive fashion may function to minimize these negative and undesirable factors.

Katz and Kahn (1966:449-450) warn that we must not "confuse individual change with change in organizational variables." Creating conditions which serve to change employees' attitudes in the direction of greater acceptance of organizational transformations on any scale does not necessarily mean that the employee will "work harder" or that the organization will become more effective than it was before the change. But logically we would not expect organizational effectiveness to decline, either. This is a signal accomplishment considered separately from other organizational benefits.

The Systemic Approach

Compared with the individual approach to planned change, the systemic approach is considered to be the more realistic and practical one. The object of change is the organization itself viewed as a complex network of departments, levels of authority, and definitions of roles. Changes in one organizational sector invariably involve adaptations and adjustments in other sectors, largely because most, if not all, organizational components (e.g., departments and work roles) are interconnected and therefore interdependent. Little is accomplished by achieving changes in individual attitudes in specific departments. The existence of an interdependent relation between departments and work roles poses a significant obstacle for the successful application of the individual approach to planned change. Consider the following example as a hypothetical case in point.

John Smith, assistant principal of a high school, enrolled in a night-school course designed to acquaint people with human-relations problems in organizations and the nature and consequences of a variety of styles of leadership. Smith acquired this information and attempted to use portions of it in his interpersonal relations with his subordinates and the principal. Since neither the subordinates nor the principal were exposed to the night course and were totally confused by Smith's new behavior in relation to them, Smith became a frequent topic of conversation among the teachers during lunch periods and coffee breaks. In time, word reached Smith that others were talking behind his back about his "new behavior." Eventually, Smith slipped back into his original pattern of behavior and no more was heard of the incident.

Judging from the situation presented above, it is apparent that other persons in the school organization were unresponsive to Smith's new behavior. One unfortunate outcome of this behavior was the ridicule of Smith. He became ostracized from teachers' activities until he brought his behavior back into harmony with the groups' expectations. Of course, we may speculate about what might have happened had *all* teachers *and* the principal attended the same night class as well. Had this been the case, it is likely that the entire organizational membership would be considerably more understanding of Smith's new behavior and possibly strongly supportive of it.

This illustration also underscores the fact that even though an agent of change is able to elicit changes in an employee's orientation to the job, this does not necessarily mean that the organization at large will allow the "new orientation" to interfere with or curtail existing and traditional functional relations with the "changed" employee. Katz and Kahn (1966:407–408) indicate the shortcomings of the individual approach to organizational change as well. They especially criticize the practice of subjecting one organizational member to T-group experiences and then reinstating this person in his former position. Focusing upon T-group experiences involving a single individual from an organization, they note that:

> powerful as this method is, its target is essentially the individual and not the organization. When the individuals return to their old structures, they step back into the same definitions of their roles. What is more basic, these roles are intimately related with a number of organizational roles; the converted returnees may want to redefine their own way of functioning, but the expectations of superiors, subordinates, and colleagues have not changed, nor has there been a change in organizational sanctions and rewards. If the person who has undergone change happens to be the head of an organization or a major unit of an organization, then organizational change may ensue. But there is no guarantee of significant organizational change even in such an instance. The old methods of operation have forces behind them other than the personal style of the leader, and these too must change to insure system change [p. 407].

Systemic changes appear to be most successful when persons at all levels of authority in the organizational hierarchy are brought together for T-group experience or "sensitivity training" (Bradford, Gibb, and Benne, 1964). This allows for new behavior to be sustained, stabilized, and supported at all organizational levels for a more prolonged period, inasmuch as each participant in the training group provides reinforcement for himself and the others.[6]

One of the primary benefits of the systemic approach to planned change is that all dimensions of organizational structure and process are considered rather than a single individual or department. At the same time, the systemic approach is more difficult to use because of the complex network of formal and informal intraorganizational factors which must be taken into account in the development of a strategy for change. In a collaborative relation with organizational leaders, the agent of change should acquire an in-depth understanding of the existing formal and informal patterns of authority and communication. The goal may be achieved most successfully by the anticipation of certain modifications in existing organizational patterns and their implications for each organizational subunit. Key personnel within each department to be affected can be assembled and briefed extensively concerning the nature and extent of proposed changes. A series of question-and-answer sessions can help to alleviate fears and anxieties associated with the impending change. With representation from all departments or organizational subunits present during such sessions, interdepartmental changes can be elaborated. The sponsors of the change can explain fully the rationale underlying each alteration in work routine and any other proposed organizational transformation. These explanations, in turn, can be relayed to lower-level personnel by their immediate supervisors or representatives, thus reducing the propensity for the circulation of distorted rumors.

OTHER APPROACHES TO PLANNED ORGANIZATIONAL CHANGE

Most of the literature dealing with planned change in organizations is directed toward individuals or small work groups, probably because such units are most accessible and malleable from the perspective of the agent of change. It logically follows, therefore, that most alternative approaches to planned organizational change center on individuals or small aggregates of individuals as opposed to major organizational variables. The belief seems to be that strategies of change fitting individuals or small groups within organizations will effect changes in target organizational variables. Below are listed some of the more popular strategies which have been and continue to be used as means of bringing about general organizational change.

T-Groups and Sensitivity Training

Since the late 1940s the National Training Laboratory located in Bethel, Maine, has been deeply involved in training persons in all types of organizations to become more proficient in dealing effectively with a wide variety of intraorganizational and interorganizational problems. Individuals representing different managerial levels and statuses within several organizations are brought together in groups of at least ten persons. The groups are unstructured in the sense that no formal leadership or plan of action is presented for them to follow. One or more trainers make up part of the group, but they remain detached as much as possible from the subsequent interaction of the group. Persons begin to share experiences with one another, and over time, each person becomes increasingly sensitive to the needs and reactions of others as well as to the impact of his own behavior on other group members.

A primary objective of such training experiences is to encourage participants to be increasingly analytical and understanding of the behavior of others, whether they be superiors or subordinates. Increased awareness of certain aspects of interpersonal situations in organizations generally leads to more effective decision making.[7]

The Case Method

Benne (1961:634) defines the "case method" as involving

> the confrontation of people in training with concrete human situations, situations with some temporal and developmental span, in which a whole complex of determinants of behavior are at work. [Persons] are asked to diagnose these situations, to analyze them in terms of why events happen as they do. If the [persons] are asked to prescribe and test verbally alternative behaviors for managing the situation confronted, they are asked to do so in terms of the diagnosis made, of the evidence available as to the dynamics of the situation, including the dynamics of the "manager" in it. Diagnosis and prescription are thus tied together in any adequate case analysis.

In Appendix I of this text are five case studies which may be approached according to the procedure outlined above.

The case method is particularly useful for inducing persons in all levels of an organizational hierarchy of authority to think about and analyze intraorganizational problems. If the problem has to do with managerial succession and its attendant conflicts with the previous work routine, a small group speculates about possible solutions and assesses the short- and long-range implications of such solutions. One major benefit of the case method is that it enhances each person's flexibility in thinking about and deciding which strategies would be most applicable to cases frequently encountered in the real world.[8] It also allows persons to see various organizational problems from several perspectives, thereby contributing to their insight into the current issues and difficulties confronting them.

This method is particularly relevant in relation to planned organizational change. Cases which pertain to the collaborative efforts of agents of change and client systems to introduce changes in organizations enable key personnel to become more sensitive to the many problems involved in the process of change. Although many of the cases are fictitious, they nevertheless provide an excellent training ground for persons to acquire certain analytical skills to be applied in actual situations at a later date.

Role Playing

This particular method of bringing about change was formally brought to bear upon interpersonal situations by Moreno (1946). Watson

(1966:171-172) discusses the value of role playing in enabling persons to empathize with others. In organizations role playing might consist of a superior and a subordinate exchanging roles temporarily in order to see how it feels to be in another's shoes on the job.

Role playing has been used to a limited degree in planned organizational change. It is particularly effective when persons at different levels in the hierarchy of authority are involved and must work together during the process of change. It aids understanding of others' roles and generally improves the relationships between roles.

Training Organizational Leaders

An alternative way of introducing change in an organization is through professional leadership. The assumption seems to be that if the organization has leadership of high quality, planned changes will be more successfully implemented.

In Chapter 7 it was observed that several kinds of leadership behavior may exist within an organization. Given the diversity of styles of leadership prevalent in organizations today, it is difficult to predict which mode of behavior would best fit a particular situation of planned change. There is little doubt that the quality of organizational leadership contributes to the success of planned change, although the precise impact of leadership quality on acceptance of changes by lower-level members is not presently known. We can only speculate about the potential rapport and trust which "successful" leaders are able to establish between themselves and their subordinates in a situation of planned change. It would seem logical to assume that greater acceptance of change would accompany action initiated by respected leaders compared with less popular ones.

The list of planned strategies for change can be extended indefinitely, although we have briefly treated some of the more popular methods. For instance, the work of Lewin (1939) in force-field analysis might have application here. Organizational behavioral states are seen as "equilibrium" conditions maintained at a given level by "driving forces" and "restraining forces." Changing an organizational state from one level to another (from one equilibrium to another) would necessitate either increasing the driving forces or decreasing (or eliminating) the restraining forces.

It is apparent that these last few strategies are designed primarily for organizational subunits rather than for the organization at large. Although many organizational researchers would prefer systemic schemes for change, particularly in the development of a general theory of organizational change, we must recognize that strategies for change at the level of small groups and individuals have far-reaching consequences for general organizational change. For this reason we have devoted considerable attention to such strategies and have noted the unique utility of each for intraorganizational planned change.

SOME POTENTIAL SOURCES OF RESISTANCE TO CHANGE

We noted earlier that bureaucratic organizations are generally sluggish when it comes to initiating change within themselves. The rigidity of the normative structure coupled with the intense adherence of organizational members to rules and rituals poses a significant obstacle to changes, regardless of their nature or magnitude. Change occurs, nevertheless, but not without incident. In addition to the routinization of organizational structure and process, subunits within organizations offer various kinds of resistance to change. Some of these are listed below.

1   Change is sometimes a threat to job security and creates anxiety for many employees.

2   Change may alter informal group relationships on the job. Since employees may derive considerable satisfaction from these associations, they are likely to resist changes which could be interpreted as potentially disruptive of such associations.

3   Change may involve additional education for remaining employees. Learning to do a new job may be acceptable to some employees as a new experience, but others may regard it with hostility and antagonism.

4   General ignorance about the nature and extent of the impending change will likely create a propensity for employees to resist it.

5   Change may signify a loss of status and prestige for certain employees as well as a gain in status for others, especially the younger workers. Few persons want to relinquish their perceived rank in the hierarchy of authority.

6   Some persons don't like to change what they do on the job regardless of whether or not the change is beneficial to them in the long run.

7   Hostility may exist among employees toward the agent of change as an "outsider." They resent his intrusion into their lives on the job.

8   Of course, informal groups in certain organizations may create some form of organized resistance to change for any reason.

9   Where there is a clear distinction between staff and line in an organization, Gardner and Whyte (1945) have observed that line personnel will resist change, particularly if it is introduced by the staff contingent. As an unwritten rule, line persons do not work smoothly with staff members.

10   In a study by Pearlin (1962a) dealing with the introduction of changes in a mental institution, it was found that those persons most likely

to resist change were at the lower levels in the hierarchy of authority and far removed from the professional goal-setters. Pearlin found that registered nurses and others with professional identifications were more understanding of the need for change and therefore less resistant to it (p. 334).

Sayles (1962:62) has observed that a considerable amount of attention has been given to introducing change into resistant organizations. It is also true that considerable interest is manifested among organizational researchers pertaining to overcoming resistance to change whenever it is found. On the basis of what has been presented here, it would seem that increased involvement of the employees in decisions directly affecting their work, early notification and dissemination of information relating to proposed changes, frequent meetings (and possibly training programs) for all levels of organizational members to fill them in on current developments concerning the change, and the gradual introduction of change in the form of "phases" would lessen considerably the various forms of resistance to change outlined above.

In Chapter 11, attention will be directed toward the topic of technological change in organizations and the mechanisms utilized by employees and management to adapt to it. Although the type of change discussed may be considered one form of planned change, the accumulated literature on the subject of technological change is ample justification for giving it a chapter to itself.

SUMMARY

All organizations, regardless of their size, shape, or complexity, are destined to change at various times and to varying degrees. Individuals and groups, as well as the organization at large, are directly and indirectly affected in different ways by organizational change. Through information acquired by researchers, we have been made increasingly aware of some of the potential implications of change in organizations for the different units of analysis.

Frequently, of course, changes occur spontaneously, or without being planned; but some change is the result of conscious, deliberate planning. Thus, a question arises as to how much human intervention (as well as what kind of intervention) should occur in planned change as compared with so-called "natural" change (e.g., labor turnover, administrative transitions, transfers, retirements, etc.). The area of planned organizational change has received a large amount of attention from professionals who try to facilitate change at the least possible personal, social, and organizational cost; but their efforts have not been unaccompanied by controversy.

This chapter has outlined some of the more important functions associated with the roles of agents of change (e.g., consultants) in relation to client systems (e.g., organizations). There are no universal guidelines for agents of change to follow, nor are there sets of evaluative criteria to cover all organizational problems. Emphasis has been placed upon the importance of the collaborative relationship between the agent of change and the client system as changes are contemplated and subsequently implemented. Various strategies for changes have been discussed briefly, including T-group interaction, case methods, and other forms of training persons to become more aware of and sensitive to processes, personalities, and relations between groups. The intelligent utilization of skills by agents of change has been stressed, and the function of such agents in "teaching" and "helping" capacities has been implicitly if not explicitly linked with their collaborative efforts.

One of our major tasks as social scientists is to understand our social world; the systematic study of organizational phenomena, including personal and interpersonal characteristics, seeks to further such understanding. The planning of change in organizations is in part the application of some of the more basic sociological principles we have developed and are currently developing. Industrial and business leaders want to have solutions to organizational problems at their disposal, and the social scientist studying organizations can be instrumental in guiding such persons to tentative answers or to possible strategies. The social scientist will make it a point to indicate to persons in need of assistance (or who represent organizations in need of assistance) that any actions which affect the lives of human subjects in any way should be explored and investigated intensively in order to determine whether or not potentially negative or harmful results will occur as a result of the change. Planned change directly involves the prediction of behavior (i.e., individual, group, or both), which generally centers on the specification of factors that precede an event to be predicted. One important implication of this chapter, however, is that we must also be concerned about the long-range outcomes and implications of our predictions.

STUDY QUESTIONS

1 What is an agent of change? What is the ideal relation between an agent of change and a client system? Discuss.
2 Why is it important to study the potential implications of planned change rather than simply say, "I want the organization changed in this or that fashion—do it!"? Explain.
3 To what extent do you feel employees should be involved in planning changes affecting their jobs? Discuss briefly. What are some potential implications of the involvement of employees for undermining the existing hierarchy of authority? Explain.

4 Is "change for the sake of change" justified in organizations in which the existing mode of thought among managers may be that "any change means progress"? Explain.

5 What are some of the forms of resistance to change in organizations? How can the organization cope with resistance to change most effectively? Explain your answer.

6 What do you see as the most important aspects of a collaborative relation between agents of change and client systems in a situation of planned change?

7 Differentiate between the individual approach and the systemic approach to planned change. Which do you feel has the greater utility for implementing change in organizations? Why?

8 Discuss the weaknesses and strengths of the following strategies for bringing about organizational change:

   a The case method.

   b T-groups.

   c Role playing.

9 How important is good leadership in planned change? Is there any specific type of leadership which is called for in general organizational change? Why or why not? Explain.

NOTES

[1] The definition of planned change presented here represents a synthesis of thought related to this conception found in various portions of the first chapter of R. Lippitt, J. Watson, and B. Westley, *The Dynamics of Planned Change: A Comparative Study of Principles and Techniques*, New York, Harcourt, Brace & World, 1958. A similar definition of planned change extracted from this volume may be found in W. G. Bennis, K. D. Benne, and R. Chin (eds.), *The Planning of Change: Reading in the Applied Behavioral Sciences*, New York, Holt, 1961:3.

[2] See for example such works as Argyris (1964-1965), Bennis (1966a), Guest (1962b), March (1965), Thompson (1967), and Whyte (1969).

[3] Training groups are designed to enable the members of small groups to improve their problem-solving skills. Miles (1959) defines training groups as "designed to help [their] members make constructive changes in their social selves by means of analysis of here-and-now experiences" (pp. 35-45). See Miles for a more complete discussion of the uses and functions of T-groups.

Agents of change functioning in the capacity of T-group coordinators are themselves trained in various centers throughout the United States in order to facilitate group problem solving and increase the skills of group participants in this regard. Instrumental in preparing persons for such skills are sites such as the National Training Laboratory in Group Development, Bethel, Maine, and the Research Center for Group Dynamics at the University of Michigan, Ann Arbor, Michigan. Each year persons qualify as group coordinators by participating in training courses offered by centers such as these. As a result, the dissemination of knowledge relating to developing the problem-solving skills of small groups is greatly increased by practicing individuals in various parts of the country.

⁴ In some cases, formal organizations hire qualified personnel to act as agents of change. This eliminates the necessity of "going outside" to seek assistance. In fact, in highly bureaucratized settings, specialized departments may exist which work exclusively toward the solution of many organizational problems.

⁵ The full study by Bavelas and Strauss is reported in Chapter 10, "Group Dynamics and Intergroup Relations" in William Foote Whyte et al., *Money and Motivation*, New York, Harper & Row, 1955, pp. 90-96.

⁶ One of the better discussions of the rationale behind this thought may be found in Katz and Kahn (1966). See especially Chapter 13, pp. 390-451.

⁷ For more extensive discussions of T-groups, see Miles (1959), Shepard (1961), and Tannenbaum, Weschler, and Masserik (1961).

⁸ The case method is given excellent coverage in Bennis, Benne, and Chin (1961), and Pigors and Pigors (1961).

Technological Change in Organizations and Adaptation of Members

INTRODUCTION

In the broadest sense technology includes methods, processes, devices, knowledge, and facilities which are used in the completion of work tasks in any organization.[1] When assembly-line production methods were first introduced, when atomic energy was discovered and harnessed, and when the first computer systems were fashioned for our business and industrial world, we experienced technological change. Technology involves virtually every aspect of getting something done.

Technology is a component of all organizations, regardless of their size, shape, and composition. Most organizations are dynamic structures, frequently changing and somewhat responsive to both external and internal variables. It seems reasonable to assume, therefore, that invention, the key to new technology, generates and promotes technological change, which, in turn, affects organizational behavior to one degree or another.

The effects of technological change on organizations are profound. Stimulated in part by the conclusions, and recommendations of the National Commission on Technology, Automation, and Economic Progress,[2] this chapter will explore a comparatively narrow range of phenomena affected by technology. Specifically, the major objectives are to (1) examine and assess the impact of technological change on organizational structure and selected organizational behaviors; (2) delineate some of the more important implications of technological change for social interaction patterns within organizations of various types; and (3) describe the means whereby organizations and their respective memberships adapt and adjust to changes attributed, directly or indirectly, to technology.

At least four arguments may be advanced in support of these objectives. First, there is a dearth of empirical research on the social effects of technological change in organizations. Second, most literature on this subject focuses upon its economic implications; the individual, the work group, and the organization are usually given only superficial attention. Third, an increase in the pace of technological change during the most recent decade has required more rapid individual, group, and organizational adaptations to its many forms. A more detailed description and analysis of such adaptations would enhance existing notions of organizational change. Finally, social scientists are actively aware of the general importance of technological change and its implications for affecting human interaction at virtually every level of organization.

TECHNOLOGY: SOME MEANINGFUL CLARIFICATIONS

Although the National Commission on Technology, Automation, and Economic Progress has alluded to several important implications of technological change for the social and economic lives of all persons, it has failed to provide a clear definition of this phenomenon. The general nature of the concept is somewhat elusive. Several writers have attempted to develop concise classifications of the term. For example, Killingsworth (1958) sees technological change as a subtopic of general economic change. Specific topics which are a part of, but subordinate to, technological change are (1) mechanization and (2) automation.

Mechanization

According to Killingsworth, "mechanization" is the use of nonanimal power sources to accomplish tasks. Steam-propelled engines, the use of compressed air to repair automobiles, airplanes, and other mechanical equipment, and the use of electricity to power addressograph machines, bookkeeping machines, computers, and typewriters are forms of mechanization.

Automation

Some researchers see automation as nothing more than an extension of mechanization, whereas others believe that the radical changes in work which have accompanied "automation" in various forms are sufficient justification for separating it from any other technological phenomena.[3]

Sultan and Prasow (1965) have been most successful in giving automation a consistent set of attributes, although their work is far from complete in the sense that little has been resolved regarding a universally acceptable definition. To illustrate the rather discouraging classification and measurement of automation, they relate the story of a man who once was asked to define an elephant. After some thought he replied, "I cannot define an elephant, but I know one when I see it."[4] Unfortunately, these researchers imply that such seems to be the present state of advance toward a general definition of automation.

In 1946 D. S. Harder, an executive of the Ford Motor Company, gave "automation" some substance by defining it as the automatic handling of parts between production units (Bright, 1958a). Subsequently, "automation" has come to refer to several things. In the discussion to follow, such phenomena as electronic-data-processing (EDP) systems, "Detroit" automation (associated with automobile assembly and other machine tool operations), and any type of closed-loop, feedback-production process which utilizes electronic sensors and paper-processing devices to regulate machines (petroleum refineries, public utilities systems, and hospitals are just a few of the many organizations employing automation in this form) will define various types of automation.[5]

A WORKING APPROACH TO TECHNOLOGICAL CHANGE IN ORGANIZATIONS

At the beginning of this book it was indicated that formal organizations consist of interrelated networks of roles and norms which form the basis for social interaction designed to achieve predetermined goals. Continuing with this perspective in the present analysis, any change in the technology of an organization will modify positively, negatively, or neutrally the existing patterns of social relations or functional role associations. More explicitly, we make tacit assumptions about people and sociofunctional group relations within all kinds of organizations. At least three of these assumptions are identified below.

Formal organizations have systems of stratification within them which develop along several different dimensions. Work roles, whether salaried, hourly, or voluntary, include different requirements as reflected by the division of labor. Levels of supervision make up another type of stratification system. Job content, job titles, and the like reinforce distinctions between organizational members.

Members (at all organizational levels) exhibit goals which are short- or long-range (or both) and which are interconnected in various ways within the organization. The organization provides the vehicle whereby members can fulfill their individual objectives, however relevant to the organization such objectives may be. While participants are on the job, their immediate or long-range objectives are inevitably linked in some way with the objectives of all other members.

Technological change of any kind necessitates individual, group, and organizational adaptations and adjustments as a type of "chain reaction" to change. Many organizations have predetermined strategies and make provisions for any required adjustments to organizational change by the membership.

Our present view requires that we examine certain implications of technological change for organizational structure, bearing in mind that organizational structure is also a component of technology. We are particularly interested in tracing the impact of structural changes to the interpersonal and personal responses to such changes. The sociological consequences of technological change in organizations have been severely neglected in the literature.

An attempt will be made in this chapter to arrive at tentative statements about the effects of technological change within organizations where there is sufficient empirical information on the subject. A word of caution is important here. It is necessary to recognize that cause-effect relations between one phenomenon and another are quite difficult to establish. As the number of variables in the social setting increases, the problem of causality becomes increasingly complex. The interrelatedness of variables most often leads to a chain reaction of events, any one of which could conceivably appear to "cause" the final outcome. We must be careful in our interpretation of the impact of technological change upon organizations externally and internally. It is impossible to understand any organizational behavior completely, given the complexities of cause-effect relations. But it will be seen that some variables contribute more to the outcome of a given event than others. An attempt will be made to specify these variables and their respective contributions in our subsequent analyses.

TECHNOLOGICAL CHANGE AND ORGANIZATIONAL BEHAVIOR

The effects of general technological change are probably being noticed most in business organizations. Certainly it cannot be disputed that an increasing number of people are gravitating toward office jobs. Hoos (1960a) reports that in 1910, 1 out of 20 people were employed in offices, compared with 1 out of 7 in 1958. Even the speculation of the early 1950s predicted that the greatest potential impact of technological change would occur in office jobs (Baldwin and Schultz, 1955:165-169). Today, we are witnessing the accuracy of such predictions.

Most formal organizations, regardless of their specific functions segmentalize their operations into several divisions. One type of divisional distinction particularly applicable to industrial settings is staff and line (Spaulding, 1961:202-205). The "staff" of an organization are usually those members responsible for planning, coordinating, and administrating. These individuals function in advisory capacities and frequently are involved in organizational paperwork. The president and his assistants, advisers, and middle-level managers are included within this rubric as well. "Line" members are typically involved in the actual production of the product, whatever it may be. In hospitals, nurses and nurses' aides might be viewed as line personnel. In factories, line employees might be the semiskilled and skilled craftsmen and machine operators and their supervisors. Usually, anyone having specific duties which directly affect production, the service rendered, or any other comparable objective would be classified as a part of line.

The distinction between staff and line has never been made explicit in the literature. For example, there are individuals who function as "men in the middle," such as first-line supervisors (Wray, 1949:298-301). Are they a part of staff or line? Neither the upper nor the lower echelons of the organization seem to want to claim them, regardless of their formal assignment in the organization. The lower-level employees view supervisors at any level as symbols of organizational authority and associate them with management, while middle-level managers and organization executives view foremen and other lower-level supervisory personnel as a part of production (i.e., line). Indeed, it is difficult to separate jobs into mutually exclusive categories with respect to direct involvement in production. While the work of line employees is typically production-centered, staff are also indirectly interested in production. Both line and staff are essential in order for the organization to achieve its overall goals. Neither would be able to operate effectively without efficient coordination between them.

In recent years the most dramatic technological change to occur in offices has been the introduction of electronic data processing (EDP). EDP has virtually revolutionized the handling and disposition of paper items in all types of businesses. "EDP" is defined as the coding and electronic manipulation of paperwork using punched cards, tapes or magnetic ink, and a related set of machines designed to interpret this information automatically.[6]

EDP handles and processes information in various forms. Information is "fed" into the machines by operators known as "programmers" or other EDP personnel, and the network of machines processes the information efficiently and accurately. The rapidity with which information is processed by EDP is many times faster than former manual paper-manipulation methods. A week's work can be processed by a computer in seconds. There is an almost limitless range of paperwork activities which can be performed by computer systems known as EDP.

Decisions made by the organizational administration to introduce technological change in this form (or any other form, for that matter) are based upon several factors. Some of the more important of these are listed below.

What is the cost of the proposed EDP system compared with present cost associated with job operations? EDP is extremely costly for any single organization, and there is much concern over whether the system will pay for itself in time by increasing the efficiency and accuracy of information processing and record keeping. After all, it would be foolish to install a costly EDP system without a substantial reduction in labor costs (i.e., employee salaries in relation to their output).

Does the organization expect to grow significantly because of the increased flexibility of services which the EDP system is capable of providing customers? An anticipation of future favorable business trends resulting from the EDP installation usually exists to justify the change. Much planning is obviously necessary in the making of these kinds of decisions.

Will there be a significant improvement in the quality and quantity of services which the organization renders the public? The efficiency of the organization may be enhanced by EDP in several respects. The bulk of paperwork is handled considerably more rapidly and accurately. The routine of handling paperwork and low-level problem solving is virtually eliminated. Simple addition, subtraction, or more complex mathematical or algebraic functions are performed by the machine rather than by error-prone employees. The greater accuracy and flexibility of such a system are indeed impressive advances over former clerical activity of the same nature.

What will be the net effect or impact of EDP on staff and line employees and their associations on the job? Will the system reduce the need for more employees, or will EDP and its accompanying advantages and flexibility in some way stimulate organizational growth to absorb originally displaced personnel? For instance, a bank in Indiana introduced drastic technological changes in the mid-1960s and many employees were left without jobs. Rather than lay off these employees, the organization was able to absorb them into newly created bank branches as a result of the improvement of their services and expansion (Champion, 1966a).

It is perhaps more meaningful to discuss technological change in organizations in terms of degree. Hoos (1961:11) states that:

the numerous adjustments in automation do not have to take place all at once. Fortunately, installation of electronic systems—at least in the office—requires time. Often the introduction of initial phases takes as long as two years. Later, new programs can be added more quickly. The organization in which the personnel and industrial relations people maintain good rapport with other divisions within the organization can do the most effective job of preserving morale, preparing employees for the new occupations, and mitigating the impact. Conversely, without an atmosphere of confidence, fear and insecurity prevail; manpower resources are wasted and costly crash programs become the inadequate surrogate for orderly planning.

SOME CONCOMITANTS OF TECHNOLOGICAL CHANGE ALONG SELECTED DIMENSIONS

Some primary spatial changes introduced by technology in organizations relate to (1) hours of work, (2) spatial relations between employees, and (3) increased dependency upon technology to accomplish tasks.

Hours of Work

Changes in hours of work are becoming commonplace in organizations undergoing changeovers to EDP systems.

Work after office hours (traditionally 8 A.M. to 5 P.M.) has often become part of an efficient cycle of operations on certain routine functions. For example, in a number of companies, computers are used during evening hours around the clock to perform runs of thousands of insurance policies to produce premium billings. In the morning, the computers' output of bills is ready for mailing by the regular daytime staff. This statement provides strong evidence that shift work is rapidly becoming an integral feature of EDP in offices. However, the implications of EDP for organizations often extend much further than the immediate labor-saving benefits of a specific office staff.

Even firms which are not partially or fully computerized but depend upon the facilities of larger organizations for work processing are not immune from being affected by this form of technology. There are accompanying new demands on and expectations of employees of such companies. Certain deadlines must be adhered to which did not exist formerly. Because of the EDP system, errors in work are readily detected. Therefore, increased accuracy and precision in manual operations are expected of office staff.

In addition, operating a computer on a twenty-four hour basis requires shift schedules and changes in hours for employees. This may mean that the organization must hire more personnel to handle work processed during the extended operating period. In many instances, radical changes in the work schedules of employees are made to adapt to the new program of operation. Employee sentiments toward such changes in their work routines are mixed. Some are given choices of accepting new working hours (e.g., midnight to 8:00 A.M.) or quitting. Other personnel are allowed to express some preference, which may be either acknowledged or ignored by higher-ups.

One implication of shift work pertains to the sex ratio of the office staff at different shifts. Night work is generally not preferred by women. Telephone operators, however, are an exception to this statement. These positions are typically filled by women, most of whom accept shift work as a basic condition of their employment. Both management and union are supportive of such conditions in employment contracts. For other types of office employees, however, there is less likelihood that women will be expected to perform duties on night shifts. The U.S. Department of Labor has noted the propensity for men to fill night positions more readily than women. In time, men will probably outnumber women in office work. Perhaps different managerial methods or supervisory styles will be practiced on day office staffs (predominantly women) as compared with night office staffs (predominantly men).

Another implication of shift work pertains to the family. Where one or both parents are employed in firms currently operating on a multishift basis, a rearrangement of family responsibilities and duties are in order. Even when only one family member has an unusual work schedule, certain difficulties are encountered as both partners attempt to adjust and adapt to new work arrangements. The real and theoretical implications of shift work for family stability or solidarity are important to consider. However, little conclusive empirical information exists at present that technological change of one sort or another causes this or that change to occur in family life. Additional study is obviously necessary.

Spatial Relations among Employees

EDP systems tend to create less need for individuals to communicate with one another about job-related matters. EDP systems usually absorb many previously related tasks into one continuous electronic function, thereby eliminating the need for much interaction between employees. The employee becomes an isolated unit in the midst of other employees. Patterns of social interaction change from employee-employee interaction to employee-machine interaction. In some office environments, office staffs undergo some degree of reorganization and reshuffling to accommodate the EDP system. Generally, fewer employees are needed after an EDP installation. The implications for the increased isolation of employees on the job as a result of EDP are perhaps better examined in the context of the functional and interpersonal conditions to be discussed in this chapter later. Suffice it to say that physical (structural) separation among employees occurs after most EDP installation. The nature and extent of job-related interaction changes as well.

Increased Technological Dependency

"Technological dependency" is the degree to which employees must rely upon a machine or system of machines to accomplish tasks according to organizational specifications and expectations. A sculptor manipulating soft clay has absolute control over the outcome of the "product." The office worker who is in charge of customer accounts must be dependent upon the EDP system to accomplish the bookkeeping function efficiently and accurately, thus meeting predetermined work deadlines. There is greater technological dependency in the latter case than in the former. The office worker activates the machinery but actually has little control over determining the ultimate quality of work performed.

Aside from the usual cost-of-living raises which employees in organizations obtain annually (if they are lucky), there is little evidence to indicate that technological change in the form of EDP results in significant pay increases for employees. What ordinarily happens is that technicians are hired to assist in the operation of the system, or present employees are trained to handle new jobs associated with EDP. It is not so much increased education as it is *different* education which employees acquire on the job in relation to the computer and technological changes of this sort. It is true, however, that people in various computer fields do command higher salaries than individuals employed without such training. The employee who sticks it out through a conversion to EDP, however, is unlikely to experience a significant increase in his salary even if he receives additional training provided by the company. The issue of whether salaries should be increased as a result of technological change must be resolved by each company individually. Blanket generalizations are far too speculative and unwarranted at the present time.

Some important processual changes in organizations associated with improvements in technology are (1) decision making, (2) number of supervisory levels, (3) type of supervision, (4) coordination between work tasks, (5) job security, and (6) job status.

Decision Making

Present indications are that computer systems such as EDP are reversing the decision-making process toward greater centralization. One of the primary functions of an EDP system is to make decisions. It is expected, therefore, that significant changes in the decision-making process of organizations using EDP will be observed. In a recent report on manpower in the United States, the U.S. Department of Labor stated that centralization of decision making (among other significant organizational changes) can be anticipated as a result of EDP in the office (U.S. Department of Labor, Bureau of Labor Statistics, 1964). A study of employees' adjustment to office automation throughout twenty private organizations showed that EDP provides a fast, accurate, reliable means of performing many tasks. More departments within the same organization are collectively relying upon the information obtained from the centralized EDP system. In this sense, greater centralization of tasks is being observed.

The centralization of decision-making power has also been observed after the installation of EDP in an airline-reservation system (U.S. Department of Labor, Bureau of Labor Statistics, No. 137, 1958). The demands for increased efficiency in flight reservations and increasingly complicated flight plans prompted the consolidation of many previously separate tasks (performed by flight clerks and ticket agents) into one electronic function, thus requiring less personnel than before as well as fewer supervisory levels.

What are some implications for employees as a result of this apparent turn toward increased centralization of decision making? One fact is that several levels of supervision are being eliminated. EDP is increasingly making routine decisions which were formerly functions of middle-level managerial personnel. From an administrative point of view, EDP is a valuable enterprise. It aids the organization in making more accurate and complete assessments of information quickly, and the decisions based upon such evaluations are generally better in quality.

The employee deprived of decision-making power may make a different interpretation of the situation, however. Much of the value a person places on his work is associated closely with his ability to control various aspects of it. Decision-making power is frequently desired by lower-level personnel, and to remove it from them leaves some degree of dissatisfaction. The result may be to encourage high labor turnover and increased production costs as employees become increasingly apathetic toward their work and lose pride in it. Argyris (1959b) has shown that at least in some instances, however, we must not be too hasty in assuming that all persons want to have a lot of responsibility in their jobs. Some employees may even be afraid of decision-making power and avoid it. He suggests that not everyone wants to make decisions on the job and that there is some degree of security in having someone else be responsible for making decisions. One cannot be blamed for wrong decisions if he did not make them in the first place. In short, decision making may be quite unimportant to many employees.

The Number of Supervisory Levels

A primary function of EDP is to centralize record processing and absorb many decisions into one electronic process. This directly affects the number of supervisory levels in the organization. As centralization of decision-making power turns upward, managers and supervisors at lower levels in the organization are left with less power. In fact, their functional necessity may be jeopardized seriously. Also, the EDP system absorbs many previously independent functions, thus requiring fewer individuals at each supervisory level. The net result is the reduction of supervisory levels in the organization. The individual occupying higher-level posts in the organization is left with fewer decisions, also. But usually his decisions are more important than formerly in the sense that they cover a greater portion of organizational work activity. As the number of supervisory levels changes, it is likely that the quality of supervision at each level will change also.

The Type of Supervision

With the advent of EDP, employees become tied to the deadlines and demands for accuracy of the EDP system itself. This may cause the worker to view his supervisor in quite a different light after technological change of this sort. The computer rechannels employees' complaints toward itself rather than toward a human being in the person of a supervisor. Also, the supervisor has a new reason for requesting work of high quality from his subordinates—the EDP system demands it.

Coordination between Tasks

A fundamental change brought about by improved technology in the office is to reduce the amount of coordination between tasks. In fact, some tasks are removed from the formal organizational interaction pattern entirely. The amount of coordination between work tasks decreases as the result of several different jobs being absorbed into EDP. A result is to leave fewer "points of friction" (where work is exchanged from one station to another) where employees potentially become irritated with one another (Strauss, 1954). As these points of friction are decreased, the result is fewer interworker arguments and an improvement in relations among employees.

Job Security

Job security deserves some mention here, particularly because of what EDP does to eliminate and change many jobs. "Job security" may be defined as the perceived assurance of continued employment and the ability to perform the job well. Job security is important to most employees, particularly those occupying office jobs. This is true partly because of the fact that there is less union representation among office workers. Furthermore, they are more vulnerable to outright dismissal compared with the average factory worker.

A major problem is to identify the target population, or those who have the most to lose as a result of EDP. EDP is geared to replace the more simple and repetitive tasks, precisely those requiring less education. It is not so much a matter of an organization's not wishing to retain older employees in new capacities as it is that the new jobs encompassed by EDP favor those who are more familiar with computer operations and have taken courses at automation training schools—the younger employees.

An argument posed by many researchers is that EDP elicits changes in the work environment which affect job security adversely. Buckingham (1962), and Hoos (1960b) independently arrived at this conclusion, particularly with reference to the older worker and the unskilled. One consequence of change which supports this notion is that EDP makes many skills obsolete. The worker possesses certain intellectual tools, but with the rapid pace of technological change, these are quickly rendered obsolete. The alternative is clear, when available: he must further prepare himself to obtain new skills so that the organization will want to retain his services. Otherwise, he will feel (as will the organization) that he is superfluous, with little or no real contribution to make to the system.

To lessen the impact of EDP on work staffs, many organizations follow the plan of retaining employees even if it means that they will have little to do after an EDP changeover. Many employees are offered new jobs in connection with the new EDP system which displaces them initially (Champion, 1966a). Though displaced temporarily, the employee somehow manages to master the new tasks and "adjusts."

In a study conducted by the U.S. Department of Labor, it was found that the effects of EDP installations in a number of business offices created only mild threats to employees' job security. In fact, it was shown that there was an increased interest on the part of management in removing potential threats to job security through job change. There was a significant willingness on the part of management to provide training for individuals to upgrade their skills to maintain their jobs. Also, many of the offices installing EDP components brought the anticipated change to the attention of their employees several months prior to the actual installation. Reassurances from management to the effect that no one would lose his job as a result of the impending EDP installation seemed to alleviate employees' insecurity on the job. More companies today are instigating programs to cushion the impact of EDP on their personnel. Some employees to be displaced are sent at the company's expense to training schools to prepare them for the change. Other employees are offered an opportunity of choosing which jobs they would like to perform after the changeover to an EDP system. Transfers, of course, are utilized when employees can be persuaded to take a job with the same company but in a different location across the country. Travel allowances and pay raises are provided as compensatory measures.

Some of the results of this managerial activity are that fewer employees in offices are perceiving technological change as a real threat to their security. More likely, the changes in jobs arouse a degree of curiosity and anxiety, as the increased necessity to adjust to the new conditions fostered by EDP becomes apparent. Job security appears to be assuming a new form as well. The cares of office workers are shifting from fears of displacement and eventual obsolescence to more immediate improvements in the work setting which will contribute to job satisfaction. The outlook for job security in relation to EDP is favorable. Increased familiarity with EDP and the growing number of training schools and programs offered by changing organizations creates more favorable conditions for adapting to technological change. EDP is less frequently viewed as a major threat to security. Rather, EDP is becoming increasingly challenging, and employees are accepting the challenge with enthusiasm.

Job Status

The status of employees in the office depends upon several factors. Perceived status is evident where the employee has some idea of how important his job is compared with the jobs of others in relation to helping the organization achieve its objectives. One's status is evident when the employee is designated by the organization as holding a particular rank or position within it. For example, the U.S. government uses ratings such as GS-9, GS-10, and GS-13 to designate individuals' different lengths of service, special abilities and skills, and educational attainment.

EDP may alter job status in several ways. It has been shown that EDP removes a degree of decision-making power from employees through the centralization of work. When the degree of one's authority to make decisions is reduced, one's status is affected—usually, it is decreased. Also when EDP is installed, a number of jobs are drastically changed and some are eliminated entirely. Some individuals find that their previous knowledge of work operations is no longer vital as a part of the daily work routine.

Fewer different jobs are generally found after EDP has been installed. This reduction of differences between occupational categories disrupts the status hierarchy to a significant degree. It brings employees closer in terms of an equalization of status through a reduction in the number of different ranks. Increased homogeneity, particularly where two or more employees of previously different status levels now perform the same job and receive the same recognition, often creates serious interpersonal problems.

The content of many jobs is changed as well. What one does has previously figured as an important indicator of his job status. Whether one is a blue-collar or a white-collar worker and whether physical or mental labor is involved in the performance of the task indicate one's status.

Changes in the office associated with the qualitative dimension are several. Among the most important changes are those pertaining to (1) job content, (2) the meaning of work, and (3) physical demands.

Job Content

It is evident that whenever technological change of any kind occurs in an organization, most jobs are affected, directly or indirectly, to one degree or another. What can be said about the effects of technological change on the content of office jobs generally, however? The fact that so many companies are at different stages of growth when significant technological changes occur, accompanied by the fact that technological change is usually a gradual process, not necessarily taking place all at once, causes many observers to conclude that very little can be said about any systematic effects of this variable upon job content. Complicating further the possibility of drawing generalizations about the effects of this phenomenon upon job content is the fact that each organization using EDP will perhaps utilize it differently. Not everyone will be similarly affected by EDP, and some departments in organizations may even remain relatively unaffected by it. Although numerous conditions must be satisfied before blanket generalizations can legitimately be made, even conservatively, the effects of EDP in offices are relatively uniform.

For the most part, jobs associated with EDP systems are repetitive. Of course, it must be admitted that many jobs unrelated to EDP are also repetitive. The impact of change on one's job, therefore, must be assessed in terms of what he did before the change. Machine tending in conjunction with an EDP operation is a fairly repetitive task. Keypunch operation is extremely repetitive. Is the consequence of EDP simply to replace one set of repetitive tasks with another set of equally repetitive jobs? On the one hand, it is argued that EDP attacks primarily the low-skilled, simple, repetitive job operations. The implication is that the jobs remaining are less repetitive than before. This is not necessarily true. Consider the following example given by Hoos (1961). In her study of the effects of office automation in a large company, she concludes that one significant reason for excessive turnover among key-punch operators was the increased monotony of tasks. She indicates that this situation existed after EDP in two other office situations as well. She says that deterioration was not only found in the surviving routine, nonsupervisory jobs, which appeared less interesting and more machine-paced than before automation, but also in the middle-management jobs outside the EDP area.

Partially offsetting the boredom and monotony associated with EDP tasks is the "halo effect" of working around computer systems. Somehow employees have developed the notion that working with EDP is rewarding and status-enhancing. Consequently, they accept the new jobs without incident, regardless of how repetitive or boring they may be.

Auxiliary positions in office settings with EDP may show little or no change in job content; rather, these jobs may require handling paper items differently. In bank work, for example, tellers continue their functions without much change. The fact that they must now relate to an EDP system makes it necessary for them to handle business transactions somewhat differently. Their basic functions remain unchanged, however.

The Meaning of Work

When technological change occurs, a change also occurs in the meaning the job has for the individual employee. If the job is transformed into one which is more repetitive than before, the worker may think his task is increasingly unimportant. Or if he accepts a new task associated with an EDP system, he may fail to comprehend how his own work relates to the total organization. He begins to wonder just how important he really is. The person who finds his job completely eliminated and is forced to accept some new menial position may have serious doubts about his necessity to the work setting.

Although machine tending is an important function in an EDP system it is often regarded as a relatively meaningless activity. The machines rarely break down or need adjustment, and therefore the services of a machine tender are seldom utilized. Such a task is comparable to a bottle inspector in a soft drink bottling plant. He watches each bottle move past him on a conveyor, attempting to spot bottling flaws and other potential problems. To decrease the extreme boredom accompanying such a task, a bottle of a competing soft drink is sometimes substituted up the line to keep the inspector on his toes and to see that he is doing his job properly.

As the machine increasingly takes over much of the job in the office, employees cannot but feel that their own jobs are less meaningful. It is difficult to measure the psychological and social implications of job change in this regard. The employee still retains some of his decision-making and problem-solving functions. The EDP system is an information processor, but the individual continues to exercise some control over the information being processed. One consequence is that the EDP system enables employees to make better and more rational decisions. Viewed from this perspective, the effects of the computer on the meaning of the job may be beneficial as well as detrimental.

Physical Demands

Almost without exception, EDP jobs are less demanding physically than the jobs they replace. Persons employed in or around EDP experience little physical strain in the performance of their tasks. What little physical labor does exist is reduced even further by EDP. Companies installing EDP equipment would do well to hire individuals who can sit for extended periods, performing routine and relatively monotonous tasks. Such is the plight of the office worker in the automated work environment.

Some of the primary interpersonal changes in the work setting resulting from technological change pertain to (1) the informal group, (2) the size of the work group, and (3) personality characteristics.

The Informal Work Group

The informal work group on the job is affected by technological change in at least three different ways. First, technological change may modify the person's job content, consequently affecting the basis for informal interactions with a particular informal group. Job content often determines one's status, and a change in status may alter an employee's informal position with others. Second, technological change may eliminate a person's job. Removing an employee from the work setting causes the most obvious form of disruption of informal groups. Finally, it is likely that a technological change may make it necessary for a person to move to some other part of the workplace, thus making it difficult, if not impossible, for him to carry on previous informal associations with other employees. The informal group, as discussed previously, performs many important functions for employees. In addition to providing each worker with informal status and recognition, the group offers security and friendship as well as a ready source of information about organizational activity. EDP systems which are geared to absorb several employee functions into one operation also cause functional separation of workers. Less formal need to communicate with others about job matters may discourage the frequency of informal associations.

The Size of the Work Group

Generally, the effect of EDP in the organization is to reduce the immediate size of the work group. Fewer workers are needed, unless, of course, the organization expands rapidly enough to absorb those employees displaced by the change. Changes in the size of the work group should act to modify the nature of supervisory practices, partly because of the new work demands under EDP and partly because there are fewer employees to supervise. The type of supervision will probably be of a general nature, because more work will be performed by the EDP system rather than the employees. It is difficult to criticize employees for work performed by EDP. The machine complex also operates on fixed schedules and employees adhere to impersonal rules and deadlines rather than to the dictates of some supervisor. They feel less pressure from the man, but more from the machine.

Personality

Undoubtedly one of the most important consequences of EDP in the office is to create conditions which conflict with particular personality systems. Little systematic study of personality in relation to technological change has been undertaken. Drawing from the few case studies in which personality variables have been investigated in relation to change, several implications for personality systems seem apparent. First, certain personality characteristics seem to cushion or intensify an employee's adaptation to technological change. Some personality traits help one to adjust and some deter one from adapting to EDP and its characteristics. We may well have to depict a typical "automation man" of the future, adaptable to the conditions which are created by technological change, especially EDP, in much the same sense that Whyte (1956) has described "the organization man."

A second implication is that the notion of "the right man for the right job" has greater merit. In relation to adapting to EDP and its conditions, personality variables seem to be quite pertinent. A third implication is that personality factors appear to be potentially useful predictors of individual adjustment to change. In a bank study previously discussed, Champion and Dager (1967a) found that definite differences in personality configuration existed between employees who adapted successfully to EDP in the workplace and those who appeared not to adapt to it. For instance, some conditions brought about by EDP systems are repetitiveness, increased isolation, and alienation. Being able to tolerate such conditions is contingent, to some extent, upon certain personality factors. Some personality characteristics lend themselves to repetitive job operations and isolative job conditions. Some people prefer to work alone while others must be around others constantly.

Anticipating employees' reactions one way or another is always helpful in the planning of change. Structuring the situation so as to maximize acceptance of change may be viewed by some as manipulating employees for the benefit of management, even though the employee benefits as well. Any attempt at planned organizational change cannot afford to ignore the contribution of personality systems as means of modifying resistance to change.

A statement from the U.S. Department of Labor, Bureau of Labor Statistics (1964), summarizes much of what has been discussed in this section. Among office workers, EDP is eliminating routine jobs and reducing the repetitive aspects of other jobs.

Electronic data processing is having its greatest effects on detailed, repetitive, manual work in functions such as accounting, addressing, billing, inventory control, payrolls, and other recordkeeping. Many clerical occupations, especially those of a service character, such as bank teller, complaint clerk, receptionist, and secretary, continue unaffected by automation. Most of the new EDP jobs, on the other hand, are at a higher level. Those of a programmer and systems analyst are in the professional category, while most of the console and peripheral equipment operators are in the upper level of clerical work. Thus, considering both the jobs eliminated and those created, the net result of the changeover to EDP is likely to be a somewhat higher average level for employees in the offices affected. There is evidence also that EDP, in eliminating many of the routine elements of office jobs, enlarges employees' personal responsibility, requires greater accuracy in office work, and imposes the necessity for workers to meet more precise deadlines. Under some circumstances, the conditions of work for clerical employees under EDP may become more similar to those of factory workers. The evidence is still far from conclusive regarding the general effects of automation on managerial personnel. In some instances, however, the introduction of EDP and the accompanying reorganization of managerial functions have led to reduced staffs in the lower and middle echelons of management [p.18].

Ordinarily, when technological change occurs in the office, it is presumed to be for the better from the standpoint of reduced production costs, increased efficiency, and greater profits, as well as increasing employees' comforts and making the work environment more attractive and challenging. Unless the company has a suggestion box, it really has little way of obtaining legitimate feedback from employees concerning the results of the changes. And even with the suggestion box, there is no guarantee that employees will convey to management the way they really feel about things. Consequently, what is intended by management may not be interpreted by employees in the same way. There exist what are commonly called "communication gaps," or breakdowns between management's motives as understood and intended by management and management's motives as understood and received by employees. A one-to-one correspondence does not always exist here.

ORGANIZATIONAL ADAPTATIONS TO TECHNOLOGICAL CHANGE

Since organizations are always changing in one way or another, employees are frequently shifted from plant to plant, from office to office, or from one type of work to another. Businesses expand and contract as the market for their goods and services changes. New organizations are continually emerging; some grow old, less competitive, and ineffective and eventually die, while others survive. It is unrealistic to argue that the employee and his work group can somehow remain immune to change in the work setting, regardless of the nature of the change. The fact that all employees, at one time or another in their careers, are directly or indirectly affected by changes in their jobs or work environment is well documented.[7]

Changes are generated by numerous factors. A new supervisor represents a change from the old one. Being placed in a new workroom with new work associates is also a change to which employees must adjust. Changes in the hierarchy of authority, promotions, or the manufacture of new products elicit modifications in one's previous work routines. In the last chapter, we examined planned organizational change from the standpoint of various strategies and potential implications. This chapter has focused upon change in organizations as the result of technology, specifically EDP. Change of this sort may result in the need for fewer employees. The likelihood is that they will be layed off or displaced. Technological change may enable the company or business to become more competitive, offering more satisfactory goods and services to consumers at less cost than before. Following an economic rationale, increased consumption of the product will likely lead to an expansion of the organization. Employees eliminated from one department or division of an organization may eventually be absorbed by a newly created one. Employees may be neither layed off nor displaced but rather asked to shift the content of their work radically. A new work role is always a possible alternative as a result of technological change, where some old jobs are rendered obsolete and new jobs are created. Sometimes, nothing whatsoever happens to the employee exposed to EDP. But other employees around them experience changes in their work roles. This affects the first employee indirectly, inasmuch as he defines himself and his work, in part, in relation to the work done around him by others.

It is recognized that adjusting to technological changes of any kind in an organization is not a unilateral process. The employer, governed by the realities of profit and loss figures, must also adapt to these changes to his best advantage. Regulating the size of the staff to fit the company's needs in the face of technological change is not an easy matter. The problem is further complicated by the presence of strong union representation or other protective employees' organizations (e.g., the American Association of University Professors in academic settings).

The remainder of this chapter will focus upon several popular strategies for adjusting to change in the organization. All of these strategies have been used in a variety of businesses and industries as means of regulating staff size. Some are more workable than others for particular kinds of organizations. Some act to benefit employees more than the organization itself; some act in the opposite fashion. In a brief discussion of each of these plans or strategies, we shall consider the advantage of each to the worker, to management, and to both as well as some general disadvantages for all concerned. The object is not to endorse any single plan or combination of plans, but rather to present each strategy in such a way so as to consider its relative merits and shortcomings more systematically and objectively. What is ideal for one work setting or company may not be for another. It is up to the individual organization to judge.

The plans for adjusting to changes which affect the number and levels of existing jobs are many. A preliminary listing of some of the more popular plans would include (1) attrition, (2) early notification of change, (3) training for new assignment and positions, (4) worker seniority rules, (5) employee consideration, (6) transferrals and relocating at company expense, (7) shift work, (8) shorter workdays, and (9) the use of temporary employees.

Attrition

"Attrition" means simply that when employees quit, die, or retire they are not replaced. The organization waits while normal turnover takes its toll, until the staff dwindles to the desired size. Known by other names, such as "silent firing" or "no-hiring policy," attrition is perhaps the most widely used method of resolving the problem of what to do with superfluous staff (Wolfbein, 1962). Compared with firing unneeded employees, attrition is the most unobtrusive way of reducing staff to the size which is more desirable (U.S. Department of Labor, Bureau of Labor Statistics, 1964, Bulletin No. 1408). Because employees are not replaced when they quit or retire, few persons notice their absence. Consequently, persons remaining with the organization are unlikely to complain. Sometimes companies, in collaboration with unions, agree to reduce the staff at a fixed rate per year. As a hypothetical example, a 2 percent reduction in staff is set as a standard. The company maintains good rapport with union officials while simultaneously achieving the desired size of staff in the long run.

An example of the use of attrition occurred at a petroleum refinery in the Midwest during the period 1956-1961 (U.S. Department of Labor, Bureau of Labor Statistics, 1964, Bulletin No. 1408). As a result of replacing old equipment with technologically superior machinery, it became necessary to decrease the refinery labor force by almost two thousand. At the same time of the changeover to improved equipment, the company had on its payroll about seven thousand employees. Over the five-year period, eighteen hundred employees were eliminated, about half as a result of attrition. "All hiring was stopped beginning in mid-1957. Soon thereafter, staffing reductions were projected and estimates were made of the number of jobs which would be vacated by quits, deaths, or retirements" (p. 11).

Attrition seems to be an expedient way of managing the cost-production balance. There is always a supply of new employees, and virtually no problems exist for most firms wanting to increase the size of their staff. Attrition is most workable where there is already a fairly rapid turnover of personnel.

A policy of attrition is beneficial to existing employees of the organization. The person can quit when he likes. In this sense, a strong psychological benefit is present. Most employees are fairly certain of retaining their own jobs. Job security exists to a high degree, even though it may be disconcerting to some workers to know that their company is no longer hiring.

Attrition is not without its shortcomings, however. In the long run, it becomes increasingly difficult for successive generations of employees to find work. As more tasks are relegated to computers and other technological devices, fewer employees are needed. Projecting the potential impact of technological changes of this type on a large scale, it is likely that in the near future, serious unemployment problems could exist, especially for persons who currently earn their living in skilled and semiskilled occupations (Brozen, 1963).

The future for employees promised their jobs in spite of drastic technological changes is not particularly pleasant either. Although they retain their job security and income, they face the possibility of performing less important jobs (Fleming, 1962:7-11).

Early Notification of Change

Frequently, organizations are able to anticipate technological changes several months in advance. The planning requisite to such a change generally involves some crude estimate of staff needs under the new system compared with existing needs. Informing the personnel to be affected of the anticipated changes and the possibility of displacement or relocation is used as an "early warning system" and as a means of encouraging a more smooth transition to the new procedures (Buckingham, 1961).

Notifying workers of changes within organizations is not new by any means. Many firms use intraorganizational newsletters as a part of this process of disseminating information. The Bank of America, the world's largest banking organization, has introduced technological changes by exposing staff members of its various branches to movies of fully automated banking systems. During the late 1950s and early 1960s this bank introduced ERMA, the "electronic recording method of accounting," to its member branches. Explanations were provided by experts associated with the electronic firm installing the system, and question-asking sessions were held to clarify any misconceptions employees held about the new system. The bank also published a monthly newsletter which kept its hundreds of branches informed regularly of current developments (Pollock, 1957).

There is sufficient reason to believe that early notification of change serves to allay anxieties and fears personnel may have concerning what they can expect (Mann, 1962). Employees' grapevines often distort information pertaining to changes in jobs. Rumor has a way of being twisted and modified as it is passed on from person to person. The more clarity employers can provide their staff pertaining to change, generally the greater cooperation they will have as they implement change in the work setting.

Some of the advantages which accrue to employees by being warned in advance of impending changes are: (1) they can make plans to adjust by upgrading their skill levels through night courses and other programs off the job; (2) they can determine their potential usefulness to the organization after the changeover and use the warning time to look for employment elsewhere; and (3) they can learn to live with the anxiety change creates (Johns, 1963).

For management, the fact that there is generally less resistance to change after early notification is an important result (President's Advisory Committee on Labor-Management Policy, 1962). Early notification may also act to increase labor turnover or stimulate the number of "early quits." As such it becomes an alternative to a strict no-hiring policy or attrition. Attrition is usually used anyway.

Training for New Assignments and Positions

Because a number of new jobs are created in the process of technological changes in the work environment, many firms have the alternative of either hiring outside personnel to fill these positions or retraining from within their own ranks. Retraining is an important means of resolving a portion of the intraorganizational unemployment difficulties. In the 1963 Manpower Report to the President (U.S. Department of Labor, Office of Manpower, Automation, and Training, 1963), the U.S. Department of Labor recommended that organizations should try to retrain as many of their own staff as possible to fill vacancies created by automation. The success of such programs is evidenced by a study of office automation (U.S. Department of Labor, Bureau of Labor Statistics, No. 137, 1960). Within one year after the installation of a computer system, about one third of the twenty-eight hundred employees of a large insurance company in units where work was directly affected had been reassigned to other positions, either within the same unit or elsewhere in the office. A majority remained in the same positions. Close to one sixth had quit, retired, died, or taken a leave of absence. Only nine persons were laid off. Employment had been reduced by about 25 percent by the end of the year.

Retraining has its advantages and disadvantages. For instance, the worker can retain his position with the organization. He does not necessarily have new knowledge and information which may prove valuable for a better job elsewhere. In any event, he becomes a more flexible employee within the labor force. Also, in retraining there is the possibility for a better-paying position with the same firm. This is contingent upon the type of job acquired compared with the one vacated. Remaining in the same social setting serves a comforting function in many cases. While job changes are viewed as threatening to the existing status quo, it is often preferable to be around old acquaintances and familiar work groups. Reshuffling work routines may result in disruptions of informal status hierarchies. As each person's job changes, so does his status in the informal group.

It is decidedly cheaper for the company to retrain existing staff. They are already familiar with former work procedures, and they are used to working with one another. Management is often able to maintain esprit de corps throughout the transition to new work methods.

Retraining offers some disadvantages. Employees may be asked to attend classes after their normal working hours, thus disrupting family routines. In some instances, employees may feel that their placement potential is not enhanced significantly by the courses offered, particularly in relation to the new jobs they will be asked to perform. Some even feel coerced into taking courses which they deem unnecessary for fear that if they don't participate, they will lose their jobs (U.S. Department of Labor, Bureau of Labor Statistics, No. 1364, 1963:17, 41). In order for retraining to be effective, it is necessary to have an educable staff. Older workers seem to have the most difficulty adjusting to changes, and consequently if there is a large proportion of older workers in an organization, retraining may be only partially effective (U.S. Department of Labor, Bureau of Labor Statistics, No. 1368, 1963). This is especially true if the worker is not able to develop competence in the new task to the satisfaction of management.

Seniority Rules

Many organizations have seniority systems based upon an employee's length of service. According to seniority rules, employees with the longest service are given priority over those with shorter service when it comes to job preferences or retention of jobs (Backman, 1962). This priority also extends to vacation times, work schedules if the organization is on a shift schedule, and better promotional opportunities in relation to other employees.

The use of seniority rules for resolving displacement problems in changing organizations is well documented (U.S. Department of Labor, Bureau of Labor Statistics, No. 1368, 1963). In the case of a petroleum refinery in the Midwest undergoing change since 1956, it was anticipated that nearly two thousand jobs would be eliminated (U.S. Department of Labor, Bureau of Labor Statistics, 1964:11-12).

> The workers to be displaced were selected on the basis of a plantwide seniority system. The company had hired all workers as laborers, and promoted them to

higher-level jobs as they were trained. Workers were chosen for dismissal on the basis of least seniority in the plant, regardless of the jobs performed. Those remaining were offered retraining by the company to fill vacated positions. The company set up an 80-hour training course on work time, prepared a 300-page textbook, and used movies, film strips, demonstrations, and field trips. Several weeks of on-the-job training were given. No age limit was set on retraining [p. 11].

Of course, seniority systems work to the advantage of the older employee. Seniority systems are mutually instituted by union and management because such systems seem to be most equitable in the making of decisions affecting the displacement of workers. Usually, there is little overt discontent among employees inasmuch as employees hired by their organization understand from the beginning that seniority is one of the major terms underlying their employment.

Seniority systems offer job security to many. The longer an employee remains with the organization, the more likely he will be to retain his position in the event of organizational disruption through technological change. It is also a built-in rewarding device for employees who accrue many years of service with the company. Seniority is also akin to our definition of the rank order of things. It is a logical system of differentiation on the job. Unfortunately, it operates to the detriment of the younger worker when mass layoffs are in order. And to complicate the situation further, there are some dysfunctional consequences for the organization. Seniority applied to displacements affects the younger, more educated worker, although the educational attainment of old and young employees appears to be increasingly similar. Currently, however, it may be argued that a type of "educational downgrading" results from the use of a seniority plan to resolve displacement problems in organizations.

Consideration of Employees

This means giving the person more say in the things that happen to him on the job, reflecting a type of humanization of the work environment and helping to solidify the employee's support for and loyalty toward the organization. This is a frequent observation in studies discussing the subject of the involvement of employees in change (Maier, 1952; Pigors and Pigors, 1961). This is manifest in the classic work *Management and the Worker* (1939), by Roethlisberger and Dickson. This book noted the fundamentals of what has since become known as the "human-relations approach" to management and was discussed in detail in an earlier chapter.

The implications of involving employees in change in organizations are many, but they almost always include increased personal satisfaction with whatever changes are made. Some people refer to involving employees in this fashion as "participative management," and they point to the social and psychological benefits to the worker because of it (Etzioni, 1964). Of course, there is always the possibility that giving employees greater consideration in decision-making power will lead to a disintegration of the effectiveness of the existing hierarchy of authority (Maier, 1965). There are undefined limits which prevail and influence the extent to which one can democratize a situation and yet maintain the existing levels of productivity and the respect and morale of the employees. Certainly there are strong arguments favoring either position.

Transferrals and Relocating at Company Expense

As one result of technological change, organizations may expand their services by creating branches elsewhere in the country. This permits one effective means of meeting and resolving the unemployment problem inasmuch as organizational officials are in the position of being able to offer employees transfers and promotions to jobs in branch operations elsewhere. Bonuses and "relocation allowances" are offered as incentives. The transfer of employees to other subunits within the same organization (e.g., General Motors), whether it be across the plant, across town, or across the country, is increasingly used in our highly mobile society.

The Internal Revenue Service is one organization utilizing the transfer method for alleviating employment problems due to EDP (U.S. Department of Labor, Bureau of Labor Statistics, No. 1364, 1963). When the IRS changed over to the electronic data processing of income tax paperwork, many new jobs were created in the IRS centers. The center in Atlanta, Georgia, offered many new responsibilities to employees:

> To facilitate transfer of employees to vacant jobs, the IRS took an inventory of the skills of employees in the affected units, made efforts to match displaced employees and job openings, gave employees counseling and guidance about job opportunities, and offered training to improve employee qualifications. The emphasis was to give employees in directly affected activities full opportunity to transfer voluntarily to other jobs, either those vacated through attrition in unaffected units or to new jobs opening in the new regional center [p. 2].

Some difficulties were encountered by the IRS, however:

> Although a number of experienced employees transferred from district offices, the response by mid-1962 was not as great as had been expected. Personal problems were reported by some employees as preventing or discouraging them

from accepting new jobs. Among the reasons cited were reluctance to sever close family ties, spouse's employment, and health and age problems. Financial burdens were important to others. Forced sale of their homes at a loss and higher living costs at Atlanta were cited by some [p. 49].

Transferrals can sometimes mean promotional opportunities to employees. In any event, continuous employment is the major benefit which they receive. Also, a transfer means something new. The psychological argument is for the need of a change from time to time. It is quite likely that the transfer will mean exposing a person to a new job not found in the present situation. For some employees, however, a transfer may result in a downgrading of their original position (Hoos, 1961).

There are other drawbacks to transferring. Family problems arise regarding relocating and finding new schools for children and new friendships. The tempo of American life is such, however, that many people are learning to cope fairly easily with changes in their environment. There are both satisfying experiences and dissatisfying ones reported by numerous workers who have transferred to new locations in a variety of work settings. It is impossible at this time to say conclusively that transferring is functional or dysfunctional to employees collectively in the long run. In many instances, it is a matter of personal taste, but the implications for management are quite clear.

Shift Work

It has been reported previously that shift work is one potential consequence of EDP. In many large organizations, shift work is more the rule than the exception. It doubles, and in some instances, triples promotional opportunities for workers. Each shift requires supervision, and labor turnover is greater during the more undesirable hours.

The fact that so many of our businesses and industries are operating on shift schedules today is evidence that shift work helps to ease the problem but not curb it. There is no doubt that shift work means employment for more people. In this sense, it helps to absorb displaced employees. The existence of several work shifts also provides diversification for more workers. At least several alternatives are available in order that people may work out a task schedule more in harmony with their particular needs and interests.

On the negative side of the ledger, shift work can be disruptive for family life. The implications for children are clear as well. Social lives require readjustments, and many of our current definitions of conventional work patterns are being drastically altered. Shift work is simply one dimension of these changing patterns.

Shorter Work Days

Proponents of the shorter workday believe that more people will be hired, that increased leisure will stimulate the need for more extensive goods and services, thereby increasing productivity, demands for goods, and more employment. Those against such a proposal argue that a shorter workday will generate inflation as a result of the rising costs of labor.

The implications of a shorter workday for employees are obvious. Employees will have increased leisure time. More leisure time would logically stimulate the market for more services, particularly in resort areas. Workers supposedly would be able to spend more time with their families, and the psychological stresses associated with physically demanding jobs would be reduced considerably. Some people question the wisdom of such logic. Levitan (1964:5) states that "it is interesting to note that in an age when the prophets of cybernetics predict the disappearance of work in our society, the number of those who work 49 hours a week or more has increased, both absolutely and relatively. Excluding agricultural workers, 10.8 million persons in 1963 worked more than 48 hours per week, and they accounted for more than a seventh of the total work force in nonagricultural employment."

Management profits from a shorter workday only if workers are able to produce more at the same time they are working less. Since physical labor is being eliminated from many jobs, it becomes a task of technology to produce and perform efficiently and profitably. Automation seems to be making an important contribution here. It is possible to question the argument that shortening the workday will automatically lead to inflation. This is true only to the extent that decreasing working hours also decreases productivity. Such a relation is unlikely with the advent of technological changes such as EDP.

The Use of Temporary Employees

The final adaptive mechanism to be discussed is the use of temporary employees. The market for temporary employees is growing. Many placement services are currently operating primarily as agencies for temporary help. Their services are to provide secretaries, laborers, technicians, clerks, and a variety of other workers for businesses and industries which require temporary increases in staff. When an employee vacations for two weeks, his work must be performed by someone else. Temporary employment agencies, though not new on the American scene, are almost always able to provide someone capable of filling in for the vacationing employee until he returns.

In a study of the IRS reported earlier in this section, one solution to the problem of changing over to EDP and having to increase staff size temporarily was to hire temporary employees (U.S. Department of Labor, Bureau of Labor Statistics, No. 1364, 1963). The study reports that:

> it was necessary to continue tax collection activities efficiently while experienced employees were being reassigned to permanent jobs before their work was shifted to computer. Management had to find a way to replace these employees without jeopardizing the job security rights of other permanent employees. One solution was to hire temporary employees for a period longer than that customarily allowed. The Civil Service Commission granted the IRS authority to hire temporary employees to do essential jobs for temporary periods which could be extended up to three years. Ordinarily, temporary appointments are limited to one year. Former IRS employees and retired workers are preferred, under arrangements with the Commission, so that training can be minimized. Employees given temporary appointments do not acquire seniority or sick leave. . . . [In this case their prolonged employment, although temporary, was sufficient to justify these fringe benefits.] Temporary employees also were placed in continuing activities where it was essential to reserve permanent job vacancies for permanent employees who would be displaced. They also filled continuing jobs in unaffected activities when the incumbents were temporarily reassigned to facilitate the changeover [pp. 20-21].

Between July 1960, near the beginning of the conversion, and July 1962, a total of 274 temporary appointments were made. The benefits of using temporary employees are chiefly restricted to management. Permanent employees are relatively unaffected. The temporary employee does not identify with the organization. He views his job as temporary, and he regards himself as expendable: "When they are through with me here, I will go where I am needed elsewhere" is a commonly expressed sentiment. There are no retirement benefits which must be paid by the hiring organization. There is seldom such a thing as sick leave. The person is paid only for the time on the job, and strict control over the hours worked is usually maintained by both the hiring company and the employment agency providing the service.

Thus it is possible for an organization to instigate a drastic change in work procedures with a minimum of negative effects on the temporary staff. Generally, disruptions of the work environment and the informal group network (if one has time to form) have no serious personal consequences for the members of the group. And since there is a continuous supply of temporary employees, there is virtually no problem in hiring and releasing them without incident.

SUMMARY

Persons and groups in organizations are usually vulnerable to being affected by changes, planned or unplanned, within the organization. We have examined various forms of change in the technology of organizations, particularly where changes displace workers or greatly modify—even eliminate—their tasks. In such situations, how resilient are individuals and groups: What kind of social and psychological impact will specific changes have? This chapter has sought to provide some of the many possible answers to these and other questions related to change and its impact.

Technological changes in the form of electronic data processing (common in banks and businesses) and "Detroit-type" automation (commonly associated with the manufacture of automobile parts) were discussed in some detail, and some indication was given of employees' responses to them. From a systemic standpoint, we can see a chain reaction: changes in one dimension of the organization will activate or necessitate changes in other dimensions. Linked with technological changes of various kinds have been changes in working hours, disruption of informal work groups, changes in the quality and type of supervision, changes in job content, changes in the amount of jurisdiction employees have over a given area of work, and changes in employees' perceptions of job security and acceptable performance.

Employees' anxieties about technological change can be allayed by early notification of changes, training for new assignments and positions, the application of rules of seniority (which benefit older, and thus possibly more threatened, employees), shift work, shorter working days, transferrals and relocations at the company's expense to avoid loss of jobs, and greater consideration of employees. Such measures suggest that organizational leaders take an active interest in preserving employees' security while striving to maintain their own position in an ever-changing economic market of supply and demand.

The economic exigencies shared by all organizations justify a chapter devoted to employees' reactions to change. From the standpoint of human (individual and social) needs, we must examine critically the psychological and social implications of general technological change and consider realistically the impact of such change upon our definitions of work and our basic economic raison d'être.

In the case studies given in Appendix I, it is suggested that the reader try to assume the identities of all persons involved in order to see the problems discussed from a variety of viewpoints. Some cases will focus upon problems at a single point in time; others deal with problems which have developed over a relatively prolonged period. Numerous alternative answers can be provided on the basis of previous reading and by applying variables in unique combinations. No single solution is necessarily the "correct" one, although some answers will be better than others. Solutions should serve as a focal point for class discussion; and their relative merits should be considered equally.

The sociology of organizations offers many opportunities for social research, as this text has indicated. More specialized articles and texts are given in the indexed bibliography (Appendix II). Much needs to be learned about the sociological aspects of organizations. It is hoped that this text has underscored the importance of considering a multiplicity of units of analysis in dealing with problems of social organizations.

STUDY QUESTIONS

1 What is included under the heading "technological change"? Do you think it is possible to devise a theory of technological change which would be generally applicable to organizations? Why or why not?

2 Describe some of the implications of EDP for changing the lives of individuals in organizations. What is the general impact of EDP upon informal group relations? Explain.

3 What mechanisms can organizations (and individuals) use to adjust to the effects of technological change? Explain each.

4 How has EDP as a part of technological change changed our definitions of work? Explain.

5 What is the general impact of EDP upon the structure of hierarchies of authority in organizations? What are some potential implications for employees in this regard? Elaborate.

6 What is meant by "attrition"? How is attrition functional and dysfunctional in relation to the security and anxiety of employees? Explain.

7 What degree of validity has the expression "automation man"? What do you think the worker of the future should be like in terms of personality for coping with the changing work environment in organizations? Elaborate.

NOTES

[1] According to the definition of "technology" used here, such aspects of organization as communication patterns (either formal or informal), authority networks, and supervisory styles (methods, forms) are considered to be components of technology. However, we have given each of these topics special consideration in earlier chapters because of their respective contributions to organizational structure and

process and because these variables have been defined by the field as central explanatory concepts in numerous books and articles.

[2] The National Commission on Technology, Automation and Economic Progress, *Technology and the American Economy,* Report of the National Commission on Technology, Automation, and Economic Progress, Vol. 1, February, 1966, Washington, D.C.; U.S. Government Printing Office. Congress gave the commission the following mandate: (1) to identify and assess the past effects and the current and prospective role and pace of technology; (2) to identify and describe the impact of technological and economic change on production and employment, including new job requirements and the major types of displacement of workers, both technological and economic, which are likely to occur during the next ten years; the specific industries, occupations, and geographic areas which are most likely to be involved; and the social and economic effects of these developments on the nation's economy, manpower, communities, families, social structure, and human values; (3) to define those areas of unmet community and human needs toward which application of new technologies might most effectively be directed, encompassing an examination of technological developments that have occurred in recent years, including those resulting from the federal government's research and development programs; (4) to assess the most effective means for channeling new technologies into promising directions, including civilian industries in which accelerated technological advancements will yield general benefits, and to assess the proper relationship between governmental and private investment in the application of new technologies to large-scale human and community needs; (5) to recommend, in addition to those actions which are the responsibility of management and labor, specific administrative and legislative steps which it believes should be taken by the federal, state, and local governments in meeting their responsibilities (a) to support and promote technological change in the interest of the continued economic growth and the improved well-being of our people, (b) to continue to adopt measures which will facilitate occupational adjustment and geographical mobility, and (c) to share the costs and help prevent and alleviate the adverse impact of change on displaced workers (p. xiv). Some of the commission's major conclusions and recommendations that (1) there has been some increase in the pace of technological change; (2) the outlook for employment and adjustment to change in the next decade depends upon the policies followed; (3) to facilitate adjustment to change as well as to improve the quality of life, adequate educational opportunity should be available to all; (4) adjustments to change requires information concerning present and future job opportunities; (5) technological and economic changes have differential geographic impacts requiring concerted regional efforts to take advantage of opportunities and avoid dislocation; (6) technology enlarges the capacities of man and extends his control over his environment; and (7) efforts should be made by employers to "humanize" the work environment by (a) adapting work to human needs, (b) increasing the flexibility of the life span of work, and (c) eliminating the distinction in the mode of payment between hourly workers and salaried employees (pp. 109-113).

[3] See especially Howard B. Jacobson and J. S. Roucek, *Automation and Society,* New York, Philosophical Library, 1959.

   [4] Joan Robinson, *Economic Philosophy,* Harmondsworth, England, Penguin Books, 1964, p. 8.

   [5] These systems are frequently considered by a majority of researchers to be forms of automation and will be treated as such. Whether or not automation must necessarily be involved in the production of tangible items such as automobile engines and parts or may be involved in paper and information processing is of little consequence. The importance of these phenomena, though different from one another in several respects, lies in how people define and interpret them. It has been said that what we define as real becomes real in its consequences. Whether or not we agree on a precise definition of "automation" does not detract from the fact that members of all organizations perceive themselves affected to one degree or another by systems which they label as "automation." Perhaps in subsequent discussion, the reader may reach contrasting conclusions about what automation is as a significant manifestation of technological change and about whether there is sufficient merit to the argument that organizational behavior is affected by it in important ways.

   [6] Automation occurs in many forms. Some applications of automation are found in industry, particularly automobile manufacture. In fact, most existing discussions of the social and economic impact of automation pertain to industrial settings. Business and service settings have been seriously neglected as targets of social inquiry into the sociological effects of automation in the form of EDP. "Detroit automation" is a term used to describe the form of automation used in factories which modifies and manipulates products and passes them from one point to another without human intervention. The present discussion emphasizes office settings instead of industrial settings. It will be observed that many statements about automation and its sociological effects in business and service institutions can also be generalized to industrial environments, even though there are obvious differences in the respective forms of automation. Looking more closely at the sociological implications of automation in office settings should give us a more balanced picture of things compared with earlier treatments of various types of technological change in the social science literature.

   Several fairly comprehensive bibliographies exist which include article references on the social and economic implications of automation. These include (1) U.S. Department of Labor, Bureau of Labor Statistics, *Implications of Automation and Other Technological Developments: A Selected Annotated Bibliography,* Bulletin No. 1319, Washington, D.C., U.S. Government Printing Office, 1962; (2) U.S. Department of Labor, Bureau of Labor Statistics, *Implications of Automation and Other Technological Developments: A Selected Annotated Bibliography,* Bulletin No. 1319-1, Washington, D.C., U.S. Government Printing Office, 1963; (3) U.S. Department of Labor, Manpower Administration, Office of Manpower, Automation, and Training, *Health and Safety Aspects of Automation and Technological Change: A Collection of Abstracts, 1956–62,* Geneva, Switzerland, International Labor Office, 1962; (4) Einar Hardin et al., *Economic and Social Implications of Automation: An Annotated Bibliography, 1957–60,* Vol. 2, East Lansing, Michigan State University, 1961.

   [7] See Walter Buckingham, "The Impact of Automation on Skills and Employment," *Computers and Automation,* April: 16–18, 1963; Louis E. Davis, "The Effects

of Automation on Job Design," *Industrial Relations,* October:53:71, 1962; Georges Friedmann, *The Anatomy of Work,* New York, Free Press, 1961: W. H. Scott, *Office Automation and the Non-manual Worker,* Paris, Organization for Economic Cooperation and Development, 1962; Jack Siegman and Bernard Karsh, "Some Organizational Correlates of White-Collar Automation," *University of Illinois Bulletin,* Reprint Series No. 110, February:108–116, 1962; Rose Wiener, "Changing Manpower Requirements in Banking," *Monthly Labor Review,* September:989–995, 1962; Sidney Goldstein, *The Norristown Study,* Philadelphia: University of Pennsylvania Press, 1961; Floyd C. Mann, "Psychological and Organizational Impacts," *Automation and Technological Change,* The American Assembly, Columbia University, Englewood Cliffs, N.J., Prentice-Hall, 1962, pp. 43–65; Walter Buckingham, *Automation: Its Impact on Business and People,* New York; Harper & Brothers, 1961; J. Garcia Santesmases, "A Few Aspects of the Impact of Automation on Society," *Impact of Science on Society,* 9:107–126, 1961; American Management Association, *Toward the Factory of the Future,* Special Report No. 28, New York, 1957; Landon L. Goodman, *Automation Today and Tomorrow,* London: Oxford University Press, 1958.

Appendix I

Case Studies

The Trainee

The Los Angeles National Bank began formal operations in June 1946. At that time, the bank consisted of two offices located in East and West Los Angeles. The formal organization of each bank branch was essentially the same. Each office was headed by a vice-president with three lending officers, an operations officer, an assistant operations officer, and twelve women performing secretarial, bookkeeping, teller, and proof-machine operations. The president of the bank was aided by two executive assistants and a board of directors.

Employees were hired to fill vacant jobs in the bank through direct application (the completion of a single personnel information form) and an interview with the vice-president (branch manager) of either branch. Applicants for various positions were hired as needed according to this informal procedure.

During the next twenty-five years, the bank expanded to nearly fifty branch offices located at various places throughout Southern California. Each branch consisted of approximately forty employees including the administrative staff. By now, the main office or central headquarters for the entire banking chain (one of the two original offices) had developed a sizable personnel department as well as an advisory staff consisting of persons with business administration, managerial-training, sociology, and psychology backgrounds. This staff successfully compiled a volume detailing the structure and procedures for all of the bank branches and jobs performed within them. This volume was known as *"The Standard Practices Handbook"* and became the major tool used for the training and development of new bank personnel.

Because of the burgeoning number of bank employees throughout all of the branches, it became necessary to develop more formalized procedures for selecting prospective job applicants as the years passed. Standardized tests of various kinds (e.g., verbal and quantitative aptitude tests and attitudes and abilities quizzes) were utilized increasingly as a means of screening potential employees. At the same time, the personnel department recognized the need to fill a growing number of administrative positions as new branches were created. This necessitated the formation of a management training program which would be designed to acquaint each trainee with all phases of banking activity and prepare him for specific future administrative posts.

Two traineeship programs were instituted. Training program A was specifically designed for college graduates, while program B was for non-college-graduates with a minimum of two years' college credit. No applicants for traineeship positions were considered without meeting these minimal qualifications. Prospective trainees were selected in much the same manner as other bank employees. However, more emphasis was placed upon their human-relations and administrative potential compared with other prospective staff members.

The time periods varied for each program. Program A (for college graduates) was to run for twelve months, while program B was established to run for twenty-four months. Both programs offered essentially the same kind of training to trainees, although trainees in program B spent twice as long in each phase of their learning of bank procedures compared with trainees in program A. The salary for trainees was differentiated by training program as well. Program A trainees were started at $525 per month, while program B trainees were started at $400 per month. Quarterly raises in salary for members of both programs brought trainees to $650 and $475 per month at the completion of their respective programs.

Three training officers were hired to direct the professional experiences of the trainees. The number of trainees at any given time, of course, depended upon the demand for administrative assistance in each of the branches. Although the trainees for both programs were under the direct supervision of their respective training officers, it was understood that the operations officer of the branch to which a trainee was assigned assumed the primary responsibility for ensuring that the trainee was exposed to all types of banking procedures and became thoroughly familiar with them. Approximately seventy-five trainees were distributed throughout the bank branches in order to receive their "on-the-job" training, and they were equally divided among the three training officers. Therefore, it was likely that any given trainee would see his training officer no more than once a month.

Each of the training programs offered different kinds of dividends. Program A resulted (at the end of the twelve-month program period) in the promotion of the trainee to the position of assistant cashier. Assistant cashiers were typically assigned lending and financial consultation functions. Members of program B were channeled toward the operations side of banking, and they became assistant operations officers or "assistants to assistants."

Members of program B were informally regarded as of "lower status" by their counterparts in program A, and bank personnel reinforced this definition by their social treatment of them. There was a certain amount of resentment directed toward *all* trainees, however, by most of the branch staff members. This seemed to be a common phenomenon throughout all of the bank branches.

One explanation for this resentment was the fact that both types of trainees began their traineeships at substantially higher salaries than the regular branch personnel assigned to train them. One typical example of such behavior was the continuing complaints of a forty-five-year-old female note teller who had to explain all aspects of her job to each management trainee. Although she had been with the bank for twelve years, her current salary was $25 lower than the starting salary of a B trainee. This obvious salary discrepancy and sex discrimination apparently were sufficient to lead the note teller to view *all* trainees categorically as incompetent idiots "not worth their salt." Resentment against trainees in many of the branches was also apparent in the form of their exclusion from informal gatherings of regular branch employees during lunch and coffee breaks.

An unusual situation developed in one bank branch, however. One particularly ambitious trainee on the B program, trainee Smith, was intent on proving to his training officer that he was highly competent in all phases of banking activity. Therefore, Smith strived to learn and to complete his various tasks as quickly as possible. He would then ask regular branch members if they had any work for him to do to fill the remaining hours of the bank day. Some tellers and bookkeepers immediately took advantage of this eager beaver and allowed him to complete some of their work which otherwise would consume much of their daily working time. After a few weeks, the trainee had "assumed" certain of the regular duties of several staff members in addition to his own, and these employees were enjoying the benefits of little work to do by having extended lunch and coffee breaks and "gab fests." One afternoon, the operations officer encountered several staff members in the bank lunchroom and inquired why they were not in the main work area performing their various roles. Their reply in unison was that "trainee Smith does our work for us and we have nothing to do."

Trainee Smith was immediately summoned into the office of the operations officer and reprimanded for doing the work of the other employees. Smith explained that he simply wanted to demonstrate that he could learn things rapidly so that his training officer would advance him more quickly through the two-year training program (the option of shortening the training program of particularly bright B trainees—who had not graduated from college—rested, in part, on the recommendation of the operations officer of the branch to which the trainee was assigned as well as on the evaluation and recommendation of the training officer in charge). Smith was told by the operations officer, "Do your own work. Furthermore, if any of your assignments *can* be completed in less than the normal allowable working hours, then work at a pace which will enable you to finish your job at the end of the day, even if it means working at a *slower pace*."

When Smith left the operations officer's desk, he felt frustrated and hurt. The next day, he was even shunned by the very people he had wanted to help earlier. Apparently, they held him accountable for their *own* reprimand by the operations officer the previous day. That afternoon, Smith's training officer, Mr. Stratton, visited the branch for the usual monthly conference with Smith and to see how his work was progressing.

QUESTIONS FOR DISCUSSION

1   What should Smith tell Stratton about the reprimand he received from his operations officer? Should he reveal that the operations officer told him to "slow down" his work pace for the good of the rest of the staff?
2   What are some strategies by which the operations officer, his assistant, or any other regular branch employee could have prevented the initial "problem"?
3   Are there any apparent communications problems which you see existing between the personnel department, the training department, the respective bank branches, and the branch managers and officers?
4   What factors—organizational, interpersonal, individual, or all three—may be brought to bear upon this problem?
5   If you were Smith, how would you have approached the situation when you first arrived at the bank branch for training? How do you think things would have turned out otherwise?

The Hadley Corporation

The Hadley Corporation is a small toy-manufacturing firm in the Southeast. Although the firm's growth pattern has not been unlike that of comparable toy companies since its inception nearly twenty years ago, the popularization of a newly created toy by this corporation has necessitated tripling its production staff over the most recent two-year period. As public demand for the new toy increased, so has the pressure for efficiency upon the production and marketing units of the organization.

The vice president in charge of production, R. J. Snell, conferred with the president of the company, Robert Sloan, and it was decided that a new position should be created to coordinate more effectively the activities of the production, supply, and marketing departments. Snell reviewed the service records of all managerial personnel to see if a person from within the firm could assume the new duties. Since most of the managerial staff had been with the corporation from the beginning and seemed to be moderately familiar with their respective work assignments and responsibilities, Snell's choice of the best candidate for coordinator of interdepartmental activities was quite difficult to make. Further conferences with the corporation president brought Snell to the conclusion that no single individual had all of the necessary skills to perform the new coordinating job adequately. Sloan instructed

Snell to seek a job candidate from outside the firm, possibly a person with some experience in human relations and a task-related administrative background. Sloan further recommended that the person have some college experience, preferably a bachelor's degree in business, sociology, or psychology, and a strong interest in working with people in a coordinating capacity.

Snell contacted his business associates with other companies and emerged with several likely prospects. After considering each of their qualifications, Snell selected Tom Blake, a rising young junior executive with a division manufacturing small parts in an electronics corporation. Blake was twenty-nine, had an MBA with an undergraduate major in sociology, and had been with the company for five years. He was in line for promotion, but because of the seniority system operative in his present firm, such advancement in the immediate future seemed highly unlikely. Therefore, Snell reasoned, his own company could successfully compete for Blake's services. Blake responded positively when approached by Snell a few weeks later. An interview with Sloan was equally fruitful, and within ninety days the Hadley Corporation employed Blake as the new coordinator.

Blake's official title was Assistant Vice-President in Charge of Product Coordination, and he was given a private office, a secretary, and two middle-level assistants to help carry out his important function. He was officially introduced to all managerial staff shortly after his arrival, and it was understood that the managers of production, supply, and marketing should "touch base" with Blake before making decisions which would affect company productivity. Each of the three managers, Rogers, Morgan, and Jefferson, assumed that Blake was their new immediate superior and intermediary between themselves and Snell. All of these men were over forty, and none had gone beyond high school in their formal academic training. In addition, Rogers, Morgan, and Jefferson were supposedly close friends of Snell and had discussed earlier among themselves which of the three would get the "nod" for the new position. Needless to say, when an "outsider" was selected over them, they were sorely disappointed. From all external appearances, however, no one would have known how each felt about the new situation.

Blake's first official act was to call a meeting with Rogers, Morgan, and Jefferson and "educate" them about how he had assisted his former company in becoming more efficient in parts manufacturing. Among other things, he indicated that he believed in "open communication" with his "subordinates," and he encouraged these men to let him know how they felt at all times about their respective departments and relations between them.

Over the next few weeks, Blake frequently visited each manager on the job and shared with him some of his own ideas about how things "could be improved around here." The marketing manager was particularly offended when Blake indicated that a different marketing perspective might increase wholesale orders substantially. Blake even went so far as to insist that Jefferson implement the new marketing strategy for a brief period and compare the results with former marketing procedures.

After ten weeks of Blake's intervention, the company developed some serious supply and demand problems. It seemed that Blake had insisted that Morgan reduce his supply inventory considerably in order to match immediate wholesale orders more closely. However, Blake did not take into account the importance of seasonal variation in product demand, and with the approaching summer months the firm overflowed with retailers' requests. The production department was unable to fulfill these requests because the supply department did not have enough of a given material on hand to complete the manufacturing process. Blake even commenced to "chew out" Morgan for letting his stock get too low, and he criticized Jefferson for not following his (Blake's) new marketing policy to the letter. Morgan immediately told Blake to "take your master's degree and go to hell!" stormed to Snell's office, and submitted his resignation. Snell was shocked, and after a few minutes with Morgan he sought out Jefferson and Rogers to investigate further the nature of Morgan's complaints.

In the meantime, Blake went directly to Sloan, the company president, and told him that Jefferson, Rogers, and particularly Morgan were not doing their jobs properly. Blake was convinced that all three were grossly incompetent in their present positions and that they ought to be replaced. He encouraged Sloan to reprimand Snell for allowing them to continue in their present posts and to question Snell directly about their work activity. Frustrated, Sloan called Snell on the interoffice phone and asked to see him at once. As Sloan and Blake waited, Snell, Morgan, Rogers, and Jefferson entered the office, all glaring at Blake.

QUESTIONS FOR DISCUSSION

1 If you were Snell, what, if anything, would you say to Sloan about Blake in his presence? How would you account for bringing Morgan, Rogers, and Jefferson along with you when Sloan assumed you would come alone?
2 If you were Sloan, what should be your opening statement to Snell? Should you have called in Snell in Blake's presence? Why or why not? After hearing Blake's complaints, how could you have acted to avert the unpleasant encounter now before you?
3 What particular behaviors apparently led to the decline in production? If you had been the company president, how would you have handled the selection of the new task coordinator? What would be some of the more important implications of your actions for organizational effectiveness?
4 To what extent do you feel that Jefferson, Morgan, and Rogers should have been consulted in Blake's selection? Why?
5 Was Blake the right man for the job? Why or why not? What could possibly account for Blake's behavior in relation to the three managers?

The Barnes Company

The following incident took place in the dispatch office of the Barnes Company, a major distributor and service center for a popular line of water-heating units and air-conditioning systems in Pittsburgh, Pennsylvania.

The dispatch office is in charge of processing complaints from customers, usually restaurants and other business establishments, who have purchased water-heating or air-conditioning units. The staff of the dispatch office consists of Frank Mattingly, a thirty-five-year-old manager; Art Jameson, a thirty-two-year-old assistant manager; and Bill Saunders, a twenty-three-year-old college junior who has taken over the job of "dispatcher" formerly occupied by a retiree. Mattingly's responsibilities include "supervising" his two subordinates and the quality of their work. He reports to the main office of the company periodically on the general efficiency of Jameson and Saunders. He has been with the Barnes Company for twelve years and has been passed over several times for promotion to a middle-level managerial position with the main office for "undisclosed reasons." He is basically unhappy with his present job assignment, and he takes a dim view of the possibility of future promotion to a more challenging and responsible position.

Jameson, on the other hand, is a five-year company veteran who is ambitious and hard-working. He aspires to a higher position within the company and "has connections" with higher-ups through his marriage to the niece of the company president. He views his present work assignment as primarily temporary and as an opportunity to gain familiarity with the dispatching aspect of the company. He has a college degree in organizational behavior and wishes eventually to become a vice-president in charge of personnel. Mattingly is very much aware of Jameson's temporary stay in his department and, at times, is openly resentful of the opportunities which Jameson has which he himself is apparently denied. Mattingly, like Jameson, also has a college degree in business administration and considers himself at least equally qualified to move up the ladder of the organizational hierarchy as Jameson.

Saunders has been with the company for four months and has only transient interactions with both Mattingly and Jameson. Mattingly is frequently out of the office, and Jameson is all too often bogged down with paperwork: processing and filing service orders and the like. Saunders, therefore, "holds down the fort" for the most part. He has been placed in charge of dispatching sixteen service trucks, each equipped with two-man teams of repair personnel who repair and provide maintenance for the heaters and air-conditioning units. Recently, Saunders was approached by Jameson with a request for assistance in completing his extensive paperwork. Saunders has been able to assist Jameson to a limited degree, although he must answer the phone during the day, take down the addresses of customer-complainants, contact service trucks by two-way radio, and then double-check at the end of the day to see if the repairs were made. During the summer months of Saunders's employment, the dispatching load has become excessive, and backlogs of service orders are running two to four days behind schedule.

In a surprisingly short period of time, Saunders has learned various aspects of both Mattingly's and Jameson's jobs to the extent that on at least two occasions, he has operated the entire office by himself when Mattingly and Jameson were simultaneously ill.

On one particularly hot Friday afternoon, Saunders was swamped with calls for service. Mattingly was, as usual, out of the office on an "official errand," and Jameson saw a burgeoning pile of service orders to process and file. In a moment of anxiety, Jameson summoned Saunders away from the phones to help him process the service orders. Saunders protested, arguing that sixteen trucks were under his direct charge and that phone orders were much heavier than usual. Jameson said, "Don't worry about it, I will assume the responsibility for any blame you might get from Mattingly." Reluctantly, Saunders began to assist Jameson. About an hour later, Red Byerly, vice-president in charge of customer relations, appeared in the dispatch office to see why his own department has just been flooded by complaints from irate customers to the effect that the service office "is not answering the phone." When he saw Saunders and Jameson sifting and sorting through the various service orders, he "blew-up" at Saunders and told him to get back to answering the phone. Saunders meekly compiled, and when Byerly asked Jameson what was going on, Jameson denied any knowledge of the fact that the calls were coming in at a heavy rate, inasmuch as his own work area was not in plain view of the flashing lights of the dispatch switchboard. [The office phones "flashed" rather than ringing. Saunders's job was to monitor the phones and observe when calls came to the dispatch office.] Since it was nearing the end of the day, Saunders and Jameson left shortly thereafter.

On Monday morning, Saunders came to work and was immediately hailed by Mattingly. Mattingly indicated that he had heard about the "big mess" last Friday, and although he was "mighty sorry," he handed Saunders his two-week notice indicating he had been fired.

QUESTIONS FOR DISCUSSION

1   If you were Saunders, what, if anything, would you say to Mattingly in your own defense? Would you incriminate Jameson, even though you were aware of his "connections" with higher-ups? How do you think Mattingly would react to such accusations in any event? Why?

2   To what extent was Jameson justified in taking Saunders off his own work assignment to give him assistance? Why do you think Jameson did not level with Byerly about what had taken place and his own part in the incident?

3   Do you feel that the dispatch office was adequately staffed to take care of the company's needs insofar as maintenance and service were concerned? What modifications or changes would you have made had you been in charge of personnel for that department? Why?

4   Should the job of "dispatcher" been assigned to Saunders in the first place? Why or why not? To what extent were the three men fulfilling their respective roles adequately? Discuss.

Case Study 4

The Jenkins Supply Company

The Jenkins Supply Company is a major supplier of school equipment (e.g., chalk, erasers, chairs, desks, and tables) for the city schools of Seattle, Washington. The company has a staff of 130, which includes five regional salesmen. Among their other sales functions, each salesman calls upon grammar schools and high schools in and around Seattle regularly in an attempt to acquaint school officials and purchasing agents with new items recently developed by various manufacturing firms.

The sales supervisor, Grady Odum, is responsible for assessing the sales effectiveness of each of his sales subordinates. He has been with the company for nearly fifteen years and was a salesman himself with the same firm some time ago. Frequently, because of a lack of paperwork, Grady visits various schools on his own as a sales representative for the company. Although this sales activity is unnecessary on his part, he has found that getting away from his office from time to time allows him to maintain his sales skills and renew friendships with school officials he formerly contacted. Unlike his subordinates, Grady is a salaried member of the organization and is entitled to no commissions on the sales he makes. His assessments of the salesmen, however, are based in large part upon their individual gross sales for a given time period, usually quarterly.

On occasion, Grady will make a "sale" at a school within the territory of one of his subordinates. Neither Grady nor the salesman assigned the school receives the benefit of commission from the sale. Typically, the salesman will have covered the school some weeks earlier and made modest sales. However, Grady's rapport and friendship with the particular school official sometimes results in "unexpected" increased purchases which exceed the original salesman's gross for that school. In spite of the fact that Grady's friendship with the school officials is the primary determinant of such increased sales, his subordinates have come to regard his activities in their areas as personally embarrassing and an infringement upon their territorial sales rights. A few have even suggested to the others that he has been systematically cutting them out of lucrative commissions on sales with the various schools and has used his manifest interest in selling as a convenient means of "spying on them."

It has been customary for salesmen to convene with their supervisor once a month to discuss any problems they might have pertaining to their work. Also, these times have been used to exchange ideas on how best to promote new products with school officials. At the most recent sales meeting, Grady launched into a lengthy discourse on salesmanship and reprimanded his subordinates collectively for their "continual failure to demonstrate good public relations skills in their school visits." He made explicit his feelings that his men were doing progressively worse in this regard as well as letting their sales momentum decline substantially. Then, to everyone's surprise and dismay, he produced a chart showing each man's sales volume for the past twelve-month period. It was very much evident from his drawings that sales for each man had, indeed, declined. He ended his speech by saying that "sales had better increase quite a bit or else!"

Tony Ramos, the senior salesman of the five, informally gathered together with his sales companions after the meeting. It was agreed that Grady should "do his supervisory chores and paperwork and keep his nose out of our territory." Ramos was selected to report to Grady's immediate superior, Frank Gilbert, concerning their supervisor's improper sales activities and "spying."

When Ramos contacted Gilbert and disclosed the suspicions of the sales group to him, Gilbert rose abruptly and told Ramos that if the men didn't like Grady's interference, they should tell Grady directly and not go behind his back with their accusations.

QUESTIONS FOR DISCUSSION

1 Should Gilbert tell Grady Odum about Ramos's visit and the nature of the conversation? Why or why not?
2 Do you feel that Ramos and the other salesmen should have leveled with their supervisor initially rather than taking their grievance to Gilbert? Why or why not?
3 What are some possible explanations for Grady Odum's behavior in relation to his subordinates? Do you feel that he is justified in visiting schools in the territory of his subordinates, even though his formal job definition does not require such visits? Why or why not?

4 Evaluate the wisdom displayed by Odum when he brought forth the sales charts in front of his subordinates. What are some potential implications of this behavior for affecting his relationship with the men? What are some potential implications of this act for interpersonal relations among the subordinates themselves?

5 Under what conditions do you feel that subordinates have a right to "go over their superior's head" with complaints? Explain and discuss.

The Salem Iron Works

In response to major technological changes in the manufacture of iron products, the Salem Iron Works executive board has decided to implement significant changes in the authority hierarchy of the organization, to redistribute existing manpower according to new job definitions and work relationships, and to reassess current company policies as they pertain to intraorganizational and interorganizational interactions.

A long-range program of change has been devised which will modify substantially, and in some cases eliminate, existing employees' work roles. All supervisors in charge of various phases of production have been briefed concerning anticipated changes, and the exectuive board has emphasized that no employees will be laid off because of the introduction of the new production technology. However, supervisors have been instructed to recommend which of the members of their work groups should have access to the new positions associated with the technological changes.

Seven out of eight production supervisors later submitted to the executive board a list of employees they believed would do well with new job assignments. None of these supervisors asked any of their subordinates whether or not they would like to perform new tasks rather than continuing after the changeover in capacities similar to the ones they fulfilled before it. The eighth supervisor, Al Langley, went around to each of his subordinates and presented them with a list of new tasks which would exist under the new production system. He asked each to give a preference as to which job they would like to have, and he gave each employee the impression that their selection "would, in all likelihood, be approved by the executive board." Al was known by his men to be a "nice guy" always willing to "go to bat" for them in matters concerning their work routine. In view of his percentage of successful attempts to get favors for his subordinates in the past, the men had little reason to believe that they would not be assigned the new tasks they wanted.

When the changeover occurred a few months later, new job assignments were posted on a public bulletin board outside the main office. Although there was some discontentment expressed by most of the employees about the new assignments each received, there was a markedly high degree of resentment among Al Langley's work crew. None of his subordinates had obtained the preferences they had expressed to him earlier. When confronted with this information by his men, Langley told them, "I've got to do what I'm told like everyone else around here. I'm sorry you didn't get what you wanted, but I did my best." Group morale became particularly low when his men discussed their plight with members of other work crews. In these instances, the other men had no "say" whatsoever in the matter of what job they would perform after the change. But most of them were fairly content with their newly assigned positions.

QUESTIONS FOR DISCUSSION

1 Under what circumstances should subordinates be allowed to participate in decisions affecting their work? Do you think Al Langley acted in accordance with the executive board's expectations when he invited his men to express a job preference for after the changeover? Why or why not? Explain.

2 What are some potential implications of Langley's behavior for his men's attitudes toward their work and toward the company? Elaborate.

3 Some persons endorse a seniority system as a means of assigning jobs to persons experiencing technological change. In effect, this means that those individuals with the most months (or years) with the company get first choice of the new jobs. Other persons feel that the new jobs should be assigned on the basis of technical competence and expert qualifications (consistent with the bureaucratic model). How do you feel job assignments should have been made in this company? Defend the method of job selection you have described.

4 Langley possibly believed that because he involved the men the way he did, they would respect him more for caring about their personal desires on the job. What general principles can be learned from his behavior under the existing circumstances and in view of the reactions of his subordinates? Explain and discuss.

Appendix II

Indexed Bibliography

The following bibliography includes approximately 1,800 references directly or indirectly related to formal organizations. This bibliography is indexed according to a variety of organizational, interpersonal, and individual variables as well as several social settings within which research was conducted (e.g., schools, hospitals, and churches).

It should be noted that the classification scheme has been constructed based upon the titles of books, papers, and articles included in the bibliography. Obviously, an article title conveys only a superficial glimpse of what the article actually contains. In all too many instances, article and book titles are grossly misleading. Also, there is always the likelihood of a reasonable amount of classification error on the part of the author. I assume full responsibility for articles which have been misclassified inadvertently.

Articles and books have also been classified according to whether the social setting studied is foreign (i.e., outside of the United States) and whether or not the research is comparative. This index should be of some value to those currently doing research in the area of formal organizations. The numbers following each variable or setting studied refer the reader to the numbered citation in the bibliography.

Bibliographical Index

The index below is divided into four sections. Section 1 contains references to articles dealing with technological change and automation (factory and office). Section 2 contains references to foreign and comparative studies. Section 3 contains references to social settings within which research was conducted (as suggested by the title of the book, article, or paper). Section 4 contains references to 76 organizational, interpersonal, and individual variables. Each number included in this index has its counterpart in the bibliography where the setting or variable can be located.

SECTION 1: TECHNOLOGICAL CHANGE AND AUTOMATION

General Technological Change: 13, 26, 38, 77, 82, 88, 110, 113, 127, 191, 220, 234, 240, 247, 251, 253, 285, 326, 358, 363, 364, 381, 419, 438, 446, 463, 489, 551, 580, 676, 709, 715, 741, 785, 803, 815, 896, 911, 975, 996, 1045, 1069, 1091, 1136, 1137, 1141, 1198, 1201, 1244, 1283, 1285, 1286, 1298, 1308, 1324, 1328, 1332, 1346, 1348, 1459, 1468, 1486, 1511, 1532, 1551, 1552, 1565, 1578, 1586, 1612, 1613, 1616, 1617, 1621, 1624, 1628, 1641, 1661, 1686, 1689, 1701, 1713, 1728.

Automation: Factory: 25, 42, 44, 45, 46, 47, 48, 71, 79, 86, 90, 156, 157, 190, 191, 211, 219, 234, 260, 284, 322, 324, 334, 367, 393, 405, 406, 415, 416, 417, 426, 438, 452, 491, 492, 494, 497, 530, 550, 552, 556, 562, 590, 606, 624, 721, 806, 846, 871, 872, 899, 921, 970, 1026, 1047, 1113, 1138, 1147, 1212, 1213, 1216, 1254, 1260, 1391, 1392, 1393, 1394, 1413, 1462, 1555, 1657, 1658, 1730, 1731, 1734, 1735.

Automation: Office: 19, 35, 36, 37, 40, 41, 43, 106, 115, 149, 153, 210, 216, 218, 239, 242, 274, 295, 296, 299, 302, 303, 304, 305, 306, 307, 363, 417, 418, 420, 448, 450, 459, 485, 501, 502, 526, 527, 605, 624, 670, 707, 708, 713, 723, 748, 761, 762, 763, 764, 808, 847, 887, 888, 891, 993, 1023, 1029, 1030, 1068, 1083, 1091, 1092, 1133, 1138, 1147, 1171, 1214, 1247, 1258, 1269, 1289, 1297, 1362, 1392, 1416, 1419, 1429, 1432, 1482, 1610, 1611, 1614, 1615, 1620, 1623, 1625, 1683, 1684, 1688.

SECTION 2: COMPARATIVE AND FOREIGN STUDIES

Comparative Studies: 10, 172, 182, 193, 255, 301, 355, 387, 444, 471, 498, 547, 569, 674, 722, 895, 901, 905, 1090, 1153, 1170, 1181, 1199, 1236, 1249, 1268, 1273, 1318, 1444, 1446, 1487, 1593, 1607, 1609, 1634, 1690, 1755.

Foreign Studies: 2, 3, 21, 22, 26, 147, 321, 349, 372, 395, 409, 451, 469, 518, 539, 580, 626, 628, 668, 699, 704, 714, 731, 752, 757, 764, 865, 870, 1136, 1224, 1225, 1262, 1268, 1388, 1389, 1399, 1414, 1465, 1480, 1602, 1603, 1663, 1690, 1725, 1739.

SECTION 3: STUDY SETTINGS

Businesses (Insurance Companies, Offices, Sales Firms, Department Stores, Etc.): 37, 62, 115, 193, 204, 214, 221, 235, 239, 285, 295, 297, 302, 303, 304, 305, 306, 364, 385, 391, 417, 448, 535, 557, 670, 748, 759, 803, 851, 948, 994, 1000, 1007, 1031, 1035, 1171, 1258, 1276, 1441, 1480, 1482, 1488, 1614, 1615, 1619, 1683, 1684, 1688, 1700, 1704, 1705.

Churches, Clergy, Funeral Parlors: 188, 249, 279, 421, 555, 669, 728, 879, 895, 1153, 1336, 1720, 1740, 1763.

Community: 104, 163, 193, 270, 358, 457, 525, 933, 977, 1128, 1154, 1348, 1449, 1593, 1750, 1758, 1760, 1775.

Factories, Industrial: 2, 3, 26, 45, 46, 53, 54, 55, 81, 82, 88, 131, 161, 183, 187, 193, 210, 223, 246, 256, 318, 319, 320, 335, 346, 351, 364, 374, 429, 430, 433, 463, 491, 492, 494, 498, 512, 515, 523, 525, 530, 537, 540, 541, 542, 545, 552, 558, 560, 593, 594, 595, 617, 618, 627, 635, 651, 652, 680, 721, 724, 732, 789, 793, 830, 844, 849, 852, 865, 871, 872, 873, 885, 908, 927, 946, 980, 1010, 1013, 1014, 1015, 1026, 1038, 1039, 1051, 1052, 1069, 1098, 1100, 1103, 1104, 1112, 1134, 1156, 1202, 1220, 1235, 1251, 1253, 1254, 1260, 1262, 1267, 1274, 1291, 1298, 1308, 1312, 1313, 1314, 1315, 1320, 1321,

1322, 1331, 1351, 1354, 1361, 1368, 1369, 1371, 1377, 1385, 1402, 1404, 1408, 1411, 1412, 1413, 1418, 1420, 1422, 1455, 1456, 1461, 1468, 1469, 1472, 1477, 1486, 1497, 1504, 1509, 1518, 1520, 1536, 1547, 1548, 1554, 1580, 1581, 1582, 1586, 1596, 1602, 1604, 1616, 1617, 1618, 1635, 1637, 1649, 1657, 1658, 1659, 1660, 1670, 1718, 1729, 1731, 1739, 1741, 1748, 1764.

Farm Laborers, Unskilled Workers: 51, 1516.

Government Agencies: 171, 875, 1088, 1144, 1269, 1610, 1615, 1623.

Hospitals, Social Service Clinics, etc.: 4, 9, 32, 58, 128, 150, 151, 158, 163, 238, 300, 338, 353, 356, 368, 380, 407, 408, 418, 461, 534, 568, 570, 572, 589, 614, 615, 688, 712, 713, 727, 798, 882, 913, 995, 1070, 1071, 1082, 1105, 1148, 1161, 1183, 1184, 1185, 1194, 1197, 1198, 1299, 1307, 1327, 1338, 1349, 1354, 1386, 1434, 1450, 1452, 1454, 1465, 1609, 1757, 1760, 1763, 1770.

Military: 6, 33, 74, 154, 159, 249, 386, 500, 810, 811, 1067, 1191, 1248, 1597.

Occupations (Cab Drivers, Cash Posters, Etc.): 193, 224, 298, 308, 334, 388, 414, 439, 440, 461, 475, 478, 519, 524, 553, 663, 733, 747, 759, 776, 894, 898, 967, 990, 1000, 1073, 1139, 1205a, 1208, 1244, 1276, 1277, 1365, 1406, 1417, 1420, 1442, 1458, 1466, 1467, 1484, 1502, 1597, 1598, 1608, 1628, 1646, 1672, 1689, 1694, 1704, 1705, 1770, 1771.

Prisons, Police Departments, Juvenile Delinquent Detention, and Correctional Facilities: 152, 198, 360, 362, 644, 825, 999, 1059, 1124, 1255, 1525, 1669, 1753, 1754, 1755, 1756.

Schools: 29, 84, 85, 146, 153, 192, 216, 268, 269, 270, 281, 283, 296, 299, 301, 307, 327, 329, 330, 331, 384, 485, 509, 636, 638, 639, 701, 702, 711, 719, 720, 1107, 1108, 1132, 1157, 1194, 1206, 1257, 1295, 1297, 1353, 1356, 1367, 1470, 1471, 1733, 1745.

Scientific Research Institutes: Governmental: 228, 229, 531.

Scientific Research Institutes: Private: 70, 93, 364, 479, 585, 772, 844, 908, 1002, 1038, 1188, 1190, 1407, 1527, 1687.

Unions: 4, 38, 211, 226, 345, 395, 496, 660, 671, 700, 840, 969, 1001, 1043, 1054, 1220, 1249, 1518, 1522, 1634, 1737, 1738.

Voluntary Associations; Other (Including Professional Associations): 13, 236, 237, 265, 312, 314, 609, 660, 807, 906, 1078, 1109, 1111, 1203, 1356, 1364, 1421, 1447, 1448, 1449, 1485, 1490, 1533, 1535, 1541, 1674, 1750, 1762, 1777.

SECTION 4: ORGANIZATIONAL, INTERPERSONAL, AND INDIVIDUAL VARIABLES

Bibliography

1 Aas, Dagfinn. 1962. "Absenteeism—A Social Fact in Need of the Theory." *Acta Sociologica,* **6**:278–286.
2 Abegglen, James C. 1957. "Subordination and Autonomy: Attitudes of Japanese Workers." *American Journal of Sociology,* **63**:181–189.
3 ———. 1958. *The Japanese Factory.* New York: Free Press.
4 Adams, F. R. 1969. "From Association to Union: Professional Organization of Asylum Attendants, 1869–1919." *British Journal of Sociology,* **20**:11–26.
5 Adams, Richard N., and Jack J. Preiss (eds.). 1960. *Human Organization Research.* Homewood, Ill.: Dorsey.
6 Adams, Stuart. 1954. "Social Climate and Productivity in Small Military Groups." *American Sociological Review,* **19**:421–425.
7 ———. 1956. "Origins of American Occupational Elites." *American Journal of Sociology,* **62**:360–368.
8 Adams, Walter. 1970. "Competition, Monopoly, and Planning," in Maurice Zeitlin (ed.), *American Society Inc.* Chicago: Markham.
9 Agnew, Paul, and Francis Hsu. 1960. "Introducing Change in a Mental Hospital." *Human Organization,* **19**:195–198.

10   Aiken, Michael, and Jerald Hage. 1966. "Organizational Alienation: A Comparative Analysis." *American Sociological Review,* **31**:497-507.

11   ———. 1968. "Organizational Interdependence and Intra-organizational Structure." *American Sociological Review,* **33**:912-930

12   ———. 1971. "The Organic Organization and Innovation." *Sociology,* **5**:63-82.

13   Akers, Ronald L. and Frederick L. Campbell. 1970. "Organizational Size, Complexity, and the Administrative Component in Occupational Associations." *Pacific Sociological Review,* **13**:241-251.

14   Albert, R. 1953. "Comments on the Scientific Function of Cohesiveness." *American Journal of Sociology,* **59**:231-234.

15   Albrow, M. C. 1964. "The Sociology of Organizations." *British Journal of Sociology,* **15**:350-357.

16   Alderfer, Clayton P. 1967. "Organizational Syndrome." *Administrative Science Quarterly,* **12**:440-460.

17   Aldrich, Howard E. 1971. "Sociable Organization: A Case Study of Mensa and Some Propositions." *Sociology and Social Research,* **55**:429-441.

18   ———. 1972. "Technology and Organizational Structure: A Reexamination of the Findings of the Aston Group." *Administrative Science Quarterly,* **17**:26-43.

19   Alexander, Tom. 1969. "Computers Can't Solve Everything." *Fortune* (October):126-129.

20   Alford, Robert R. 1969. "Bureaucracy and Participation in Four Wisconsin Cities." *Urban Affairs Quarterly,* **5**:5-30.

21   Alger, Chadwick F. 1962. "External Bureaucracy in U.S. Foreign Affairs." *Administrative Science Quarterly,* **7**:50-78.

22   ———. 1970. "Research on Research: Decade of Quantitative and Field Research on International Organizations." *International Organization,* **24**:414-450.

23   Allen, Phillip J. 1962. "Growth of Strata in Early Organizational Development." *American Journal of Sociology,* **68**:34-46.

24   Alutto, Joseph A., and James A. Belasco. 1972. "A Typology for Participation in Organizational Decision Making." *Administrative Science Quarterly,* **17**:117-125.

25   Amber, G. H. and P. S. Amber. 1958. "The Anatomy of Automation." *Electrical Manufacturing,* **61**:78-83.

25a   ———. *Anatomy of Automation.* Englewood Cliffs, N. J.: Prentice-Hall.

26   Ancona, L., et al. 1957. *Iron and Steel Workers' Attitudes in the Face of Technological Changes.* Milan, Italy: Institute of Psychology, Catholic University of the Sacred Heart.

27   Anderson, B. D. 1971. "Reactions to a Study of Bureaucracy and Alienation." *Social Forces,* **49**:614-621.

28   ———, Anderson, B., et al. 1966. "Status Classes in Organizations." *Administrative Science Quarterly,* **11**:264-283.

29   Anderson, James G. 1968. *Bureaucracy in Education.* Baltimore: The Johns Hopkins Press.
30   Anderson, Nels. 1961. *Work and Leisure.* New York: Free Press.
31   Anderson, Richard. 1965. *Management Strategies.* New York: McGraw-Hill.
32   Anderson, Theodore, and Seymour Warkov. 1961. "Organizational Size and Functional Complexity: A Study of Administration in Hospitals." *American Sociological Review,* **26**:23–28.
33   Andreski, Stanislav. 1968. *Military Organization and Society.* London: Routledge.
34   Andrews, Frank M. and Donald C. Pelz. 1961. "Dimensions of Organizational Atmosphere." Ann Arbor, Mich.: Institute for Social Research.
35   Anonymous. 1962. *Data Processing Yearbook, 1962–63.* Detroit: American Data Processing, Inc.
36   ————. 1961. *Advances in EDP and Information Systems,* AMA Management Report No. 62. New York: American Management Association.
37   ————. 1962. "A Computer Market Survey: The Banking Industry." *Computers and Automation* (October):14–20.
38   ————. 1962. "Adaptation to Technological Change under Collective Bargaining." Proceedings of the Twelfth Annual Labor-Management Conference. Morgantown, W.Va.: Institute of Industrial Relations.
39   ————. 1971. "Other Recent ASQ Articles Relevant to Leadership Behavior." *Administrative Science Quarterly,* **16**:122–126.
40   ————. 1962. "Airline Passenger Processing: It Takes Nerves of Steel—Literally!" *Systems Management* (March): 13–15.
41   ————. 1962. "A New Systems Concept for Retail Automation." *Data Processing* (December): 42–44.
42   ————. 1955. "A Review of Automatic Technology." *Monthly Labor Review,* **78**:637–644.
43   ————. 1962. "A Survey of Airline Reservation Systems." *Datamation* (June):53–55.
44   ————. 1956. "Automation: A Brief Survey of Recent Developments." *International Labor Review,* **74**:384–404.
45   ————. 1962. "Automation and the Foreman." *Manage* (February):23–25.
46   ————. 1957. "Automation in New York State: Cooperative Action by Industry and Labor in the Age of Automation." *Industrial Bulletin,* **36**:3–7.
47   ————. 1962. "Automation: Outlook for Youth." *American Child* (November):1–15.
48   ————. 1962. "Automation: The Benefits and Problems Incident to Automation and Other Technological Advances." Report from the President's Advisory Committee on Labor-Management Policy. Washington, D.C.: U.S. Government Printing Office.
49   Anshen, Melvin. 1962. "Managerial Decisions," in John T. Dunlop (ed.), *Automation and Technological Change.* Englewood Cliffs, N.J.: Prentice-Hall.
50   Apel, Hans. 1962. "Should We Shorten the Workweek?" *Challenge* (March): 28–31.

51 Apodaca, Anacleto, 1952. "Corn and Custom: The Introduction of Hybrid Corn to Spanish American Farmers in New Mexico," in Edward H. Spicer (ed.), *Human Problems in Technological Change: A Casebook.* New York: Russell Sage.

52 Applewhite, Philip B. 1965. *Organizational Behavior.* Englewood Cliffs, N.J.: Prentice-Hall.

53 Arensberg, Conrad M. 1957. *Research in Industrial Human Relations.* New York: Harper.

54 ——— and D. McGregor. 1942. "Determination of Morale in an Industrial Company." *Applied Anthropology,* **1**:12-34.

55 Argyle, Michael. 1953. "The Relay Assembly Test Room in Retrospect." *Occupational Psychology,* **27**:98-103.

56 ———, Godfrey Gardner, and Frank Cioffi. 1958. "Supervisory Methods Related to Productivity, Absenteeism, and Labor Turnover." *Human Relations,* **11**:23-40.

57 Argyris, Chris. 1954. "The Fusion of an Individual with the Organization." *American Sociological Review,* **19**:267-272.

58 ———. 1956. *Diagnosing Human Relations in Organizations: A Case Study of a Hospital.* New Haven, Conn.: Labor Management Center, Yale University.

59 ———. 1957a. *Personality and Organization.* New York: Harper.

60 ———. 1957b. "The Individual and Organization: Some Problems of Mutual Adjustment." *Administrative Science Quarterly,* **2**:1-24.

61 ———. 1958a. "Creating Effective Research Relationships in Organizations." *Human Organization,* **17**:34-40.

62 ———. 1958b. "Some Problems in Conceptualizing Organizational Climate: A Case Study of a Bank." *Administrative Science Quarterly,* **2**:501-520.

63 ———. 1959a. "Individual and Organization: An Empirical Test." *Administrative Science Quarterly,* **4**:145-167.

64 ———. 1959b. "Understanding Human Behavior in Organizations: One Viewpoint," in Mason Haire (ed.), *Modern Organizational Theory.* New York: Wiley.

65 ———. 1960a. "Personal vs. Organizational Goals." *Yale Scientific,* Winter: 40-50.

66 ———. 1960b. *Understanding Organizational Behavior.* Homewood, Ill.: Dorsey.

67 ———. 1962. *Interpersonal Competence and Organizational Effectiveness.* Homewood, Ill.: Dorsey.

68 ———. 1964. *Integrating the Individual and the Organization.* New York: Wiley.

69 ———. 1965. *Organization and Innovation.* Homewood, Ill.: Dorsey.

70 ———. 1969. "On the Effectiveness of Research and Development Organizations." *American Scientist,* **56**:344-355.

71 Ashburn, Anderson. 1962. "Detroit Automation." *The Annals of the American Academy of Political and Social Science* (March):21-28.

72 Assael, Henry. 1969. "Constructive Role of Interorganizational Conflict." *Administrative Science Quarterly,* **14**:573-583.

73 Atkinson, John W., and D. Cartwright. 1964. "Some Neglected Variables in Contemporary Conceptions of Decision and Performance." *Psychological Reports,* **14**:575-590.

74 Aubert, Vilhelm, and Oddvar Arner. 1958. "On the Social Structure of a Ship." *Acta Sociologica,* **3**:200-219.

75 Babchuk, Nicholas, and William J. Goode. 1951. "Work Incentives in a Self-determined Group." *American Sociological Review,* **16**:679-687.

76 Bachman, Jerald G., Clagett G. Smith, and J. A. Slesinger. 1966. "Control, Performance, and Satisfaction: An Analysis of Structural and Individual Effects." *Journal of Personality and Social Psychology,* **4**:127-136.

77 Backman, Jules. 1961. "Cushioning the Impact of Technological Change." *Labor Law Journal* (September):731-746.

78 Baehr, Melany E., and Richard Renck. 1958. "Definition and Measurement of Employee Morale." *Administrative Science Quarterly,* **3**:157-184.

79 Bagrit, Sir Leon. 1965. *The Age of Automation.* New York: New American library.

80 Baker, Alton W., and Ralph C. Davis. 1954. *Ratio of Staff to Line Employees and Stages of Differentiation of Staff Functions.* Columbus: Bureau of Business Research, College of Commerce and Administration, Ohio State University.

81 Baker, Helen, and Robert France. 1954. *Centralization and Decentralization in Industrial Relations.* Princeton, N. J.: Industrial Relations Section, Princeton University.

82 Baker, H. C., and S. Mitchell. 1960. "Some Factors Affecting Technical Process in the Cutlery Industry." *Occupational Psychology,* **34**:45-54.

83 Bakke, E. Wight. 1950. *Bonds of Organization.* New York: Harper.

84 Baldridge, J. Victor (ed.). 1971a. *Academic Governance in the Administration of Higher Education.* Berkeley, Calif.: McCutchan Publishing Corporation.

85 ———. 1971b. *Power and Conflict in the University.* New York: Wiley.

86 Baldwin, George B., and George P. Schultz. 1955. "Automation: A New Dimension to Old Problems." *Monthly Labor Review,* **78**:165-169.

87 Balfour, W. Campbell. 1953. "Productivity and the Worker." *British Journal of Sociology,* **4**:257-265.

88 Banks, Olive. 1960. *The Attitudes of Steelworkers to Technological Change.* Liverpool: Liverpool University Press.

89 Barach, Arnold, et al. 1962. *1975 and the Change to Come.* New York: Harper.

90 Barkin, Solomon. 1963. "The Challenge of Automation for Labor." *The Voice of America Forum Lectures.* Washington, D.C.: U.S. Information Agency.

91 Barnard, Chester I. 1938. *The Functions of the Executive.* Cambridge, Mass.: Harvard.

92 ———. 1949. *Organization and Management.* Cambridge, Mass.: Harvard.

93 Barnes, Louis B. 1960. *Organizational Systems and Engineering Groups: A Comparative Study of Two Technical Groups in Industry.* Boston: Harvard University Graduate School of Business Administration.

94 Reference omitted.
95 Barrett, Jon. 1970. *Individual Goals and Organizational Objectives.* Ann Arbor, Mich.: Institute for Social Research.
96 Barth, Ernest A. T. 1963. "The Causes and Consequences of Interagency Conflict." *Social Science Review,* **37**:51-57.
97 Barton, Allen. 1961. *Organizational Measurement.* New York: College Entrance Examination Board.
98 ———. 1966. "Comments on Hage's 'An Axiomatic Theory of Organization.' " *Administrative Science Quarterly,* **11**:134-139.
99 Basil, Douglas C. 1971. *Leadership Skills for Executive Action.* Washington, D.C.: The American Management Association, Inc.
100 Bass, Bernard M. 1952. "Ultimate Criteria of Organizational Worth." *Personnel Psychology,* **5**:157-173.
101 ———. 1960. *Leadership, Psychology, and Organization Behavior.* New York: Harper.
102 ———. 1965. *Organizational Psychology.* Boston: Allyn and Bacon.
103 Bates, Frederick. 1956. "Position, Role, and Status: A Reformulation of the Concept." *Social Forces,* **34**:313-321.
104 ———. 1960. "Institutions, Organizations, and Communities: A General Theory of Complex Structure." *Pacific Sociological* **3**:59-70.
105 Baty, Gordon B., et al. 1971. "Personnel Flows as Interorganizational Relations." *Administrative Science Quarterly,* **16**:430-443.
106 Bauer, W. F., D. L. Gerlough, and J. W. Granholm. 1961. "Advanced Computer Applications." *Proceedings of the IRE* (January):296-304.
107 Baum, B. H. 1961. *Decentralization of Authority in a Bureaucracy.* Englewood Cliffs, N.J.: Prentice-Hall.
108 Baumgartel, Howard. 1953. "The Survey Feedback Experiment: A Study of a Program for the Use of Attitude Survey Data in a Large Organization." Ann Arbor, Mich.: Institute for Social Research.
109 ———. 1957. "Leadership Style as a Variable in Research Administration." *Administrative Science Quarterly,* **2**:344-360.
110 ——— and Gerald Goldstein. 1961. "Some Human Consequences of Technological Change." *Personnel Administration* (July-August):32-40.
111 Bavelas, Alex. 1948. "Some Problems of Organizational Change." *Journal of Social Issues,* **3**:48-52.
112 ———. 1960. "Leadership: Man and Function." *Administrative Science Quarterly,* **4**:491-498.
113 Beal, G. M. and E. M. Rogers. 1958. "The Scientist as a Referent in the Communication of New Technology." *Public Opinion Quarterly,* **22**:556-563.
114 Beal, George, et al. 1967. *System Linkages among Women's Organizations.* Ames: Department of Sociology and Anthropology, Iowa State University.
115 Becker, Ester R., and E. P. Murphy. 1957. *The Office in Transition: Meeting the Problems of Automation.* New York: Harper.
116 Becker, Howard. 1962. "The Nature of a Profession," in *Education for the Professions.* Chicago: 61st Yearbook for the Society for the Study of Education.

117   Becker, H. S., et al. 1956. "The Development of Identification with an Occu-
      pation." *American Journal of Sociology,* **61**:289-298.
118   Becker, Joseph M., et al. 1965. *Programs to Aid the Unemployed in the 1960's.*
      Kalamazoo, Mich.: W. E. Upjohn Institute for Employment Research.
119   Becker, Selwyn W., and N. Baloff. 1969. "Organizational Structure and Com-
      plex Problem-Solving." *Administrative Science Quarterly,* **14**:260-271.
120   —— and Gerald Gordon. 1966. "Entrepreneurial Theory of Formal Or-
      ganization—Part 1: Patterns of Formal Organizations." *Administrative Sci-
      ence Quarterly,* **11**:315-344.
121   —— and Frank Stafford. 1967. "Some Determinants of Organizational
      Success." *Journal of Business,* **40**:511-518.
122   Beckett, John A. 1971. *Management Dynamics: The New Synthesis.* New
      York: McGraw-Hill.
123   Bell, Daniel. 1956. *Work and Its Discontents.* Boston: Beacon Press.
124   Bell, Gerald D. 1967a. "Determinants of Span of Control." *American Journal
      of Sociology,* **73**:100-109.
125   ——. 1967b. *Organizations and Human Behavior: A Book of Readings.* En-
      glewood Cliffs, N.J.: Prentice-Hall.
126   Bell, Wendell, and Maryanne T. Force. 1956. "Social Structure and Participa-
      tion in Different Types of Formal Associations." *Social Forces,* **34**:345-350.
127   Bello, Francis. 1962. "The Technology Behind Productivity." *Monthly Labor
      Review* (August):865-867.
128   Ben-David, Joseph. 1958. "The Professional Role of the Physician in Bureau-
      cratized Medicine: A Study of Role Conflict." *Human Relations,* **2**:901-911.
129   Bendix, Reinhard. 1945. "Bureaucracy and the Problem of Power." *Public
      Administration Review,* **5**:194-209.
130   ——. 1947. "Bureaucracy: The Problem and Its Setting." *American Socio-
      logical Review,* **12**:493-507.
131   ——. 1963. *Work and Authority in Industry: Ideologies of Management in the
      Course of Industrialization.* New York: Harper & Row.
132   ——. 1968. "Bureaucracy." *International Encyclopedia of the Social Sci-
      ences.* New York: Macmillan.
133   Benne, Kenneth D. 1961. "Three Pivotal Functions in Planned Change:
      Training, Consulting, and Research," Research Papers and Technical Notes
      No. 28. Boston: Boston University Human Relations Center.
134   —— and P. Sheats. 1948. "Functional Roles of Group Members." *Journal
      of Social Issues,* **4**:42-45.
135   Bennis, Warren G. 1959. "Leadership Theory and Administrative Behavior:
      The Problem of Authority." *Administrative Science Quarterly,* **4**:259-301.
136   ——. 1963. "New Role for the Behavioral Sciences: Effecting Organiza-
      tional Change." *Administrative Science Quarterly,* **8**:125-165.
137   ——. 1965. "Theory and Method in Applying Behavioral Science to
      Planned Organizational Change." *The Journal of Applied Behavioral Science,*
      1:337-360.
138   ——. 1966a. *Changing Organizations.* New York: McGraw-Hill.

139 ———. 1966b. *Essays on the Development and Evolution of Human Organiza-tion.* New York: McGraw-Hill.

140 ———. 1969a. "Organizational Developments and the Fate of Bureaucracy," in L. L. Cummings and W. E. Scott (eds.), *Organizational Behavior and Hu-man Performance.* Homewood, Ill.: Dorsey-Irwin.

141 ———. 1969b. "Post-Bureaucratic Leadership." *Transaction,* **6**:44-51.

142 ———. 1970a. "A Funny Thing Happened on the Way to the Future." *American Psychologist,* **25**:595-608.

143 ———. 1970b. *American Bureaucracy.* Chicago: Aldine.

144 Kenneth Benne, and Robert Chin (eds.). 1961. *The Planning of Change: Read-ings in Applied Behavioral Science.* New York: Holt.

145 ——— and Philip Slater. 1968. *The Temporary Society.* New York: Harper & Row.

146 Berg, Curt. 1968. "Case Studies in Organizational Research and Education." *Acta Sociologica,* **11**:1-11.

147 Berger, Monroe. 1957. "Bureaucracy East and West." *Administrative Science Quarterly,* **1**:518-529.

148 Berk, Bernard B. 1966. "Organizational Goals and Inmate Organization." *American Journal of Sociology,* **71**:522-534.

149 Berkeley, Edmund C. 1962. *The Computer Revolution.* Garden City, N.Y.: Doubleday.

150 Berkowitz, Norman J., and Warren G. Bennis. 1961. "Interaction Patterns in Formal Service-Oriented Organizations." *Administrative Science Quarterly,* **6**:25-50.

151 ———, Warren G. Bennis, and N. Malone. 1958. "Reference Groups and Loyalties in the Outpatient Department." *Administrative Science Quarterly,* **2**:481-500.

152 Besco, Robert O., and C. H. Lawshe. 1959. "Foreman Leadership as Per-ceived by Superiors and Subordinates." *Personnel Psychology,* **12**:573-582.

153 Beshers, James M. 1968. *Computer Methods in the Analysis of Large Scale Social Systems.* Cambridge, Mass.: M.I.T.

154 Biderman, Albert D., and Laure M. Sharp. 1967. "The Convergence of Mili-tary and Civilian Occupational Structures: Evidence from Studies of Military Retired Employment." *American Journal of Sociology,* **73**:381-399.

155 Bidwell, Charles E. 1966. "Values, Norms, and the Integration of Complex Systems." *Sociological Quarterly,* **7**:119-136.

156 Billeau, I. John. 1962. *The Challenges and Opportunities of Automation.* New York: U.S. Industries, Inc.

157 Bittel, L. R., M. G. Melden, and R. S. Rice. 1957. *Practical Automation: Methods for Increasing Plant Productivity.* New York: McGraw-Hill.

158 Black, Bertram J., and Harold M. Kasi. 1963. "Interagency Cooperation in Rehabilitation and Mental Health." *Social Science Review,* **37**:26-32.

159 Blake, Joseph A. 1970. "The Organization as an Instrument of Violence: The Military Case." *Sociological Quarterly,* **11**:331-350.

160 Blake, Robert R. 1964. *The Managerial Grid.* Houston: Gulf Publishing Com-pany.

161   ——— et al. 1964. *Managing Intergroup Conflict in Industry.* Houston: Gulf.
162   Blakelock, E. 1959. "Satisfaction with Shift Work." *Study of Work Life and Life Satisfaction,* Report No. 3. Ann Arbor, Mich.: Institute for Social Research.
163   Blankenship, L., and Ray Elling. 1962. "Organizational Support and Community Power Structure: The Hospital." *Journal of Health and Human Behavior,* **3**:257-269.
164   Blankenship, Vaughn, and Raymond Miles. 1968. "Organizational Structure and Managerial Decision Behavior." *Administrative Science Quarterly,* **13**:106-120.
165   Blau, Peter M. 1953. "Orientation of College Students toward International Relations." *American Journal of Sociology,* **59**:205-214.
166   ———. 1955. *The Dynamics of Bureaucracy.* Chicago: The University of Chicago Press.
167   ———. 1957. "Formal Organization: Dimensions of Analysis." *American Journal of Sociology,* **63**:58-69.
168   ———. 1960a. "A Theory of Social Integration." *American Journal of Sociology,* **65**:545-556.
169   ———. 1960b. "Patterns of Deviation in Work Groups." *Sociometry,* **23**:245-261.
170   ———. 1962. "Studies on Formal Organizations." *American Journal of Sociology,* **68**:289-290.
171   ———. 1963. *The Dynamics of Bureaucracy: A Study of Interpersonal Relations in Two Government Agencies.* Chicago: The University of Chicago Press.
172   ———. 1965. "The Comparative Study of Organizations." *Industrial and Labor Relations Review,* **18**:323-338.
173   ———. 1968. "The Hierarchy of Authority in Organization." *American Journal of Sociology,* **73**:453-467.
174   ———. 1970a. "A Formal Theory of Differentiation in Organizations." *American Sociological Review,* **35**:201-218.
175   ———. 1970b. "Decentralization in Bureaucracies," in Mayer N. Zald (ed.), *Power in Organizations.* Nashville, Tenn.: Vanderbilt University Press.
176   ———. 1971. "Comments on Two Mathematical Formulations of the Theory of Differentiation in Organizations." *American Sociological Review,* **36**:304-307.
177   ———. 1972. "Interdependence and Hierarchy in Organizations." *Social Science Research,* **1**:1-24.
178   ——— and O. Dudley Duncan. 1967. *The American Occupational Structure.* New York: Wiley.
179   ———, Wolf Heydebrand, and Robert D. Stouffer. 1966. "The Structure of Small Bureaucracies." *American Sociological Review,* **31**:179-191.
180   ——— and Marshall W. Meyer. 1971. *Bureaucracy in Modern Society* (2d ed.). New York: Random House.
181   ——— and Richard A. Schoenherr. 1971. *The Structure of Organizations.* New York: Basic Books.

182 ——— and W. Richard Scott. 1962. *Formal Organizations: A Comparative Approach.* San Francisco: Chandler.

183 Blauner, Robert. 1964. *Alienation and Freedom: The Factory Worker and His Industry.* Chicago: The University of Chicago Press.

184 ———. 1966. "Work Satisfaction Trends in Modern Society," in Walter Fogel and Archibald Kleigartner (eds.), *Contemporary Labor Issues.* Belmont, Calif.: Wadsworth.

185 Blegen, Hans M. 1968. "The Systems Approach to the Study of Organizations." *Acta Sociologica,* **11**:12–30.

186 Blood, Milton R., and Charles L. Haslin. 1967. "Alienation, Environmental Characteristics, and Worker Responses." *Journal of Applied Psychology,* **51**:284–290.

187 Blumberg, Paul. 1969. *Industrial Democracy: The Sociology of Participation.* New York: Schocken Books.

188 Bock, E. Wilbur. 1967. "The Female Clergy: A Case of Professional Marginality." *American Journal of Sociology,* **72**:531–539.

189 Boehm, George A. 1962. "Helping the Executive to Make Up His Mind." *Fortune* (April):128–131.

190 Bogardus, E. S. 1958. "Social Aspects of Automation." *Sociology and Social Research,* **42**:358–363.

191 Bok, Derek, and Max D. Kossoris. 1963. *Methods of Adjusting to Automation and Technological Change: A Review of Selected Methods Prepared for the President's Committee on Labor-Management Policy.* Washington, D.C.: U.S. Government Printing Office.

192 Boland, Walter R. 1971. "Size, Organization, and Environmental Mediation: A Study of Colleges and Universities," in J. Victor Baldridge (ed.), *Academic Governance in the Administration of Higher Education.* Berkeley, Calif.: McCutchan Publishing Corporation.

193 Bonjean, Charles M. 1966. "Mass, Class, and the Industrial Community: A Comparative Analysis of Managers, Businessmen, and Workers." *American Journal of Sociology,* **72**:149–162.

194 ———, Grady D. Bruce, and J. Allen Williams, Jr. 1967. "Social Mobility and Job Satisfaction: A Replication and Extension." *Social Forces,* **45**:492–501.

195 ——— and Michael D. Grimes. 1970. "Bureaucracy and Alienation: A Dimensional Approach." *Social Forces,* **48**:365–373.

196 ——— and———. 1971. "Some Issues in the Study of Bureaucracy and Alienation." *Social Forces,* **49**:622–630.

197 ———, Richard J. Hill, and S. Dale McLemore. 1967. *Sociological Measurement: An Inventory of Scales and Indices.* San Francisco: Chandler.

198 Bordua, David J., and Albert J. Reiss. 1966. "Command, Control and Charisma: Reflections on Police Bureaucracy." *American Journal of Sociology,* **72**:68–76.

199 Borgatta, E. F., A. S. Couch, and R. F. Bales. 1954. "Some Findings Relevant to the Great Man Theory of Leadership." *American Sociological Review,* **19**:755–759.

200 Borhek, J. T. 1965. "Role Orientations and Organizational Stability." *Human Organization,* **24**:322–338.

201 Boulding, Kenneth. 1953. *Organizational Revolution.* New York: Harper.

202 ———. 1964. "A Pure Theory of Conflict Applied to Organizations," in Robert P. Kahn and Kenneth E. Boulding (eds.), *Power and Conflict.* New York: Basic Books.

203 Bowers, David G. 1963. "Self-esteem and the Diffusion of Leadership Style." *Journal of Applied Psychology,* **47**:135–140.

204 ———. 1964. "Organizational Control in an Insurance Company." *Sociometry,* **27**:230–244.

205 ———. 1964b. "Self-esteem and Supervision." *Personnel Administration,* **27**:23–36.

206 ——— and Stanley Seashore. 1966. "Predicting Organizational Effectiveness with a Four-Factor Theory of Leadership." *Administrative Science Quarterly,* **11**:238–263.

207 ——— and ———. 1967. "Peer Leadership within Work Groups." *Personnel Administration,* **30**:45–50.

208 Bowers, Raymond V. (ed.). 1966. *Studies on Behavior in Organizations.* Athens: University of Georgia Press.

209 Bradford, L., J. Gibb, and K. Benne (eds). 1964. *T-Group Theory and Laboratory Method: Innovation and Re-education.* New York: Wiley.

210 Brady, Robert A. 1961. *Organization, Automation, and Society: The Scientific Revolution in Industry.* Berkeley: University of California Press.

211 Brager, George. 1967. "Commitment and Conflict in a Normative Organization." *American Sociological Review,* **34**:482–491.

212 Brayfield, A. H., and W. H. Crockett. 1955. "Employee Attitudes and Employee Performance." *Psychological Bulletin,* **52**:396–424.

213 ——— and Harold F. Rothe. 1951. "The Brayfield-Rothe Index of Job Satisfaction." *Journal of Applied Psychology,* **35**:307–311.

214 Breed, Warren. 1955. "Social Control in the Newsroom: A Functional Analysis." *Social Forces,* **33**:326–335.

215 Brewer, John. 1971. "Flow of Communications, Expert Qualifications, and Organizational Authority Structures." *American Sociological Review,* **36**:475–484.

216 Brickman, William W. 1966. *Automation, Education, and Human Values.* New York: School and Society Books, Inc.

217 Bridges, Edwin M., Wayne J. Doyle, and David J. Mahan. 1968. "Effects of Hierarchical Differentiation on Group Productivity, Efficiency, and Risk-Taking." *Administrative Science Quarterly,* **13**:305–319.

218 Bright, J. R. 1958a. *Automation and Management.* Boston: Division of Research, Graduate School of Business Administration, Harvard University.

219 ———. 1958b. "Does Automation Raise Skill Requirements?" *Harvard Business Review,* **36**:85–98.

220 ———. (ed.). 1962. *Technological Planning on the Corporate Level.* Boston: Harvard University Graduate School of Business Administration.

221   Brinkerhoff, Merlin B. 1972. "Hierarchical Status, Contingencies, and the Administrative Staff Conference." *Administrative Science Quarterly,* 17:395-407.

222   ——— and Phillip Kunz. 1972. *Complex Organizations and Their Environments.* Dubuque, Iowa: Wm. C. Brown Company Publishers.

223   Brooks, Thomas R. 1962. "Bleaching the Blue Collar." *Dun's Review and Modern Industry* (January):58-64.

224   Broom, Leonard, and J. H. Smith. 1963. "Bridging Occupations." *British Journal of Sociology,* 14:321-334.

225   Brouillette, John R., and E. L. Quarantelli. 1971. "Types of Patterned Variation in Bureaucratic Adaptations to Organizational Stress." *Sociological Inquiry,* 41:39-46.

226   Brown, Julia S. 1956. "Union Size as a Function of Intra-Union Conflict." *Human Relations,* 9:75-89.

227   Brown, Michael E. 1969. "Identification and Some Conditions of Organizational Involvement." *Administrative Science Quarterly,* 14:346-356.

228   Brown, Paula. 1954. "Bureaucracy in a Government Laboratory." *Social Forces,* 32:259-268.

229   ——— and Clovis Shepard. 1956. "Factionalism and Organizational Change in a Research Laboratory." *Social Problems,* 3:235-243.

230   Brown, Roger. 1965. *Social Psychology.* New York: Free Press.

231   Brown, Wilfred. 1960. *Explorations in Management.* New York: Wiley.

232   ———. 1965. *Explorations in Management.* Harmondsworth, England: Penguin.

233   Browne, C. G., and B. J. Neitzel. 1952. "Communication, Supervision, and Morale." *Journal of Applied Psychology,* 36:86-91.

234   Brozen, Yale. 1963. *Automation: The Impact of Technological Change.* Washington, D.C.: American Enterprise Institute for Public Policy Research.

235   Bruce, Grady D., et al. 1966. "Job Satisfaction among Independent Businessmen: A Correlative Study." *Sociology and Social Research,* 52:195-204.

236   Bucher, Rue and Joan Stelling. 1967. "Characteristics of Professional Organizations." Paper presented at the 62d Annual Meetings of the American Sociological Association.

237   ——— and ———. 1969. "Characteristics of Professional Organizations." *Journal of Health and Social Behavior,* 10:3-15.

238   ———. 1970. "Social Process and Power in a Medical Study," in Mayer Zald (ed.), *Power in Organizations.* Nashville, Tenn.: Vanderbilt University Press.

239   Buckingham, Walter. 1961. *Automation: Its Impact on Business and People.* New York: Harper.

240   ———. 1962a. "Technology in a Changing Economy," in *Challenge to Labor Education in the 60's.* Washington, D.C.: National Institute of Labor Education.

241   ———. 1962b. "The Great Employment Controversy." *The Annals of the American Academy of Political and Social Science* (March):46-52.

242   ———. 1963. "The Impact of Automation on Skills and Employment." *Computers and Automation* (April):16-18.

243 Buckley, Walter. 1968. *Modern Systems Research for the Behavioral Sciences.* Chicago: Aldine.

244 Bucklow, A. Maxine. 1966. "New Role for the Work Group." *Administrative Science Quarterly,* **11**:59-78.

245 Bullock, R. P. 1952. *Social Factors Related to Job Satisfaction.* Columbus: Ohio State University, Bureau of Business Research.

246 Burak, Elmer H. 1967a. "Industrial Management in Advanced Production Systems: Some Theoretical Concepts and Preliminary Findings." *Administrative Science Quarterly,* **12**:479-500.

247 ———. 1967b. "Technology and Supervisory Functions: A Preliminary View." *Human Organization,* **26**:256-264.

248 Burby, Raymond J. 1968. *Managing With People.* Reading, Mass.: Addison-Wesley.

249 Burchard, Waldo. 1954. "Role Conflict of Military Chaplains." *American Sociological Review,* **19**:528 535.

250 Burke, Kenneth. 1935. *Permanence and Change.* New York: New Republic.

251 Burlingame, John F. 1961. "Information Technology and Decentralization." *Harvard Business Review* (November-December):121-126.

252 Burns, Tom. 1954. "The Reference of Conduct in Small Groups: Cliques and Cabals in Occupational Milieux." *Human Relations,* **7**:73-97.

253 ———. 1956. "The Social Character of Technology." *Impact of Science on Society,* **7**:147-165.

254 ———. 1961. "Micropolitics: Mechanisms of Institutional Change." *Administrative Science Quarterly,* **6**:257-281.

255 ———. 1967. "The Comparative Study of Organizations," in Victor H. Vroom (ed.), *Methods of Organizational Research.* Pittsburgh: University of Pittsburgh Press.

256 ———. 1969. *Industrial Man: Selected Readings.* Baltimore: Penguin.

257 ——— and G. M. Stalker. 1961. *The Management of Innovation.* London: Tavistock Publications.

258 Burnstein, Eugene, and Robert B. Zajonc. 1965. "Individual Task Performance in a Changing Social Structure." *Sociometry,* **28**:16-29.

259 Bursk, Edward C., and T. B. Blodgett. 1971. *Developing Executive Leaders.* Cambridge, Mass.: Harvard.

260 Burtle, James. 1957. "Automation: The Guaranteed Wage and the Hours of Work." *International Labour Review,* **75**:495-513.

261 Caldwallader, M. L. 1959. "The Cybernetic Analysis of Change in Complex Social Organizations." *American Journal of Sociology,* **65**:154-157.

262 Caldwell, Robert G., and James A. Black. 1971. *Juvenile Delinquency.* New York: Ronald.

263 Campbell, A. 1953. "Administering Research Organizations." *American Psychologist,* **8**:225-230.

264 Campbell, Donald T. 1970. "Considering the Case against Experimental Evaluations of Social Innovations." *Administrative Science Quarterly,* **15**:110-118.

265 Campbell, Frederick L., and Ronald L. Akers. 1970. "Size and the Administrative Component in Occupational Associations." *Sociological Quarterly,* **11**:435-451.

266 Campbell, H. 1953. "Some Effects of Joint Consultation on the Status and Role of the Supervisor." *Occupational Psychology,* **27**:200-206.

267 Campbell, John P., and Marvin D. Dunnette. 1968. "Effectiveness of T-Group Experiences in Managerial Training and Development." *Psychological Bulletin,* **70**:73-104.

268 Campbell, Roald, John E. Corbally, Jr. and John A. Ranseyer. 1967. *Introduction to Educational Administration.* Boston: Allyn and Bacon.

269 —— and Donald H. Layton. 1969. *Policy Making for American Education.* Chicago: The University of Chicago Press.

270 —— and John A. Ranseyer. 1955. *The Dynamics of School-Community Relationships.* New York: Allyn and Bacon.

271 Cangelosi, Vincent E., and William R. Dill. 1965. "Organizational Learning: Observations toward a Theory." *Administrative Science Quarterly,* **10**:175-203.

272 Cannon, Martin J. 1970. "An Analysis of Organizational Size and Organizational Performance." Paper presented at the American Sociological Association Meetings in Washington, D.C.

273 Cantor, Nathaniel. 1958. *The Learning Process for Managers.* New York: Harper.

274 Caples, W. G. 1960. "Automation in Theory and Practice." *Business Topics,* **8**:7-19.

275 Caplow, Theodore. 1953. "The Criteria of Organizational Success." *Social Forces,* **32**:1-9.

276 ——. 1957. "Organizational Size." *Administrative Science Quarterly,* **1**:484-505.

277 ——. 1964. *Principles of Organization.* New York: Harcourt, Brace & World.

278 Carey, Alex. 1967. "The Hawthorne Studies: A Radical Criticism." *American Sociological Review,* **32**:403-416.

279 Carey, Raymond, 1972. "Correlates of Satisfaction in the Priesthood." *Administrative Science Quarterly,* **17**:185-195.

280 Carlson, Earl R. 1960. "Clique Structure and Member Satisfaction in Groups." *Sociometry,* **23**:327-337.

281 Carlson, Richard O. 1961. "Successions and Performance among School Superintendents." *Administrative Science Quarterly,* **6**:210-227.

282 ——. 1962. *Executive Succession and Organization Change.* Chicago: The University of Chicago Press.

283 ——. 1964. "Environmental Constraints and Organizational Consequences: The Public School and Its Clients." *Behavioral Science and Educational Administration.* Chicago: National Society for the Study of Education.

284 Carras, William. 1965. *Automation: What Happened to the Hand at the Automat?* New York: Macmillan.

285 Carter, C. F., and B. R. Williams. 1959. "The Characteristics of Technically Progressive Firms." *Journal of Industrial Economics,* 7:87-103.
286 Cartwright, D. 1951. "Achieving Change in People: Some Applications of Group Dynamics Theory." *Human Relations.* 4:381-392.
287 ———. 1957. "Sociology, Psychology, and Group Processes." *Annual Review of Psychology,* 8:211-236.
288 ———. 1959. "Power: A Neglected Variable in Social Psychology," in D. Cartwright (ed.), *Studies in Social Power.* Ann Arbor, Mich.: Research Center for Group Dynamics.
289 ——— and A. Zander (eds.). 1960. *Group Dynamics: Research and Theory* (2d ed.). New York: Row, Peterson.
290 Carzo, Rocco, Jr. 1963. "Some Effects of Organization Structure on Group Cohesiveness." *Administrative Science Quarterly,* 7:393-424.
291 ——— and John Yanouzas. 1967. *Formal Organization: A Systems Approach.* Homewood, Ill.: Dorsey.
292 ——— and ———. 1969. "Effects of Flat and Tall Organization Structure." *Administrative Science Quarterly,* 14:178-191.
293 ——— and ———. 1970. "Justification for the Carzo-Yanouzas Experiment on Flat and Tall Structures." *Administrative Science Quarterly,* 15:235-241.
294 Cattell, Raymond B. 1951. "Concepts and Methods for Measuring Leadership in Terms of Group Syntality." *Human Relations,* 4:161-184.
295 Champion, Dean J. 1966a. "Organization Size and Degree of Automation as Determinants of Depersonalization and Role Performance in Six Banks and a Computer Center." Paper presented at the American Sociological Association Meetings, Miami, Fla.
296 ———. 1966b. "Registration and Regimentation." *Medical Opinion and Review,* 1:72-77.
297 ———. 1968. "Informal-Formal Complementarity in a Telephone Company." Unpublished paper, Knoxville, Tenn.: University of Tennessee.
298 ———. 1970a. "Who Practices Where and Why?: Surprise in Appalachia." *Medical Opinion and Review,* 6:26-29.
299 ———. 1970b. "Uniformity and Depersonalization: Some Consequences of Automation on the Campus." *The Southern Journal of Educational Research,* 4:97-106.
300 ——— and H. Betterton. 1974. "On Organizational Size and Administrative Ratios: A Critical Examination of General and Specialized Hospitals." *Pacific Sociological Review,* 17:98-107.
301 ——— and Lynn J. Champion. 1973. "A Comparative Study of Large University and Small College Faculty." The Southern Journal of Educational Research, 7:114-126.
302 ——— and Edward Z. Dager. 1965. "Some Impacts of Office Automation upon Status, Role Change, and Depersonalization." Paper presented at the American Sociological Association Meetings, Chicago, Ill.

303 —— and ——. 1966. "Automation Man in the Counting House." *Transaction,* **3**:34-36.

304 —— and ——. 1967a. "Depersonalization: Some Implications for Bank Employees." *Journal of Industrial Engineering,* **18**:223-226.

305 —— and ——. 1967b. "Pressures and Performance: Automation and the Bank Employee." *The Banker's Magazine,* **150**:97-102.

306 —— and ——. 1967c. "Some Impacts of Office Automation upon Status Role Change, and Depersonalization." *Sociological Quarterly,* **8**:71-84.

307 —— and E. Gordon Ericksen. 1967. "Automated Registration: The Education of Automation Man." *Liberal Education,* **53**:357-364.

308 —— and Donald B. Olsen. 1971. "Physician Recruitment in Southern Appalachia: Some Recruitment Factors." *Journal of Health and Social Behavior,* **12**:243-252.

309 Chandler, Alfred D. 1963. *Strategy and Structure.* Garden City, N.Y.: Doubleday.

310 Chant, N. S. F. 1932. "Measuring Factors That Make a Job Interesting." *Personnel Journal,* **11**:1-4.

311 Chapin, F. Stuart. 1951. "The Growth of Bureaucracy: An Hypothesis." *American Sociological Review,* **16**:835-856.

312 ——. 1956. "The Formalization Process in Voluntary Organizations." *Social Forces,* **34**:342-344.

313 ——. 1957. "The Optimum Size of Institutions: A Theory of the Large Group." *American Journal of Sociology,* **62**:449-460.

314 —— and John E. Tsouderos. 1955. "Formalization Observed in Ten Voluntary Associations: Concepts, Morphology, and Process." *Social Forces,* **33**:306-309.

315 Chapple, Eliot D. 1962. "Quantitative Analysis of Complex Organizations Systems." *Human Organization,* **21**:67-87.

316 Child, John. 1972. "Organization Structure and Strategies of Control: A Replication of the Aston Study." *Administrative Science Quarterly,* **17**:163-177.

317 Childers, Grant W., et al. 1971. "System Size and Structural Differentiation in Military Organizations: Testing a Baseline Model of the Division of Labor." *American Sociological Review,* **76**:813-830.

318 Chinoy, Ely. 1952. "The Tradition of Opportunity and the Aspirations of Automobile Workers." *American Journal of Sociology,* **57**:453-459.

319 ——. 1955. *Automobile Workers and the American Dream.* Garden City, N.Y.: Doubleday.

320 Chowdhry, Kamla. 1953. *An Analysis of the Attitudes of Textile Workers and the Effect of These Attitudes on Working Efficiency.* Ahmedabad, India: Atira Research Institute.

321 —— and A. K. Pal. 1957. "Production Planning and Organizational Morale: A Case Study from India." *Human Organization,* **15**:11-16.

322 Chwalek, Henryka. 1965. *Productivity and Automation.* Madison: Center for Productivity Motivation, School of Commerce, University of Wisconsin.

323   Cicourel, Aaron V. 1958. "Front and Back of Organizational Leadership: A Case Study." *Pacific Sociological Review*, 1:54-58.

324   Clague, Ewan. 1964. "Measurement of Technological Change." Paper presented at Conference of Employment Problems of Automation and Advanced Technology. Geneva, Switzerland: International Institute for Labor Studies.

325   ———— and Leon Greenberg, 1962a. "Employment," in John T. Dunlop (ed.), *Automation and Technological Change*. Englewood Cliffs, N.J.: Prentice-Hall.

326   ———— and ————. 1962b. "Technological Change and Employment." *Monthly Labor Review* (July): 742-746.

327   Clark, Burton. 1956a. *Adult Education in Transition*. Berkeley: University of California Press.

328   ————. 1956b. "Organizational Adaptation and Precarious Values." *American Sociological Review*, 21:327-336.

329   ————. 1960a. "The 'Cooling Out' Function in Higher Education." *American Journal of Sociology*, 65:569-576.

330   ————. 1960b. *The Open Door College: A Case Study*. New York: McGraw-Hill.

331   ————. 1965. "Interorganizational Patterns in Education." *Administrative Science Quarterly*, 10:224-237.

332   Clark, Peter A. and Janet R. Ford. 1970. "Methodological and Theoretical Problems in the Investigation of Planned Organizational Change." *Sociological Review*, 18:29-52.

333   Clark, Peter B., and James Q. Wilson. 1961. "Incentive Systems: A Theory of Organizations." *Administrative Science Quarterly*, 6:129-166.

334   Clayton, Curtis T. 1962. "Automatic Ships—Only Hope for the U.S. Merchant Marine?" *Control Engineering* (July):73-76.

335   Cleland, Sherill. 1955. *The Influence of Plant Size on Industrial Relations*. Princeton, N.J.: Princeton University Press.

336   Coates, Charles H., and Roland J. Pellegrin. 1957. "Executives and Supervisors: Informal Factors in Differential Bureaucratic Promotion." *Administrative Science Quarterly*, 2:200-215.

337   Coch, L. and J. R. P. French. 1948. "Overcoming Resistance to Change." *Human Relations*, 1:512-533.

338   Coe, Rodney M. (ed). 1970. *Planned Change in the Hospital: Case Studies of Organizational Innovation*. New York: Praeger.

339   Cogan, Morris L. 1953. "Toward a Definition of a Profession." *Harvard Educational Review*, 23:33-50.

340   Cohen, Arthur M. 1962. "Changing Small Group Communication Networks." *Administrative Science Quarterly*, 6:443-462.

341   ————, Ernest L. Robinson, and Jack L. Edwards. 1969. "Experiments in Organizational Embeddedness." *Administrative Science Quarterly*, 14:208-221.

342   Cohen, Harry. 1965. *The Demonics of Bureaucracy*. Ames: University of Iowa Press.

343 ———. 1970. "Bureaucratic Flexibility: Some Comments on Robert Merton's Bureaucratic Structure and Personality." *British Journal of Sociology,* 21:390-399.

344 Coleman, James S. 1958. "Relational Analysis: A Study of a Social Organization with Survey Methods." *Human Organization,* 17:28-36.

345 Coleman, John R. 1956. "The Compulsive Pressures of Democracy in Unionism." *American Journal of Sociology.* 61:519-526.

346 Collins, Orvis, Melville Dalton, and Donald Roy. 1946. "Restriction of Output and Social Cleavage in Industry." *Applied Anthropology,* 5:1-14.

347 Comrey, A. L., W. S. High, and R. C. Wilson, 1955. "Factors Influencing Organizational Effectiveness." *Personnel Psychology,* 8:79-99.

348 ———, J. M. Pfiffner, and W. S. High. 1954. *Factors Influencing Organizational Effectiveness.* Los Angeles: University of Southern California, Office of Naval Research.

349 Constas, Helen. 1961. "U.S.S.R. from Charismatic Sect to Bureaucratic Society." *Administrative Science Quarterly,* 6:282-298.

350 Cooley, C. H. 1909. *Social Organization.* New York: Scribner, pp. 145-156.

351 Cooper, Robert. 1966. "Leaders, Task Relevance and Subordinate Behavior in Industrial Work Groups." *Human Relations.* 19:57-84.

352 Cooper, William W., et al. 1964. *New Perspectives in Organizational Research.* New York: Wiley.

353 Corwin, Ronald G. 1961. "The Professional Employee: A Study of Conflict in Nursing Roles." *American Journal of Sociology,* 66:604-615.

354 ———. 1969. "Patterns of Organizational Conflict." *Administrative Science Quarterly,* 14:507-521.

355 ———. 1972. "Strategies for Organizational Innovation: An Empirical Comparison." *American Sociological Review,* 37:441-454.

356 Coser, Rose L. 1958. "Authority and Decision-Making in a Hospital." *American Sociological Review,* 23:56-63.

357 Costello, Timothy W., et al. 1963. "An Analysis of Attitudes toward a Planned Merger." *Administrative Science Quarterly,* 8:507-521.

358 Cottrell, W. F. 1951. "A Case Study in the Reaction to Technological Change: Death by Dieselization." *American Sociological Review,* 16:358-365.

359 Craig, John G., and Edward Gross. 1970. "The Forum Theory of Organizational Democracy: Structural Guarantees as Time Related Variables." *American Sociological Review,* 35:19-33.

360 Cressey, Donald R. 1958. "Achievement of an Unstated Organizational Goal: An Observation of Prisons." *Pacific Sociological Review,* 1:43-49.

361 ———. 1959. "Contradictory Directives in Complex Organizations: The Case of a Prison." *Administrative Science Quarterly,* 4:1-19.

362 ——— (ed.). 1961. *The Prison: Studies in Institutional Organization and Change.* New York: Holt.

363 Cross, M. O., Jr. 1960. "Automation: The New Technology." *Business Topics,* 8:59-68.

364   Crossman, Edward. 1966. "Evaluation of Change in Skill Profile and Job Content Due to Technological Change: Methodology and Pilot Results from the Banking, Steel and Aerospace Industries." Berkeley, Calif.: Office of Manpower Policy, Evaluation, and Research.

365   Crozier, Michael, 1961. "Human Relations at the Management Level." *Human Organization,* 20:51-64.

366   ———. 1964. *The Bureaucratic Phenomenon.* Chicago: The University of Chicago Press.

367   ——— and G. Friedmann. 1958. "The Social Consequences of Automation: Foreward." *International Social Science Bulletin,* 10:7-17.

368   Cumming, Elaine, and John Cumming. 1962. "The Organization of the Large Mental Hospital." *Human Organization,* 21:97-101.

369   ———, Lois Dean, and David S. Newell. 1958. "What is Morale? A Case History of a Validity Problem." *Human Organization,* 17:3-8.

370   Cummings, Larry L., and Aly M. ElSalmi. 1970. "The Impact of Role Diversity, Job Level, and Organizational Size on Managerial Satisfaction." *Administrative Science Quarterly,* 15:1-11.

371   ——— and W. E. Scott. 1969. *Readings in Organizational Behavior and Human Performance.* Homewood, Ill.: Dorsey.

372   Cutwright, Phillips. 1968. "Occupational Inheritance: A Cross-National Analysis." *American Journal of Sociology,* 73:400-416.

373   Cyert, Richard M., and James G. March. 1963. *A Behavioral Theory of the Firm.* Englewood Cliffs, N.J.: Prentice-Hall.

374   Dahrendorf, Ralf. 1959. *Class and Class Conflict in Industrial Society.* Stanford, Calif.: Stanford.

375   Dale, Ernest, 1960. *The Great Organizers.* New York: McGraw-Hill.

376   Dalton, Gene, Louis B. Barnes, and Abraham Zaleznik. 1968. *The Distribution of Authority in Formal Organizations.* Boston: Division of Research, Graduate School of Business Administration, Harvard University.

377   Dalton, Melville. 1950. "Conflicts Between Staff and Line Managerial Officers." *American Sociological Review,* 15:342-351.

378   ———. 1955. "Industrial Controls and Personal Relations." *Social Forces,* 35:244-249.

379   ———. 1959. *Men Who Manage.* New York: Wiley.

380   Daniels, Morris J. 1962. "Levels of Organization in the Role Position of the Staff Nurse." *Social Forces,* 40:242-248.

381   Dankert, C. E. 1959. "Technological Change and Unemployment." *Labor Law Journal,* 10:393-404.

382   ———. 1962. "Shorter Hours, in Theory and Practice." *Industrial and Labor Relations Review* (April): 307-322.

383   ———, Floyd C. Mann, and Herbert R. Northrup. 1965. *Hours of Work.* New York: Harper & Row.

384   Darkenwald, Gordon G., Jr. 1971. "Organizational Conflict in Colleges and Universities." *Administrative Science Quarterly,* 16:407-412.

385 David, James W., and Kenneth M. Dolbeare. 1968. *Little Groups of Neighbors: The Selective Service System.* Chicago: Markham Publishing Company.

386 Davies, Arthur K. 1948. "Bureaucratic Patterns in the Navy Officer Corps." *Social Forces,* **27**:143-153.

387 Davies, I. 1967. "Introducing Comparative Sociology." *British Journal of Sociology,* **18**:443-450.

388 Davis, Fred. 1959. "The Cabdriver and His Fare: Facets of a Fleeting Relationship." *American Journal of Sociology,* **65**:158-165.

389 Davis, Keith. 1953. "Management Communication and the Grapevine." *Harvard Business Review* (September-October): 44-49.

390 ———. 1962. *Human Relations at Work.* New York: McGraw-Hill.

391 ——— and Robert L. Blomstrom. 1966. *Business and Its Environment.* New York: McGraw-Hill.

391a Davis, Keith, and William G. Scott. 1969. *Human Relations and Organizational Behavior: Readings and Comments,* (3d ed.). New York: McGraw-Hill.

392 Davis, Louis E. 1957. "Job Design and Productivity: A New Approach." *Personnel,* **33**:418-430.

393 ———. 1962. "The Effects of Automation on Job Design." *Industrial Relations* (October):53-71.

394 ——— and Ernst S. Valfer. 1966. "Studies in Supervisory Job Design." *Human Relations,* **19**:339-352.

395 Davis, Stanley. 1968. "Management's Effects on Worker Organizations in Developing Countries." *Human Organization,* **27**:21-29.

396 Day, Robert, and Robert L. Hamblin. 1964. "Some Effects of Close and Punitive Styles of Supervision." *American Journal of Sociology,* **69**:499-510.

397 Delaney, William. 1960. "Some Field Notes on the Problem of Access in Organizational Research." *Administrative Science Quarterly,* **5**:448-457.

398 ———. 1963. "Development and Decline of Patrimonial and Bureaucratic Administrations." *Administrative Science Quarterly,* **7**:458-501.

399 Delbecq, Andre L. 1968. "How Informal Organization Evolves: Interpersonal Choice and Subgroup Formation." *Business Perspectives* (Spring):17-21.

400 Demerath, Nicholas J., and Richard A. Peterson (eds.). 1967. *Systems, Change and Conflict.* New York: Free Press.

401 ——— and John W. Thibaut. 1956. "Small Groups and Administrative Organizations." *Administrative Science Quarterly,* **1**:139-154.

402 ——— and Victor Thiessen. 1966. "On Spitting against the Wind: Organizational Precariousness and American Irreligion." *American Journal of Sociology,* **71**:674-687.

403 Denhardt, Robert B. 1968. "Bureaucratic Socialization and Organizational Accommodation." *Administrative Science Quarterly,* **13**:441-450.

404 ———. 1970. "Leadership Style, Worker Involvement, and Deference to Authority." *Sociology and Social Research,* **54**:172-180.

405 Denise, Malcolm L. 1962a. "Automation and Unemployment: A Manage-

ment Viewpoint." *The Annals of the American Academy of Political and Social Science* (March):90-99.

406 ———. 1962b. "Unemployment and Automation." *The Personnel Administrator* (May-June):18-21.

407 Denman, Loretta. 1963. "Mental Patients as 'Line Workers,' 'Machines,' and 'Outputs.' " *Journal of Health and Human Behavior,* **4**:211-214.

408 Dent, J. K., and R. G. Griffith. 1957. "Employee Health Services: A Study of Managerial Attitudes and Evaluations." Ann Arbor, Mich.: Institute for Social Research.

409 Denton, Charles F. 1969. "Bureaucracy in an Immobilist Society: The Case of Costa Rica." *Administrative Science Quarterly,* **14**:418-425.

410 Deutsch, Morton. 1949a. "An Experimental Study of the Effects of Cooperation and Competition upon Group Process." *Human Relations,* **2**:199-232.

411 ———. 1949b. "A Theory of Cooperation and Competition." *Human Relations,* **2**:129-152.

412 Deutscher, Verda, and Irwin Deutscher. 1955. "Cohesion in a Small Group: A Case Study." *Social Forces,* **33**:336-341.

413 Dickson, Donald T. 1968. "Bureaucracy and Morality: An Organizational Perspective on a Moral Crusade." *Social Problems,* **16**:143-156.

414 Dibble, Vernon K. 1968. "Occupations and Ideologies." *American Journal of Sociology,* **68**:229-241.

415 Diebold, John. 1955. "Integrating Automation into Our Economy." *Monthly Labor Review,* **78**:526-527.

416 ———. 1958. "Automation as a Challenge to Management." *International Social Science Bulletin,* **10**:37-43.

417 ———. 1959. *Automation: Its Impact on Business and Labor.* Washington, D.C.: National Planning Association.

418 ———. 1962a. "Automation: Its Implications for Counseling." *Occupational Outlook Quarterly* (September):3-6.

419 ———. 1962b. "The Application of Information Technology." *The Annals of the American Society of Political and Social Science,* (March):38-45.

420 ———. 1964. *Beyond Automation's Managerial Problems.* New York: McGraw-Hill.

421 Dill, William R., et al. 1962. *The New Managers.* Englewood Cliffs, N.J.: Prentice-Hall.

422 Dimock, Dudley G. 1971. "Sensitivity Training as a Method of Increasing On-the-Job Effectiveness." *Sociological Inquiry,* **41**:227-236.

423 Downs, Anthony. 1967. *Inside Democracy.* Boston: Little, Brown.

424 Drabek, Thomas E., and Eugene J. Haas. 1969. "Laboratory Simulation of Organizational Stress." *American Sociological Review,* **34**:222-236.

425 Draper, Jean D., and George B. Strother. 1963. "Testing a Model for Organizational Growth." *Human Organization,* **22**:180-194.

426 Dreher, C. 1957. *Automation: What It Is, How It Works, Who Can Use It.* New York: Norton.

427   Driver, Michael J., and Siegfried Streufert. 1969. "Integrative Complexity: An Approach to Individuals and Groups as Information-Processing Systems." *Administrative Science Quarterly,* **14**:272-285.

428   Drucker, Peter. 1946. *Concept of the Corporation.* Boston: Beacon Press.

429   Dubin, Robert. 1949. "Decision Making by Management in Industrial Relations." *American Journal of Sociology,* **54**:292-297.

430   ———. 1956. "Industrial Worker's Worlds: A Study of the Central Life Interests of Industrial Workers." *Social Problems.* 3:131-142.

431   ———. 1959. "Human Relations in Formal Organizations." *Review of Educational Research,* **29**:357-366.

432   ———. 1962. "Power, Function, and Organization." *Pacific Sociological Review,* **6**:16-24.

433   ———. 1965a. "Industrial Conflict: The Power of Prediction." *Industrial and Labor Relations Review,* **18**:352-363.

434   ———. 1965b. "Supervision and Productivity," in Robert Dubin et al. (eds.). *Leadership and Productivity.* San Francisco: Chandler Publishing Company.

435   ———. 1969. *Theory Building.* New York: Free Press.

436   Duffy, N. F. 1960. "Occupational Status, Job Satisfaction, and Levels of Aspiration." *British Journal of Sociology,* **11**:348-355.

437   Dunkerley, David. 1972. *The Study of Organizations.* London: Routledge.

438   Dunlop, John. T. 1962. *Automation and Technological Change.* Englewood Cliffs, N.J.: Prentice-Hall.

439   Dunn, S. S. 1947. "A Study of Work Practices." *Bulletin of Industrial Psychological Personnel Practice* 3:21-29.

440   Dunnette, Marvin, John P. Campbell, and Milton D. Hakel. 1967. "Factors Contributing to Job Satisfaction and Job Dissatisfaction in Six Occupational Groups." *Organizational Behavior and Human Performance,* **2**:143-174.

441   ———, John Campbell, and Chris Argyris. 1968. "A Symposium: Laboratory Training." *Industrial Relations,* **8**:1-48.

442   Durkheim, Émile (translated by George Simpson). 1933. *On the Social Division of Labor in Society.* New York: Macmillan.

443   ———. 1951. *Suicide.* Glencoe, Ill.: Free Press.

444   Dutton, John M., and Richard E. Walton. 1966. "Interdepartmental Conflict and Cooperation: Two Contrasting Studies." *Human Organization,* **25**:207-220.

445   Dyer, William G. 1960. "Looking at Conflict." *Adult Leadership,* **9**:79-80.

446   Earl of Halsbury. 1957. "Integrating Social and Technical Change." *Impact of Science on Society,* **3**:3-15.

447   Eckerman, William C. 1963. "The Relation of Need Achievement to Production, Job Satisfaction, and Psychological Stress." Unpublished doctoral dissertation, University of Michigan, Ann Arbor.

448   Eckert, James B., and Robert R. Wyand. 1962. "Automating at Commercial Banks." *Federal Reserve Bulletin* (November):1408-1420.

449   Edwards, John. 1969. "Organizational and Leadership Status." *Sociological Inquiry,* **39**:49-56.

450   Edwards, M. L. 1960. "Is Automation as Big a Problem as It Appears?" *Balance Sheet,* **42**:4-5.

451   Ehrmann, Henry W. 1961. "French Bureaucracy and Organized Interests." *Administrative Science Quarterly,* **5**:534-555.

452   Einzig, P. 1957. *The Economic Consequences of Automation.* New York: Norton.

453   Eisenstadt, S. N. 1959. "Bureaucracy, Bureaucratization, and Debureaucratization." *Administrative Science Quarterly,* **4**:302-320.

454   ———. 1968. "Some Reflections on the Variability of Development and Organizational Structure." *Administrative Science Quarterly,* **13**:491-499.

455   Eitzen, D. Stanley, and Norman R. Yetman. 1972. "Managerial Change, Longevity, and Organizational Effectiveness." *Administrative Science Quarterly,* **17**:110-116.

456   Elling, Ray H. 1961. "Organizational Differentiation and Support: A Conceptual Framework." *Administrative Science Quarterly,* **6**:185-209.

457   ———. 1962. "Organizational Support and Community Power Structure." *Journal of Health and Social Behavior,* **3**:257-269.

458   Emerson, Richard M. 1962. "Power Dependence Relations." *American Sociological Review,* **27**:31-41.

459   Emery, F. E., and Julius Marek. 1962. "Some Socio-Technical Aspects of Automation." *Human Relations,* **15**:17-25.

460   ——— and E. L. Trist. 1965. "The Causal Texture of Organizational Environments." *Human Relations,* **18**:21-32.

461   Engel, Gloria V. 1969. "The Effect of Bureaucracy on the Professional Autonomy of Physicians." *Journal of Health and Social Behavior,* **10**:30-41.

462   ———. 1970. "Professional Autonomy and Bureaucratic Organization." *Administrative Science Quarterly,* **15**:12-21.

463   Enos, J. L. 1958. "A Measure of the Rate of Technological Progress in the Petroleum Refining Industry." *Journal of Industrial Economics,* **6**:180-197.

464   Entwisle, Doris R., and John Walton. 1961. "Observations on the Span of Control." *Administrative Science Quarterly,* **5**:522-533.

465   Ephron, Lawrence, R. 1961. "Group Conflict in Organizations: A Critical Appraisal of Recent Theories." *Berkeley Journal of Sociology,* **6**:53-72.

466   Etzioni, Amitai. 1958a. "Human Relations and the Foreman." *Pacific Sociological Review,* **1**:33-38.

467   ———. 1958b. "Lower Levels of Leadership in Industry." *Sociology and Social Research,* **43**:209-212.

468   ———. 1959a. "Authority Structure and Organizational Effectiveness." *Administrative Science Quarterly,* **4**:43-67.

469   ———. 1959b. "The Functional Differentiation of Elites in the Kibbutz." *American Journal of Sociology,* **64**:476-487.

470   ———. 1960. "Two Approaches to Organizational Analysis: A Critique and a Suggestion." *Administrative Science Quarterly,* **5**:257-278.

471   ———. 1961a. *A Comparative Analysis of Complex Organizations.* New York: Free Press.

472   ———. 1961b. *Complex Organizations.* New York: Holt.

473   ———. 1964. *Modern Organizations.* Englewood Cliffs, N.J.: Prentice-Hall.

474   ———. 1965a. "Dual Leadership in Complex Organizations." *American Sociological Review,* **30**:688-698.

475   ———. 1965b. "Social Analysis as a Sociological Vocation." *American Journal of Sociology,* **70**:613-625.

476   ———. 1969a. *A Sociological Reader on Complex Organizations.* New York: Holt.

477   ———. 1969b. *Readings on Modern Organizations.* Englewood Cliffs, N.J.: Prentice-Hall.

478   ———. 1969c. *The Semiprofessions and Their Organization.* New York: Free Press.

479   Evan, William M. 1962. "Role Strain and the Norm of Reciprocity in Research Organizations." *American Journal of Sociology,* **68**:346-354.

480   ———. 1965. "Superior-Subordinate Conflict in Research Organizations." *Administrative Science Quarterly,* **10**:52-64.

481   ———. 1966a. "Organizational Lag." *Human Organization,* **25**:51-53.

482   ———. 1966b. "The Organizational Set: Toward a Theory of Interorganizational Relations," in James D. Thompson (ed.), *Approaches to Organizational Design.* Pittsburgh: University of Pittsburgh Press.

483   ——— and Mildred A. Schwartz. 1964. "Law and the Emergence of Formal Organizations." *Sociology and Social Research,* **48**:270-280.

484   ——— and Roberta G. Simmons. 1969. "Organizational Effects of Inequitable Rewards: Two Experiments in Status Inconsistency." *Administrative Science Quarterly,* **14**:224-237.

485   Evans, Luther H., and George E. Arnstein (eds.). 1962. *Automation and the Challenge to Education.* Washington, D.C.: National Educational Association.

486   Ewan, Robert B., et al. 1966. "An Empirical Test of the Herzberg Two-Factor Theory." *Journal of Applied Psychology,* **50**:544-550.

487   Ewing, David W. 1964. *The Managerial Mind.* New York: Macmillan.

488   Fabricant, Solomon. 1959. *Basic Facts on Productivity Change,* Occasional Paper No. 63. New York: National Bureau of Economic Research.

489   ———. 1965. *Measurement of Technological Change.* Washington, D.C.: U.S. Department of Labor, Office of Manpower, Automation, and Training, Seminar on Manpower Policy and Program.

490   Fathi, Asghar. 1968. "Marginality, Leadership, and Directed Change." *Human Organization,* **27**:143-146.

491   Faunce, William A. 1958a. "Automation and the Automobile Worker." *Social Problems,* **6**:68-77.

492   ———. 1958b. "Automation in the Automobile Industry: Some Consequences for In-Plant Social Structure." *American Sociological Review,* **23**:401-407.

493   ———. 1959a. "Automation's Many Implications." *Industrial Union Department Digest* (AFL-CIO), (Spring):90-99.

494 ———. 1959b. "The Automobile Industry: A Case Study in Automation," in H. B. Jacobson and J. S. Roucek (eds.), *Automation and Society*. New York: Philosophical Library.

495 ———. 1960. "Social Stratification and Attitude toward Change in Job Content." *Social Forces*, **39**:140–148.

496 ———. 1962. "Size of Locals and Union Democracy." *American Journal of Sociology*, **68**:291–298.

497 ——— et al. 1962. "Automation and the Employee." *Annals of the American Academy of Political and Social Science*, **34**:60–68.

498 ——— and William H. Form. 1969. *Comparative Perspectives on Industrial Society*. Boston: Little, Brown.

499 Fayol, H. 1949. *General and Industrial Management*. London: Sir Isaac Pitman & Sons, Ltd.

500 Feld, M. D. 1959. "Information and Authority: The Structure of Military Organization." *American Sociological Review*, **24**:15–22.

501 Ferguson, M. P. 1957. "Automation: The Management Approach." *Michigan Business Review*, **9**:1–10.

502 Ferguson, William A. 1962. "Establishing Centralized Data Processing." *Automation* (May):50–56.

503 Ferman, Patricia R. 1966. "Comments on Hage's 'An Axiomatic Theory of Organizations.'" *Administrative Science Quarterly*, **11**:139–141.

504 Fesler, J. W. 1960. "Leadership and Its Context." *Public Administration Review*, **20**:122.

505 Festinger, Leon. 1950. "Informal Social Communication." *Psychology Review*, **57**:271–282.

506 Fiedler, Fred E. 1967. *A Theory of Leadership Effectiveness*. New York: McGraw-Hill.

507 Fiedler, R. E. 1965. "Engineer the Job to Fit the Manager." *Harvard Business Review*, **43**:115–122.

508 Filley, Alan C., and Robert J. House. 1969. *Managerial Processes and Organizational Behavior*. Glenview, Ill.: Scott, Foresman.

509 Findikyan, N. and S. B. Sells. 1966. "Organizational Structure and Similarity in Campus Student Organizations." *Journal of Organizational Behavior and Human Performance*, **1**:169–190.

510 Finer, Herman. 1945. "Critics of Bureaucracy." *Political Science Quarterly*, **60**:100–112.

511 Fisher, J. 1963. "Leadership, Education, and Our Racial Predicament." *South Atlantic Quarterly*, **62**:532–538.

512 Flanders, A. 1965. *Industrial Relations, What Is Wrong with the System?* London: Faber.

513 Fleishman, Edwin A. 1953. "Leadership Climate, Human Relations Training, and Supervisory Behavior." *Personnel Psychology*, **6**:205–222.

514 ——— and E. F. Harris. 1962. "Patterns of Leadership Behavior Related to Employee Grievances and Turnover." *Personnel Psychology*, **15**:43–56.

515 ———, E. F. Harris, and H. E. Burtt. 1955. *Leadership and Supervision in Industry.* Columbus: Bureau of Educational Research, Ohio State University.

516 ——— and David Peters. 1962. "Interpersonal Values, Leadership Attitudes, and Managerial Success." *Personnel Psychology,* **15**:127-143.

517 Fleming, R. W. 1962. "The Problem of the Displaced Worker." *Atlantic Economic Review* (March):7-11.

518 Fleming, William G. 1966. "Authority, Efficiency, and Role Stress: Problems in the Development of East African Bureaucracies." *Administrative Science Quarterly,* **11**:386-404.

519 Flittie, Edwin, and Jan Nelson. 1968. "The Truck Driver: A Sociological Analysis of an Occupational Role." *Sociology and Social Research,* **52**:205-210.

520 Foa, Uriel G. 1955. "The Foreman-Worker Interaction: A Research Design." *Sociometry,* **18**:226-244.

521 ———. 1956. "A Test of the Foreman-Worker Relationship." *Personnel Psychology,* **9**:469-486.

522 ———. 1960. "Some Correlates of the Empathy of the Workers with the Foreman." *Journal of Applied Psychology,* **44**:6-10.

523 Form, William H., and J. A. Geschwender. 1962. "Social Reference Basis of Job Satisfaction: The Case of Manual Workers." *American Sociological Review,* **27**:351-362.

524 ——— and Delbert C. Miller. 1949. "Occupational Career Pattern as a Sociological Instrument." *American Journal of Sociology,* **54**:317-329.

525 ——— and ———. 1960. *Industry, Labor and the Community.* New York: Harper & Row.

526 Foster, David. 1963. *Modern Automation.* London: Sir Isaac Pitman & Sons, Ltd.

527 ———. 1968. *Automation in Practice.* New York: McGraw-Hill.

528 Fouraker, Lawrence E., and J. M. Stopford. 1968. "Organizational Structure and Multinational Strategy." *Administrative Science Quarterly,* **13**:47-64.

529 Fournet, G. P., M. K. Distefano, and M. W. Pryer. 1966. "Job Satisfaction: Issues and Problems." *Personnel Psychology,* **19**:165-183.

530 Francois, William. 1964. *Automation: Industrialization Comes of Age.* New York: Collier.

531 Frandsen, Walter J. 1969. *Relationships of Attitudes, Role Perceptions, and Overt Behaviors of Scientists, Managers, and Administrators.* San Diego, Calif.: U.S. International University.

532 Frank, Gunder A. 1958. "Goal Ambiguity and Conflicting Standards: An Approach to the Study of Organizations." *Human Organization,* **17**:8-13.

533 Frank, Lawrence K. 1954. "The Interdisciplinary Frontiers in Human Relations Studies." *Journal of Human Relations* (Fall):9-23.

534 Freidson, Eliot (ed.). 1963. *The Hospital in Modern Society.* New York: Free Press.

535 French, Cecil. 1963. "Some Structural Aspects of a Retail Sales Group." *Human Organization,* **22**:146-151.

536 French, J. R. P. , Jr. 1958. "Legitimate Power, Coercive Power, and Observability in Social Influence." *Sociometry*, **21**:83-97.

537 ——— et al. 1958. "Employee Participation in a Program of Industrial Change." *Personnel*, **35**:291-301.

538 ——— et al. 1966. "Participation and the Appraisal System." *Human Relations*, **19**:3-20.

539 ———, J. Israel, and D. Aos. 1960. "An Experiment on Participation in a Norwegian Factory." *Human Relations*, **13**:3-19.

540 ——— and Robert L. Kahn. 1962. "A Programmatic Approach to Studying Industrial Environment and Mental Health." *Journal of Social Issues*, **18**:1-47.

541 ———, ———, and F. C. Mann (eds.). 1962 "The Industrial Environment and Mental Health." *Journal of Social Issues*, **18**:(entire volume).

542 ———, ———, ———, and D. M. Wolfe. 1959. "The Effects of the Industrial Environment on Mental Health," Working Paper No. 1, Ann Arbor, Mich.: Institute for Social Research.

543 ———, H. W. Morrison, and G. Levinger. 1960. "Coercive Power and Forces Affecting Conformity." *Journal of Abnormal and Social Psychology*, **61**:93-101.

544 ——— and B. Raven. 1959. "The Bases of Social Power." Ann Arbor, Mich.: Institute for Social Research.

545 ——— and I. C. Ross. 1958. "Employee Participation in a Program of Industrial Change." *Personnel Magazine*, **35**:16-29.

546 Friedlander, Frank. 1964. "Job Characteristics as Satisfiers and Dissatisfiers." *Journal of Applied Psychology*, **48**:388-392.

547 ———. 1965. "Comparative Work Value Systems." *Personnel Psychology*, **18**:1-20.

548 ——— and H. Pickle. 1968. "Components of Effectiveness in Small Organizations." *Administrative Science Quarterly*, **13**:289-304.

549 ——— and E. Walton. 1964. "Positive and Negative Motivations toward Work." *Administrative Science Quarterly*, **9**:194-207.

550 Friedman, Jack J. 1962. "The Other Side of Automation." *Dun's Review and Modern Industry* (May):42-44.

551 Friedmann, Georges. 1952. "Technological Change and Human Relations." *British Journal of Sociology*, **3**:95-116.

552 ———. 1955. *Industrial Society: The Emergence of the Human Problems of Automation*. New York: Free Press.

553 ———. 1961. *The Anatomy of Work*. New York: Free Press.

554 Froomkin, Joseph, and A. J. Jaffe. 1953. "Occupational Skill and Socioeconomic Structure." *American Journal of Sociology*, **59**:42-48.

555 Fulton, R. L. 1961. "The Clergyman and the Funeral Director: A Study of Role Conflict." *Social Forces*, **39**:317-323.

556 Gabor, Dennis. 1962. "Inventing the Future," in Morris Philipson (ed.), *Automation: Implications for the Future*. New York: Vintage Books.

557 Gaiennie, L. R. 1954. "Organization Control in Business." *Journal of Applied Psychology*, **38**:289-292.

558 Galbraith, Kenneth. 1967. *The New Industrial State.* Boston: Houghton Mifflin.

559 Gamson, Zelda F. 1958. "Organizational Responses to Members." *Sociological Inquiry,* **9**:139-149.

560 Gardner, Burleigh B. 1945. *Human Relations in Industry.* Chicago: Irwin.

561 —— and William F. Whyte. 1945. "The Man in the Middle: Position and Problems of the Foreman." *Journal of Applied Anthropology,* **4**:1-28.

562 Gass, J. R. 1958. "Research into the Social Effects of Automation." *International Social Science Bulletin,* **10**:70-82.

563 Gawthrop, Louis C. 1969. *Bureaucratic Behavior in the Executive Branch: An Analysis of Organizational Change.* New York: Free Press.

564 Gellerman, Saul W. 1963. *Motivation and Productivity.* New York: American Management Association.

565 ——. 1968. *Management by Motivation.* New York: American Management Association.

566 George, Claude S., Jr. 1968. *The History of Management Thought.* Englewood Cliffs, N.J.: Prentice-Hall.

567 George, Julius R., and Lloyd K. Bishop. 1971. "Relationship of Organizational Structure and Teacher Personality Characteristics to Organizational Climate." *Administrative Science Quarterly,* **16**:467-475.

568 Georgopoulos, Basil S. 1964. "Hospital Organization and Administration: Prospects and Perspectives." *Hospital Administration Quarterly,* **9**:23-35.

569 ——. 1969. "Normative Structure Variables and Organizational Behavior: A Comparative Study." *Human Relations,* **18**:155-169.

570 ——. 1972. *Organization Research on Health Institutions.* Ann Arbor, Mich.: Institute for Social Research.

571 ——, B. P. Indik, and Stanley E. Seashore. 1960. "Some Models of Organizational Effectiveness." Ann Arbor, Mich.: Survey Research Center.

572 —— and Floyd C. Mann, 1962. "The Hospital as an Organization." *Hospital Administration Quarterly,* **7**:50-64.

573 —— and A. S. Tannenbaum. 1957. "Study of Organizational Effectiveness." *American Sociological Review,* **22**:534-540.

574 Gerth, H. H., and C. Wright Mills. 1946. *From Max Weber: Essays in Sociology.* New York: Oxford University Press.

575 Getzels, J. W., and E. G. Guba. 1954. "Role, Role Conflict, and Effectiveness: An Empirical Study." *American Sociological Review,* **19**:164-175.

576 Ghiselli, Edwin E. 1966. *Validity of Occupational Aptitude Tests.* New York: Wiley.

577 Ghorpade, Jasingh. 1970. "Study of Organizational Effectiveness: Two Prevailing Viewpoints." *Pacific Sociological Review,* **13**:21-40.

578 Gibb, Cecil A. 1947. "The Principles and Traits of Leadership." *Journal of Abnormal and Social Psychology,* **42**:267-284.

579 ——. 1969. "Leadership," in Gardner Lindzey and E. Aronson (eds.), *The Handbook of Social Psychology,* Vol. IV (2d ed.). Reading, Mass.: Addison-Wesley.

580   Gibbs, Jack P., and Harley L. Browning. 1966. "The Division of Labor, Tech-
       nology, and the Organization of Production in Twelve Countries." *American
       Sociological Review,* **31**:81-92.
581   Gibson, R. Oliver. 1966. "Toward a Conceptualization of Absence Behavior
       of Personnel in Organizations." *Administrative Science Quarterly,* **11**:107-133.
582   Giese, W. J., and H. W. Ruter. 1949. "An Objective Analysis of Morale."
       Journal of Applied Psychology, **33**:421-427.
583   Gilbreth, F. B., and L. M. Gilbreth. 1917. *Applied Motion Study.* New York:
       Sturgis and Walton.
584   Ginzberg, E., and W. Reilley. 1957. *Effecting Change in Large Organizations.*
       New York: Columbia.
585   Glaser, Barney G. 1963a. "Attraction, Autonomy and Reciprocity in the Sci-
       entist-Supervisory Relationship." *Administrative Science Quarterly,* **8**:379-398.
586   ———. 1963b. "The Local-Cosmopolitan Scientist." *American Journal of So-
       ciology,* **69**:249-256.
587   ———. 1964. *Organizational Scientists: Their Professional Careers.* Indianapo-
       lis: Bobbs-Merrill.
588   ——— (ed.). 1968. *Organizational Careers: A Sourcebook for Theory.* Chicago:
       Aldine.
589   Glaser, William A. 1970. *Social Settings and Medical Organization.* New
       York: Atherton.
590   Glazier, William. 1962. "Automation and Joblessness." *Atlantic Monthly* (Au-
       gust):43-47.
591   Gold, David. 1964. "Criticism of an Empirical Assessment of the Concept
       Bureaucracy on Conceptual Independence and Empirical Independence."
       American Journal of Sociology, **70**:223-226.
592   Goldman, Daniel R. 1973. "Managerial Mobility Motivations and Central
       Life Interests." *American Sociological Review,* **38**:119-126.
593   Goldthorpe, J. H. 1959. "Technical Organization as a Factor in Supervisor-
       Worker Conflict: Some Observations on a Study Made in the Mining Indus-
       try." *British Journal of Sociology,* **10**:213-230.
594   ———. 1966. "Attitudes and Behavior of Car Assembly Workers: A Deviant
       Case and a Theoretical Critique." *British Journal of Sociology,* **17**:227-244.
595   ——— et al. 1968. *The Affluent Worker: Industrial Attitudes and Behavior.*
       London: Cambridge.
596   Golembiewski, Robert T. 1962. *Behavior and Organization.* Chicago: Rand
       McNally.
597   ———. 1967. *Organizing Men and Power: Patterns of Behavior and Line-Staff
       Models.* Chicago: Rand McNally.
598   ———. 1970. "The Persistence of Laboratory Induced Changes in Organiza-
       tional Styles." *Administrative Science Quarterly,* **15**:330-340.
599   ——— and Stokes B. Carrigan. 1970. "Planned Change in Organizational
       Style Based on the Laboratory Approach." *Administrative Science Quarterly,*
       15:79-93.
600   Goodacre, D. M. 1960. "Changing On-the-Job Behavior: How and Where to
       Start." *Personnel,* **37**:58-62.

601 Goode, William J. 1960. "A Theory of Role Strain." *American Sociological Review,* **25**:483-496.

602 ———. 1967. "The Protection of the Inept." *American Sociological Review,* **32**:5-18.

603 ——— and Irving Fowler. 1949. "Incentive Factors in a Low-Morale Plant." *American Sociological Review,* **14**:618-624.

604 ——— and Paul K. Hatt. 1952. *Methods in Social Research.* New York: McGraw-Hill.

605 Goodman, Edith H. 1963. "The Effects of Computers on Corporate Management." *Data Processing* (January):11-29.

606 Goodman, L. L. 1957. *Man and Automation.* Harmondsworth, England: Penguin.

607 Goodman, Paul S. 1970. "The Natural Controlled Experiment in Organizational Research." *Human Organization,* **29**:197-203.

608 Goodwin, H. F. 1958. "Work Simplification." *Factory Management and Maintenance* (July):72-106.

609 Gordon, C. Wayne, and N. Babchuck. 1959. "A Typology of Voluntary Organizations." *American Sociological Review,* **24**:22-29.

610 Gordon, G. G. 1966. "The Relationships of Satisfiers and Dissatisfiers to Productivity, Turnover, and Morale." Paper presented at the American Psychological Association Meetings, Chicago, Ill.

611 Gordon, Gerald, and Selwyn Becker. 1964. "Organizational Size and Managerial Succession: A Reexamination." *American Journal of Sociology,* **70**:215-222.

612 Gore, William J. 1964. *Administrative Decision Making.* New York: Wiley.

613 ——— and Fred S. Silander. 1959. "Bibliographical Essay on Decision Making." *Administrative Science Quarterly,* **4**:97-121.

614 Goss, M. 1961. "Influence and Authority among Physicians in an Outpatient Clinic." *American Sociological Review,* **26**:39-50.

615 ———. 1963. "Patterns of Bureaucracy among Hospital Staff and Physicians," in Eliot Freidson (ed.), *The Hospital in Modern Society.* New York: Free Press.

616 Gould, Nathan, and Murray Melbin. 1964. "Formal Structure and Rational Organization Theory." *Human Organization,* **23**:305-311.

617 Gouldner, Alvin W. 1954a. *Patterns of Industrial Bureaucracy.* New York: Free Press.

618 ———. 1954b. *Wildcat Strike.* Yellow Springs, Ohio: Antioch Press.

619 ———. 1957. "Cosmopolitans and Locals: Toward an Analysis of Latent Social Roles." *Administrative Science Quarterly,* **2**:281-306.

620 ———. 1958. "Cosmopolitans and Locals: Toward an Analysis of Latent Social Roles." *Administrative Science Quarterly,* **2**:444-480.

621 ———. 1959. "Organizational Analysis," in Robert K. Merton et al. (eds.), *Sociology Today.* New York: Basic Books.

622 ———. 1960a. "The Norm of Reciprocity." *American Sociological Review,* **25**:161-178.

623   ——. 1960b. "Dimensions of Organizational Commitment." *Administrative Science Quarterly,* **4**:468–490.
624   Grabbe, Eugene. 1957. *Automation in Business and Industry.* New York: Wiley.
625   Graham, W. K. 1968. "Description of Leader Behavior and Evaluation of Leaders as a Function of LPC." *Personnel Psychology,* **21**:457–464.
626   Granick, David. 1960. *The Red Executive: A Study of the Organization Man in Russian Industry.* New York: Columbia.
627   Graves, Bennie. 1970. "Particularism, Exchange and Organizational Efficiency: A Case Study of a Construction Industry." *Social Forces,* **49**:72–81.
628   Greenberg, Martin H. 1970. *Bureaucracy and Development: A Mexican Case Study.* Lexington, Mass.: Heath Lexington Books.
629   Greene, Charles N., and Dennis W. Organ. 1973. "An Evaluation of Causal Models Linking the Received Role with Job Satisfaction." *Administrative Science Quarterly,* **18**:95–103.
630   Greiner, Larry E. 1967. "Patterns of Organizational Change." *Harvard Business Review,* **45**:119–130.
631   Gross, B. M. 1964. *The Managing of Organizations: The Administrative Struggle.* New York: Free Press.
632   ——. 1965. "What are Your Organization's Objectives? A General Systems Approach to Planning." *Human Relations,* **18**:195–216.
633   ——. 1968. *Organizations and Their Managing.* New York: Free Press.
634   Gross, Edward. 1953. "Some Functional Consequences of Primary Controls in Formal Work Organizations." *American Sociological Review,* **28**:368–373.
635   ——. 1955. "Some Suggestions for the Legitimation of Industrial Studies in Sociology." *Social Forces,* **33**:233–239.
636   ——. 1968. "Universities as Organizations: A Research Approach." *American Sociological Review,* **33**:518–544.
637   ——. 1969. "The Definition of Organizational Goals." *British Journal of Sociology,* **20**:277–294.
638   —— and Paul V. Grambsch. 1968. *University Goals and Academic Power.* Washington, D.C.: American Council on Education.
639   Gross, George R. 1970. "The Organizational Set: A Study of Sociology Departments." *The American Sociologist,* **5**:25–29.
640   Gross, M. L. 1962. *The Brainwatchers.* New York: Random House.
641   Gross, Neal, and William E. Martin. 1952. "On Group Cohesiveness." *American Journal of Sociology,* **57**:546–564.
642   —— et al. 1958. *Explorations in Role Analysis.* New York: Wiley.
643   Grusky, Oscar. 1959a. "Organizational Goals and the Behavior of Informal Leaders." *American Journal of Sociology,* **65**:59–67.
644   ——. 1959b. "Role Conflict in Organization: A Study of Prison Camp Officials." *Administrative Science Quarterly,* **3**:452–472.
645   ——. 1960. "Administrative Succession in Formal Organizations." *Social Forces,* **39**:105–115.
646   ——. 1961. "Corporate Size, Bureaucratization, and Managerial Succession." *American Journal of Sociology,* **67**:261–269.

647　———. 1963. "Managerial Succession and Organizational Effectiveness." *American Journal of Sociology,* **69**:21-31.

648　———. 1966. "Career Mobility and Organizational Commitment." *Administrative Science Quarterly,* **10**:488-503.

649　——— and George A. Miller. 1970. *The Sociology of Organizations: Basic Studies.* New York: Free Press.

650　Guba, Egon G. 1958. "Morale and Satisfaction: A Study in Past-Future Time Perspective." *Administrative Science Quarterly,* **3**:195-209.

651　Guest, Robert H. 1954. "Work Careers and Aspirations of Automobile Workers." *American Sociological Review,* **19**:155-163.

652　———. 1955. "Men and Machines: An Assembly-Line Worker Looks at His Job." *Personnel,* **31**:496-503.

653　———. 1957. "Job Enlargement—A Revolution in Job Design." *Personnel Administration,* **20**:9-16.

654　———. 1962a. "Managerial Succession in Complex Organizations." *American Journal of Sociology,* **68**:47-56.

655　———. 1962b. *Organizational Change: The Effect of Successful Leadership.* Homewood, Ill.: Dorsey.

656　Guetzkow, Harold. 1965. "The Creative Person in Organizations," in Gary A. Steiner (ed.), *The Creative Organization.* Chicago: The University of Chicago Press.

657　———. 1966. "Relations among Organizations," in Raymond V. Bowers (ed.), *Studies on Behavior in Organizations.* Athens: University of Georgia Press.

658　Gulick, L., and L. Urwick (eds.). 1937. *Papers on the Science of Administration.* New York: Institute of Public Administration, Columbia University.

659　Gullahorn, John T. 1956. "Measuring Role Conflict." *American Journal of Sociology,* **61**:299-303.

660　Gusfield, Joseph R. 1955. "Social Structure and Moral Reform: A Study of the Woman's Christian Temperance Union." *American Journal of Sociology,* **61**:221-232.

661　———. 1957. "The Problem of Generations in an Organizational Structure." *Social Forces,* **35**:323-330.

662　———. 1958. "Equalitarianism and Bureaucratic Recruitment." *Administrative Science Quarterly,* **2**:521-541.

663　———. 1961. "Occupational Roles and Forms of Enterprise." *American Journal of Sociology,* **66**:571-580.

664　Haas, J. Eugene, and Thomas E. Drabek. 1973. *Complex Organizations: A Sociological Perspective.* New York: Macmillan.

665　———, Richard Hall, and Norman Johnson. 1963. "Size of Supportive Component in Organizations: A Multi-Organizational Analysis." *Social Forces,* **42**:9-17.

666　———, ———, and ———. 1966. "Toward an Empirically Derived Taxonomy of Organizations," in Raymond V. Bowers (ed.), *Studies on Behavior in Organizations.* Athens: University of Georgia Press.

667   ——, ——, and ——. 1967. "Organizational Size, Complexity, and Formalization." *American Sociological Review,* **32**:903-912.

668   Habens, A. Eugene, and Harry Potter. 1967. "Organizational and Societal Variables in Conflict Resolution: An International Comparison." *Human Organization,* **26**:126-131.

669   Habenstein, Robert. 1963. "Conflicting Organizational Patterns in Funeral Directing." *Human Organization,* **22**:126-132.

670   Haddy, Pamela. 1958. "Some Thoughts on Automation in a British Office." *Journal of Industrial Economics,* **6**:161-170.

671   Hagburg, Eugene C. 1966. "Correlates of Organizational Participation: An Examination of Factors Affecting Union Membership Activity." *Pacific Sociological Review,* **9**:15-21.

672   Hage, Jerald. 1965. "An Axiomatic Theory of Organizations." *Administrative Science Quarterly,* **10**:289-320.

673   ——. 1966. "Rejoinder." *Administrative Science Quarterly,* **11**:141-146.

674   —— and Michael Aiken. 1967a. "Program Change and Organizational Properties: A Comparative Analysis." *American Journal of Sociology,* **72**:503-519.

675   —— and ——. 1967b. "Relationship of Centralization to Other Structural Properties." *Administrative Science Quarterly,* **12**:72-92.

676   —— and ——. 1969. "Routine, Technology, Social Structure, and Organizational Goals." *Administrative Science Quarterly,* **14**:366-377.

677   —— and ——. 1970. *Social Change in Complex Organizations.* New York: Random House.

678   Hagstrom, Warren, and Hanan Selvin. 1963. "The Empirical Classification of Formal Groups." *American Sociological Review,* **28**:399-411.

679   Haimann, Theo, and William G. Scott. 1970. *Management in the Modern Organization.* Boston: Houghton Mifflin.

680   Haire, Mason. 1955. "Size, Shape, and Function in Industrial Organizations." *Human Organization,* **14**:17-22.

681   ——. 1959. *Modern Organization Theory.* New York: Wiley.

682   ——. 1963. "Philosophy of Organizations," in D. M. Bowerman and F. M. Fillerup (eds.), *Management: Organization and Planning.* New York: McGraw-Hill.

683   Hall, Douglas T., and Edward E. Lawler. 1970. "Job Characteristics and Pressures and the Organizational Integration of Professionals." *Administrative Science Quarterly,* **15**:271-281.

684   —— and Roger Mansfield. 1971. "Organizational and Individual Response to External Stress." *Administrative Science Quarterly,* **16**:533-547.

685   —— and Benjamin Schneider. 1972. "Correlates of Organizational Identification as a Function of Career Pattern and Organizational Type." *Administrative Science Quarterly,* **17**:340-350.

686   ——, ——, and Harold T. Nygren. 1970. "Personal Factors in Organizational Identification." *Administrative Science Quarterly,* **15**:176-190.

687 Hall, John W. 1972. "A Comparison of Halpin and Croft's Organizational Climates with Likert's Organizational Systems." *Administrative Science Quarterly,* **17**:586-590.

688 Hall, Oswald. 1946. "The Informal Organization of the Medical Profession." *Canadian Journal of Economics and Political Science,* **12**:30-44.

689 Hall, Richard H. 1962. "Intraorganizational Structural Variation: Application of the Bureaucratic Model." *Administrative Science Quarterly,* **7**:295-308.

690 ———. 1963a. "Bureaucracy in Small Organizations." *Sociology and Social Research,* **48**:38-46.

691 ———. 1963b. "The Concept of Bureaucracy: An Empirical Assessment." *American Journal of Sociology,* **69**:32-40.

692 ———. 1967. "Some Organizational Considerations in the Professional-Organizational Relationship." *Administrative Science Quarterly,* **12**:461-478.

693 ———. 1968. "Professionalization and Bureaucratization." *American Sociological Review,* **33**:92-104.

694 ———. 1972a. *Organizations: Structure and Process.* Englewood Cliffs, N.J.: Prentice-Hall.

695 ———. 1972b. *The Formal Organization.* New York: Basic Books.

696 ——— et al. 1967. "Organizational Size, Complexity, and Formalization." *American Sociological Review,* **32**:903-912.

697 ———, J. Eugene Haas, and Norman J. Johnson. 1967. "Examination of the Blau-Scott and Etzioni Typologies." *Administrative Science Quarterly,* **12**:118-139.

698 ——— and Charles Tittle. 1966. "A Note on Bureaucracy and Its Correlates." *American Journal of Sociology,* **72**:267-272.

699 Haller, Archibald O., and David M. Lewis. 1967. "The Hypothesis of Intersocietal Similarity in Occupational Prestige Hierarchies." *American Journal of Sociology,* **72**:210-216.

700 Halpern, Richard S. 1961. "Employee Unionization and Foreman's Attitudes." *Administrative Science Quarterly,* **6**:73-88.

701 Halpin, A. W. 1956. *The Leadership Behavior of School Superintendents.* Columbus: Ohio State University Press.

702 ——— et al. 1963. *The Organizational Climate of Schools.* Danville, Ill.: Interstate.

703 Hamilton, Richard F. 1963. "Income Differences Between Skilled and White Collar Workers." *British Journal of Sociology,* **14**:363-373.

704 ———. 1965. "Affluence and the Worker: The West German Case." *American Journal of Sociology,* **71**:144-152.

705 Hammond, Phillip E. 1966. "Secularization: Incorporation, and Social Relations." *American Journal of Sociology,* **72**:188-194.

706 Hampton, David R., Charles E. Summer, and Ross A. Webber. 1968. *Organizational Behavior and the Practice of Management.* Glenview Ill.: Scott, Foresman.

707   Hardin, E. 1960a. "Computer Automation, Work Environment, and Employee Satisfaction." *Industrial and Labor Relations Review,* **13**:559-567.

708   ———. 1960b. "The Reactions of Employees to Office Automation." *Monthly Labor Review,* **83**:925-932.

709   ——— et al. 1961. *Economic and Social Implications of Automation: An Annotated Bibliography.* East Lansing: Labor and Industrial Relations Center, Michigan State University.

710   ——— and G. L. Hershey. 1960. "Accuracy of Employee Reports on Changes in Pay." *Journal of Applied Psychology,* **44**:269-275.

711   Harper, Dean. 1965. "The Growth of Bureaucracy in School Systems." *American Journal of Economics and Sociology,* **24**:261-272.

712   ——— and F. Emmert. 1963. "Work Behavior in a Service Industry." *Social Forces,* **42**:216-225.

713   Hart, D. J., and W. M. Lifton. 1958. "Of Things to Come: Automation and Counseling." *Personnel and Guidance Journal,* **37**:282-287.

714   Hartmann, Heinz. 1959. *Authority and Organization in German Management.* Princeton, N.J.: Princeton University Press.

715   Harvey, E. 1968. "Technology and the Structure of Organizations." *American Sociological Review,* **33**:247-259.

716   Harvey, O. J. 1953. "Status Relations in Informal Groups." *American Sociological Review,* **18**:357-367.

717   Hasenfeld, Yeheskel. 1972. "People-Processing Organizations: An Exchange Approach." *American Sociological Review,* **37**:256-263.

718   Hauser, Philip M. 1954. "Changes in the Labor Force Participation of the Older Worker." *American Journal of Sociology,* **59**:312-323.

719   Havelock, Ronald G., and Mary C. Havelock. 1972. *Training for Change Agents: A Guide to the Design of Training Programs in Education and Other Fields.* Ann Arbor, Mich.: Institute for Social Research.

720   Hawley, Amos, Walter Boland, and Margaret Boland. 1965. "Population Size and Administration in Institutions of Higher Education." *American Sociological Review,* **30**:252-255.

721   Hawley, George. 1959. *Automation and Manufacturing Process.* New York: Reinhold.

722   Heady, Ferrel. 1959. "Bureaucratic Theory and Comparative Administration." *Administrative Science Quarterly,* **3**:509-525.

723   Hearle, Edward, and Raymond J. Mason. 1961. "Data Processing: Its Future in State Government." *State Government* (Winter):47-51.

724   Hegland, Tore, and Borre Nylehn. 1968. "Adjustment of Work Organizations to Critical Environmental Factors." *Acta Sociologica,* **11**:31-54.

725   Hemphill, J. K. 1956. *Group Dimensions: A Manual for Their Measurement.* Columbus: Bureau of Business Research, Ohio State University.

726   Hendershot, Gerry E., and Thomas F. James. 1972. "Size and Growth as Determinants of Administrative-Production Ratios in Organizations." *American Sociological Review,* **37**:149-153.

727 Henry, Jules. 1954. "The Formal Structure of a Psychiatric Hospital." *Psychiatry,* **17**:139–151.

728 Herb, Terry. 1972. "Organizational Effectiveness: The Case of the Southern Baptist Convention." *L.S.U. Journal of Sociology,* **2**:48–59.

729 Hermann, Charles F. 1963. "Some Consequences of Crisis Which Limit the Viability of Organizations." *Administrative Science Quarterly,* **8**:61–82.

730 Hershey, Paul, et al. 1969. *Management of Organizational Behavior.* Englewood Cliffs, N.J.: Prentice-Hall.

731 Herzberg, Frederick. 1965a. "Motivation to Work among Finnish Supervisors." *Personnel Psychology,* **18**:393–402.

732 ———. 1965b. "The New Industrial Psychology." *Industrial and Labor Relations Review,* **18**:364–376.

733 ———. 1966. *Work and the Nature of Man.* New York: World Publishing.

734 ———. 1968. "One More Time: How Do You Motivate Employees?" *Harvard Business Review,* **46**:53–62.

735 ——— et al. 1957. *Job Attitudes: Review of Research and Opinion.* Pittsburgh: Psychological Service of Pittsburgh.

736 ——— et al. 1959. *Motivation to Work.* New York: Wiley.

737 Hetzler, Stanley A. 1955. "Variations in Role-Playing Patterns among Different Echelons of Bureaucratic Leaders." *American Sociological Review,* **20**:700–706.

738 Hicks, Herbert G. 1972. *The Management of Organizations: A Systems and Human Resources Approach.* New York: McGraw-Hill.

739 Hickson, D. J. 1966. "Convergence in Organizational Theory." *Administrative Science Quarterly,* **11**:224–237.

740 ——— et al. 1971. "A Strategic Contingencies Theory of Intraorganizational Power." *Administrative Science Quarterly,* **16**:216–229.

741 ———, D. S. Pugh, and D. C. Pheysey. 1969. "Operations Technology and Organization Structure: An Empirical Reappraisal." *Administrative Science Quarterly,* **14**:378–397.

742 Hilgendorf, E. L., and B. L. Irving. 1969. "Job Attitude Research: A New Conceptual and Analytical Model." *Human Relations,* **22**:415–426.

743 Hill, Walter A., and Douglas M. Egan (eds.). 1967. *Readings in Organizational Theory: A Behavioral Approach.* Boston: Allyn and Bacon.

744 Hills, R. J. 1969. *Toward a Science of Organization.* Eugene: University of Oregon Center for the Advanced Study of Educational Administration.

745 Hinings, C. R., and Gloria Lee. 1971. "Dimensions of Organizational Structure and Their Context: A Replication." *Sociology,* **5**:83–112.

746 ———, D. S. Pugh, D. J. Hickson, and C. Turner. 1967. "An Approach to the Study of Bureaucracy." *Sociology,* **1**:61–72.

747 Hirsch, Paul. 1970 *The Structure of the Popular Music Industry: The Filtering Process by Which Records are Preselected for Public Consumption.* Ann Arbor, Mich.: Institute for Social Research.

748 Hirsch, Phil. 1962. "Automation, Clerks, and Bookkeepers." *The New Republic* (May):13-14.

749 Hocking, William E. 1941. "The Nature of Morale." *American Journal of Sociology.* **47**:302-320.

750 Hodge, Robert W., and P. Hodge. 1965. "Occupational Assimilation as a Competitive Process." *American Journal of Sociology,* **71**:249-264.

751 ———, Paul M. Siegel, and Peter H. Rossi. 1964. "Occupational Prestige in the United States—1925-63." *American Journal of Sociology,* **70**:286-302.

752 Hoffman, Stanley. 1970. "International Organization and the International System." *International Organization,* **24**:389-413.

753 Holdaway, Edward A., and Thomas A. Blowers. 1971. "Administrative Ratios and Organizational Size: A Longitudinal Examination." *American Sociological Review,* **36**:278-286.

754 Hollander, E. P. 1964. *Leaders, Groups, and Influence.* New York: Oxford University Press.

755 ———. 1971. "Style, Structure, and Setting in Organizational Leadership." *Administrative Science Quarterly,* **16**:1-9.

756 ——— and James W. Julian. 1969. "Contemporary Trends in the Analysis of Leadership Processes." *Psychological Bulletin,* **71**:387-397.

757 Holter, Harriet. 1965. "Attitudes Towards Employee Participation in Company Decision-Making Processes: A Study of Nonsupervisory Employees in Some Norwegian Firms." *Human Relations,* **18**:297-321.

758 Homans, George. 1950. *The Human Group.* New York: Harcourt, Brace & World.

759 ———. 1954. "The Cash Posters: A Study of Working Girls." *American Sociological Review,* **19**:724-733.

760 ———. 1961. *Social Behavior: Its Elementary Forms.* New York: Harcourt, Brace & World.

761 Hoos, Ida. 1960a. "Impact of Automation on Office Workers." *International Labor Review,* **82**:363-388.

762 ———. 1960b. "When the Computer Takes Over the Office." *Harvard Business Review,* **38**:102-112.

763 ———. 1961. *Automation in the Office.* Washington, D.C.: Public Affairs Press.

764 ——— and B. L. Jones. 1963. "Office Automation in Japan." *International Labour Review,* **87**:551-572.

765 Hopkins, Terrence K. 1962. "Bureaucratic Authority: The Convergence of Weber and Barnard," in Amitai Etzioni (ed.), *Complex Organizations.* New York: Holt.

766 Hopper, E. 1965. "Some Effects of Supervisory Style: A Sociological Analysis." *British Journal of Sociology.* **16**:189-205.

767 Hoppock, R. 1935. *Job Satisfaction.* New York: Harper.

768 House, Robert J. 1968. "Leadership Training: Some Dysfunctional Consequences." *Administrative Science Quarterly,* **12**:556-571.

769 ——— and John B. Miner. 1969. "Merging Management and Behavioral Theory: The Interaction between Span of Control and Group Size." *Administrative Science Quarterly,* **14**:451–465.

770 ——— and Lawrence A. Wigdor. 1967. "Herzberg's Dual Factor Theory of Job Satisfaction and Motivation: A Review of the Evidence and a Criticism." *Personnel Psychology,* **20**:369–389.

771 Hovland, C. I., et al. 1960. "*Attitude, Organization and Change.* New Haven, Conn.: Yale University Press.

772 Howton, William F. 1963. "Work Assignment and Interpersonal Relations in a Research Organization: Some Participant Observations." *Administrative Science Quarterly,* **7**:502–520.

773 ———. 1971. *Functionaries.* Chicago: Quadrangle.

774 Hrebiniak, Lawrence G., and Joseph A. Alutto. 1972. "Personal and Role-Related Factors in the Development of Organizational Commitment." *Administrative Science Quarterly,* **17**:555–573.

775 Hughes, E. C. 1952. "The Sociological Study of Work." *American Journal of Sociology,* **57**:423–426.

776 ———. 1958. *Men and Their Work.* Glencoe, Ill.: Free Press.

777 ———. 1962. "Disorganization and Reorganization." *Human Organization,* **21**:154–161.

778 Hulin, Charles L., and Milton R. Blood. 1968. "Job Enlargement, Individual Differences, and Worker Responses." *Psychological Bulletin,* **69**:41–55.

779 Humble, J. W. 1965. *Improving Management Performance.* London: B.I.M.

780 ———. 1970. *Management by Objectives in Action.* New York: McGraw-Hill.

781 Hummon, Norman P. 1970. "Criticism of 'Effects of Flat and Tall Organizational Structure.'" *Administrative Science Quarterly,* **15**:230–234.

782 ———. 1971. "A Mathematical Theory of Differentiation in Organizations." *American Sociological Review,* **36**:297–303.

783 Hunt, J. G. 1971. "Leadership Style Effects at Two Managerial Levels in a Simulated Organization." *Administrative Science Quarterly,* **16**:476–485.

784 ——— and J. W. Hill. 1969. "The New Look in Motivation Theory for Organizational Research." *Human Organization,* **28**:100–109.

785 Hunt, R. G. 1970. "Technology and Organization." *Academy of Management Journal,* **13**:235–253.

786 Huse, Edgar F., and James L. Bowditch. 1973. *Behavior in Organizations: A Systems Approach to Managing.* Reading, Mass.: Addison-Wesley.

787 Indik, B. P. 1963a. "Some Effects of Organization Size on Member Attitude and Behavior." *Human Relations,* **16**:369–384.

788 ———. 1963b. "There is No 'Pat' Answer to the Supervision Question." *Personnel Administration,* **26**:15–19.

789 ———. 1964a. "Relationship between Job-Related Stress and Strain in Industrial Workers." *Journal of Industrial Psychology,* **2**:22–27.

790 ———. 1964b. "Relationship between Organization Size and the Supervision Ratio." *Administrative Science Quarterly,* **9**:301–312.

791   ———. 1965. "Organization Size and Member Participation—Some Empirical Tests of Alternative Explanations." *Human Relations,* **18**:339-350.

792   ———, B. S. Georgopoulos, and Stanley Seashore. 1961. "Superior-Subordinate and Performance." *Journal of Personnel Psychology,* **14**:367-374.

793   Ingham, Geoffrey K. 1970. *Size of Industrial Organization and Worker Behavior.* Cambridge, England: Cambridge University Press.

794   Inkeles, Alex and Peter H. Rossi. 1956. "National Comparisons of Occupational Prestige." *American Journal of Sociology,* **61**:329-339.

795   Inkson, J. H., D. S. Pugh, and D. J. Hickson. 1970. "Organizational Context and Structure: An Abbreviated Replication." *Administrative Science Quarterly,* **15**:318-329.

796   Jackson, Jay M. 1959. "Reference Group Processes in a Formal Organization." *Sociometry,* **22**:307-327.

797   Jackson, John A. (ed.). 1970. *Professions and Professionalization.* London: Cambridge University Press.

798   Jacobs, Jerry. 1969. "Symbolic Bureaucracy: A Case Study of a Social Welfare Agency." *Social Forces,* **47**:413-422.

799   Jacobson, E. 1951a. "Communication Practices in Complex Organizations." *Journal of Social Issues,* **7**:28-40.

800   ———. 1951b. "Communication Structure and Attitudes in Large Organizations." Ann Arbor, Mich.: Institute for Social Research.

801   ———. 1952. "A Method for Studying the Relationship between Communication Structure and Attitudes in Complex Organizations." Ann Arbor, Mich.: Institute for Social Research.

802   ——— et al. 1951. "Human Relations in Large Organizations." *Journal of Social Issues,* **7**:1-14.

803   ——— et al. 1959. "Employee Attitudes toward Technological Change in a Medium Sized Insurance Company." *Journal of Applied Psychology,* **42**:349-354.

804   ———, W. Charters, and S. Lieberman. 1951. "The Use of the Role Concept in the Study of Complex Organizations." *Journal of Social Issues,* **7**:18-27.

805   ——— and Stanley Seashore. 1951. "Communication Practices in Complex Organizations." *Journal of Social Issues,* **7**:28-40.

806   Jacobson, Howard B., and Joseph S. Roucek (eds.). 1959. *Automation and Society.* New York: Philosophical Library.

807   Jacoby, Arthur, and N. Babchuck. 1963. "Instrumental and Expressive Voluntary Associations." *Sociology and Social Research,* **47**:461-471.

808   Jakubauskas, E. B. 1958. "Adjustment to an Automatic Air Line Reservation System." *Monthly Labor Review,* **81**:1014-1016.

809   James, T. F. 1972. "The Administrative Component in Organizations. *Sociological Quarterly,* **13**:533-539.

810   Janowitz, Morris. 1959. "Changing Patterns of Organizational Authority: The Military Establishment." *Administrative Science Quarterly,* **3**:473-493.

811   ———. 1960. *The Professional Soldier.* New York: Free Press.

812   ——— and William Delany. 1957. "Bureaucrat and the Public: A Study of Informational Perspectives." *Administrative Science Quarterly,* **2**:141-162.

813   Jasinski, Frank J. 1956a. "Foreman Relationships Outside the Work Group." *Personnel,* **33**:130-136.
814   ———. 1956b. "Use and Misuse of Efficiency Controls." *Harvard Business Review,* **34**:105-112.
815   ———. 1959. "Adapting Organization to New Technology." *Harvard Business Review,* **37**:79-86.
816   Johns, Roy. 1963. *Confronting Organizational Change.* New York: New York Association Press.
817   Johnson, Norman. 1966. "Toward a Taxonomy of Organizations." Unpublished Ph.D. dissertation, Ohio State University, Columbus.
818   Johnson, Peter A. 1960. "The Marginal Man Revisited." *Pacific Sociological Review,* **3**:71-74.
819   Jones, Garth N. 1965. "Strategies and Tactics of Planned Organizational Change." *Human Organization,* **24**:192-200.
820   ———. 1968. *Planned Organizational Change: A Study in Change Dynamics.* London: Routledge.
821   Josephson, Eric. 1952. "Irrational Leadership in Formal Organizations." *Social Forces,* **31**:109-117.
822   Julian, Joseph. 1966. "Compliance Patterns and Communication Blocks in Complex Organizations." *American Sociological Review,* **3**:382-389.
823   ———. 1968. "Organizational Involvement and Social Control." *Social Forces,* **47**:12-16.
824   ———. 1969. "Some Determinants of Dissensus on Role Prescriptions within and between Four Organizational Positions." *Sociological Quarterly,* **10**:177-189.
825   Juris, Hervey A., and Kay B. Hutchison. 1970. "The Legal Status of Municipal Police Employee Organizations." *Industrial and Labor Relations Review,* **23**:352-366.
826   Kaczka, Eugene A., and Roy V. Kirk. 1967. "Managerial Climate, Work Groups and Organizational Performance." *Administrative Science Quarterly,* **12**:253-272.
827   Kahn, Robert L. 1955. *Leadership Patterns and Organizational Effectiveness.* Ann Arbor, Mich.: Institute for Social Research.
828   ———. 1956. "The Prediction of Productivity." *Journal of Social Issues,* **12**:41-49.
829   ———. 1957. "Employee Motivation," in *Addresses on Industrial Relations,* 1957 Series. Ann Arbor, Mich.: Bureau of Industrial Relations, University of Michigan.
830   ———. 1958. "Human Relations on the Shop Floor," in E. M. Hugh-Jones (ed.), *Human Relations and Modern Management.* Amsterdam: North Holland Publishing Company.
831   ———. 1959. "The Administrative Statesman," Review of P. Selznick's *Leadership in Administration. Contemporary Psychology,* **4**:4-5.
832   ———. 1960. "Productivity and Job Satisfaction." *Personnel Psychology,* **13**:275-287.

833   ———. 1963. "Role Conflict and Ambiguity in Large Organizations." Proceedings of the Comité International l'Organisation Scientifique 13th Annual International Management Congress.

834   ———. 1964. *Conflict and Ambiguity: Studies in Organizational Roles and Personnel Stress.* New York: Wiley.

835   ——— et al. (eds.). 1959. *Employment Relations Research Studies: A Summary and Appraisal.* New York: Harper.

836   ——— and Elise Boulding (eds.). 1964. *Power and Conflict in Organizations.* New York: Basic Books.

837   ——— and Daniel Katz. 1951. "Some Relationships between Organizational Characteristics and Productivity." Ann Arbor, Mich.: Institute for Social Research.

838   ———, Floyd C. Mann, and Stanley Seashore (eds.). 1956. "Human Relations Research in Large Organizations." *Journal of Social Issues,* **12**:(entire issue).

839   ——— and N. Morse. 1951. "The Relation of Productivity to Morale." *Journal of Social Issues,* **7**:8-17.

840   ——— and A. S. Tannenbaum. 1957. "Union Leadership and Member Participation." *Personnel Psychology,* **10**:277-292.

841   Kahn, Robert P., J. Diedrick Snoek, and Robert A. Rosenthal. 1964. *Organizational Stress: Studies in Role Conflict and Ambiguity.* New York: Wiley.

842   Kaplan, Berton H. 1968a. "A Commentary on Organization and Social Development." *Administrative Science Quarterly,* **13**:484-490.

843   ———. 1968b. "Notes on a Non-Weberian Model of Bureaucracy: The Case of Development Bureaucracy." *Administrative Science Quarterly,* **13**:471-483.

844   Kaplan, Norman. 1965. "Professional Scientists in Industry." *Social Problems,* **13**:88-97.

845   Karpick, Lucien. 1968. "Expectations and Satisfaction and Work." *Human Relations,* **21**:327-350.

846   Karsh, B. 1957. "The Meaning of Work in an Age of Automation." *Current Economic Comment,* **19**:3-13.

847   ——— and J. Shegman. 1964. "Functions of Ignorance in Introducing Automation." *Social Problems,* **12**:141-150.

848   Kasl, S. V., and J. R. P. French, Jr. 1962. "The Effects of Occupational Status on Physical and Mental Health." *Journal of Social Issues,* **18**:67-89.

849   Katz, Daniel, 1954. "Satisfaction and Deprivations in Industrial Life," in A. Kornhauser et al. (eds.), *Industrial Conflict.* New York: McGraw-Hill.

850   ———. 1964. "The Motivational Basis of Organizational Behavior." *Behavioral Science,* **9**:131-146.

851   ——— et al. 1950. *Productivity, Supervision, and Morale in an Office Situation.* Ann Arbor, Mich.: Institute for Social Research.

852   ——— et al. 1951. *Productivity, Supervision, and Morale among Railroad Workers.* Ann Arbor, Mich.: Institute for Social Research.

853   ——— and Robert L. Kahn. 1952. "Human Organization and Worker Motivation." Ann Arbor, Mich.: Industrial Relations Research Organization, University of Michigan.

854 —— and ——. 1966. *The Social Psychology of Organizations.* New York: Wiley.

855 Katz, F. E. 1958. "Occupational Contact Networks." *Social Forces,* **37**:52-55.

856 ——. 1965. "Explaining Informal Work Groups in Complex Organizations: The Case for Autonomy in Structure." *Administrative Science Quarterly,* **10**:204-223.

857 ——. 1967. "Do Administrative Officials Believe in Bureaucracy? A Pilot Study." *Sociological Inquiry,* **37**:205-209.

858 ——. 1968. *Autonomy and Organization: The Limits of Social Control.* New York: Random House.

859 Katzell, R. A. 1962. "Contrasting Systems of Work Organization." *American Psychologist,* **17**:102-108.

860 ——, R. S. Barrett, and T. C. Parker. 1961. "Job Satisfaction, Job Performance, and Situation Characteristics." *Journal of Applied Psychology,* **45**:65-72.

861 Kaufman, Herbert, and David Seidman. 1970. "The Morphology of Organizations." *Administrative Science Quarterly,* **15**:439-452.

862 Kaufman, Herbert. 1964. "Organization Theory and Political Theory." *American Political Science Review,* **58**:5-14.

863 Kaufmann, Carl B. 1967. *Man Incorporate: The Individual and His Work in an Organized Society.* Garden City-N.Y.: Doubleday.

864 Kavanagh, Michael J. 1972. "Leadership Behavior as a Function of Subordinate Competence and Task Complexity." *Administrative Science Quarterly,* **17**:591-600.

865 Kavcic, Bogdan, Veljko Rus, and A. S. Tannenbaum. 1971. "Control, Participation, and Effectiveness in Four Yugoslav Industrial Organizations." *Administrative Science Quarterly,* **16**:74-87.

866 Kaye, C. 1954. "The Effects on Organizational Goal Achievement of a Change in the Structure of Roles." Ann Arbor, Mich.: Institute for Social Research.

867 Kelley, Harold H. 1951. "Communication in Experimentally Created Hierarchies." *Human Relations,* **4**:39-56.

868 Kelly, Joe. 1969. *Organizational Behavior.* Homewood, Ill.: Dorsey.

869 Kennedy, J. E., and H. E. O'Neill. 1958. "Job Content and Workers' Opinions." *Journal of Applied Psychology,* **42**:372-375.

870 Kerr, Clark and Abraham Siegel. 1954. "The Interindustry Propensity to Strike: An International Comparison," in A. Kornhauser et al. (eds.). *Industrial Conflict.* New York: McGraw-Hill.

871 Killingsworth, Charles C. 1958. "Automation in Manufacturing." Industrial Relations Research Association Annual Proceedings, Publication No. 22.

872 ——. 1962. "Industrial Relations and Automation." *Annals of the American Academy of Political and Social Science* (March):68-80.

873 Kipnis, David. 1964. "Mobility Expectations and Attitudes toward Industrial Structure." *Human Relations,* **17**:57-71.

874 Kish, Leslie. 1965. "Sampling Organizations and Groups of Unequal Sizes." *American Sociological Review,* **30**:564-572.

875   Klatzky, S. R. 1970a. "Organizational Inequality: The Case of the Public Employment Agencies." *American Journal of Sociology,* 76:474-491.

876   ———. 1970b. "Relationship of Organizational Size to Complexity and Coordination." *Administrative Science Quarterly* 15:428-438.

877   Klein, M. W., M. H. Berkowitz, and M. F. Malone. 1961. "Judgments on Organizational Performance." *Sociology and Social Research,* 46:26-35.

878   Knowles, K. G. 1954. "Strike Proneness and Its Determinants." *American Journal of Sociology,* 60:213-229.

879   Knudsen, Dean K. 1968. "Sect, Church, and Organizational Change." *Sociological Focus,* 2:11-17.

880   Koivisto, W. A. 1953. "Value, Theory, and Fact in Industrial Sociology." *American Journal of Sociology,* 58:564-572.

881   Kalaja, Jiri. 1963. "An Organization Seen as a Structure of Decision Making." *Human Relations,* 16:351-357.

882   Kong-Ming New, Peter, and J. Thomas May. 1965. "Organization under Stress: An Analysis of the Local Board of Health." *Journal of Health and Human Behavior,* 6:226-234.

883   Koontz, Harold, and Cyril O'Donnell. 1968. *Principles of Management: An Analysis of Managerial Functions.* New York: McGraw-Hill.

884   Korman, Abraham K. 1966. "Consideration, Initiating Structure, and Organizational Criteria: A Review." *Personnel Psychology,* 19:349-361.

885   Kornhauser, Arthur, et al. (eds.). 1954. *Industrial Conflict.* New York: McGraw-Hill.

886   Krause, Elliot A. 1968. "Functions of Bureaucratic Ideology: Citizen Participation." *Social Problems,* 16:129-142.

887   Kraut, Allen I. 1962. "How EDP Is Affecting Workers and Organizations." *Personnel,* 39:38-50.

888   Kremers, John, and Paul C. Durkee. 1962. "Electronic Data Processing in the Bell System." *Bell Telephone Magazine* (Winter):12-20.

889   Kriesberg, Louis. 1962. "Careers, Organization Size, and Succession." *American Journal of Sociology,* 68:355-359.

890   Krohn, Roger. 1971. "Conflict and Function: Some Basic Issues in Bureaucratic Theory." *British Journal of Sociology,* 22:115-132.

891   Krugman, H. E. 1957. "Just Like Running Your Own Little Store . . ." *Personnel,* 34:46-50.

892   Krupp, Sherman. 1961. *Patterns in Organizational Analysis.* New York: Holt.

893   Kuethe, James L., and Bernard Levenson. 1965. "Conceptions of Organizational Worth." *American Journal of Sociology,* 70:342-348.

894   Kunz, Phillip. 1969. "Sponsorship and Organizational Stability: Boy Scout Troops." *American Journal of Sociology,* 74:666-675.

895   ——— and Merlin R. Brinkerhoff. 1970. "Growth in Religious Organizations: A Comparative Study." *Social Science,* 45:215-221.

896   Labovitz, S., and Jack Gibbs. 1964. "Urbanization, Technology, and the Division of Labor: Further Evidence." *Pacific Sociological Review,* 7:3-9.

897   ——— and Robert Hagedorn. 1971. *Introduction to Social Research.* New York: McGraw-Hill.

898 Ladinsky, Jack, and Joel B. Grossman. 1966. "Organizational Consequences of Professional Consensus: Lawyers and Selection of Judges." *Administrative Science Quarterly,* **11**:79-106.

899 Laird, Donald. 1964. *How to Get Along with Automation.* New York: McGraw-Hill.

900 Lammers, C. J. 1967. "Power and Participation in Decision Making in Formal Organizations." *American Journal of Sociology,* **73**:201-216.

901 ———. 1969. "Strikes and Mutinies: A Comparative Study of Organizational Conflicts between Rulers and Ruled." *Administrative Science Quarterly,* **14**:558-572.

902 Landsberger, Henry A. 1958. *Hawthorne Revisited.* Ithaca, N.Y.: Cornell University Press.

903 ———. 1961a. "Horizontal Dimension in Bureaucracy." *Administrative Science Quarterly,* **6**:299-332.

904 ———. 1961b. "Parson's Theory of Organizations," in Max Black (ed.), *The Social Theories of Talcott Parsons.* Englewood Cliffs, N.J.: Prentice-Hall.

905 ———. 1970. *Comparative Perspectives on Formal Organization.* Boston: Little, Brown.

906 Landy, David, and Sara E. Singer. 1961. "The Social Organization and Culture of a Club for Former Mental Patients." *Human Relations,* **14**:31-41.

907 Lanzetta, John T., and T. Roby. 1956. "Group Performance as a Function of Work Distribution Patterns and Task Load." *Sociometry,* **19**:95-104.

908 LaPorte, Todd R. 1965. "Conditions of Strain and Accommodation in Industrial Research Organizations." *Administrative Science Quarterly,* **10**:21-38.

908a Larke, Alfred G. 1954. "What Makes a Good Foreman?" *Dun's Review and Modern Industry* (July):73-76.

909 Larson, William R. 1958. "Social Desirability as a Latent Variable in Medical Questionnaire Responses." *Pacific Sociological Review,* **1**:30-32.

910 Laumann, Edward O. 1965. "Subjective Social Distance and Urban Occupational Stratification." *American Journal of Sociology,* **71**:26-36.

911 Lave, Lester B. 1966. *Technological Change: Its Conception and Measurement.* Englewood Cliffs, N.J.: Prentice-Hall.

912 Lawler, Edward E., and Lyman W. Porter. 1967. "The Effect of Performance on Job Satisfaction." *Industrial Relations,* **7**:20-28.

913 Lawler, Edward J. 1970. "Intraorganizational Powerlessness among Social Workers: A Test of the Professional-Bureaucratic Hypothesis." Paper presented at the Society for the Study of Social Problems (SSSP) Meetings.

914 Lawrence, P. R. 1958. *The Changing of Organizational Behavior Patterns: A Case Study of Decentralization.* Boston: Harvard Business School, Division of Research.

915 ——— and Jay W. Lorsch. 1967a. "Differentiation and Integration in Complex Organizations." *Administrative Science Quarterly,* **12**:1-47.

916 ——— and ———. 167b. *Organization and Environment: Managing Differentiation and Integration.* Cambridge, Mass.: Harvard Graduate School of Business Administration.

917 ——— and John A. Seiler. 1965. *Organizational Behavior and Administration: Cases, Concepts, and Research Findings*. Homewood, Ill.: Dorsey-Irwin.

918 Lawshe, C. H., and Bryant F. Nagle. 1953. "Productivity and Attitude toward Supervisors." *Journal of Applied Psychology*, 37:159–162.

919 Lawson, Edwin D. 1965. "Change in Communication Nets: Performance and Morale." *Human Relations*, 18:139–147.

920 Learned, Edmund P., and A. T. Sproat. 1966. *Organization Theory and Policy: Notes for Analysis*. Homewood, Ill.: Irwin.

921 Leaver, Eric W. 1962. "The Next Fifteen Years of Automation." *Automation* (November):52–58.

922 Leavitt, Harold J. 1962. "Unhuman Organizations." *Harvard Business Review*, 40:90–98.

923 ——— (ed.). 1963. *The Social Science of Organizations*, Englewood Cliffs, N.J.: Prentice-Hall.

924 ——— and Louis R. Pondy (eds.). 1964. *Readings in Managerial Psychology*. Chicago: The University of Chicago Press.

925 ——— and T. Whisler. 1958. "Management in the 1980's." *Harvard Business Review*, 36:41–48.

926 Lefton, Mark, and William R. Rosengren. 1966. "Organizations and Clients: Lateral and Longitudinal Dimensions." *American Sociological Review*, 31:802–810.

927 Lehman, Edward W. 1968. "Opportunity, Mobility, and Satisfaction within an Industrial Organization." *Social Forces*, 46:492–501.

928 Lennerlof, Lennart. 1968. *Supervision: Situation, Individual, Behavior, Effect*. Stockholm: Swedish Council for Personnel Administration.

929 Lenski, G. E. 1956a. "Social Participation and Status Crystallization." *American Sociological Review*, 21:458–464.

930 ———. 1956b. "Status Crystallization: A Non-Vertical Dimension of Social Status." *American Sociological Review*, 19:15–21.

931 Levin, Jack, and Gerald Taube. 1970. "Bureaucracy and the Socially Handicapped: A Study of Lower Status Tenants in Public Housing." *Sociology and Social Research*, 54:209–219.

932 Levine, Joel H. 1972. "The Sphere of Influence." *American Sociological Review*, 37:14–27.

933 Levine, Sol, et al. 1963. "Community Interorganizational Problems in Providing Medical Care and Social Services." *American Journal of Public Health*, 53:1183–1195.

934 ——— and Paul E. White. 1961. "Exchange as a Conceptual Framework for the Study of Organization Relationships." *Administrative Science Quarterly*, 5:583–601.

935 Levinson, D. J. 1959. "Role, Personality, and Social Structure in the Organizational Setting." *Journal of Abnormal Social Psychology*, 58:170–180.

936 Levinson, Harry. 1965. "Reciprocation: The Relationship between Man and Organization." *Administrative Science Quarterly*, 9:370–390.

937 ———. 1968. *The Exceptional Executive*. Cambridge, Mass.: Harvard.

938   —— et al. 1972. *Organizational Diagnosis.* Cambridge, Mass.: Harvard.

939   Levinson, Robert F. 1967. *The Knack of Developing and Using Management Savvy.* West Nyack, N.Y.: Parker Publishing Company.

940   Levitan, Sar A. 1964. *Reducing Worktime as a Means to Combat Unemployment.* Kalamazoo, Mich.: W. E. Upjohn Institute for Employment Research.

941   Levy, Philip, and Derick Pugh. 1969. "Scaling and Multivariate Analyses and the Study of Organizational Variables." *Sociology,* 3:193-213.

942   Lewin, Kurt, 1939. "Field Theory and Experiment in Social Psychology: Concepts and Methods." *American Journal of Sociology,* 44:868-896.

943   ——. 1947. "Group Decision and Social Change," in T. M. Newcomb and E. L. Hartley (eds.), *Readings in Social Psychology.* New York: Holt.

944   Lewis, Lionel S., and Joseph Lopreato. 1963. "Functional Importance and Prestige of Occupations." *Pacific Sociological Review,* 6:55-56.

945   Libo, Lester M. 1954. *Measuring Group Cohesiveness.* Ann Arbor, Mich.: Institute for Social Research.

946   Lieberman, S. 1951. "An Analysis of Role Change in a Factory Situation." Ann Arbor, Mich.: Institute for Social Research.

947   ——. 1956. "The Effects of Changes in Roles on the Attitudes of Role Occupants." *Human Relations,* 9:385-402.

948   ——. 1961. "The Division of Labor in Banking." *American Journal of Sociology,* 66:491-496.

946   —— and James F. O'Connor. 1972. "Leadership and Organizational Performance: A Study of Large Organizations." *American Sociological Review,* 37:117-130.

950   Likert, Rensis. 1954a. "A Neglected Factor in Communications." *Communications Review,* 2:3.

951   ——. 1954b. "Understanding Human Behavior." *Michigan State Bar Journal,* 33:13-19.

952   ——. 1957. "Organizational Aspects of Human Behavior," in *Industry and the Human Being in an Automated World.* A Transcript of the Second Ann Arbor Industry-Education Symposium. Ann Arbor Mich.: Industry Program of the College of Engineering, University of Michigan.

953   ——. 1958a. "Effective Supervision: An Adaptive and Relative Process." *Personnel Psychology,* 11:317-332.

954   ——. 1958b "Measuring Organizational Performance." *Harvard Business Review,* 36:41-50.

955   ——. 1959a. "An Emerging Theory of Management Applicable to Public Administration," in D. L. Bower and R. H. Healy (eds.), *Administrative Leadership in Government: Selected Papers.* Ann Arbor, Mich.: Institute of Public Administration.

956   ——. 1959b. "Management, Measurement and Motivation," in F. E. May (ed.), *Increasing Sales Efficiency: Conference on Sales and Marketing Management.* Ann Arbor: Bureau of Business Research, University of Michigan.

957   ——. 1961a. "An Emerging Theory of Organization Behavior and Management," in L. Petrullo and B. M. Bass (eds.), *Leadership and Interpersonal Behavior.* New York: Holt.

958 ———. 1961b. *New Patterns of Management.* New York: McGraw-Hill.

959 ———. 1962. "Supervision." *International Science and Technology* (March):57–62.

960 ———. 1967. *The Human Organization: Its Management and Value.* New York: McGraw-Hill.

961 ——— and David Bowers. 1960. "Organization Theory and Human Resources Accounting." *American Psychologist,* **24**:585–592.

962 ——— and ———. 1970. "Conflict Strategies Related to Organizational Theories of Management Systems." Ann Arbor, Mich.: Institute for Social Research.

963 ——— and Stanley Seashore. 1956. "Motivation and Morale in the Public Service." *Public Personnel Review,* **17**:268–274.

963a Linton, Ralph. 1936. *The Study of Man.* New York: Appleton.

964 Lippitt, Gordon L. 1955. "What Do We Know about Leadership?" *National Education Association Journal* (December):556–557.

965 Lippitt, Ronald. 1962. "Unplanned Maintenance and Planned Change in the Work Processes," in *National Conference on Social Welfare: Social Work Practice.* New York: Columbia.

966 ———, Jean Watson, and B. Westley. 1958. *The Dynamics of Planned Change: A Comparative Study of Principles and Techniques.* New York: Harcourt, Brace, & World.

967 Lipset, Seymour M., and Reinhard Bendix. 1952a. "Social Mobility and Occupational Career Patterns." *American Journal of Sociology,* **57**:366–374.

968 ——— and ———. 1952b. "Social Mobility and Occupational Career Patterns: II—Social Mobility." *American Journal of Sociology,* **57**:494–504.

969 ———, Martin A. Trow, and James S. Coleman. 1956. *Union Democracy.* Glencoe, Ill.: Free Press.

970 Lipstreu, O. 1960. "Training Implications of Automation." *Journal of American Society of Training Directors,* **14**:48–51.

971 Litterer, Joseph A. 1963. *Organizations: Structure and Behavior.* New York: Wiley.

972 ———. 1965. *The Analysis of Organizations.* New York: Wiley.

973 ———. 1973. *The Analysis of Organizations* (2d ed.). New York: Wiley.

974 Litwak, Eugene. 1961. "Models of Bureaucracy which Permit Conflict." *American Journal of Sociology,* **67**:177–184.

975 ———. 1967. "Technological Innovation and Theoretical Functions of Primary Groups and Bureaucratic Structures." *American Journal of Sociology,* **73**:468–481.

976 ——— and Lydia F. Hylton. 1962. "Interorganizational Analysis: A Hypothesis on Coordinating Agencies." *Administrative Science Quarterly,* **6**:395–420.

977 ——— and Henry J. Meyer. 1966. "A Balance Theory of Coordination between Bureaucratic Organizations and Community Primary Groups." *Administrative Science Quarterly,* **11**:33–58.

978 Litwin, George H., and Robert A. Stringer. 1968. *Motivation and Organizational Climate.* Cambridge, Mass.: Division of Research, Graduate School of Business Administration, Harvard University.

979 —— and Renato Tagiuri. 1968. *Organizational Climate: Explorations of a Concept.* Cambridge, Mass.: Division of Research, Graduate School of Business Administration, Harvard University.

980 Lodahl, Thomas M. 1964. "Patterns of Job Attitudes in Two Assembly Technologies." *Administrative Science Quarterly,* **8**:482-519.

981 Loomis, Charles P. 1960. *Social Systems: Essays on Their Persistence and Change.* Princeton, N.J.: Van Nostrand.

982 Lopez, Felix M. 1970. *The Making of a Manager.* Washington, D.C.: American Management Association.

983 Lorsch, Jay W. 1965. *Product Innovation and Organization.* New York: Macmillan.

984 —— and Paul R. Lawrence. 1965. "Organizing for Product Innovation." *Harvard Business Review,* **43**:109-122.

985 Lowin, Aaron, William J. Hrapchak, and Michael J. Kavanagh. 1969. "An Experimental Investigation of Leadership Traits." *Administrative Science Quarterly,* **14**:238-253.

986 Lowry, R. 1967. "Functions of Alienation in Leadership." *Sociology and Social Review,* **46**:426-435.

987 Lucio, William H., and John D. McNeil. 1969. *Supervision: A Synthesis of Thought and Action,* New York: McGraw-Hill.

988 Luecke, David S. 1973. "The Professional as Organizational Leader." *Administrative Science Quarterly,* **18**:86-94.

989 Lyden, Fremont J., et al. (eds.). 1969. *Policies, Decisions, and Organization.* New York: Appleton-Century-Crofts.

990 Lyman, Elizabeth L. 1955. "Occupational Differences in the Value Attached to Work." *American Journal of Sociology,* **61**:138-144.

991 Lynton, Rolf P. 1969. "Linking an Innovative Subsystem into the System." *Administrative Science Quarterly,* **14**:398-417.

992 Lystad, Mary H., and Robert C. Stone. 1956. "Bureaucratic Mass Media: A Study in Role Definitions." *Social Forces,* **34**:356-361.

993 MacBride, Robert. 1967. *The Automated State: Computer Systems as a New Force in Society.* Philadelphia: Chilton.

994 MacDonald, Keith, and W. Nichols. 1969. "Employee Involvement: A Study of Drawing Offices." *Sociology,* **3**:233-238.

995 MacGuire, Jullian M. 1968. "The Function of the 'Set' in Hospital Controlled Schemes of Nurse Training." *British Journal of Sociology,* **19**:271-283.

996 MacKenzie, W. J. M. 1967. "Technology and Organization," in W. J. M. MacKenzie (ed.), *Politics and Social Science.* London: Penguin.

997 MacKinney, A. C., P. F. Wernimont, and W. O. Galitz. 1962. "Has Specialization Reduced Job Satisfaction?" *Personnel,* **39**:8-17.

998 MacNeil, Kenneth, and James D. Thompson, 1971. "The Regeneration of Social Organizations." *American Sociological Review,* **36**:624-637.

999 McCleery, R. H. 1957. *Policy Change in Prison Management.* East Lansing: Government Research Bureau, Michigan State University.

1000 McCormack, Thelma. 1956. "The Druggist's Dilemma: Problems of a Marginal Occupation." *American Journal of Sociology,* **61**:308-315.

1001   McCormick, B. 1960. "Managerial Unionism in the Coal Industry." *British Journal of Sociology* 11:356-369.
1002   McEwen, William J. 1956. "Position Conflict and Professional Orientation in a Research Organization." *Administrative Science Quarterly,* 1:208-224.
1003   McFarland, David D. 1968. "Measuring the Permeability of Occupational Structures: An Information Theoretic Approach." *American Journal of Sociology,* 74:41-61.
1004   McGregor, Douglas. 1960. *The Human Side of Enterprise.* New York: McGraw-Hill.
1005   McKelrey, William W. 1969. "Expectational Noncomplementarity and Style of Interaction between Professional and Organization." *Administrative Science Quarterly,* 14:21-32.
1006   McKinney, John C. 1966. *Constructive Typology and Social Theory,* New York: Appleton-Century-Crofts.
1007   McMurry, Robert N. 1958. "Recruitment, Dependency, and Morale in the Banking Industry." *Administrative Science Quarterly,* 3:87-117.
1008   McNulty, James E. 1962. "Organizational Change in Growing Enterprises." *Administrative Science Quarterly,* 7:1-21.
1009   McWhinney, W. H. 1965. "On the Geometry of Organizations." *Administrative Science Quarterly* 10:347-363.
1010   Magistretti, Franca. 1955. "Sociological Factors in the Structuring of Industrial Worker's Teams." *American Journal of Sociology,* 60:536-540.
1011   Mahoney, Thomas A., and William Weitzel. 1969. "Managerial Models of Organizational Effectiveness." *Administrative Science Quarterly,* 14:357-365.
1012   Maier, Norman R. F. 1952. *Principles of Human Relations.* New York: Wiley.
1013   ———. 1955. *Psychology in Industry.* Boston: Houghton Mifflin.
1014   ———. 1965. *Psychology in Industry* (2d ed.). Boston: Houghton Mifflin.
1015   ———. 1973. *Psychology in Industry* (3d ed.). Boston: Houghton Mifflin.
1016   ———, L. Richard Hoffman, and William H. Reed. 1963. "Superior-Subordinate Communication: The Relative Effectiveness of Managers Who Held Their Subordinate's Positions." *Personnel Psychology,* 16:1-11.
1017   Maiolo, John R. 1970. "Organization for Social Action: Some Consequences of Competition for Control." *Sociological Quarterly,* 11:463-473.
1018   Maniha, John and Charles Perrow. 1965. "Reluctant Organization and the Aggressive Environment." *Administrative Science Quarterly,* 10:238-257.
1019   Mann, Floyd C. 1951. "Changing Superior-Subordinate Relationships." *Journal of Social Issues* 7:56-63.
1020   ———. 1953. "Work Satisfactions as Related to Aspirations and Achievements." Ann Arbor, Mich.: Institute for Social Research.
1021   ———. 1957. "Studying and Creating Change: A Means of Understanding Social Organization," in C. W. Arensberg et al. (eds.), *Research in Industrial Human Relations.* New York: Harper.
1022   ———. 1962. "Psychological and Organizational Impacts," in John T. Dunlop (ed.), *Automation and Technological Change.* Englewood Cliffs, N.J.: Prentice-Hall.

1023 —— et al. 1956. "Individual and Organizational Correlates of Automation." *Journal of Social Issues,* **12**:7-17.

1024 —— et al. 1971. *The Productivity of Work Groups.* Ann Arbor, Mich.: Institute for Social Research.

1025 —— and J. Dent. 1954. "The Supervisor: Member of Two Organizational Families." *Harvard Business Review,* **32**:103-112.

1026 —— and I. R. Hoffman. 1960. *Automation and the Worker: A Study of Social Change in Power Plants.* New York: Holt.

1027 ——, B. P. Indik, and Victor Vroom. 1963. *Productivity of Work Groups.* Ann Arbor: Survey Research Center, University of Michigan.

1028 —— and F. W. Neff. 1961. *Managing Major Change in Organizations.* Ann Arbor, Mich.: The Foundation for Research on Human Behavior.

1029 —— and Lawrence K. Williams. 1958. "Organizational Impact of White Collar Automation." *Industrial Relations Research Association Annual Proceedings,* Publication No. 22.

1030 —— and ——. 1960. "Observations on the Dynamics of a Change to Electronic Data Processing Equipment." *Administrative Science Quarterly,* **5**:217-256.

1031 —— and ——. 1962 "Some Effects of the Changing Work Environment in the Office." *Journal of Social Issues,* **18**:90-101.

1032 Mann, Roland. 1971. *The Arts of Top Management: A McKinsey Anthology.* New York: McGraw-Hill.

1033 Mannheim, Bilha F., et al. 1967. "Instrumental Status of Supervisors as Related to Workers' Perceptions and Expectations." *Human Relations,* **20**:387-397.

1034 March, James G. 1955. "Group Autonomy and Internal Group Control." *Social Forces,* **33**:322-326.

1035 ——. 1962. "The Business Firm as a Political Coalition." *Journal of Politics,* **24**:662-678.

1036 —— (ed.). 1965. *The Handbook of Organizations.* Chicago: Rand McNally.

1037 —— and Herbert A. Simon. 1958. *Organizations.* New York: Wiley.

1038 Marcson, S. 1960. *The Scientist in American Industry: Some Organizational Determinants in Manpower Utilization.* Princeton, N.J.: Industrial Relations Section, Princeton University.

1039 ——. 1961. "Organization and Authority in Industrial Research." *Social Forces,* **40**:72-80.

1040 Marcus, Philip. 1960. "Expressive and Instrumental Group: Toward a Theory of Group Structure." *American Journal of Sociology,* **66**:54-59.

1041 ——. 1961. "Supervision and Group Process." *Human Organization,* **20**:15-19.

1042 ——. 1962. "Group Cohesion and Worker Productivity: A Dissenting View." *Personnel Administration,* **25**:44-48.

1043 ——. 1966. "Union Conventions and Executive Boards: A Formal Analysis of Organizational Structure." *American Sociological Review,* **31**:61-70.

1044 ——— and Dora Marcus. 1965. "Control in Modern Organizations." *Public Administration Review,* **25**:121-127.

1045 Marek, Julius. 1967. "Technological Development, Organization, and Interpersonal Relations." *Acta Sociologica,* **10**:224-257.

1046 Mark, Harold, and Merlin Taber. 1967. "Typology of Organizational Data." *Sociological Focus,* **1**:21-31.

1047 Markham, Charles. 1964. *Jobs, Men and Machines: Problems of Automation.* New York: Praeger.

1048 Markley, O. W. 1967. "A Simulation of the SIVA Model of Organizational Behavior." *American Journal of Sociology,* **73**:339-347.

1049 Marriott, R. 1949. "Size of Working Group and Output." *Occupational Psychology,* **23**:47-57.

1050 Marrow, Alfred J., David G. Bowers, and Stanley E. Seashore. 1967. *Management by Participation.* New York: Harper & Row.

1051 Martin, F. N. 1951. "Human Relations in Industry." *British Journal of Sociology,* **2**:354-359.

1052 Martin, Norman H., and Anselm L. Strauss. 1956. "Patterns of Mobility within Industrial Organizations." *Journal of Business of the University of Chicago,* **29**:249-260.

1053 Martin, R. T., and J. C. Murray. 1958. "Morale among Railway Workers." *Personnel Practices Bulletin,* **14**:58-63.

1054 Martin, Roderick. 1968. "Union Democracy: An Explanatory Framework." *Sociology,* **2**:205-220.

1055 Martindale, Don. 1966. *Institutions, Organizations, and Mass Society.* Boston: Houghton Mifflin.

1056 Marwell, Gerald, and Jerald Hage. 1970. "The Organization of Role-Relationships: A Systematic Description." *American Sociological Review,* **35**:884-900.

1057 Maslow, Abraham. 1954. *Motivation and Personality.* New York: Harper.

1058 Massie, Joseph. 1965. "Management Theory," in James G. March (ed.), *Handbook of Organizations.* Chicago: Rand McNally.

1059 Mathiesen, Thomas. 1971. *Across the Boundaries of Organizations: An Exploratory Study of Communication Patterns in Two Penal Institutions.* Berkeley, Calif.: The Glendessary Press.

1060 Mayer, K., and S. Goldstein. 1961. *The First Two Years: Problems of Small Firm Growth and Survival,* Small Business Research Series No. 2 Washington, D.C.: U.S. Government Printing Office.

1061 Mayhew, Bruce H., and Louis N. Gray. 1968. "Internal Control Relations in Administrative Hierarchies: A Critique." *Administrative Science Quarterly,* **14**:131-133.

1062 ——— et al. 1972. "System Size and Structural Differentiation in Formal Organizations: A Baseline Generator for Two Major Theoretical Propositions." *American Sociological Review,* **37**:629-633.

1063 Mayhew, Leon H., and Albert J. Reiss. 1969. "The Social Organization of Legal Contracts." *American Sociological Review,* **34**:309-318.

1064 Mayo, Elton. 1945. *The Social Problems of an Industrial Civilization.* Cambridge, Mass.: Harvard.

1065 Mechanic, David. 1962. "Sources of Power and Lower Participants in Complex Organizations." *Administrative Science Quarterly,* 7:349-364.

1066 ———. 1963. "Some Considerations in the Methodology of Organizational Studies," in H. Leavitt, *The Social Science of Organizations.* Englewood Cliffs, N.J.: Prentice-Hall.

1067 Medalia, Nahum Z., and Delbert C. Miller. 1955. "Human Relations Leadership and the Association of Morale and Efficiency in Work Groups: A Controlled Study with Small Military Units." *Social Forces,* 33:348-352.

1068 Meggison, L. C. 1960. "The Human Consequences of Automation." *Personnel,* 37:18-26.

1069 Meissner, Martin. 1969. *Technology and the Worker: Technical Demands and Social Processes in Industry.* San Francisco: Chandler.

1070 Melbin, Murray. 1961. "Organizational Practice and Individual Behavior: Absenteeism among Psychiatric Aides." *American Sociological Review,* 26:14-23.

1071 Melio, Nancy. 1971. "Health Care Organizations and Innovation." *Journal of Health and Social Behavior,* 12:163-173.

1072 Mellinger, G. 1957. "Interpersonal Trust as a Factor in Communications." *Journal of Abnormal and Social Psychology,* 52:304-309.

1073 Meltzer, Leo, and James Salter. 1962. "Organizational Structure and the Performance and Job Satisfactions of Physiologists." *American Sociological Review,* 27:351-362.

1074 Mercer, Jane R., and Edgar W. Butler, 1967. "Disengagement of the Aged Population and Response Differentials in Survey Research." *Social Forces* 46:89-96.

1075 Merton, Robert K. 1940. "Bureaucratic Structure and Personality." *Social Forces,* 18:560-568.

1076 ———. 1957. *Social Theory and Social Structure.* Glencoe, Ill.: Free Press.

1077 ——— et al. 1952. *Reader in Bureaucracy.* Glencoe, Ill.: Free Press.

1078 Messinger, S. L. 1955. "Organizational Transformation: A Case Study of a Declining Social Movement." *American Sociological Review,* 20:3-10.

1079 Metzler, William 1963. "Relocation of the Displaced Worker." *Human Organization,* 22:142-145.

1080 Metzner, H., and F. C. Mann. 1953. "Employee Attitudes and Absence." *Personnel Psychology* 6:467-485.

1081 ———, F. C. Mann, and H. Baumgartel, 1957. "The Supervisor and Absence Rates." *Supervisory Management,* 2:7-14.

1082 Meyer, John W. 1968. "Collective Disturbances and Staff Organizations on Psychiatric Wards: A Formalization." *Sociometry,* 31:211-228.

1083 Meyer, Marshall W. 1968a. "Automation and Bureaucratic Structure." *American Journal of Sociology,* 74:256-264.

1084 ———. 1968b. "Expertness and the Span of Control." *American Sociological Review,* 33:944-950.

1085 ———. 1968c. "Two Authority Structures of Bureaucratic Organizations." *Administrative Science Quarterly,* **13**:211–229.

1086 ———. 1971a. "Some Constraints in Analyzing Data on Organizational Structures: A Comment on Blau's Paper." *American Sociological Review,* **36**:294–303.

1087 ——— (ed.). 1971b. *Structures, Symbols, and Systems: Readings on Organizational Behavior.* Boston: Little, Brown.

1088 ———. 1972a. *Bureaucratic Structure and Authority: Coordination and Control in 254 Government Agencies.* New York: Harper & Row.

1089 ———. 1972b. "Size and the Structure of Organizations: A Causal Analysis." *American Sociological Review,* **37**:434–441.

1090 Meyer, Paul. 1957. *Administrative Organization: A Comparative Study of the Organization of Public Administration.* London: Stevens & Sons, Ltd.

1091 Michael, Donald N. 1962a. *Cybernation: The Silent Conquest.* Santa Barbara, Calif.: Fund for the Republic, Inc.

1092 ———. 1962b. *Psychological Adjustments to Automation.* Washington, D.C.: The Voice of America Forum Lectures, U.S. Information Agency.

1093 Miles, Matthew B. 1959. *Learning How to Work in Groups.* New York: Bureau of Publications, Teachers College, Columbia University.

1094 Miles, Raymond E. 1965. "Human Relations or Human Resources?" *Harvard Business Review,* **43**:148–155.

1095 Mill, John Stuart. 1930. *A System of Logic,* (8th ed.). New York: Longmans.

1096 Miller, David W. and Martin K. Starr. 1967. *The Structure of Human Decisions.* Englewood Cliffs, N.J.: Prentice-Hall.

1097 Miller, Delbert C. 1970. *Handbook of Research Design and Social Measurement.* New York: McKay.

1098 ——— and William Form. 1964. *Industrial Sociology: The Sociology of Work Organizations.* New York: Harper & Row.

1099 Miller, E. J., and A. K. Rice. 1967. *Systems of Organization: The Control of Task and Sentiment Boundaries.* New York: Tavistock Publications.

1100 Miller, George A. 1967. "Professionals in Bureaucracy: Alienation among Industrial Scientists and Engineers." *American Sociological Review,* **32**:755–768.

1101 ——— and L. Wesley Wager. 1971. "Adult Socialization, Organizational Structure, and Role Orientations." *Administrative Science Quarterly,* **16**:151–163.

1102 Miller, John P., and Lincoln J. Fry. 1973. "Social Relations in Organizations: Evidence for the Weberian Model." *Social Forces,* **51**:305–319.

1103 ——— and Sanford Labovitz. 1971. "Industrialization, Urbanization, and Deviant Behavior." *Pacific Sociological Review,* **14**:177–195.

1104 Mills, C. Wright. 1970. "The Contribution of Sociology to Studies of Industrial Relations." *Berkeley Journal of Sociology,* **15**:11–32.

1105 Misler, Elliot G., and Asher Tropp. 1956. "Status and Interaction in a Psychiatric Ward." *Human Relations,* **9**:187–205.

1106 Misumi, J., and S. Shiraskashi. 1966. "An Experimental Study of the Effects of Supervisory Behavior on Productivity and Morale in a Hierarchical Organization." *Human Relations,* **19**:297-307.

1107 Moeller, G. 1962. "Bureaucracy and Teacher's Sense of Power." *Administrator's Notebook,* **11**:1-4.

1108 ——— and W. W. Charters. 1966. "Relation of Bureaucratization to Sense of Power among Teachers." *Administrative Science Quarterly,* **10**:444-465.

1109 Montagna, Paul D. 1968. "Professionalization and Bureaucratization in Large Professional Organizations." *American Journal of Sociology,* **74**:138-145.

1110 Mooney, J. D., and A. C. Reilley. 1939. *The Principles of Organization.* New York: Harper.

1111 Moore, Joan W. 1961. "Patterns of Women's Participation in Voluntary Organizations." *American Journal of Sociology,* **66**:592-598.

1112 Moore, Wilbert E. 1947. "Current Issues in Industrial Sociology." *American Sociological Review,* **12**:651-657.

1113 Moos, S. 1957. "The Scope of Automation." *Economic Journal,* **67**:26-39.

1114 Morane, J. H. 1967. *A Sociology of Human Systems.* New York: Appleton-Century-Crofts.

1115 Moreno, J. L. 1934. *Who Shall Survive?* Washington, D.C.: Nervous and Mental Disease Monograph No. 58.

1116 ———. 1946. "Sociogram and Sociomatrix." *Sociometry,* **9**:348-349.

1117 Morse, Chandler. 1961. "The Individual and Pattern Variables." in Max Black (ed.) *The Social Theories of Talcott Parsons.* Englewood Cliffs, N.J.: Prentice-Hall.

1118 Morse, Nancy C. 1953. *Satisfaction in the White Collar Job.* Ann Arbor: Survey Research Center, University of Michigan.

1119 ———. 1954. "What Workers Want." *Michigan Business Review,* **6**:19-21.

1120 ———, Floyd Mann, and Robert Kahn. 1952. "The Meaning of Morale." Ann Arbor, Mich.: Institute for Social Research.

1121 ——— and E. Reimer. 1956. "The Experimental Change of a Major Organizational Variable." *Journal of Abnormal Psychology,* **52**:120-129.

1122 ———, E. Reimer, and A. Tannenbaum. 1951. "Regulation and Control in Hierarchical Organizations." *Journal of Social Issues,* **7**:41-48.

1123 ——— and R. Weiss. 1955. "The Function and Meaning of Work and the Job." *American Sociological Review,* **20**:191-198.

1124 Mouledous, Joseph C. 1963. "Organizational Goals and Structural Change: A Study of The Organization of a Prison Social System." *Social Forces,* **41**:283-290.

1125 Mouzelis, Nicos P. 1967. *Organization and Bureaucracy.* London: Routledge.

1126 ———. 1968. *Organization and Bureaucracy: An Analysis of Modern Theories.* Chicago: Aldine.

1127 Mulder, N., et al. 1971. "An Organization in Crisis and Non-Crisis Situations." *Human Relations,* **24**:19-41.

1128 Mulford, Charles L. 1967. "Consideration of the Instrumental and Expressive Roles of Community Influentials and Formal Organizations." *Sociology and Social Research,* **51**:141-147.

1129   Mullen, James H. 1966a. "Personality Polarization as an Equilibrating Force in a Large Organization." *Human Organization,* **25**:330-338.

1130   ———. 1966b. *Personality and Productivity in Management.* New York: Columbia.

1131   Mumford, Enid. 1970. "Job Satisfaction—A New Approach Derived from an Old Theory." *Sociological Review,* **18**:71-101.

1132   Musgrave, P. W. 1968. *The School as an Organization.* London: Macmillan.

1133   Myers, Charles A. (ed.). 1968. *The Impact of Computers on Management.* Cambridge, Mass.: M. I. T.

1134   ——— and John G. Turnbull. 1956. "Line and Staff in Industrial Relations." *Harvard Business Review,* **34**:113-124.

1135   Myers, M. S. 1964. "Who Are Your Motivated Workers?" *Harvard Business Review,* **42**:73-88.

1136   Nash, Manning. 1958. "Machine Age Maya: The Industrialization of a Guatemalan Community," Memoirs No. 87. Menasha, Wis.: American Anthropological Association.

1137   National Commission on Technology, Automation and Economic Progress. 1966. *Technology and the American Economy.* Washington, D.C.: U.S. Government Printing Office.

1138   Naville, P. 1958. "The Structure of Employment and Automation." *International Social Science Bulletin,* **10**:16-29.

1139   Neff, W. S. 1968. *Work and Human Behavior.* New York: Atherton.

1140   Neiman, L. J., and J. W. Hughes. 1951. "The Problem of the Concept of Role: A Resurvey of the Literature." *Social Forces,* **30**:141-149.

1141   Neuloh, O. 1958. "Paving the Way for Technological Change." *Personnel,* **34**:21-26.

1142   Newcomb, Theodore M., Ralph H. Turner, and P. E. Converse. 1965. *Social Psychology: The Study of Human Interaction.* New York: Holt.

1143   Niles, Mary C. 1949. *Middle Management: The Job of the Junior Administrator.* New York: Harper.

1144   Nonet, Philippe. 1969. *Administrative Justice: Advocacy and Change in Government Agencies.* New York: Russell Sage.

1145   Norman, Robert M., et al. 1965. *Structure Models: An Introduction to the Theory of Directed Graphs.* New York: Wiley.

1146   Normann, Richard. 1971. "Organizational Innovativeness: Product Variation and Reorientation." *Administrative Science Quarterly,* **16**:203-215.

1147   Northrup, H. R. 1958. "Automation: Effects on Labor Force, Skills, and Employment." Industrial Relations Research Association Annual Proceedings, Publication No. 22.

1148   Oaklander, Harold, and Edwin A. Fleishman. 1964. "Patterns of Leadership Related to Organizational Stress in Hospital Settings." *Administrative Science Quarterly,* **8**:520-532.

1149   Obrochta, Richard J. 1960. "Foreman-Worker Attitude Patterns." *Journal of Applied Psychology,* **44**:88-91.

1150   O'Connell, Jeremiah. 1968. *Managing Organizational Innovation.* Homewood, Ill.: Dorsey-Irwin.

1151 O'Donavan, T. R. 1960. *Organizational Behavior and Change Program Bibliography.* Ann Arbor, Mich.: Survey Research Center.

1152 ———. 1962. "Socioeconomic and Educational Factors Influencing Achievement Levels of Individuals in Large Scale Organizations." *Sociology and Social Research,* **46**:416-425.

1153 ——— and Arthur X. Deegan. 1964. "A Comparative Study of the Orientations of a Selected Group of Church Executives." *Sociology and Social Research,* **48**:330-339.

1154 Olmstead, Donald W. 1954 "Organizational Leadership and Social Structure in a Small City." *American Sociological Review* **19**:273-281.

1155 Olsen, Marvin E. 1968. *The Process of Social Organization.* New York: Holt.

1156 Opsahl, R. L., and M. D. Dunnette. 1966. "The Role of Financial Compensation in Industrial Motivation." *Psychological Bulletin,* **66**:94-118.

1157 Page, Charles H. 1951. "Bureaucracy in Higher Education." *The Journal of Higher Education,* **5**:91-100.

1158 Pages, M. 1959. "The Sociotherapy of the Enterprise: The Conditions of Psychosocial Change in Industrial Concerns and the Role of the Social Psychologist as an Agent of Social Change." *Human Relations,* **12**:317-334.

1159 Palisi, B. 1970. "Some Suggestions about the Transitory Permanence Dimension of Organizations." *British Journal of Sociology,* **21**:200-206.

1160 Palola, Ernest G. 1967. "Organizational Types and Role Strains: An Experimental Study of Complex Organizations." *Sociology and Social Research,* **51**:171-184.

1161 ——— and William Larsen. 1965. "Some Dimensions of Job Satisfaction among Hospital Personnel." *Sociology and Social Research,* **49**:201-213.

1162 Palumbo, D. J. 1960. *Structure and Process in Modern Societies.* New York: Free Press.

1163 ———. 1969. "Power and Role Specificity in Organizational Theory." *Public Administration Review,* **29**:237-248.

1164 Parker, S. R. 1964. "Type of Work, Friendship Patterns, and Leisure." *Human Relations,* **17**:215-219.

1165 Parker, Treadway C. 1963. "Relationships among Measures of Supervising Behavior, Group Behavior, and Situational Characteristics." *Personnel Psychology,* **16**:319-334.

1166 Parris, Crawley A. 1969. *Mastering Executive Arts and Skills.* West Nyack, N.Y.: Parker Publishing Company.

1167 Parsons, T. 1951. *The Social System.* Glencoe, Ill.: Free Press.

1168 ———. 1956a. "Suggestions for a Sociological Approach to the Theory of Organizations." *Administrative Science Quarterly,* **1**:63-85.

1169 ———. 1956b. "Suggestions for a Sociological Approach to the Theory of Organization—II." *Administrative Science Quarterly,* **1**:225-239.

1170 ———. 1966. *Societies: Evolutionary and Comparative Perspectives.* Englewood Cliffs, N.J.: Prentice-Hall.

1171 Paschell, W., and D. P. Willis. 1958. "How Automation Will Affect Office Workers." *Occupational Outlook Quarterly,* **2**:3-9.

1172 Patchen, M. 1958. "The Effect of Reference Group Standards on Job Satisfactions." *Human Relations,* **11**:303-314.

1173 ———. 1960. "Absence and Employee Feelings about Fair Treatment." *Personnel Psychology,* **13**:349-360.

1174 ———. 1962. "Supervisory Methods and Group Performance Norms." *Administrative Science Quarterly,* **7**:275-294.

1175 ———. 1963. "Alternative Questionnaire Approaches to the Measurement of Influence in Organizations." *American Journal of Sociology,* **64**:41-52.

1176 ———. 1964. "Participation in Decision Making and Motivation: What Is the Relation?" *Personnel Administration,* **24**:24-31.

1177 ———, Donald C. Pelz, and Craig W. Allen. 1971. *Some Questionnaire Measures of Employee Motivation and Morale: A Report on Their Reliability and Validity.* Ann Arbor, Mich.: Institute for Social Research.

1178 Patten, Thomas, Jr. 1967. "Organizational Processes and the Development of Managers: Some Hypotheses." *Human Organization,* **26**:242-255.

1179 Pavalko, Ronald M. 1971. *Sociology of Occupations and Professions.* Itasca, Ill.: F. E. Peacock Publishers, Inc.

1180 Payne, Raymond. 1954. "An Approach to the Study of the Relative Prestige of Formal Organizations." *Social Forces,* **32**:244-247.

1181 Peabody, Robert L. 1962. "Perceptions of Organizational Authority: A Comparative Analysis." *Administrative Science Quarterly,* **6**:463-482.

1182 ———. 1964. *Organizational Authority.* New York: Atherton.

1183 Pearlin, Leonard I. 1962a. "Sources of Resistance to Change in a Mental Hospital." *American Journal of Sociology,* **68**:325-334.

1184 ———. 1962b. "Alienation from Work: A Study of Nursing Personnel." *American Sociological Review,* **27**:314-326.

1185 ——— and Morris Rosenberg. 1962. "Nurse-Patient Social Distance and the Structural Context of a Mental Hospital." *American Sociological Review,* **27**:56-65.

1186 Pelz, Donald C. 1951. "Leadership within a Hierarchical Organization." *Journal of Social Issues,* **7**:49-55.

1187 ———. 1952. "Influence: A Key to Effective Leadership in the First Line Supervisor." *Personnel,* **29**:209-217.

1188 ———. 1956. "Some Social Factors Related to Performance in a Research Organization." *Administrative Science Quarterly,* **1**:310-325.

1189 ———. 1957. "Motivation of the Engineering and Research Specialist." *Improving Managerial Performance,* American Management Association General Management Series No. 186.

1190 ——— and Frank M. Andrews. 1966. *Scientists in Organizations: Productive Climates for Research and Development.* New York: Wiley.

1191 Pennington, Leon. 1943. *The Psychology of Military Leadership.* Englewood Cliffs, N.J.: Prentice-Hall.

1192 Pennock, George A. 1930. "Industrial Research at Hawthorne." *Personnel Journal,* **8**:296-313.

1193 Peres, Sherwood H. 1962. "Performance Dimensions of Supervisory Positions." *Personnel Psychology,* **15**:405–410.

1194 Perlstadt, Harry. 1972. "Goal Implementation and Outcome in Medical Schools." *American Sociological Review,* **37**:73–82.

1195 Perrow, Charles. 1961a. "The Analysis of Goals in Complex Organizations." *American Sociological Review,* **26**:854–866.

1196 ———. 1961b. "Organizational Prestige: Some Functions and Dysfunctions." *American Journal of Sociology,* **66**:335–341.

1197 ———. 1963. "Goals and Power Structures: A Historical Case Study," in Eliot Freidson (ed.), *The Hospital in Modern Society.* New York: Free Press.

1198 ———. 1965. "Hospitals, Technology, Goals and Structure," in James March (ed.), *Handbook of Organizations.* Chicago: Rand McNally.

1199 ———. 1967. "A Framework for the Comparative Analysis of Organizations." *American Sociological Review,* **32**:194–209.

1200 ———. 1968. "Organizational Goals," in *International Encyclopedia of the Social Sciences* (rev. ed.). New York: Macmillan.

1201 ———. 1968b. "The Effects of Technological Change on the Structure of Business Firms," in B. C. Roberts (ed.), *Industrial Relations: Contemporary Issues.* New York: Macmillan.

1202 ———. 1970a. "Departmental Power and Perspective in Industrial Firms," in Mayer Zald (ed.) *Power in Organizations.* Nashville, Tenn.: Vanderbilt.

1203 ———. 1970b. "Members as a Resource in Voluntary Organizations," in W. Rosengren and M. Lefton (eds.), *Organizations and Clients.* Columbus, Ohio: Merrill.

1204 ———. 1970c. *Organizational Analysis: A Sociological View.* Belmont, Calif.: Wadsworth.

1205 ———. 1972. *Complex Organizations: A Critical Essay.* Glenview, Ill.: Scott, Foresman.

1205a Perrucci, Robert (ed.). 1969. *The Engineers and the Social System.* New York: Wiley.

1206 ——— and Richard A. Mannweiler. 1968. "Organization Size, Complexity, and Administrative Succession in Higher Education." *Sociological Quarterly,* **9**:343–355.

1207 Peter, Lawrence J., and Raymond Hull. 1969. *The Peter Principle.* New York: Morrow.

1208 Peterson, Richard A., and David G. Berger. 1971. "Entrepreneurship in Organizations: Evidence from the Popular Music Industry." *Administrative Science Quarterly,* **16**:97–107.

1209 Petrello, Luigi. 1961. *Leadership and Interpersonal Behavior.* New York: Holt.

1210 Pfeffer, Jeffrey. 1972. "Merger as a Response to Organizational Interdependence." *Administrative Science Quarterly,* **17**:382–394.

1211 Pheysey, Diana C., Roy L. Payne, and Derek S. Pugh. 1971. "Influence of Structure at Organizational and Group Levels." *Administrative Science Quarterly,* **16**:61–73.

1212 Philipson, Morris (ed.). 1962. *Automation: Implications for the Future.* New York: Vintage Books.

1213 Phillips, A. 1957. *Automation: Its Impact on Economic Growth and Stability.* New York: American Enterprises Association.

1214 Pierce, G. 1967. *Data Processing for Guidance and Counseling Handbook.* Detroit: Automated Education Center.

1215 Pigors, Paul and Faith Pigors. 1961. *Case Method in Human Relations: The Incident Process.* McGraw-Hill.

1216 Pollock, F. 1957. *Automation: A Study of its Economic and Social Consequences.* New York: Praeger.

1217 Pondy, Louis. 1967. "Organizational Conflict: Concepts and Models." *Administrative Science Quarterly,* **12**:296-320.

1218 ———. 1969a. "Effects of Size, Complexity, and Ownership on Administrative Intensity." *Administrative Science Quarterly,* **14**:47-61.

1219 ———. 1969b. "Varieties of Organizational Conflict." *Administrative Science Quarterly,* **14**:499-506.

1220 Popiel, Gerald. 1955. "Bureaucracy in the Mass Industrial Union." *American Journal of Economics and Sociology,* **15**:49-58.

1221 Porter, L. W. 1962. "Job Attitudes in Management: Perceived Deficiencies in Need Fulfillment as a Function of Job Level." *Journal of Applied Psychology,* **56**:375-384.

1222 ——— and ——— E. E. Lawler. 1965. "Properties of Organization Structure in Relation to Job Attitudes." *Psychological Bulletin,* **64**:23-51.

1223 ——— and ———. 1968. *Managerial Attitudes and Performance.* Homewood, Ill.: Irwin.

1224 ——— and J. Siegel. 1965. "Relationships of Tall and Flat Organizational Structures to the Satisfactions of Foreign Managers." *Personnel Psychology,* **18**:379-392.

1225 Porterfield, Austin, and Jack P. Gibbs. 1960. "Occupational Prestige and Social Mobility of Suicides in New Zealand." *American Journal of Sociology,* **66**:147-152.

1226 Presthus, Robert V. 1950. "Social Bases of Bureaucratic Organization." *Social Forces,* **38**:103-109.

1227 ———. 1958. "Toward a Theory of Organizational Behavior." *Administrative Science Quarterly,* **3**:48-72.

1228 ———. 1960. "Authority in Organizations." *Public Administration Review,* **20**:86-91.

1229 ———. 1965. *The Organizational Society.* New York: Vintage Books.

1230 Price, James L. 1965. "The Use of New Knowledge in Organizations." *Human Organization,* **23**:224-234.

1231 ———. 1968a. "Design of Proof in Organizational Research." *Administrative Science Quarterly,* **13**:121-134.

1232 ———. 1968b. *Organizational Effectiveness: An Inventory of Propositions.* Homewood, Ill.: Irwin.

1233   ———. 1968c. "Rejoinder to Starbuck." *Administrative Science Quarterly,* 13:162-166.
1234   ———. 1968d. "The Impact of Departmentalization on Interoccupational Cooperation." *Human Organization,* 27:362-368.
1235   Pruden, Henry O., and Richard M. Reese. 1972. "Interorganizational Role-Set Relations and the Performance and Satisfaction of Industrial Salesmen." *Administrative Science Quarterly,* 17:601-609.
1236   Przeworski, Adam, and Henry Teune. 1970. *The Logic of Comparative Social Inquiry.* New York: Wiley.
1237   Pugh, D. S. 1966. "Modern Organization Theory: A Psychological and Sociological Study." *Psychological Bulletin,* 66:235-251.
1238   ———. 1969a. "Organizational Behavior: An Approach from Psychology." *Human Relations,* 22:345-354.
1239   ———. 1969b. "An Empirical Taxonomy of Structures of Work Organizations." *Administrative Science Quarterly,* 14:115-126.
1240   ——— et al. 1963. "Conceptual Scheme for Organizational Analysis." *Administrative Science Quarterly,* 8:289-315.
1241   ——— et al. 1968. "Dimensions of Organizational Structure." *Administrative Science Quarterly,* 13:65-104.
1242   ——— et al. 1969. "The Context of Organizational Structures." *Administrative Science Quarterly,* 14:91-114.
1243   Putman, Mark L. 1930. "Improving Employee Relations." *Personnel Journal,* 8:314-325.
1244   Pym, Denis. 1966. "Technology, Effectiveness and Predisposition towards Work Change among Mechanical Engineers." *Journal of Management Studies,* 3:304-311.
1245   Quarantelli, E. L., and John R. Brouillette. 1971. "Types of Patterned Variation and Bureaucratic Adaptations to Organizational Stress." *Sociological Inquiry,* 41:39-46.
1246   Quinn, A. P., and R. L. Kahn. 1967. "Organizational Psychology." *Annual Review of Psychology,* 18:437-466.
1247   Quinn, Francis X. (ed.). 1962. *The Ethical Aftermath of Automation.* Westminster, Md.: Newman.
1248   Randell, Seppo. 1967. "On Some Social Influences of the Military Organization." *Acta Sociologia,* 10:274-298.
1249   Raphael, Edna. 1967. "The Anderson-Warkov Hypothesis in Local Unions: A Comparative Study." *American Sociological Review,* 32:768-776.
1250   Raven, Bertram H., and J. R. P. French, Jr. 1958. "Legitimate Power, Coercive Power, and Observability in Social Influence." *Sociometry,* 21:83-97.
1251   Read, William H. 1962. "Upward Communication in Industrial Hierarchies." *Human Relations,* 15:3-15.
1252   Record, Jane C. 1967. "The Research Institute and the Pressure Group," in Gideon Sjoberg's (ed.), *Ethics, Politics, and Social Research.* Cambridge, Mass.: Schenkman.

1253 Reeves, Tom K., and Barry A. Turner. 1972. "A Theory of Organization and Behavior in Batch Production Factories." *Administrative Science Quarterly,* 17:81-98.

1254 Reid, P. C. 1960. "Supervision in an Automated Plant." *Supervisory Management* (August):2-10.

1255 Reid, William. 1964. "Interagency Coordination in Delinquency Prevention and Control." *Social Service Review,* 38:418-428.

1256 Reimer, E., and N. Morse. 1956. "The Experimental Change of a Major Organizational Variable." *Journal of Abnormal and Social Psychology,* 52:120-129.

1257 Reiss, Albert J., Jr. 1965. *Schools in a Changing Society.* New York: Free Press.

1258 Reistad, Dale L. 1961. *Banking Automation and the Magnetic Ink Character Recognition Program.* Detroit: Detroit Research Institute.

1259 Reitzes, Dietrich. 1953. "The Role of Organizational Structures." *Journal of Social Issues,* 9:37-44.

1260 Rezler, J. 1958. "The Impact of Automation on the Stability of Manufacturing Employment." *Current Economic Comment,* 20:55-62.

1261 Rhenman, Eric. 1967. "Organizational Goals." *Acta Sociologica,* 10:275-287.

1262 Rice, A. K. 1953. "Productivity and Social Organization in an Indian Weaving Mill." *Human Relations,* 6:279-329.

1263 ———. 1963. *The Enterprise and Its Environment.* London: Tavistock Publications.

1264 ———. 1965. *Learning for Leadership: Interpersonal and Intergroup Relations.* London: Tavistock Publications.

1265 Rice, George H., Jr., and Dean W. Bishoprick. 1971. *Conceptual Models of Organization.* New York: Appleton-Century-Crofts.

1266 Rice, Linda E., and Terence R. Mitchell. 1973. "Structural Determinants of Individual Behavior in Organizations." *Administrative Science Quarterly* 18:56-70.

1267 Richardson, Frederick L., and Charles R. Walker. 1948. *Human Relations in an Expanding Company.* New Haven, Conn.: Labor and Management Center, Yale University.

1268 Richardson, Stephen A. 1956. "Organizational Contrasts on British and American Ships." *Administrative Science Quarterly,* 1:189-207.

1269 Riche, R. W., and W. E. Alli. 1960. "Office Automation in the Federal Government." *Monthly Labor Review,* 83:933-938.

1270 Ritzer, George, and Harrison M. Trice. 1969. *An Occupation in Conflict: A Study of a Personnel Manager.* Ithaca: New York State School of Industrial and Labor Relations, Cornell University.

1271 Rizzo, John R., Robert J. House, and Sidney I. Lirtzman. 1970. "Role Conflict and Ambiguity in Complex Organizations." *Administrative Science Quarterly,* 15:150-163.

1272 Roach, Darrell E. 1958. "Dimensions of Employee Morale." *Personnel Psychology,* 11:419-451.

1273 Roberts, Karlene. 1970. "On Looking at an Elephant: An Evaluation of Cross-Cultural Research Related to Organizations." *Psychological Bulletin,* 74:327–330.

1274 Robertson, Leon, and James C. Rodgers. 1966. "Distributive Justice in Informal Organization in a Freight Warehouse Work Crew." *Human Organization,* 25:221–224.

1275 Robinson, Alan H., and Ralph P. Connors. 1963. "Job Satisfaction Research of 1962." *Personnel and Guidance Journal,* 42:136–142.

1276 Rodgers, David, and Ivar Berg, Jr. 1961. "Occupation and Ideology: The Case of the Small Businessman." *Human Organization,* 20:103–111.

1277 Roe, Ann. 1956. *The Psychology of Occupations.* New York: Wiley.

1278 Roethlisberger, Fritz J. 1941. *Management and Morale.* Cambridge, Mass.: Harvard.

1279 ———. 1945. "The Foreman: Master and Victim of Double Talk." *Harvard Business Review,* 23:283–298.

1280 ———. 1968. *Man in Organization.* Cambridge, Mass.: Harvard.

1281 ——— and William J. Dickson. 1939. *Management and the Worker.* Cambridge, Mass.: Harvard.

1282 Rogers, David. 1968. *110 Livingstone St.* New York: Random House.

1283 Rogers, E. M. 1958a. "A Conceptual Variable Analysis of Technological Change." *Rural Sociology,* 23:136–145.

1284 ———. 1962. *Diffusion of Innovations.* New York: Free Press.

1285 ——— and G. M. Beal. 1958. "The Importance of Personal Influence in the Adoption of Technological Changes." *Social Forces,* 36:329–335.

1286 Rogers, J. 1958. *Automation: Technology's New Face.* Berkeley, Calif.: Institute of Industrial Relations.

1287 Rokeach, Milton. 1968. *Beliefs, Attitudes and Values: A Theory of Organization and Change.* San Francisco: Jossey-Bass.

1288 Ronan, W. W. 1970. "Individual and Situational Variables Relating to Job Satisfaction." *Journal of Applied Psychology Monograph,* 54:Part II.

1289 Ronayne, M. F. 1960. "The Personnel Side of Automatic Data Processing." *Public Personnel Review,* 21:243–248.

1290 Roney, James G., Jr. 1965. "A Case of Administrative Structure." *Human Organization,* 24:346–352.

1291 Ronken, Harriet O., and P. R. Lawrence. 1952. *Administering Change: A Case Study of Human Relations in a Factory.* Boston: Harvard Graduate School of Business Administration.

1292 Roos, Leslie L., Jr. 1972. "Politics, Organizations, and Choice: Applications of an Equilibrium Model." *Administrative Science Quarterly,* 17:529–543.

1293 ——— and Noralous R. Roos. 1970. "Administrative Change in a Modernizing Society." *Administrative Science Quarterly,* 15:69–78.

1294 Rose, Jerry D. 1969. "The Attribution of Responsibility for Organizational Failure." *Sociology and Social Research,* 53:323–332.

1295 Rosen, Bernard, and Allen Bates. 1967. "The Structure of Socialization in Graduate School." *Sociological Inquiry,* 37:71–84.

1296   Rosen, R. A. 1970. "Foreman Role Conflict: An Expression of Contradictions in Organizational Goals." *Industrial and Labor Relations Review,* **23**:541-552.

1297   Rosenberg, Jerry M. 1966. *Automation, Manpower, and Education.* New York: Random House.

1298   Rosenbloom, Richard S., and F. W. Wolek. 1970. *Technology and Information Transfer: A Survey of Practice in Industrial Organizations.* Boston: Harvard.

1299   Rosengren, William R. 1964. "Communication, Organization, and Conduct in the Therapeutic Milieu." *Administrative Science Quarterly,* **9**:70-90.

1300   ———. 1967. "Structure, Policy, and Style: Strategies of Organizational Control." *Administrative Science Quarterly,* **12**:140-164.

1301   ———. 1968. "Organizational Age, Structure, and Orientations toward Clients." *Social Forces,* **47**:1-11.

1302   ———. 1971. "The Rhetoric of Value Transfer in Organizations." *Sociological Inquiry,* **41**:47-56.

1303   ——— and Mark Lefton. 1970. *Organizations and Clients.* Columbus, Ohio: Merrill.

1304   Rosner, Martin M. 1968. "Economic Determinants of Organizational Innovation." *Administrative Science Quarterly,* **12**:614-625.

1305   Ross, I. C., and A. Zander. 1957. "Need Satisfactions and Employee Turnover." *Personnel Psychology,* **10**:327-338.

1306   Rossel, Robert D. 1970. "Instrumental and Expressive Leadership in Complex Organizations." *Administrative Science Quarterly,* **15**:306-317.

1307   Roth, Julius. 1962. "Management Bias in the Study of Medical Treatment." *Human Organization,* **21**:47-50.

1308   Rothberg, H. J. 1957. "Labor Adjustments for Changes in Technology in an Oil Refinery." *Monthly Labor Review,* **80**:1083-1087.

1309   Rothman, Robert A., and Robert Perrucci. 1970. "Organizational Careers and Professional Expertise." *Administrative Science Quarterly,* **15**:282-294.

1310   Rourke, Francis E. 1961. *Secrecy and Publicity: Dilemmas of Democracy.* Baltimore: Johns Hopkins.

1311   Rowland, Virgil K. 1958. *Improving Managerial Performance.* New York: Harper.

1312   Roy, Donald F. 1952. "Quota Restriction and Goldbricking in a Machine Shop." *American Journal of Sociology,* **57**:427-442.

1313   ———. 1954. "Efficiency and the Fix: Informal Intergroup Relations in a Piecework Machine Shop." *American Journal of Sociology,* **60**:255-266.

1314   ———. 1960. "Banana Time: Job Satisfaction and Informal Interaction." *Human Organization,* **18**:158-168.

1315   ———. 1970. "Sex in the Factory." Paper presented at the Southern Sociological Society Meetings, Atlanta, Ga.

1316   Rubenstein, Alberta H., and Chadwick J. Haberstroh. 1966. *Some Theories of Organization.* Homewood, Ill.: Dorsey.

1317   Rubinton, Earl. 1965. "Organizational Strains and Key Roles." *Administrative Science Quarterly,* **9**:350-369.

1318   Rushing, William A. 1966a. "Organizational Rules and Surveillance: Propositions in Comparative Organizational Analysis." *Administrative Science Quarterly,* **10**:423-443.

1319   ———. 1966b. "Organizational Size and Administration: The Problems of Causal Homogeneity and a Heterogeneous Category." *Pacific Sociological Review,* **9**:100-108.

1320   ———. 1967a. "The Effects of Industry Size and Division of Labor on Administration." *Administrative Science Quarterly,* **12**:273-295.

1321   ———. 1967b. "Two Patterns of Industrial Administration." *Human Organization,* **26**:32-39.

1322   ———. 1968. "Hardness of Material as Related to Division of Labor in Manufacturing Industries." *Administrative Science Quarterly,* **13**:229-245.

1323   ———. 1969. "Organizational Size, Rules and Surveillance," in J. A. Litterer (ed.), *Organizations: Structure and Behavior.* New York: Wiley.

1324   Ruttenberg, S. H. 1959. "Economics and Social Implications of the New Technology." *Monthly Labor Review,* **82**:164-165.

1325   Sadler, P. F., and B. A. Barry. 1970. *Organizational Development.* London: Longman Group.

1326   Sales, Stephen M. 1966. "Supervisory Style and Productivity: Review and Theory." *Personnel Psychology,* **19**:275-286.

1327   ———. 1969. "Organizational Role as a Risk Factor in Coronary Disease." *Administrative Science Quarterly,* **14**:325-337.

1328   Salter, W. E. G. 1960. *Productivity and Technological Change.* London: Cambridge University Press.

1329   Samuel, Yitzhak, and B. F. Mannheim. 1970. "A Multidimensional Approach toward a Typology of Bureaucracy." *Administrative Science Quarterly,* **15**:216-229.

1330   Sawthrop, Louis. 1969. *Bureaucratic Behavior in the Executive Branch: An Analysis of Organizational Change.* New York: Free Press.

1331   Sayles, Leonard. 1958a. *Behavior of Industrial Work Groups.* New York: Wiley.

1332   ———. 1958b. "Introduction to Technology, Social Relations, and Performance." *Human Organization,* **17**:2.

1333   ———. 1962. "The Change Process in Organizations." *Human Organization,* **21**:62-67.

1334   ———. 1964. *Managerial Behavior: Administration in Complex Organizations.* New York: McGraw-Hill.

1335   ———. 1966. *Human Behavior in Organizations.* Englewood Cliffs, N.J.: Prentice-Hall.

1336   Scanzoni, John. 1965. "Innovation and Constancy in the Church-Sect Typology." *American Journal of Sociology,* **71**:320-327.

1337   Schacter, Stanley, et al. 1951. "An Experimental Study of Cohesiveness and Productivity." *Human Relations.* **4**:229-238.

1338   Scheff, Thomas J. 1961. "Control over Policy by Attendants in a Mental Hospital." *Journal of Health and Human Behavior,* **2**:93-105.

1339   Schein, Edgar H. 1960. "Interpersonal Communication, Group Solidarity, and Social Influence." *Sociometry,* **23**:148-161.

1340   ———. 1965. *Organizational Psychology.* Englewood Cliffs, N.J.: Prentice-Hall.

1341   ——— and Warren G. Bennis. 1965. *Personal and Organizational Change Through Group Methods: The Laboratory Approach.* New York: Wiley.

1342   ——— and J. Steven Ott. 1962. "The Legitimacy of Organizational Influence." *American Journal of Sociology,* **67**:682-689.

1343   Schlesinger, L., et al. 1960. "Leader-Member Interaction in Management Committees." *Journal of Abnormal and Social Psychology,* **61**:360-364.

1344   Schmidt, Stuart M., and T. A. Kochan. 1972. "Conflict: Toward Conceptual Clarity." *Administrative Science Quarterly,* **17**:359-370.

1345   Schneider, Eugene V. 1950. "Limitations on Observation in Industrial Sociology." *Social Forces,* **28**:279-284.

1346   Schon, Donald A. 1967. *Technology and Change: The New Heraclitus.* New York: Delacorte Press.

1347   Schriver, William R. 1966. "The Prediction of Worker Productivity." *Human Organization,* **25**:339-343.

1348   Schroeder, H. H. 1957. "Employee and Community Relations Problems Resulting from Technological Developments." *Michigan Business Review,* **9**:18-24.

1349   Schulman, Jay. 1969. *Remaking an Organization: Innovation in a Specialized Psychiatric Hospital.* Albany: State University of New York Press.

1350   Schwartz, Michael. 1964. "Reciprocities Multiplier: An Empirical Evaluation." *Administrative Science Quarterly,* **9**:264-277.

1351   Schwartz, M. M., E. Jenusaitis, and H. Stark. 1963. "Motivational Factors among Supervisors in a Utility Industry." *Personnel Psychology,* **16**:45-53.

1352   Schwartzbaum, Allan, and Leopold Gruenfeld. 1969. "Factors Influencing Subject-Observer Interaction in an Organizational Study." *Administrative Science Quarterly,* **14**:443-450.

1353   Scott, Joseph W., and M. El-Assal. 1969. "Multiversity, University Size, University Quality, and Student Protest: An Empirical Study." *American Sociological Review,* **34**:702-722.

1354   Scott, Robert A. 1967a. "The Factory as a Social Service Organization: Goal Displacement in Workships for the Blind." *Social Problems,* **15**:160-175.

1355   ———. 1967b. "The Selection of Clients by Social Welfare Agencies: The Case of the Blind." *Social Problems.* **14**:248-257.

1356   Scott, William A. 1965. *Values and Organizations: A Study of Fraternities and Sororities.* Chicago: Rand McNally.

1357   Scott, William G. 1961. "Organizational Theory: An Overview and an Appraisal." *Academy of Management Journal,* **4**:7-27.

1358   ———. 1965. *The Management of Conflict.* Homewood, Ill.: Dorsey-Irwin.

1359   ———. 1967. *Organizational Theory: A Behavioral Analysis for Management.* Homewood, Ill.: Dorsey.

1360   ———. 1969. *Organization Concepts and Analysis.* Belmont, Calif.: Dickenson.

1361 Scott, W. H. 1959. "The Aims of Industrial Sociology: Some Reflections." *British Journal of Sociology,* **10**:193-203.

1362 ———. 1962. *Office Automation and the Non-Manual Worker.* Paris: Organization for Economic Cooperation and Development.

1363 Scott, W. Richard. 1963. "Field Work in a Formal Organization." *Human Organization,* **22**:162-168.

1364 ———. 1965. "Reactions to Supervision in a Heteronomous Professional Organization." *Administrative Science Quarterly,* **10**:65-81.

1365 ———. 1966. "Professionals in Bureaucracies: Areas of Conflict," in H. M. Vollmer and D. L. Mills (eds.). *Professionalization.* Englewood Cliffs, N.J.: Prentice-Hall.

1366 ——— et al. 1967. "Organizational Evaluation and Authority." *Administrative Science Quarterly,* **12**:93-117.

1367 Scurrah, Martin J., M. Shani, and C. Zipfel. 1971. "Influence of Internal and External Change Agents in a Simulated Educational Organization." *Administrative Science Quarterly,* **16**:113-121.

1368 Seashore, Stanley E. 1954a. "Group Cohesiveness as a Factor in Industrial Morale and Productivity." *American Psychologist,* **9**:468.

1369 ———. 1954b. *Group Cohesiveness in the Industrial Work Group.* Ann Arbor, Mich.: Institute for Social Research.

1370 ———. 1955. "Teamwork: Key to Production?" *Adult Leadership,* **3**:20-21.

1371 ———. 1956. "Interaction between Research and Application in Industry in the Field of Human Relations," in *Report of the International Conference on Human Relations.* Nijmegen, Netherlands: International Conference on Human Relations.

1372 ———. 1957. "Administrative Leadership and Organizational Effectiveness," in R. Likert and S. P. Hayes (eds.), *Some Applications of Behavioral Research.* Paris: UNESCO Publications Division.

1373 ———. 1958. "The Scientific Study of Social Behavior." *Industrial and Labor Relations Review,* **12**:148-149.

1374 ———. 1964a. *Assessing Organization Performance with Behavioral Measurements.* Ann Arbor, Mich.: Foundation for Research on Human Behavior.

1375 ———. 1964b. "Field Experiments with Formal Organizations." *Human Organization,* **23**:164-170.

1376 ———. 1965. "Criteria of Organizational Effectiveness." *Michigan Business Review,* **17**:26-30.

1377 ———. 1971. *Group Cohesiveness in the Industrial Work Group.* Ann Arbor, Mich.: Institute for Social Research.

1378 ——— and David G. Bowers. 1963. *Changing the Structure and Functioning of an Organization.* Ann Arbor, Mich.: Institute for Social Research.

1379 ——— and ———. 1970. "Durability of Organizational Change." *American Psychologist,* **25**:227-233.

1380 ———, B. P. Indik, and B. S. Georgopoulos. 1960. "Relationships among Criteria of Job Performance." *Journal of Applied Psychology,* **44**:195-202.

1381 ——— and R. J. McNeill (eds.). 1970. *The Management of Urban Crisis.* New York: Free Press.

1382   —— and E. Yuchtman. 1967. "Factorial Analysis of Organizational Performance." *Administrative Science Quarterly,* **12**:377–395.

1383   Seeman, Melvin. 1958. "Social Mobility and Administrative Behavior." *American Sociological Review,* **23**:633–642.

1384   ——. 1959. "On the Meaning of Alienation." *American Sociological Review,* **24**:783–791.

1385   ——. 1967. "On the Personal Consequences of Alienation in Work." *American Sociological Review,* **32**:273–285.

1386   —— and J. Evans. 1961. "Stratification and Hospital Care." *American Sociological Review,* **26**:67–79.

1387   —— J. Evans, and Edna Rodgers. 1960. "The Measurement of Stratification in Formal Organizations." *Human Organization,* **19**:90–96.

1388   Segal, Bernard E. 1969a. "Dissatisfaction and Desire for Change among Chilean Hospital Workers." *American Journal of Sociology,* **75**:375–388.

1389   ——. 1969b. "Hierarchy and Work Dissatisfaction in a Chilean Hospital." *Social Forces,* **48**:193–202.

1390   Seiler, John A. 1967. *Systems Analysis in Organizational Behavior.* Homewood, Ill.: Dorsey.

1391   Seldin, Joel. 1965. *Automation: The Challenge of Men and Machines.* New York: Coward-McCann.

1392   Seligman, Ben B. 1962a. "Automation Comes to the Supermarket." *Challenge* (November):25–29.

1393   ——. 1962b. "Man, Work, and the Automated Feast." *Commentary* (July):9–19.

1394   ——. 1966. *Most Notorious Victory: Man in an Age of Automation.* New York: Free Press.

1395   Selltiz, Claire, et al. 1959. *Research Methods in Social Relations.* New York: Holt.

1396   Selvin, Hanan, et al. 1963. "The Empirical Classification of Formal Groups." *American Sociological Review,* **28**:399–411.

1397   Selznick, Philip. 1943. "An Approach to a Theory of Bureaucracy." *American Sociological Review,* **8**:47–54.

1398   ——. 1948. "Foundations for the Theory of Organizations." *American Sociological Review,* **13**:23–35.

1399   ——. 1952. *The Organization Weapon: A Study of Bolshevik Strategy and Tactics.* Santa Monica, Calif.: Rand Corporation.

1400   ——. 1957. *Leadership in Administration: A Sociological Interpretation.* New York: Harper and Row.

1401   ——. 1966. *TVA and Grass Roots: A Study in the Sociology of Formal Organizations.* Berkeley: University of California Press.

1402   ——. 1969a. *Law, Society, and Industrial Justice.* New York: Russell Sage.

1403   ——. 1969b. "Rejoinder to Wohlin," in A. Etzioni (ed.), *A Sociological Reader on Complex Organizations.* New York: Holt.

1404   Sengupta, A. K. 1969. "Some Features on Malfunctioning of an Industrial Organization." *Sociological Bulletin,* **18**:122–137.

1405 Sheldon, Mary E. 1971. "Investments and Involvements as Mechanisms Producing Commitment to the Organization." *Administrative Science Quarterly,* **16**:143–150.

1406 Shepard, Clovis R. 1961. "Orientations of Scientists and Engineers." *Pacific Sociological Review,* **4**:79–83.

1407 ——— and Paula Brown. 1956. "Status, Prestige, and Esteem in a Research Organization." *Administrative Science Quarterly* **1**:340–360.

1408 Shepard, Herbert A. 1956a. "Nine Dilemmas in Industrial Research." *Administrative Science Quarterly,* **1**:295–309.

1409 ———. 1956b. "Patterns of Organization for Applied Research and Development: Superiors and Subordinates in Research." *Journal of Business,* **29**:261–267.

1410 Shepard, Jon M. 1971. "On Alex Carey's Radical Criticism of the Hawthorne Studies." *Academy of Management Journal,* **14**:23–32.

1411 ———. 1972. *Organizational Issues in Industrial Society.* Englewood Cliffs, N.J.: Prentice-Hall.

1412 Sheppard, H. L. 1954. "Approaches to Conflict in American Industrial Sociology." *British Journal of Sociology,* **5**:324–341.

1413 Shils, Edward B. 1963. *Automation and Industrial Relations.* New York: Holt.

1414 Shor, Edgar L. 1960. "Thai Bureaucracy." *Administrative Science Quarterly,* **5**:66–86.

1415 Shull, Fremont A., et al. 1970. *Organizational Decision-Making.* New York: McGraw-Hill.

1416 Shultz, G. P., and T. L. Whisler (eds.). 1960. *Management Organization and the Computer.* Glencoe, Ill.: Free Press.

1417 Shuval, Judith T. 1963. "Occupational Interests and Sex Role Congruence." *Human Relations,* **16**:171–182.

1418 Siegel, Laurence. 1969. *Industrial Psychology.* Homewood, Ill.: Irwin.

1419 Siegman, Jack, and Bernard Karsh. 1962. "Some Organizational Correlates of White Collar Automation," Bulletin No. 11. Urbana: University of Illinois.

1420 Silberman, Charles E. 1965. "The Comeback of the Blue-Collar Worker." *Fortune* (February):153–155.

1421 Sills, David L. 1957. *The Volunteers.* New York: Free Press.

1422 Silverman, David. 1952. "Formal Organization or Industrial Sociology: Towards a Social Action Analysis of Organizations." *Sociology,* **2**:221–238.

1423 Simmel, Georg. 1903. "The Number of Members as Determining the Sociological Form of the Group." *American Journal of Sociology,* **8**:1–46.

1424 Simmons, Roberta G. 1968. "The Role Conflict of the First-Line Supervisor: An Experimental Study." *American Journal of Sociology,* **73**:482–495.

1425 Simon, H. A. 1947. *Administrative Behavior.* New York: Macmillan.

1426 ———. 1957. *Models of Man.* New York: Wiley.

1427 ———. 1960. *The New Science of Management Decision.* New York: Harper.

1428 ———. 1961. *Administrative Behavior* (2d ed.). New York: Macmillan.

1429 ———. 1962. "The Corporation: Will It Be Managed by Machines?" in Morris Philipson (ed.), *Automation: Implications for the Future.* New York: Vintage Books.

1430 ———. 1964. "On the Concept of Organizational Goal." *Administrative Science Quarterly,* **9**:1-22.

1431 ———. 1965a. *Administrative Behavior: A Study of Decision-Making Processes in Administration Organization.* New York: Free Press.

1432 ———. 1965b. *The Shape of Automation for Men and Management.* New York: Harper & Row.

1433 ———, D. W. Smithburg, and V. A. Thompson. 1950. *Public Administration.* New York: Knopf.

1434 Simpson, Ida H. 1967. "Patterns of Socialization into Professions: The Case of Student Nurses." *Sociological Inquiry,* **37**:47-54.

1435 Simpson, Richard L. 1959. "Vertical and Horizontal Communication in Formal Organizations." *Administrative Science Quarterly,* **4**:188-196.

1436 ——— and W. H. Gulley. 1962. "Goals, Environmental Pressures, and Organizational Characteristics." *American Sociological Review,* **27**:344-350.

1437 ——— and Ida H. Simpson. 1964. *Social Organization and Behavior.* New York: Wiley.

1438 Sirota, D. 1959. "Some Effects of Promotional Frustration on Employee's Understanding of and Attitudes toward Management." *Sociometry,* **22**:273-278.

1439 Slesinger, J. A., and E. P. Harburg. 1964. "Organizational Stress: A Force Requiring Management Control." *Personnel Administration,* **27**:35-39.

1440 ——— and ———. 1968. "Organizational Change and Executive Behavior." *Human Organization,* **27**:95-109.

1441 Smigel, Erwin O. 1960. "The Impact of Recruitment on the Organization of the Large Law Firm." *American Sociological Review,* **25**:56-66.

1442 ——— et al. 1963. "Occupational Sociology: A Reexamination." *Sociology and Social Research,* **47**:472-477.

1443 Smith, Adam. 1904. *Treatise on the Wealth of Nations.* London: Methuen.

1444 Smith, Clagett G. 1966. "Comparative Analysis of Some Conditions and Consequences of Intraorganizational Conflict." *Administrative Science Quarterly,* **10**:504-529.

1445 ——— and Ogus N. Ari. 1964. "Organizational Control Structure and Member Concensus." *American Journal of Sociology,* **69**:623-638.

1446 ——— and A. S. Tannenbaum. 1963. "Organizational Control Structure: A Comparative Analysis." *Human Relations,* **16**:299-316.

1447 ——— and ———. 1965. "Some Implications of Leadership and Control for Effectiveness in a Voluntary Organization." *Human Relations,* **18**:265-272.

1448 Smith, David H. 1966a. "A Psychological Model of Individual Participation in Formal Voluntary Associations." *American Journal of Sociology,* **72**:249-266.

1449 ———. 1966b. "The Importance of Formal Voluntary Organizations for Society." *Sociology and Social Research,* **50**:483-495.

1450 Smith, Dorothy E. 1965. "Front Line Organization of the State Mental Hospital." *Administrative Science Quarterly* **10**:381-399.

1451 Smith, Edmund A. 1957. "Bureaucratic Organization: Selective or Saturative." *Administrative Science Quarterly,* **2**:361-375.

1452 Smith, Gilbert. 1970. *Social Work and the Sociology of Organizations.* London: Routledge.

1453 Smith, Harvey L. 1955. "Two Lines of Authority Are One Too Many." *Modern Hospital,* **84**:59–64.

1454 ———. 1958. "Two Lines of Authority: The Hospital's Dilemma," in E. G. Jaco (ed.), *Patients, Physicians, and Illness: Sourcebook in Behavioral Science and Medicine.* Glencoe, Ill.: Free Press.

1455 Smith, J. H. 1955. "The Scope of Industrial Relations." *British Journal of Sociology,* **6**:80–85.

1456 ———. 1959. "New Ways in Industrial Sociology." *British Journal of Sociology,* **10**:244–252.

1457 ———. 1960. "Sociology and Management Studies." *British Journal of Sociology,* **11**:103–111.

1458 ———. 1961. "Managers and the Married Women Workers." *British Journal of Sociology,* **12**:12–22.

1459 Smith, Michael A. 1968. "Process Technology and Powerlessness." *British Journal of Sociology,* **19**:76–88.

1460 Smith, Peter B., et al. 1969. "Relationships between Managers and Their Work Associates." *Administrative Science Quarterly,* **14**:338–345.

1461 Smith, P. C., and C. J. Cranny. 1968. "Psychology of Men at Work." *Annual Review of Psychology,* **19**:467–496.

1462 Snyder, John I., Jr. 1962. "The Impact of Automation." *Challenge* (May):20–23.

1463 Soemardjan, Selo. 1957. "Bureaucratic Organization in a Time of Revolution." *Administrative Science Quarterly,* **2**:182–199.

1464 Sofer, C. 1963. *The Organization From Within.* Chicago: Quadrangle.

1465 Sofer, Cyril. 1955. "Reactions to Administrative Change: A Study of Staff Relations in Three British Hospitals." *Human Relations,* **8**:291–231.

1466 ———. 1970. *Men in Mid-Career.* Cambridge, Mass.: Harvard.

1467 Solomon, David N. 1960. "Professional Persons in Bureaucratic Organizations." *Public Aid in Illinois,* **27**:4–11.

1468 Solow, R. M. 1957. "Technological Change and the Aggregate Production Function." *Review of Economics and Statistics,* **39**:312–320.

1469 Sorensen, Robert C. 1951. "The Concept of Conflict in Industrial Sociology." *Social Forces,* **29**:263–267.

1470 Spaeth, Joel. 1968. "Occupational Prestige Expectations among Male College Graduates." *American Journal of Sociology,* **73**:548–558.

1471 ———. 1970. "Occupational Attainment among College Male Graduates." *American Journal of Sociology,* **75**:632–644.

1472 Spaulding, Charles B. 1961. *An Introduction to Industrial Sociology.* San Francisco: Chandler.

1473 Spencer, Herbert. 1882. *The Study of Sociology.* London: Routledge.

1474 ———. 1898. *Principles of Sociology,* Vol. I. New York: Appleton.

1475 Spencer, Martin A. 1970. "Weber on Legitimate Norms and Authority." *The British Journal of Sociology,* **21**:123–134.

1476   Spreitzer, Elmer A. 1971. "Organizational Goals and Patterns of Informal Organization." *Journal of Health and Social Behavior,* **12**:73–80.

1477   Stagner, Ross. 1950. "Psychological Aspects of Industrial Conflict: Motivation." *Personnel Psychology,* **3**:1–15.

1478   Stanton, Erwin S. 1960. "Company Policies and Supervisors' Attitudes toward Supervision." *Journal of Applied Psychology,* **44**:22–26.

1479   Starbuck, William H. 1965. "Organizational Growth and Development," in James G. March (ed.), *Handbook of Organizations.* Chicago: Rand McNally.

1480   ———. 1966. "The Efficiency of British and American Retail Employees." *Administrative Science Quarterly,* **11**:345–385.

1481   ———. 1968. "Some Comments, Observations and Objections Stimulated by 'Design of Proof in Organization Research.' " *Administrative Science Quarterly,* **13**:135–161.

1482   Steiber, J. 1958. "Automation and the White Collar Worker." *Personnel,* **34**:8–17.

1483   Steiner, Gary A. 1965. *The Creative Organization.* Chicago: The University of Chicago Press.

1484   Stewart, C. M. 1961. "Future Trends in the Employment of Married Women." *British Journal of Sociology,* **12**:1–11.

1485   Stewart, Donald D. 1951. "The Place of Volunteer Participation in a Bureaucratic Organization." *Social Forces,* **29**:311–317.

1486   Stewart, Michael. 1957. "Resistance to Technological Change in Industry." *Human Organization,* **16**:36–39.

1487   Stinchcombe, Arthur L. 1959. "Bureaucratic and Craft Administration of Production: A Comparative Study." *Administrative Science Quarterly,* **4**:168–187.

1488   ———. 1960. "The Sociology of Organization and the Theory of the Firm." *Pacific Sociological Review,* **3**:75–82.

1489   ——— et al. 1968. "Demography of Organizations." *American Journal of Sociology,* **74**:221–229.

1490   Stoddard, Ellwyn R. 1969. "Some Latent Consequences of Bureaucratic Efficiency in Disaster Relief." *Human Organization,* **28**:177–189.

1491   Stogdill, Ralph M. 1949. "The Sociometry of Working Relationships in Formal Organizations." *Sociometry,* **12**:75–82.

1492   ———. 1965. *Managers, Employees, and Organizations.* Columbus: Bureau of Business Research, Ohio State University.

1493   ———. 1971. "Dimensions of Organization Theory," in James D. Thompson and Victor Vroom (eds.), *Organizational Design and Research.* Pittsburgh: University of Pittsburgh Press.

1494   ——— and A. E. Coons. 1957. *Leadership Behavior: Its Description and Measurement.* Columbus: Bureau of Business Research, Ohio State University.

1495   Stone, Robert C. 1952a. "Conflicting Approaches to the Study of Worker-Management Relations." *Social Forces,* **31**:117–126.

1496   ———. 1952b. "Mobility Factors as They Affect Workers' Attitudes and Conduct toward Incentive Systems." *American Sociological Review,* **17**:58–64.

1497 ———. 1953. "Factory Organization and Vertical Mobility." *American Sociological Review,* **18**:28-35.

1498 Storing, Herbert J. 1962. "The Science of Administration: Herbert A. Simon," in Herbert J. Storing (ed.), *Essays on the Scientific Study of Politics.* New York: Holt.

1499 Strauss, George. 1954. "The Set-Up Man: A Case Study of Organizational Change." *Human Organization.* **13**:17-25.

1500 ———. 1957a. "The Changing Role of the Working Supervisor." *Journal of Business of the University of Chicago,* **30**:202-211.

1501 ———. 1957b. "The Scanlon Plan: Some Organizational Problems." *Human Organization,* **16**:15-23.

1502 ———. 1962. "Tactics of Lateral Relationship: The Purchasing Agent." *Administrative Science Quarterly,* **7**:161-186.

1503 ———. 1963. "Some Notes on Power Equalization," in H. Leavitt (ed.), *The Social Science of Organizations.* Englewood Cliffs, N.J.: Prentice-Hall.

1504 ———. 1968. "1968 Style Industrial Relations." *Human Relations,* **7**:262-272.

1505 ———. 1969. "Human Relations: 1968 Style." *Industrial Relations,* **7**:262-276.

1506 ——— and Alex Bavelas. 1955. "Group Dynamics and Intergroup Relations," in William F. Whyte, *Money and Motivation.* New York: Harper & Row.

1507 Street, D., R. D. Vinter, and C. Perrow. 1966. *Organization for Treatment.* New York: Free Press.

1508 Student, Kurt R. 1968. "Supervisory Influence and Work Group Performance." *Journal of Applied Psychology* **52**:188-194.

1509 Styler, W. E. 1953. "Manual Workers and the W. E. A." *British Journal of Sociology,* **4**:79-83.

1510 Stymne, Bengt. 1968. "Interdepartmental Communication and Intraorganizational Strain." *Acta Sociologica,* **11**:82-100.

1511 Sultan, Paul E. and Paul Prasow. 1965. *Automation: Some Classification and Measurement Problems.* Institute of Industrial Relations, Univ. of California, Los Angeles, Calif.

1512 Summer, Charles E. 1956. *Factors in Effective Administration.* New York: Graduate School of Business Administration, Columbia University.

1513 Suojanen, W. W. 1955. "The Span of Control: Fact or Fable?" *Advanced Management,* **20**:5-13.

1514 ———. 1957. "Leadership, Authority, and the Span of Control." *Advanced Management,* **22**:17-22.

1515 Susman, Gerald I. 1970. "The Concept of Status Congruence as a Basis to Predict Task Allocations in Autonomous Work Groups." *Administrative Science Quarterly,* **15**:164-175.

1516 Sutton, Willis, and D. C. Dubey. 1965. "A Rural Man in the Middle." *Human Organization,* **24**:148-158.

1517 Swanson, Guy E. 1971. "An Organizational Analysis of Collectivities." *American Sociological Review,* **36**:607-624.

1518 Sykes, A. J. M. 1960. "Trade Union Workshop Organization in the Printing Industry: The Chapel." *Human Relations,* **13**:49-65.

1519 ———. 1962. "The Effect of a Supervisory Training Course in Changing Supervisors' Perceptions and Expectations of the Role of Management." *Human Relations,* **15**:227-243.

1520 ———. 1964 "A Study of Changing the Attitudes and Stereotypes of Industrial Workers." *Human Relations,* **17**:143-154.

1521 ———. 1965 "Economic Interest and the Hawthorne Researchers: A Comment." *Human Relations,* **18**:253-263.

1522 ———. 1967. "The Cohesion of a Trade Union Workshop Organization." *Sociology,* **1**:141-163.

1523 ———. 1969a. "Navies: Their Social Relations." *Sociology,* **3**:21-35.

1524 ———. 1969b. "Navies: Their Work Attitudes." *Sociology,* **3**:157-172.

1525 Sykes, Gresham M. 1958. *The Society of Captives: A Study of Maximum Security Prisons.* Princeton, N.J.: Princeton University Press.

1526 Taeuber, Alma F., Karl E. Taeuber, and Glen Cain. 1966. "Occupational Assimilation and the Competitive Process." *American Journal of Sociology,* **72**:273-285.

1527 Tagiuri, Renato. 1965. "Value Orientations and the Relationship of Managers to Scientists." *Administrative Science Quarterly,* **10**:39-51.

1528 Talacchi, Sergio. 1960. "Organization Size, Individual Attitudes and Behavior: An Empirical Study." *Administrative Science Quarterly,* **5**:389-420.

1529 Tannenbaum, Arnold S. 1956. "The Concept of Organizational Control." *Journal of Social Issues,* **12**:50-60.

1530 ———. 1957a. "Personality Change as a Result of an Experimental Change of Environmental Conditions." *Journal of Abnormal and Social Psychology,* **52**:404-406.

1531 ———. 1957b. "The Application of Survey Techniques to the Study of Organizational Structure and Functioning." *Public Opinion Quarterly,* **21**:439-442.

1532 ———. 1961a. "Adaptability of Older Workers to Technological Change: Performance in Retraining." Paper presented to the International Congress of Applied Psychology, Copenhagen.

1533 ———. 1961b. "Control and Effectiveness in a Voluntary Organization." *American Journal of Sociology,* **67**:33-46.

1534 ———. 1962a. "Control in Organizations: Individual Adjustment and Organizational Performance." *Administrative Science Quarterly,* **7**:236-257.

1535 ———. 1962b. "Reactions of Members of Voluntary Groups: A Logarithmic Function of Size of Group." *Psychological Reports,* **10**:113-114.

1536 ———. 1966a. *Social Psychology of the Work Organization.* Belmont, Calif.: Wadsworth.

1537 ———. 1966b. "Organizational Theory and Organizational Practice." *Management International Review,* **5**:121-135.

1538 ———. 1966c. "The Control-Satisfaction Relationship Across Varied Areas of Experience." *Delta Pi Epsilon Journal,* **8**:16-25.

1539 ———. 1968. *Control in Organizations.* New York: McGraw-Hill.

1540 —— and Jerald G. Bachman. 1964. "Structural vs. Individual Effects." *American Journal of Sociology,* **69**:585-595.
1541 —— and ——. 1966. "Attitude Uniformity and Role in a Voluntary Organization." *Human Relations,* **19**:309-322.
1542 —— and B. S. Georgopoulos. 1957. "The Distribution of Control in Formal Organizations." *Social Forces,* **36**:44-50.
1543 —— and Robert L. Kahn. 1957. "Organization Control Structure." *Human Relations,* **10**:127-140.
1544 —— and Clagett G. Smith. 1964. "The Effects of Member Influence in an Organization: Phenomenology Versus Organization Structure." *Journal of Abnormal and Social Psychology,* **69**:401-410.
1545 Tannenbaum, Robert, Irving R. Weschler, and Fred Masserik. 1961. *Leadership and Organization: A Behavioral Science Approach.* New York: McGraw-Hill.
1546 Taub, Richard P. 1969. *Bureaucrats Under Stress.* Berkeley: University of California Press.
1547 Tausky, Curt. 1969. "Meanings of Work Among Blue Collar Men." *Pacific Sociological Review,* **12**:49-55.
1548 ——. 1970. *Work Organizations: Major Theoretical Perspectives.* Itasca, Ill.: F. E. Peacock.
1549 —— and Eugene B. Piedmont. 1968. "The Meaning of Work and Unemployment: Implications for Mental Health." *International Journal of Social Psychiatry,* **14**:44-49.
1550 Taylor, F. W. 1911. *The Principles of Scientific Management.* New York: Harper.
1551 Taylor, James C. 1971a. "Some Effects of Technology in Organizational Change." *Human Relations,* **24**:105-123.
1552 ——. 1971b. *Technology and Planned Organizational Change.* Ann Arbor, Mich.: Institute for Social Research.
1553 —— and David G. Bowers. 1972. *Survey of Organizations.* Ann Arbor, Mich.: Institute for Social Research.
1554 Telly, Charles S., W. L. French, and W. G. Scott. 1971. "The Relationship of Inequity to Turnover among Hourly Workers." *Administrative Science Quarterly,* **16**:164-172.
1555 Terborgh, George W. 1966. *The Automation Hysteria.* New York: Norton.
1556 Terreberry, Shirley. 1968. "Evolution of Organizational Environments." *Administrative Science Quarterly,* **12**:590-613.
1557 Terrien, Frederic. 1959. "Too Much Room at the Top?" *Social Forces,* **37**:298-305.
1558 —— and Donald Mills. 1955. "The Effect of Changing Size on the Internal Structure of Organizations." *American Sociological Review,* **20**:11-13.
1559 Thomas, Edwin J. 1959. "Role Conception and Organization Size." *American Sociological Review,* **24**:30-37.
1560 Thomas, R. Murray. 1962. "Reinspecting a Structural Position on Occupational Prestige." *American Journal of Sociology,* **67**:561-565.

1561 Thomas, W. I. 1923. *The Unadjusted Girl.* Boston: Little, Brown.
1562 Thompson, James D. (ed.). 1956. "Authority and Power in Identical Organizations." *American Journal of Sociology,* **62**:290-301.
1563 ———. 1967. *Organizations in Action.* New York: McGraw-Hill.
1564 ——— (ed.). 1971. *Approaches to Organizational Design.* Pittsburgh: University of Pittsburgh Press.
1565 ——— and F. L. Bates. 1957. "Technology, Organization, and Administration." *Administrative Science Quarterly,* **2**:325-343.
1566 ——— and W. J. McEwen. 1958. "Organizational Goals and Environment: Goal Setting as an Interaction Process." *American Sociological Review,* **23**:23-31.
1567 ——— and Arthur Tuden. 1959. "Strategies, Structures, and Processes of Organizational Decision," in James D. Thompson (ed.). *Comparative Studies in Administration.* Pittsburgh: University of Pittsburgh Press.
1568 Thompson, John W. 1963. "The Importance of Opposites in Human Relationships." *Human Relations,* **16**:161-169.
1569 Thompson, Victor A. 1961a. "Hierarchy, Specialization, and Organizational Conflict." *Administrative Science Quarterly,* **5**:485-521.
1570 ———. 1961b. *Modern Organization.* New York: Knopf.
1571 ———. 1962. "Organizations and Output Transactions." *American Journal of Sociology,* **68**:309-324.
1572 ———. 1965. "Bureaucracy and Innovation." *Administrative Science Quarterly,* **10**:1-20.
1573 ———. 1969. *Bureaucracy and Innovation.* University: University of Alabama Press.
1574 Thornton, Russell. 1970. "Organizational Involvement and Commitment to Organization and Profession." *Administrative Science Quarterly,* **15**:417-427.
1575 Timperley, S. R. 1970. "A Study of Self-Governing Work Groups." *Sociological Review,* **18**:259-281.
1576 Tolstoi, Leo N. (ed.), 1928. "The Tsar and the Elephants," in M. Komroff (ed.), *The Great Fables of all Nations.* New York: Tudor Publishing Company.
1577 Tosi, H., and H. Patt. 1967. "Administrative Ratios and Organizational Size." *Academy of Management Journal,* **10**:161-168.
1578 Touraine, Alain, et al. 1965. *Workers' Attitudes to Technical Change: An Integrated Survey of Research.* Paris: Organization for Economic Cooperation and Development.
1579 Trahair, Richard C. S. 1968. "The Workers' Judgment of Their Job as a Variable in Work Role Analysis." *Human Relations,* **21**:141-162.
1580 Treiman, Donald J. 1970. "Industrialization and Social Stratification." *Sociological Inquiry,* **40**:207-234.
1581 Triandis, Harry C. 1958. "Attitude Change through Training in Industry." *Human Organization,* **17**:27-30.
1582 ———. 1959. "Differential Perceptions of Certain Jobs and People by Managers, Clerks, and Workers in Industry." *Journal of Applied Psychology,* **43**:221-225.

1583 ——— 1967. "Interpersonal Relations and International Organization." *Organizational Behavior and Human Performance,* **2**:26-55.

1584 ———. 1971. "Notes on the Design of Organizations," in J. D. Thompson (ed.), *Approaches to Organizational Design.* Pittsburgh: University of Pittsburgh Press.

1585 Trice, Harrison M., et al. 1969. "The Role of Ceremonials in Organizational Behavior." *Industrial and Labor Relations Review,* **23**:40-51.

1586 Trist, E. L., and E. K. Bamforth. 1951. "Some Social and Psychological Consequences of the Longwall Method of Coal-Getting." *Human Relations,* **4**:3-38.

1587 ——— et al. 1963. *Organizational Choice.* London: Tavistock Publications.

1588 Troxell, J. P. 1954. "Elements of Job Satisfaction." *Personnel,* **31**:199-205.

1589 Trumbo, Donald A. 1961. "Individual and Group Correlates of Attitudes toward Work-Related Change." *Journal of Applied Psychology,* **45**:338-344.

1590 Tsouderos, John. 1955. "Organizational Change in Terms of a Series of Selected Variables." *American Sociological Review,* **20**:206-210.

1591 Tudor, Bill. 1972. "A Specification of Relationships between Job Complexity and Powerlessness." *American Sociological Review,* **37**:596-604.

1592 Tullock, Gordon. 1965. *The Politics of Bureaucracy.* Washington, D.C.: The Public Affairs Press.

1593 Turk, Herman. 1970. "The Interorganizational Networks in Urban Society: Initial Perspectives and Comparative Research." *American Sociological Review,* **35**:1-9.

1594 Turner, Arnold. 1961. "What is Feedback?" in Robert F. Weeks et al. (eds.), *Machines and the Man: A Sourcebook on Automation.* New York: Appleton-Century-Crofts.

1595 Turner, Arthur N. 1955. "Interaction and Sentiment in the Foreman-Worker Relationship." *Human Organization,* **14**:10-16.

1596 ———. 1957. "Foreman, Job, and Company." *Human Relations,* **10**:99-112.

1597 Turner, Ralph H. 1947. "The Navy Disbursing Officer as a Bureaucrat." *American Sociological Review,* **12**:342-348.

1598 ———. 1964. "Some Aspects of Women's Ambition." *American Journal of Sociology,* **70**:271-285.

1599 Udell, Jon G. 1967. "Empirical Test of Hypotheses Relating to Span of Control." *Administrative Science Quarterly,* **12**:420-439.

1600 Udy, Stanley H., Jr. 1958. "Bureaucratic Elements in Organizations: Some Research Findings." *American Sociological Review,* **23**:415-418.

1601 ———. 1959a. "Bureaucracy and Rationality in Weber's Theory." *American Sociological Review,* **24**:761-765.

1602 ———. 1959b. *Organization of Work: A Comparative Analysis of Production among Non-Industrial Peoples.* New Haven, Conn.: HRAF Press.

1603 ———. 1959c. "The Structure of Authority in Nonindustrial Production Organizations." *American Journal of Sociology,* **64**:582-584.

1604 ———. 1961. "Technical and Institutional Factors in Production Organization: A Preliminary Model." *American Journal of Sociology,* **67**:247-260.

1605 ———. 1962. "Administrative Rationality. Social Setting, and Organizational Development." *American Journal of Sociology,* **68**:299–308.

1606 ———. 1965a. "Dynamic Inferences from Static Data." *American Journal of Sociology,* **70**:625–628.

1607 ———. 1965b. "The Comparative Analysis of Organizations," in James G. March (ed.), *Handbook of Organizations.* Chicago: Rand McNally.

1608 ———. 1970. *Work in Traditional and Modern Society.* Englewood Cliffs, N.J.: Prentice-Hall.

1609 Ullman, Leonard P. 1967. *Institution and Outcome: A Comparative Study of Psychiatric Hospitals.* Elmsford, N.Y.: Pergamon.

1610 U.S. Civil Service Commission, Bureau of Programs and Standards. 1958. *Personnel Impact of Automation in the Federal Service.* Washington, D.C.: U.S. Government Printing Office.

1611 U.S. Congress. 1960. *Office Automation and Employee Job Security.* Hearings before the Subcommittee on Census and Government Statistics of the Committee on Post Office and Civil Service, House of Representatives, 86th Congress. Washington, D.C.: U.S. Government Printing Office.

1612 U.S. Department of Labor, Bureau of Labor Statistics. 1962. *Employer Attitudes toward Advance Notice of Technological Change.* Washington, D.C.: U.S. Government Printing Office.

1613 ———. 1963. *Work Force Adjustments to Technological Change: Selected Employer Procedures,* No. E-215. Washington, D.C.: U.S. Government Printing Office.

1614 ———. 1960. *Adjustments to the Introduction of Office Automation,* Report No. 137. Washington, D.C.: U.S. Government Printing Office.

1615 ———. 1963. *Impact of Office Automation in the Internal Revenue Service,* Bulletin No. 1364. Washington, D.C.: U.S. Government Printing Office.

1616 ———. 1962. *Impact of Technological Change and Automation in the Pulp and Paper Industry,* Bulletin No. 1347. Washington, D.C.: U.S. Government Printing Office.

1617 ———. 1965. *Manpower Planning to Adapt to New Technology of Electric and Gas Utility,* Report No. 293. Washington, D.C.: U.S. Government Printing Office.

1618 ———. 1957. *A Case Study of a Modernized Petroleum Refinery,* Report No. 120. Washington, D.C.: U.S. Government Printing Office.

1619 ———. 1958. *A Case Study of an Automatic Airline Reservation System.* Washington, D.C.: U.S. Government Printing Office.

1620 ———. 1960. *Impact of Automation,* Bulletin No. 1287. Washington, D.C.: U.S. Government Printing Office.

1621 ———. 1963. *Industrial Retraining Programs for Technological Change,* Bulletin No. 1368. Washington, D.C.: U.S. Government Printing Office.

1622 ———. 1964. *Experiences of Workers after Layoff,* Bulletin No. 1408. Washington, D.C.: U.S. Government Printing Office.

5555

1623 U.S. Department of Labor, Office of Manpower, Automation and Training. 1963. *Automatic Data Processing in the Federal Government: Its Manpower Requirements,* Report No. 6. Washington, D.C.: U.S. Government Printing Office.

1624 ———. 1964. *Productivity, Changing Technology, and Employment: A Report to the President.* Washington, D.C.: U.S. Government Printing Office.

1625 ———. 1962. *Automation, Productivity, and Manpower Problems.* Washington, D.C.: U.S. Government Printing Office.

1626 ———. 1963. *Manpower and Training: Trends, Outlook, and Programs,* Research Bulletin No. 2. Washington, D.C.: U.S. Government Printing Office.

1627 ———. 1963. *Manpower Report to the President and a Report on Manpower Requirements, Utilization, Resources, and Training.* Transmitted to Congress March, 1963. Washington, D.C.: U.S. Government Printing Office.

1628 U.S. Department of Labor, Women's Bureau. 1963. *Women Telephone Workers and Changing Technology,* Bulletin No. 286. Washington, D.C.: U.S. Government Printing Office.

1629 Urwick, Lyndall F. 1943. *The Elements of Administration.* New York: Harper.

1630 ———. 1956. "The Manager's Span of Control." *Harvard Business Review,* **34**:39-47.

1631 ——— and Edward Brech. 1948. *The Making of Scientific Management,* Vol. III. London: Management Publications Trust.

1632 Uyeki, Eugene. 1964. "Organizational Behavior and Preventive Intervention." *Human Organization,* **23**:11-15.

1633 Vander Zaden, J. W. 1959. "Resistance and Social Change." *Social Forces,* **37**:312-315.

1634 Van de Vall, Mark. 1970. *Labor Organizations: A Macro- and Micro-Sociological Analysis on a Comparative Basis.* London: Cambridge University Press.

1635 Vincent, M. J., and J. Mayers. 1959. *New Foundations for Industrial Sociology.* Princeton, N.J.: Van Nostrand.

1636 Viteles, Morris S. 1953. *Motivation and Morale in Industry.* New York: Norton.

1637 ———. 1954. *Motivation and Morale in Industry.* London: Staples.

1638 Vollmer, Howard M. 1960. *Employee Rights and the Employment Relationship.* Berkeley: University of California Press.

1639 ———. 1965. "Some Comments on 'The Professionalization of Everyone?' " *American Journal of Sociology,* **70**:480-481.

1640 ———. 1966. *Professionalization.* Englewood Cliffs, N.J.: Prentice-Hall.

1641 ——— and Donald L. Mills. 1962. "Nuclear Technology and the Professionalization of Labor." *American Journal of Sociology,* **67**:690-696.

1642 Vroom, Victor H. 1959. "Some Personality Determinants of the Effects of Participation." *Journal of Abnormal and Social Psychology,* **59**:322-327.

1643 ———. 1960a. "Employee Attitudes," in R. Gray (ed.), *The Expanding Frontiers of Industrial Relations.* Pasadena, Calif.: California Institute of Technology.

1644 ———. 1960b. *Some Personality Determinants of the Effects of Participation.* Englewood Cliffs, N.J.: Prentice-Hall.

1645 ———. 1960c. "The Effects of Attitudes on Perception of Organizational Goals." *Human Relations,* **13**:229-240.

1646 ———. 1964. *Work and Motivation.* New York: Wiley.

1647 ———. 1966. "A Comparison of Static and Dynamic Correlational Methods in the Study of Organizations." *Journal of Organizational Behavior and Human Performance,* **1**:55-70.

1648 ———. 1967. *Methods of Organizational Research.* Pittsburgh: University of Pittsburgh Press.

1649 ——— and R. F. Maier. 1961. "Industrial Social Psychology." *Annual Review of Psychology,* **12**:413-446.

1650 ——— and Floyd C. Mann. 1960. "Leader Authoritarianism and Employee Attitudes." *Personnel Psychology,* **13**:125-140.

1651 Wade, L. L. 1967. "Professionals in Organizations: A Neoteric Model." *Human Organization,* **26**:40-46.

1652 Wager, Wesley, and E. G. Palola. 1964. "The Miniature Replica Model and Its Use in Laboratory Experiments of Complex Organizations." *Social Forces,* **42**:418-429.

1653 ———. 1965. "Leadership Style, Hierarchical Influence, and Supervisory Role Obligations." *Administrative Science Quarterly,* **9**:391-420.

1654 ———. 1971. "The Expansion of Organizational Authority and Conditions Affecting Its Denial." *Sociometry,* **34**:91-113.

1655 Waldo, Dwight. 1968. *The Novelist on Organization and Administration.* Berkeley: Institute of Governmental Studies, University of California.

1656 Walker, Charles R. 1950. "The Problem of the Repetitive Job." *Harvard Business Review,* **28**:54-58.

1657 ———. 1957. *Toward the Automatic Factory: A Case Study of Men and Machines.* New Haven, Conn.: Yale University Press.

1658 ———. 1958. "Life in the Automatic Factory: A Case Study of Men and Machines." *Harvard Business Review,* **36**:111-119.

1659 ——— and R. H. Guest. 1952. *The Man on the Assembly Line.* Cambridge, Mass.: Harvard.

1660 ——— and ———. 1956. *The Foreman on the Assembly Line.* Cambridge, Mass.: Harvard.

1661 ——— and Adelaide G. Walker (eds.). 1962. *Modern Technology and Civilization: An Introduction to Human Problems in the Machine Age.* New York: McGraw-Hill.

1662 Walker, K. F., and J. Lumsden. 1963. "Employees, Job Satisfaction, and Attitudes: A Survey." *Business Review* (March):20-24.

1663 Wallace, Michael D., and David J. Singer. 1970. "Intergovernmental Organization in the Global System: 1815-1964: A Quantitative Description." *International Organization,* **24**:239-287.

1664 Walter, Benjamin. 1966. "Internal Control Relations in Administrative Hierarchies." *Administrative Science Quarterly,* **11**:179-206.

1665   ———. 1969. "On Sampling, Measures and Aggregations." *Administrative Science Quarterly,* **14**:131–133.

1666   Walton, Clarence C. 1967. *Corporate Social Responsibility.* Belmont, Calif.: Wadsworth.

1667   Walton, Richard E., and John N. Dutton. 1969. "The Management of Inter-department Conflict: A Model and Review." *Administrative Science Quarterly,* **14**:73–90.

1668   ———, ———, and Thomas P. Cafferty. 1969. "Organizational Context and Interdepartmental Conflict." *Administrative Science Quarterly,* **14**:522–543.

1669   Ward, David A., and Gene G. Kassebaum. 1965. *Women's Prison: Sex and Social Structure.* Chicago: Aldine.

1670   Ward, J. T. 1970. *The Factory System.* New York: Barnes & Noble.

1671   Wardwell, Walter I. 1955. "Social Integration, Bureaucratization, and the Professions." *Social Forces,* **33**:356–359.

1672   Warner, Malcolm. 1971. "Organizational Context and Control of Policy in the Television Newsroom." *British Journal of Sociology,* **22**:283–294.

1673   Warner, W. Keith, and Eugene A. Havens. 1967. "Goal Displacement and the Intangibility of Organizational Goals." *Administrative Science Quarterly,* **12**:539–555.

1674   ——— and Sidney Miller. 1964. "Organizational Problems in Two Types of Voluntary Associations." *American Journal of Sociology,* **74**:654–657.

1675   Warner, W. Lloyd, et al. (eds.). 1967. *The Emergent American Society: Large-Scale Organizations.* New Haven, Conn.: Yale University Press.

1676   Warren, Donald I. 1966. "Social Relations of Peers in a Formal Organization Setting." *Administrative Science Quarterly,* **11**:440–478.

1677   ———. 1968. "Power, Visibility, and Conformity in Formal Organizations." *American Sociological Review,* **33**:951–970.

1678   ———. 1969. "The Effects of Power Bases and Peer Groups on Conformity in Formal Organizations." *Administrative Science Quarterly,* **14**:544–557.

1679   Warren, Roland L. 1967. "The Intraorganizational Field as a Focus for Investigation." *Administrative Science Quarterly,* **12**:369–419.

1680   Warriner, Charles K. 1965. "The Problem of Organizational Purpose." *Sociological Quarterly,* **6**:139–146.

1681   Watson, Goodwin. 1966. *Social Psychology: Issues and Insights.* New York: Lippincott.

1682   Webb, E. J., et al. 1966. *Unobtrusive Measures: Nonreactive Research in the Social Sciences.* Chicago: Rand McNally.

1683   Weber, C. E. 1959. "Impact of Electronic Data Processing on Clerical Skills." *Personnel Administration,* **22**:20–27.

1684   Weber, C. I. 1959. "Change in Managerial Manpower with Mechanization of Data Processing." *Journal of Business,* **32**:151–163.

1684a Weber, Max. 1946. "Bureaucracy" in H. H. Gerth and C. Wright Mills (eds.), *From Max Weber: Essays in Sociology.* New York: Oxford University Press. Press.

1685   Weber, Max. 1947. *The Theory of Social and Economic Organization.* New York: Oxford University Press.

1686 Weeks, Robert. 1961. *Machines and the Man.* New York: Appleton-Century-Crofts.

1687 Weick, Karl E. 1969. "Laboratory Organizations and Unnoticed Causes." *Administrative Science Quarterly,* **14**:294–304.

1688 Weinberg, E. 1960. "Experiences with the Introduction of Office Automation." *Monthly Labor Review,* **83**:376–380.

1689 ———. 1962. *The Effects of Technology on Employment of the Handicapped.* Paper presented before the Mountain States Regional Meeting before the President's Committee on Employment of the Handicapped, Pueblo, Colorado.

1690 Weintraub, D., and F. Bernstein. 1966. "Social Structure and Modernization: A Comparative Study of Two Villages." *American Journal of Sociology,* **71**:509–521.

1691 Weiss, Edward C. 1957. "Relation of Personnel Statistics to Organizational Structure." *Personnel Psychology,* **10**:27–42.

1692 Weiss, Robert S. 1956. *Processes of Organization.* Ann Arbor, Mich.: Institute for Social Research.

1693 ——— and E. Jacobson. 1955. "A Method for the Analysis of the Structure of Complex Organizations." *American Sociological Review,* **20**:661–668.

1694 ——— and Robert L. Kahn. 1960. "Definitions of Work and Occupation." *Social Problems,* **8**:142–151.

1695 Weissenberg, Peter. 1971. *Introduction to Organizational Behavior.* Scranton, Pa.: The International Textbook Company.

1696 Weldon, Peter D. 1972. "An Examination of the Blau-Scott and Etzioni Typologies: A Critique." *Administrative Science Quarterly,* **17**:76–78.

1697 Wells, W. D., and G. Smith. 1960. "Four Semantic Rating Scales Compared." *Journal of Applied Psychology,* **44**:393–397.

1698 Wernimont, P. F. 1966. "Intrinsic and Extrinsic Factors in Job Satisfaction." *Journal of Applied Psychology,* **50**:41–50.

1699 Westby, David L. 1966. "A Typology of Authority in Complex Organizations." *Social Forces,* **44**:484–491.

1700 Whisler, Thomas L. 1964. "Measuring Centralization of Control in Business Organizations," in W. W. Cooper et al. (eds.), *New Perspectives in Organization Research.* New York: Wiley.

1701 ———. 1970. *Information Technology and Organization Change.* Belmont, Calif.: Wadsworth.

1702 White, Harrison. 1966. "Management Conflict and Sociometric Structure." *American Journal of Sociology,* **67**:185–199.

1703 White, R. K., and R. Lippitt. 1960. *Autocracy and Democracy.* New York: Harper.

1704 Whyte, William Foote. 1948. *Human Relations in the Restaurant Industry.* New York: McGraw-Hill.

1705 ———. 1949. "The Social Structure of the Restaurant." *American Journal of Sociology,* **54**:302–310.

1706 ———. 1955. *Money and Motivation.* New York: Harper.

1707 ———. 1956. "Human Relations Theory: A Progress Report." *Harvard Business Review,* **34**:125-132.

1708 ———. 1959. *Man and Organization: Three Problems in Human Relations in Industry.* Homewood, Ill.: Irwin.

1709 ———. 1965. "A Field in Search of a Focus." *Industrial and Labor Relations Review,* **18**:305-322.

1710 ———. 1967. "Models for Building and Changing Organization." *Human Organization,* **26**:22-31.

1711 ———. 1969. *Organization Behavior: Theory and Application.* Homewood, Ill.: Dorsey-Irwin.

1712 Whyte, William H., Jr. 1957. *Organization Man.* New York: Doubleday.

1713 Wiebe, G. D. 1961. "A Strategy for Social Psychological Research on Technological Innovation." *Journal of Social Issues,* **27**:56-64.

1714 Wieland, George F. 1969. "The Determinants of Clarity in Organizational Goals." *Human Relations,* **22**:161-172.

1715 ———. 1970. "Note on Interdependent Contacts and Coordination in Organizations." *Psychological Reports,* **27**:747-751.

1716 Wilensky, Harold L. 1957. "Human Relations in the Workplace," in C. Arensberg et al. (eds.), *Research in Industrial Human Relations: A Critical Appraisal.* New York: Harper.

1717 ———. 1964. "The Professionalization of Everyone?" *American Journal of Sociology,* **70**:137-158.

1718 ——— and Charles N. Lebeaux. 1965. *Industrial Society and Social Welfare.* New York: Free Press.

1719 ———. 1967. *Organizational Intelligence.* New York: Basic Books.

1720 Wilken, Paul H. 1971. "Size of Organizations and Member Participation in Church Congregations." *Administrative Science Quarterly,* **16**:173-179.

1721 Willerman, B. 1952. "Motivating Workers for Productivity." *Modern Industry,* **23**:65-68.

1722 Williams, B., and H. J. Leavitt.1947. "Group Opinion as a Predictor of Military Leadership." *Journal of Consulting Psychology,* **11**:283-291.

1723 Williams, D. C. S. 1956. "Effects of Competition between Groups in a Training Situation." *Occupational Psychology,* **30**:85-93.

1724 Williams, Lawrence K., L. R. Hoffman, and F. C. Mann. 1959. "An Investigation of the Control Graph: Influence in a Staff Organization." *Social Forces,* **37**:189-195.

1725 ———, William F. Whyte, and Charles S. Green. 1966. "Do Cultural Differences Affect Workers' Attitudes?" *Industrial Relations,* **5**:105-116.

1726 Williams, Virgil. 1965. "Leadership Types, Role Differentiation." *Social Forces,* **45**:380-389.

1727 Willmott, P. 1956. "Social Grading by Manual Workers." *British Journal of Sociology,* **7**:337-345.

1728 Wilson, G. W. 1958. "Technological Change and Unemployment." *Current Economic Comment,* **20**:47-54.

1729   Wilson, Robert C., H. P. Beem, and A. L. Comrey. 1953. "Factors Influencing
       Organizational Effectiveness: A Survey of Skilled Tradesmen." *Personnel Psy-
       chology,* **6**:313-325.
1730   Winthrop, H. 1958. "Some Psychological and Economic Assumptions Under-
       lying Automation." *American Journal of Economics and Sociology,*
       17:399-412.
1731   ———. 1959. "Automation: And the Future of Personnel and Industrial Psy-
       chology." *Personnel and Guidance Journal,* **37**:326-333.
1732   Wofford, J. C. 1971. "Managerial Behavior, Situational Factors, and Produc-
       tivity and Morale." *Administrative Science Quarterly,* **16**:10-18.
1733   Wolcott, Harry F. 1970. "An Ethnographic Approach to the Study of School
       Administrators." *Human Organization,* **29**:115-122.
1734   Wolfbein, Seymour L. 1961. "Automation and the Labor Force." *Challenge*
       (October):24-28.
1735   ———. 1962. "Automation and Skill." *Annals of the American Academy of
       Political and Social Science* (March):53-59.
1736   ——— (ed.). 1970. *Emerging Sectors of Collective Bargaining.* Braintree,
       Mass.: D. H. Mark Publishing Company.
1737   Wolin, Sheldon S. 1960. "A Critique of Organizational Theories." *Politics and
       Vision: Continuity and Innovation in Western Political Thought.* Boston: Little,
       Brown.
1738   Won, George and D. Yamamura. 1968. "Career Orientation of Local Union
       Leadership: A Case Study." *Sociology and Social Research,* **52**:243-252.
1739   Wood, James R., and Eugene A. Weinstein. 1966. "Industrialization, Values
       and Occupational Evaluation in Uruguay." *American Journal of Sociology,*
       72:146-157.
1740   ——— and Mayer N. Zald. 1966. "Aspects of Racial Integration in the Meth-
       odist Church: Sources of Resistance to Organizational Policy." *Social Forces,*
       45:255-265.
1741   Woodward, Joan. 1965. *Industrial Organization: Theory and Practice.* London:
       Oxford University Press.
1742   Worsnop, Richard L. 1962. "Shorter Hours of Work." *Editorial Research Re-
       ports* (June):419-435.
1743   Worthy, James. 1950. "Organizational Structure and Employee Morale."
       American Sociological Review, **15**:169-179.
1744   Wray, Donald E. 1949. "Marginal Men of Industry: The Foremen." *Ameri-
       can Journal of Sociology,* **54**:298-301.
1745   Wright, Charles R. 1967. "Changes in Occupational Commitment of Gradu-
       ate Sociology Students: A Research Note." *Sociological Inquiry,* **37**:55-62.
1746   Wright, Q. 1951. "The Nature of Conflict." *Western Political Quarterly,*
       4:193-209.
1747   Wyatt, S. F., and J. M. Langdon. 1937. "Fatigue and Boredom in Repetitive
       Work." *Industrial Health Research Board Report,* **77**:43-46.
1748   Wyatt, S., and R. Marriott. 1961. *A Study of Attitudes to Factory Work.* Lon-
       don: Tavistock Publications.

1748a ———. 1965. "The Study of Work Organization and Supervisory Behavior."*Human Organization,* **23**:245-253.

1749 Yanouzas, John. 1969. A Comparative Study of Work Organization and Supervisory Behavior." *Human Organization,* **27**:245-253.

1750 Young, Ruth C., and Olaf F. Larson. 1965. "The Contribution of Voluntary Organizations to Community Structure." *American Journal of Sociology,* **71**:178-186.

1751 Yuchtman, Ephraim, and Stanley Seashore. 1967. "A System Resource Approach to Organizational Effectiveness." *American Sociological Review,* **32**:891-903.

1752 Zajonc, Robert, and Donald M. Wolfe. 1966. "Cognitive Consequences of a Person's Position in a Formal Organization." *Human Relations,* **19**:139-150.

1753 Zald, Mayer N. 1960. "The Correctional Institution for Juvenile Offenders: An Analysis of Organizational 'Character.' " *Social Problems,* **8**:57-67.

1754 ———. 1962. "Power Balance and Staff Conflict in Correctional Institutions." *Administrative Science Quarterly,* **7**:22-49.

1755 ———. 1963a. "Comparative Analysis of Measurement of Organizational Goals: The Case of Correctional Institutions for Delinquents." *Sociological Quarterly,* **4**:206-230.

1756 ———. 1963b. "Organizational Control Structures in Five Correctional Institutions." *American Journal of Sociology,* **68**:335-345.

1757 ———. 1965. "Who Shall Rule? A Political Analysis of Succession in a Large Welfare Organization." *Pacific Sociological Review,* **8**:52-60.

1758 ———. 1967. "Urban Differentiation, Characteristics of Boards of Directors, and Organizational Effectiveness." *American Journal of Sociology,* **73**:261-272._

1759 ——— (ed.). 1968a. *Power in Organizations.* Nashville, Tenn.: Vanderbilt.

1760 ———. 1969b. "The Structure of Society and Social Service Integration." *Social Science Quarterly,* **50**:557-567.

1761 ———. 1969c. "The Power and Functions of Boards of Directors: A Theoretical Synthesis." *American Journal of Sociology,* **75**:97-111.

1762 ——— and Roberta Ash. 1966. "Social Movement Organizations: Growth, Decay, and Change." *Social Forces,* **46**:327-341.

1763 ——— and Patricia Denton. 1963. "From Evangelism to General Service: The Transformation of the YMCA." *Administrative Science Quarterly,* **8**:214-234.

1764 Zaleznik, Abraham. 1958. *A Case Study of Work and Social Behavior in a Factory Group.* Boston: Graduate School of Business Administration, Harvard University.

1765 ———. 1965. "Interpersonal Relations in Organizations," in James G. March (ed.), *Handbook of Organizations.* Chicago: Rand McNally.

1766 ——— et al. 1958. *Motivation, Productivity, and Satisfaction of Workers.* Boston: Graduate School of Business Administration, Harvard University.

1767 Zalkind, Sheldon, and T. W. Costello. 1962. "Perceptions: Some Recent Research and Implications for Administration." *Administrative Science Quarterly,* **7**:218-235.

1768   Zand, Dale E., Fred I. Steele, and S. S. Zalkind. 1969. "The Impact of an Organizational Development Program on Perceptions of Interpersonal, Group, and Organizational Functioning." *Journal of Applied Behavioral Science,* **5**:393–410.

1769   Zander, Alvin. 1961. "The Nature and Consequences of Leadership." *Michigan Business Review,* **13**:29–32.

1770   ―――― et al. 1957. *Role Relations in the Mental Health Professions.* Ann Arbor, Mich.: Institute for Social Research.

1771   ――――, A. R. Cohen, and E. Scotland. 1959. "Power and the Relations among Professions," in D. Cartwright (ed.), *Studies in Social Power.* Ann Arbor, Mich.: Research Center for Group Dynamics.

1772   ―――― and Herman M. Medow. 1963. "Individual and Group Levels of Aspiration." *Human Relations,* **16**:89–105.

1773   ――――, ――――, and Ronald Efron. 1965. "Observers' Expectations as Determinants of Group Aspirations." *Human Relations,* **18**:273–287.

1774   ―――― and Donald M. Wolfe. 1964. "Administrative Rewards and Coordination among Committee Members." *Administrative Science Quarterly,* **9**:50–69.

1775   Zeitlin, Maurice. 1970. *American Society, Inc.* Chicago: Markham Publishing Company.

1776   Ziller, Robert C. 1964. "Individuation and Socialization: A Theory of Assimilation in Large Organizations." *Human Relations,* **17**:341–360.

1777   Zurcher, Louis. 1968. "Social Psychological Functions of Ephemeral Roles: A Disaster Work Crew." *Human Organization,* **27**:281–297.

1778   Zwerman, William L. 1970. *New Perspectives on Organizational Theory: An Empirical Reconsideration of the Classical and Marxian Analyses.* Minneapolis: Greenwood Publishing Company.

Name Index

Haas, Eugene J., 65-69, 76, 86, 88, 330, 341-343
Habens, A. Eugene, 342
Habenstein, Robert, 342
Haberstroh, Chadwick J., 14, 22, 27, 372
Haddy, Pamela, 342
Hagburg, Eugene C., 342
Hage, Jerald, 42, 98, 311, 342, 360
Hagedorn, Robert, 82, 352
Hagstrom, Warren, 342
Haimann, Theo, 342
Haire, Mason, 101, 313, 342
Hakel, Milton D., 331
Hall, Douglas T., 342
Hall, John W., 343
Hall, Oswald, 343
Hall, Richard H., 2, 27, 60, 65-69, 76, 86-88, 90, 319, 341-343
Haller, Archibald O., 343
Halpern, Richard S., 343
Halpin, A. W., 343
Hamblin, Robert L., 130, 170, 329
Hamilton, Richard F., 343
Hammond, Phillip E., 343
Hampton, David R., 343
Harburg, E. P., 378
Harder, D. S., 250
Hardin, Einar, 279, 344
Harper, Dean, 216, 344
Harris, E. F., 49, 111-112, 334-335
Hart, D. J., 344
Hartley, E. L., 355
Hartmann, Heinz, 344
Harvey, E., 101-102, 344
Harvey, O. J., 344
Hasenfeld, Yeheskel, 344
Haslin, Charles L., 319
Hatt, Paul K., 339
Hauser, Philip M., 344
Havelock, Mary C., 344
Havelock, Ronald G., 344

Havens, Eugene A., 389
Hawley, Amos, 344
Hawley, George, 344
Hayes, S. P., 375
Heady, Ferrel, 344
Healy, R. H., 355
Hearle, Edward, 344
Hegland, Tore, 344
Hemphill, J. K., 167, 344
Hendershot, Gerry E., 344
Henry, Jules, 345
Herb, Terry, 345
Hermann, Charles F., 345
Hershey, G. L., 344
Hershey, Paul, 345
Herzberg, Frederick, 200, 205, 207-208, 216, 223, 345
Hetzler, Stanley A., 345
Heydebrand, Wolf, 318
Hicks, Herbert G., 219-220, 345
Hickson, D. J., 102, 118-119, 345, 348
High, W. S., 327
Hilgendorf, E. L., 114-115, 199, 345
Hill, J. W., 113, 199-201, 223, 347
Hill, Richard J., 122
Hill, Walter A., 345
Hills, R. J., 345
Hinings, C. R., 88, 345
Hirsch, Paul, 345
Hirsch, Phil, 346
Hitler, Adolf, 147
Hocking, William E., 346
Hodge, P., 346
Hodge, Robert W., 346
Hoffman, I. R., 359
Hoffman, Richard, 358, 391
Hoffman, Stanley, 346
Holdaway, Edward A., 346
Hollander, E. P., 170, 346
Holter, Harriet, 217-218, 346

Subject Index

Competition:
  defined, 99
  interorganizational, 55–56, 99,
    101
  intraorganizational, 99
Complexity:
  and A/P ratio, 8, 154–155
  and effectiveness, 196
  functional, 54, 134–135
  horizontal, 87, 91
  organizational, 8, 40, 65, 87–88,
    99–100, 154
  and organizational size, 40,
    154–155
  and span of control, 91
  vertical, 87
Compliance-involvement typology,
    169
  characteristics of, 70–72
  compliance defined, 67
  congruent types, 70
  criticisms of, 71–72
  defined, 67, 70–72
  incongruent types, 70
  involvement, 70
Concomitant variation, 80
Confidentiality of research
    information, 128
Conflict:
  within authority hierarchies, 49,
    120
  of goals, 99
  interdepartmental, 54
  interpersonal, 54, 99
  intraorganizational, 99–100
  and levels of aspiration, 113–114
  organizational, 48
  and role clarity, 99
Conformity, 49
  and bureaucracy, 35, 38
  and commitment, 118

Conformity:
  factors promoting, 146, 149–150,
    192
  and role specificity, 118
Control:
  over behavior, 168
  formal as opposed to informal,
    184
  over groups in organizations, 91,
    168
  spans of, 91, 184
  structures of, 158–159, 184
Conversion operations (see
    Automation)
Cooperation, intraorganizational,
    32, 46
Coordination, 32
  and communication, 176
  interdepartmental, 54, 176, 258
  interpersonal, 46, 54
  organizational, 1, 46, 52, 154,
    158–159, 180
  and technological change, 258
Corporation organizations, 66
Correctional institutions (see Prison
    organizations)
Cui Bono? (who benefits?), 72–73

Data collection in field research, 19,
    134
  analysis, 80
Deadlines, 211
  and anxiety, 211
  and technological change, 254
Debureaucratization, 89–90
  and bureaucracy, 90
  defined, 90
  examples, 90
Decentralization, 90–91
  decision making as related to,
    159
  defined, 91

Norms:
  deviation from, 88, 209
  group, 109, 216-217
  group cohesion and, 209-210
  implications of, 216-217
  individual, 88
  organizational, 88, 153, 168
  sanctions imposed for violation
    of, 88
Norwegian factory (footwear), 115

Oak Ridge, Tennessee, National
  Laboratories, 42
Occupations, 116
  airplane pilots, 150
  engineers, 120
  newsmen, 192
  politicians, 50
  prestige, 116-117
  psychiatric social workers, 50
  salesmen, 50
  scientists, 51, 118, 120
  status, 116
Official authority and bureaucracy,
  35
Open-systems models, 28-59
  characteristics of, 28
  natural-systems model, 55-58
Organic analogy, 55-58
"Organization man," 6
Organizational adaptability, 9, 144
Organizational age, 144
Organizational analysis, 121
Organizational behavior, 8, 86,
  92-98, 104, 137, 197
  criticisms of term, 92
  and leadership, 166, 168
  organizational climate and, 92-93
  organizational effectiveness and,
    93-95
  organizational goals and, 95-98
  (*See also specific* Variable
    headings)

Organizational change, 44, 86,
  98-104, 112
  acceptance of, 233-234
  adaptation of membership to, 55,
    205-206, 243-244
  administrative succession and,
    101
  Bennis's acceptance conditions,
    234
  bureaucratization and, 90
  case method, 241
  characteristics of successful,
    230-235
  as a continuing process, 2, 57
  factors which influence, 196-197
  functional approaches to,
    235-240
  Greiner's six phases of success
    patterns, 233
  individual-interpersonal
    approach, 235-238
  Jones's six major elements of,
    232-233
  labor turnover and, 98-99
  measuring, 98-104
  organizational conflict and,
    99-100
  organizational flexibility and, 100
  organizational growth and, 101
  organizational technology and,
    101-104
  other approaches to, 240-243
  planned, 55
  potential sources of resistance to,
    243-244
  power relations and, 145
  role playing and, 241-242
  and skill levels, 205-206
  studies of, 126
  systemic approach to, 238-240
  technological change as related
    to, 55, 160
  (*See also* Technological
    change)

Research findings:
  validity and reliability of
    measures related to, 136
Research problems in studying
  organizations:
  alternative appeals and
    approaches, 124-125
  gaining access to organizations,
    123-126
  guarantees of anonymity,
    125-126
  introduction to organizations
    initially, 124
  obtaining formal approval, 124,
    127
  using the prestige of sponsoring
    agency, 124
  utilizing friends and associates to
    study their organizations,
    124
Resistance to change, 38, 190, 195
  departmentalization and, 100
  group cohesion and, 209
  intraorganizational conflict and,
    100
  involvement in decision making
    and, 236
  technological change and, 264,
    269
  voluntary organizations and, 100
Responsibility, 205
Rest pauses, 46
"Restraining forces," 242
Restriction of output, 61-62, 210
Retirements, 1, 269
Retraining, 269-270
  (See also Organizational
    Adaptability; Technological
    Change)
Rewards:
  bonuses, 33
  compliance through, 70

Rewards:
  job satisfaction and, 214-217
  in organizations, 1, 52-53, 71,
    214-217
  power and, 149
    (See also Power)
  variations in, 216-217
Role:
  authority based on, 148
  clarity, 32
  conflict, 119
  definition of, 88, 119
  expectations, 118-119
  interdependency of roles, 9, 148
  performance, 113, 117-120
Role clarity (see Role specificity)
Role conflict, 119-120
  defined, 119
  examples, 119-120
  implications of, 119-120
  interpersonal relations and, 120
  job satisfaction and, 120
  role performance and, 119-120
  work group effectiveness and,
    120
Role definitions
  conflict and, 119-120
  legal-rational authority and, 148
  productivity and, 117-118
  specificity or clarity and, 118-119
  (See also specific Variable
    headings)
Role specificity, 118-119
  authority and, 118-119
  defined, 118-119
  examples of, 118-119, 186-187
  role performance and, 118
Routine (see Work routine)
Rules:
  bureaucracy and, 34, 37-39,
    51-52, 90, 153, 161, 174